Studies in Neurolinguistics

VOLUME 4

PERSPECTIVES IN
NEUROLINGUISTICS AND PSYCHOLINGUISTICS

Harry A. Whitaker, Series Editor
DEPARTMENT OF PSYCHOLOGY
THE UNIVERSITY OF ROCHESTER
ROCHESTER, NEW YORK

HAIGANOOSH WHITAKER and HARRY A. WHITAKER (Eds.).
Studies in Neurolinguistics, Volumes 1, 2, and 3
NORMAN J. LASS (Ed.). Contemporary Issues in Experimental Phonetics
JASON W. BROWN. Mind, Brain, and Consciousness: The Neuropsychology
of Cognition
SIDNEY J. SEGALOWITZ and FREDERIC A. GRUBER (Eds.). Language Devel-
opment and Neurological Theory
SUSAN CURTISS. Genie: A Psycholinguistic Study of a Modern-Day "Wild
Child"
JOHN MACNAMARA (Ed.). Language Learning and Thought
I. M. SCHLESINGER and LILA NAMIR (Eds.). Sign Language of the Deaf:
Psychological, Linguistic, and Sociological Perspectives
WILLIAM C. RITCHIE (Ed.). Second Language Acquisition Research: Issues
and Implications
PATRICIA SIPLE (Ed.). Understanding Language through Sign Language
Research
MARTIN L. ALBERT and LORAINE K. OBLER. The Bilingual Brain: Neuro-
physiological and Neurolinguistic Aspects of Bilingualism
HAIGANOOSH WHITAKER and HARRY A. WHITAKER (Eds.). Studies in Neuro-
linguistics, Volume 4

In preparation

TALMY GIVON. On Understanding Grammar
CHARLES J. FILLMORE, DANIEL KEMPLER and WILLIAM S.-Y. WANG (Eds.).
Individual Differences in Language Ability and Language Behavior

Studies in Neurolinguistics

Volume 4

Edited by

HAIGANOOSH WHITAKER

HARRY A. WHITAKER

Department of Psychology
The University of Rochester
Rochester, New York

ACADEMIC PRESS   New York   San Francisco   London   1979

A Subsidiary of Harcourt Brace Jovanovich, Publishers

ACADEMIC PRESS, INC.
111 Fifth Avenue, New York, New York 10003

United Kingdom Edition published by
ACADEMIC PRESS, INC. (LONDON) LTD.
24/28 Oval Road, London NW1   7DX

Library of Congress Cataloging in Publication Data
Main entry under title:

Studies in Neurolinguistics.

(Perspectives in neurolinguistics and psycholinguistics)
Includes bibliographies and indexes.
1. Speech, Disorders of. 2. Languages--Physiological
aspects. 3. Neuropsychology. I. Whitaker, Haiganoosh.
II. Whitaker, Harry A. [DNLM: 1. Language.
2. Neurophysiology. WL102 S933]
RC423.S74   616.8'552   75-13100
ISBN 0-12-746304-6 (v.4)

PRINTED IN THE UNITED STATES OF AMERICA

79 80 81 82   9 8 7 6 5 4 3 2 1

Contents

3 Structure in a Manual Communication System Developed Without a Conventional Language Model: Language Without a Helping Hand 125

Susan Goldin-Meadow

List of Contributors

Temple Baker (241), Department of Foreign Languages and Linguistics, The University of Texas at Arlington, Arlington, Texas 76019

D. Frank Benson (293), The Neurobehavioral Center, Boston Veterans Administration Hospital, and Neurology Department, Boston University School of Medicine, Boston, Massachusetts 02130

Hugh W. Buckingham, Jr. (269, 329), Department of Audiology and Speech Sciences, Purdue University, West Lafayette, Indiana 47907

Maureen Dennis (211), Department of Psychology, The Hospital for Sick Children, Toronto, Ontario M5G 1X8, Canada

William Orr Dingwall (1), Linguistics Program, University of Maryland, College Park, Maryland 20742

Susan Goldin-Meadow (125), Department of Education, The University of Chicago, Chicago, Illinois 60637

Dennis L. Molfese (225), Department of Psychology, Southern Illinois University, Carbondale, Illinois 62901

Victoria J. Molfese (225), Department of Psychology, Southern Illinois University, Carbondale, Illinois 62901

Francis J. Pirozzolo (97), Department of Neurology, Minneapolis Veterans Administration Hospital, Minneapolis, Minnesota 55417

Keith Rayner (97), Department of Psychology, University of Massachusetts, Amherst, Massachusetts 01003

Renee Freedman Stern (241), Program in Communication Disorders, The University of Texas at Dallas, Dallas, Texas 75235

Hanna K. Ulatowska (241), Program in Communication Disorders, The University of Texas at Dallas, Dallas, Texas 75235

Haiganoosh Whitaker (329), Department of Psychology, The University of Rochester, Rochester, New York 14627

Harry A. Whitaker (329), Department of Psychology, The University of Rochester, Rochester, New York 14627

Carole Ann Wiegel-Crump (211), Troy University, European Division, Soesterberg, The Netherlands, and The International School, Amsterdam, The Netherlands

Preface

This is the fourth in a series of volumes of original research and review papers in neurolinguistics. The continuation of the series will mark an expansion of the scope of the series: This will be the last volume devoted exclusively to language phenomena. In subsequent volumes, all research areas in the field of neuropsychology will be represented. The series will be retitled *Studies in Neurolinguistics and Neuropsychology*. This expansion of coverage is warranted by the almost phenomenal growth of neuro- psychology over the past few years. Neurological, linguistic, psychological, and speech pathology societies all include sections in their annual meetings devoted to papers on neuropsychological and neurolinguistic topics.

As in the three previous volumes, the present work is heterogeneous both in theoretical perspective and in topical coverage. In our opinion, this accurately reflects the discipline today: It is not working under a uniform paradigm and there are not a few, narrowly defined areas of research. There is another, pragmatic reason for the inclusion of multiple topics in this, as in the other volumes. As editors, we believe it is our responsibility to make important review and research papers available to the scholarly community as quickly as possible. Withholding a paper from publication for a long period of time in order to pair it with another paper on a similar topic does not serve anyone's interests. As before, we continue to solicit and are always receptive to all scholarly approaches and perspectives to any topic in the field of human brain and behavioral relationships.

In Chapter 1, Dingwall reviews the history of studies on, and the evidence for, "The Evolution of Human Communication Systems." Fully appreciating the interdisciplinary complexity, he develops a framework for analyzing communication systems and examines the behavioral and neuro- logical homologies among man, apes, and other species.

In Chapter 2, Pirozzolo and Rayner consider the problem of "The Neural Control of Eye Movements in Acquired and Developmental Read- ing Disorders," referring both to the literature and their own experimental research data. They argue that dyslexia is not caused by abnormal eye movements, although two types of dyslexic subjects do appear to have predictable differences in their eye movements during reading.

In Chapter 3, Goldin-Meadow addresses an unusual topic, "Structure in a Manual Communication System Developed Without a Conventional Language Model." The basic focus is on the role of linguistic input in language acquisition. She establishes the criteria for determining that the signs used by the children in her study do have communicative function and a linguistic (phrase) structure.

In Chapter 4, Dennis and Weigel-Crump address a question first formulated by Hughlings Jackson in the nineteenth century. "Aphasic Dissolution and Language Acquisition" is a study of the regression hypothesis. The evidence indicates that there is little unequivocal support for the regression hypothesis.

In Chapter 5, Molfese and Molfese analyze "VOT Distinctions in Infants." Voice onset time, a basic acoustic cue for distinguishing stop consonant pairs such as /b,p/, has recently been used in a number of infant studies in order to assess prelanguage linguistic abilities. The authors report their evidence that the VOT discrimination is made by 2–5-month-old infants, but not newborns, thus questioning the innateness of this sensory process.

In Chapter 6, Ulatowska, Baker, and Stern look at the "Disruption of Written Language in Aphasia." They review the nature of agraphia in the broader context of written language and its relation to spoken language, and present an analysis of aphasic writing. Of particular note is the detailed syntactic analysis, not generally found in analyses of agraphia.

In Chapter 7, Buckingham considers "Linguistic Aspects of Lexical Retrieval in the Posterior Fluent Aphasias." Both a psycholinguistic and a neurolinguistic framework are given for the nature of lexical items (words) in language and in a grammar. These frameworks are then applied to the analysis of the anomic aphasia usually seen in patients with lesions to the posterior language zones. Various hypotheses concerning aspects of word finding, lexical retrieval, are discussed.

In Chapter 8, Benson complements Chapter 7 with "Neurologic Correlates of Anomia." The clinically distinct types, methods for diagnosing, and the anatomic correlates of the anomias, are all reviewed in detail. Benson concludes that anomia is not a unitary, specific aphasic disturbance, but has many varieties as well as many clinico–anatomical correlations.

In Chapter 9, "On Linguistic Perseveration," Buckingham, Whitaker, and Whitaker present the first review of this phenomenon. Perseveration does not appear to have a distinct localization. Different linguistic units are subject to perseveration in aphasic patients, most noticeably phonemes, syllables, and words. Illustrative examples and theoretical conclusions are given.

Clinicians and research scientists will find the material in this and the previous volumes of interest. Clinical neurologists and speech pathologists will find new theories and methods derived from the behavioral sciences. Linguists will find important new data against which performance models of language must be tested; they will also welcome insights into the language-research techniques of neuropsychologists. Psychologists will find insights into language structure and brain function, which represent the best of the interdisciplinary focus that is neurolinguistics. The most obvious goal of neurolinguistics and neuropsychology is a synthesis of the brain sciences, the behavioral sciences, and the clinical sciences. It does not matter whether one's primary interest is in language, the brain, or in the therapy and rehabilitation of the brain-damaged patient. As in the previous three volumes of this series, we hope that the reader will perceive a sense of the scope as well as the interest and excitement of many of the topics in this field.

Figure, Table, and Quotation Credits

FIGURES

Figure 1.2, page 11   From Van Sommers, P. 1972. *The biology of behavior*. New York: Wiley.

Figure 1.4, page 17   From Rosen, S.I. 1974. *Introduction to the primates: Living and fossil*. Englewood Cliffs, New Jersey: Prentice-Hall. Credit is given to LeGros Clark.

Figure 1.6, page 24   From van Lawick-Goodall, J. 1971. *In the shadow of man*. Boston: Houghton Mifflin.

(b)   From Goodall, Vanne (Ed.). 1975. *The quest for man*. New York: Praeger.

(c), (f), (i)   From Albrecht, H., & Dunnett, S. 1971. *Chimpanzees in western Africa*. Munchen: R. Piper.

(d), (e), (g), (h)   From van Lawick-Goodall, J., & van Lawick, H. 1965. New discoveries among Africa's chimpanzees. *National Geographic, 128*(6), 802–831. Photographs by Baron Hugo van Lawick, © National Geographic Society.

Figure 1.7, page 28   From Chevalier-Skolnikoff, S. 1973. Facial expression of emotion in nonhuman primates. In P. Ekman (Ed.), *Darwin and facial expression*. New York: Academic Press. Drawn by Eric Stoelting.

Figure 1.8, page 38   Reproduced from LIFE Magazine (February 11, 1972) by permission of Time Inc.

Figure 1.9, page 43   From Jordan, J. 1971. Studies on the structure of the organ of voice and vocalization in chimpanzees. *Folia Morphologica* (Warsaw), *30*, 97–136; 222–248; 323–340.

Figure 1.11, page 44   From Fink, B. R. 1975. *The human larynx*. New York: Raven.

Figure 1.12, page 49
(A)   From Lieberman, P., & Crelin, E. 1971. On the speech of Neanderthal man. *Linguistic Inquiry, 11*, 208.

(B,C)   From Du Brul, E. L. 1976. Biomechanics of speech sounds. *Annals of the New York Academy of Sciences, 280*, 631–642.

Figure 1.13, page 54   From Passingham, R. E., & Ettlinger, G. 1974. A comparison of cortical functions in man and other primates. *International Review of Neurobiology, 16*, 233–299.

Figure 1.14, page 57	From Passingham, R. E. 1975. Changes in the size and organization of the brain in man and his ancestors. *Brain Behavior Evolution*, *11*, 73–90. Reprinted by permission of S. Karger AG, Basel.
Figure 1.15, page 57	From Passingham, R. E. 1975. Changes in the size and organization of the brain in man and his ancestors. *Brain Behavior Evolution*, *11*, 73–90. Reprinted by permission of S. Karger AG, Basel.
Figure 1.18, page 74	From Marler, P. 1975. On the origin of speech from animal sounds. Reprinted from *The role of speech in language* edited by J. Kavanagh & J. Cutting, by permission of The M.I.T. Press, Cambridge, Massachusetts.

TABLES

Table 1.2, page 12	From Lasker, G. Ward. 1976. *Physical anthropology*. New York: Holt.
Table 1.7, page 50	From Prestrude, A. M. 1970. Sensory capacities of the chimpanzee: A review. *Psychological Bulletin*, *74*, 47–67. Copyright 1970 by the American Psychological Association. Reprinted by permission.

QUOTATIONS

Pages 39–40	From Rumbaugh, D., & Gill, T. 1976. Language and the acquisition of language-types by a chimpanzee (*Pan*). *Annals of the New York Academy of Sciences*, *280*, 90–123.
Page 270	From Chomsky, N. 1976. On the biological basis of language capacities. In R. W. Rieber (Ed.), *The neuropsychology of language*. New York: Plenum. Reprinted by permission of the author and publisher.
Page 329	Reprinted by permission from Goldstein, Kurt. 1948. *Language and language disturbances*. New York: Grune & Stratton.

Contents of Previous Volumes

VOLUME 3

Studies in Neurolinguistics

VOLUME 4

1 The Evolution of Human Communication Systems

William Orr Dingwall
UNIVERSITY OF MARYLAND

INTRODUCTION

> . . . it is of as little use to be a good reasoner when there are no facts
> to reason upon, as it is to be a good bricklayer when there are no
> bricks to be built with.
>
> [Edward B. Tylor, 1878, p. 15]

The topic of this chapter has engaged philosophers since the beginning of recorded history and, no doubt, before. As is the wont of philosophers (and some of the most renowned of all time have turned their attention to this problem), many, widely divergent, often conflicting, solutions have been proposed.[1] Some of the more frequent elements that figure in these solutions are present in Table 1.1, lest it be imagined that current views, to be touched on later, are overly original. These themes, as in some vast intellectual fugue, are introduced alone or in conjunction only to disappear, reappear in transposition or in totally new combinations depending on the times. It is not my purpose here to survey this complex segment of the history of ideas.[2]

---

[1] For example, Johann Süssmilch argues that the perfection of structure which characterizes language clearly indicates that it was designed by a rational being. Since man without language is not such a being, it follows that only God could have created language. Jacob Grimm, on the other hand, holds that language had to be man's creation since to assume it is a divine gift makes man God's equal and to assume it is innate makes him identical to a beast.

[2] A recent, literate account is available in Stam (1976). Some other sources include Aarsleff (1967, 1976), Bolinger (1975), Borst (1957–61), Critchley (1960), Diamond (1959), Gray and

1

TABLE 1.1   The Evolution of Human Communication Systems: Some Recurrent Themes.

Environmental	Behavioral	Psychological	Physiological	Supernatural
Climate change	Innate cries	Growth in	Vocal tract	Divine creation
Habitat Change	(Interjections)	cognitive	changes	
	Babbling	abilities	Increase in	
	Gesture		relative	
	Song		brain size	
	Imitation		Restructuring	
	(Onomatopoeia)		of the brain	
	Upright		Neotony (pedo-	
	locomotion		morphism)	
	Invention			
	Convention			
	(Social			
	contract)			
	Social			
	organization			
	Play			
	Tool-making			
	and use			
	Hunting			
	Cooperative labor			
	in general			

Whether taken singly or arranged in complex causal chains, in the absence of "hard" facts and an overall framework within which they could be interpreted, there were few if any constraints imposed on solutions fashioned from the elements in Table 1.1. It is this state of affairs that Tylor laments in the opening quotation and that led, in large part, to the banning of speculation on this topic altogether. It is with this subject that we shall begin our discussion.

The Fall and Rise of a Question

THE BANNING OF THE QUESTION

In 1866, what Stam (1976) refers to as the **annihilation of the question,** took place. In the second bylaw of its constitution, the Société de linguistique de Paris, which had been founded the year before, stated "**Article II:** The Society will accept no communication dealing with . . . the origin of language . . . ." This ban was to be reconfirmed in 1911. The Philological Society of London, albeit unofficially, followed suit. Comment-

Wise (1959), Hewes (1973), Hoepp (1970), Marx (1967), Moran and Gode (1966), Pulgram (1970), Stross (1976), Wescott (1967). A comprehensive bibliography is provided in Hewes (1975).

ing on Max Müller's attack on evolutionary theory, Alexander Ellis, the president of the Society, concluded that: "We shall do more by tracing the historical growth of one single work-a-day tongue, than by filling waste-paper baskets with reams of paper covered with speculations on the origin of all tongues."

Even if the weight of Tylor's argument or scepticism concerning the more "imaginative" solutions to the question[3] might move the reader to sympathize with such a ban, it seems evident upon reflection that is was ill-conceived and strangely inopportune.

First of all, lack of empirical evidence need not impede brilliant insight, any more than the presence of such evidence necessarily guarantees its correct interpretation. Relying on logical argument alone, Leucippus was able to develop the atomic theory, while Aristotle, able to rely on the results of numerous dissections, failed to discover the correct function of the brain, imagining it to be the cooling system of the body. Historical aspects of any endeavor whether in the natural or human sciences are forced to operate with less than a complete set of facts. This does not and should not rule out investigation of the origin of the universe, of life, or of any aspect of behavior such as human communication.

Second, it is becoming clear that it is unlikely that we shall ever be able to fully explain any but the most trivial aspects of human behavior either diachronically or synchronically. We must be satisfied with models that more or less closely approximate the phenomenon we seek to explain. The convergence of evidence from as many sources as become available will continue to play an important role in chosing among conflicting hypotheses (see Rose, 1973).

Third, the Ban of 1866 was inopportune in that it was imposed just at the time when a mass of new facts relevant to the question was becoming available as well as a comprehensive framework within which to interpret them. In 1859 *The Origin of Species* was published by Charles Darwin, culminating over 100 years of discussion of evolution (see Mayr, 1972). While it scarcely mentioned man, it nevertheless laid the foundations for the rational investigation of the origin of his communicative behavior. Just three years before the Ban, T. H. Huxley, Darwin's Bulldog, published his brilliant work on man's place in nature, wherein he collected a vast amount of behavioral, anatomical, and paleontological evidence for man's descent from a common ancestor with the apes. His method, which foreshadows that

[3] One such "imaginative" solution was proposed in a two volume work by the Scotch autodidact, Alexander Murray. This work demonstrates that current languages are but dialects of one original language made up of nine primordial syllables: AG, BAG, DWAG, GWAG, LAG, MAG, NAG, RAG, and SWAG all of which partake of the semantic features: *striking* or *pressing*.

of this chapter, quite correctly arrives at the conclusion that the gorilla and chimpanzee share a closer relationship to man than they do to other apes and monkeys. The last section of Huxley's work highlights the fact that, as early as 1829, fossil remains of what was eventually to be termed *Homo sapiens neanderthalensis* had been uncovered. Finally, in 1871, we have Darwin's own contribution to the evolution of man, followed one year later by his important work *The Expressions of the Emotions in Man and Animals.* In both these works, the evolution of human communication systems was discussed in some detail.

Finally, it might be argued that although linguists undoubtedly felt at the time of the Ban that they were in the vanguard of science because of the successes of the comparative method, they were actually in the process of isolating themselves from the mainstream of the human sciences by a misinterpretation of evolutionary theory. It was widely felt that language could be regarded as a natural organism, whose structure could be validly studied in isolation from the beings that produced it and from the contexts within which it was produced. To quote Schleicher (1873): "Languages are natural organisms, which, unregulated by the will of man, arise according to certain laws, grow and develop, and then become old and die out [p. 7]." It is only now beginning to dawn upon us how mistaken this notion is.[4]

THE RATIONALE FOR THE BAN

Although other disciplines that abided more closely by the teachings of biology continued their interest in the evolution of human communication systems, linguistics itself gradually abandoned all research into this topic. Thus one is lucky to find any reference to it in modern texts on linguistics. Those that do mention the subject do so only as an excuse for cataloguing the reasons against pursuing such a question.

First, it is usually pointed out that written evidence for language can only be traced back some 5000 years, to the earliest writings of the Sumerians. This may not be completely true, as we shall see below when we discuss Marshack's recent findings indicating that symbolic notations existed at a much earlier date. Also it overlooks the fact that the development of writing itself may contain hints as to how communication systems in general may have evolved (see Pfeiffer's [1969] interesting comments on this topic, which will be expanded on later). Second, it is customary to point out that the reconstruction of protolanguages can shed little light on the primitive stages of language, as they tend to be more complex than their modern descendants. The heuristics of comparative reconstruction are un-

[4] This misinterpretation was aided and abetted by both Darwin and Haeckel, who unfortunately bowed to the authority of Schleicher (who was little better than Aristotle in the interpretation of empirical evidence).

likely to lead to any other result. Internal reconstruction applied to the results of the comparative method (see Lehmann, 1955) could lead to such simplification however. Thus Lehmann postulates but a single vowel phoneme for the "prestress" stage of pre-Indo-European. Further, both Bender (1973) and Kiparsky (1976) agree that the methods of reconstruction can push back our knowledge of language at most some 20–30 thousand years. This may be all that is necessary if we are to accept Lieberman's argument against true language in some fossil hominids generally assigned to the subspecies *Homo sapiens neanderthalensis*. Third, we learn that there are no truly primitive languages extant today. Thus, the Tasaday, even though they live in what is equivalent to a stone age culture, presumably have a language which has the same potential for the efficient transfer of complex information as English. I am inclined to believe that any member of the species *Homo sapiens sapiens,* which the Tasaday surely are, possesses such a communication system simply by virtue of being members of the species. This supposition is based on the known range of cognitive capacities in our species and has nothing to do with the degree of primitiveness of human communication systems, for which linguists have no measures whatsoever. Finally, it is standard to point out that structures relevant to speech and language do not fossilize. While this is true to some extent, it underestimates the abilities of investigators to utilize what evidence is available in the fossil record to reconstruct these missing structures. After all, linguists are not the only scholars privileged to reconstruct lost features! This objection also overlooks the possibility of deriving evidence from extant species vis-à-vis the structures in question, namely the vocal tract, ear, and nervous system.

NEW SOURCES OF EVIDENCE RELEVANT TO THE QUESTION

Despite the Ban and the ensuing, progressively increasing, neglect of the topic by most linguists, there has been a resurgence of interest in the evolution of human communication systems. Two august societies: the American Anthropological Association and the New York Academy of Sciences have recently provided fora for the review of current research on the topic (see Wescott, 1974; Harnad, Steklis, & Lancaster, 1976). New books have begun appearing on the topic, and it has even become respectable once more to treat it in linguistics texts (see Bolinger, 1975). The basic reason for this rebirth of interest is the great expansion of relevant data from a wide variety of disciplines. This is coupled with an intellectual climate that increasingly pushes towards merger of, or at least increased cooperation among, disciplines dealing with animal (including human) behavior (see Wilson, 1975; Mason & Lott, 1976).

What then is the make-up of this expanded data base? Some of its major components are listed in outline form below:

1. rapidly expanding fossil evidence coupled with increased ability to date it accurately
2. reconstructions of the brain, as well as peripheral structures, based on fossil evidence
3. increased data from the neurosciences:
   a. comparative neurological studies
   b. neurolinguistic studies
   c. research in experimental phonetics and hearing and speech science
4. biochemical studies of the relatedness of animal species
5. studies of nonhuman primates in the wild and in the laboratory leading to increased knowledge of their complex behaviors in general and their communicative behavior in particular
6. studies of signing and nonverbal communicative behavior in general in human and nonhuman primates
7. renewed research on the effects of isolation on the development of communicative behavior
8. increasing knowledge of the normal ontogenesis of language in humans
9. studies of vocal learning in nonprimates particularly birds
10. investigation of the graphic behavior of early hominids
11. research on language universals
12. increased understanding of linguistic structures and their complexity

Many of these sources of information will be tapped at various points in this discussion. Some, such as language universals, are of questionable relevance. Such universals, if they indeed exist, may well result from the fortuitous overlap of behaviors constrained by species-specific neural and peripheral structures. There is no reason to believe such universals provide any insight into the make-up of the primordial structure (see Kiparsky [1976] for a different argument leading to the same conclusion).

It should be cautioned that we are at a primitive stage in the evaluation of almost every item on this list and that reevaluation of current evidence, as well as the rapid accretion of new evidence, may well vastly alter our perspective of things in the future.

For many centuries biology consisted solely of the accumulation of data such as those just listed. With the advent of the theory of evolution, it gained a framework within which such facts could be interpreted. Since certain aspects of this framework are crucial to our investigation, we now turn to a discussion of it.

The Evolutionary Approach

The fact that almost all the evidence listed in the previous section derives from disciplines other than linguistics should not be surprising. As noted, with the imposition of the Paris Ban, linguists gradually turned their backs on the question of language origins. They also effectively turned their backs on biology with their treatment of language as an organism that can be studied in isolation. This odd view persists (see, for example, Stevick, 1963) despite cogent arguments raised against it (see Hockett, 1957). Insofar as an evolutionary approach to human communication has even been considered, most linguists have adopted the discontinuity view of Lenneberg (1967) and Chomsky (1972). This view stresses that human language is not only species-specific, but also that the structures that subserve it are task-specific, that is, distinct from other mental functions. As we shall see, this view derives from an overly restrictive concept of language, which is then further held to be either present or absent as a totality in a given species (see Dingwall, 1975). Since it is felt that human communication either has no evolutionary history or that that history is irrevocably lost to us, no serious attempt has been made by linguists to investigate the origin of language within the framework provided by evolutionary theory. In this section, recent work on the concept of behavioral homology, which makes available a methodology for such an investigation, will be reviewed.

First of all, let us consider briefly some of the basic elements of modern evolutionary theory as it applies within biology. This theory seeks to account for changes that take place within populations of plants and animals over time. The individuals making up such populations at any given moment display wide variability in both **phenotype** (morphology and behavior) as well as **genotype** (the sum of inherited genetic material). The phenotype variance observed is determined by the variance in the genotype plus the variance in the environment, as well as their interaction. This fact may be expressed mathematically as: $\sigma^2 p = \sigma^2 g + \sigma^2 e + \sigma^2 ge$ (see Murphy, 1973; Whalen, 1971). Genotypic variance is due not only to such factors as **recombination** and **crossing over** which occur during reproduction but also to various types of random genetic changes collectively termed **mutations**. These latter constitute the primary source of new genetic material.

If we were to draw samples at random from populations of plants and animals over time, we might observe patterns such as those in Figure 1.1. Here we see a simple instance of divergent development from a population sample with a single mode vis-à-vis the characteristic in question to one with an overlapping bimodal distribution. As an example, we know that cats and dogs are descended from a common ancestor. Yet they have clearly diverged in many characteristics, one of which is snout size. Dogs (excluding those with atypical characteristics cultivated by man) have a long snout,

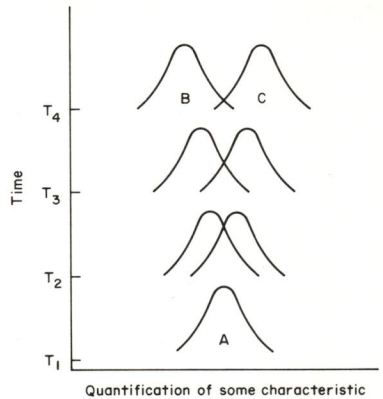

Figure 1.1. Divergence of population samples over time.

while cats have a short one. This, like other changes over time, is the result of natural selection. Certain phenotypes have a better chance of survival because of their higher degree of adaptedness to their environment. The selection of certain phenotypes over others changes the make-up of the genotype variance in the population, because such phenotypes have a greater opportunity to reproduce. Hutchinson (1974) believes that a change in hunting habits (tracking prey over long distances rather than stalking and pouncing upon it) may have originally produced the selective advantage for large versus small snouts. This is a typical example of behavioral evolution preceding structural change.

Other patterns of evolution besides divergence may occur. There may be a simple change in a population. This is typified by a gradual change such as that from A to B in Figure 1.1 without a split of the population into C. This may be the course followed in the shift in the hominid line from *Homo erectus* to *Homo sapiens neanderthalensis.* Finally, there may be very little or no change over time if environmental factors remain relatively stable. Thus, the lamp shell *Lingula,* which lives in a deep sea environment, has changed very little in over 500 million years.

Thus there are two main forces in evolution: **variation** created by random factors and a filter whose properties are determined by factors that may be subsumed under the rubric of **natural selection,** which maintains or alters distributions of characteristics in various ways.

THE PRIMATE RADIATION

One of the outcomes of the gradual accrual of divergent characteristics is the radiation of species, that is, the development of populations that do not interbreed. Such populations may be separated in time (*Homo erectus* versus *Homo sapiens neanderthalensis,* presumably) or may be coextant (cats and dogs). The barriers to interbreeding involve a number of factors termed **isolating mechanisms** (see Hutchinson, 1974, 193ff.; Avers, 1974, 225ff.).

In Figure 1.2 we have a simplified representation, in the .form of a phylogenetic tree, of such a radiation of species within the subphylum *vertebrata.* In the bottom half of the figure are more detailed trees for the class of mammals and the order of primates, to which the hominids (modern man together with his fossil ancestors) ultimately belong. It should be noted that the primate lineages constitute early offshoots of the insectivores (represented today by such animals as shrews and hedgehogs). Leaving aside the issue of whether the tarsiers are to be grouped with the prosimian suborder (represented in this figure by lemurs and lorises) or form a separate suborder of their own, the remaining primate suborder is that of the *anthropoidea,* from which first the New World Monkeys (e.g., squirrel monkeys and capuchins) and then the Old World Monkeys (e.g., macaques and baboons) split, leaving the super-family *hominoidea*.

At this point the tree diagram has been revised in order to bring it into greater accord with current thought. A considerable volume of morphological, biochemical, and behavioral evidence points to a closer relation between the Great Apes (chimpanzees, gorillas, and orangutans) and man than between the Lesser Apes (gibbons and siamangs) and man. Further, among the Great Apes, the African varieties (chimpanzee and gorilla) appear to be somewhat closer relatives of man than the Asian variety (orangutan) (see Figure 1.2b).

The biochemical evidence derives from three basic types of comparisons. One involves combining single strands from the DNA of two species. Such strands will recombine except at those points at which they are chemically different. A second method involves comparing the sequencing of amino acids in various types of protein molecules, such as those found in the blood (hemoglobin). Finally, the immunological approach involves injecting a protein, such as serum-albumin, taken from one species into an animal from another species. This will result in antibodies being produced. Reactions to serum containing such antibodies can be used to gauge the relationships between various animals and the donor of the serum-albumin.

Evidence derived from these techniques is impressive in that (1) phylogenetic trees drawn on the basis of this evidence accord well with those such as that in Figure 1.2 based on other independent sources of data and (2) as Table 1.2 demonstrates, biochemical evidence drawn from a number of divergent sources is remarkably consistent. The immunological distances (ID) and percentage of differing amino acids (AAD) between man and a wide assortment of primates works out as follows:

		ID	AAD
Man———————Chimp		7	.27
Gorilla		9	.65
Orang		12	2.75
Gibbon		15	2.38
Old World Monkey		32	3.89
New World Monkey		58[5]	8.78[6]

Because of the great similarity of these measures among the chimpanzee, the gorilla, and man, Goodman (1974) has gone so far as to suggest that the former two be reclassified as hominids, leaving only the orangutan in the pongid family. Others point out that the organismal difference between the pongids and hominids is sufficiently great to make us believe that the macromolecular differences cannot be telling the whole story. King and Wilson (1975) suggest that the true differences may lie in regulatory genes. This may turn out to be true, but, on the other hand, after our survey of behavioral and morphological differences, the reader may be willing to agree with Washburn and Moore (1974) that most of the differences relate to superficial matters of appearance that came late in evolution.

There is also an apparent lack of consistency between dates derived from the fossil record and from biochemical measures. Perhaps this can be explained by various factors such as increased gestational and generation lengths that may have decelerated molecular evolution in hominoids (see Goodman, 1974; as well as Sarich, 1974; Wilson & Sarich, 1969; and Byles, 1976).

Although for some the ability of the scientist to produce amino acids under conditions thought to have existed on this planet before life began or the demonstrated presence of DNA in the cells of all living matter may constitute convincing evidence for the theory of evolution, for most it is probably the existence of fossil plants and animals of no longer extant varieties—particularly the existence of fossil man. Whereas the biochemical data has had the effect of pushing the date of the ape–man split forward in time, more and more fossil discoveries have pushed back the date of the emergence of man.

Figure 1.3 provides a chronology of the more important fossil hominids, based in part on Campbell (1972). There has been no attempt to construct a phylogenetic tree, as this appears premature at this point. Most authorities agree that the earliest fossils classifiable as hominid are those of the genus *Ramapithecus,* found in Asia, Africa, and Europe. As we have only jaw fragments and teeth, there is no way of determining cranial capacity or

[5] From Sarich (1969).
[6] From Goodman (1974).

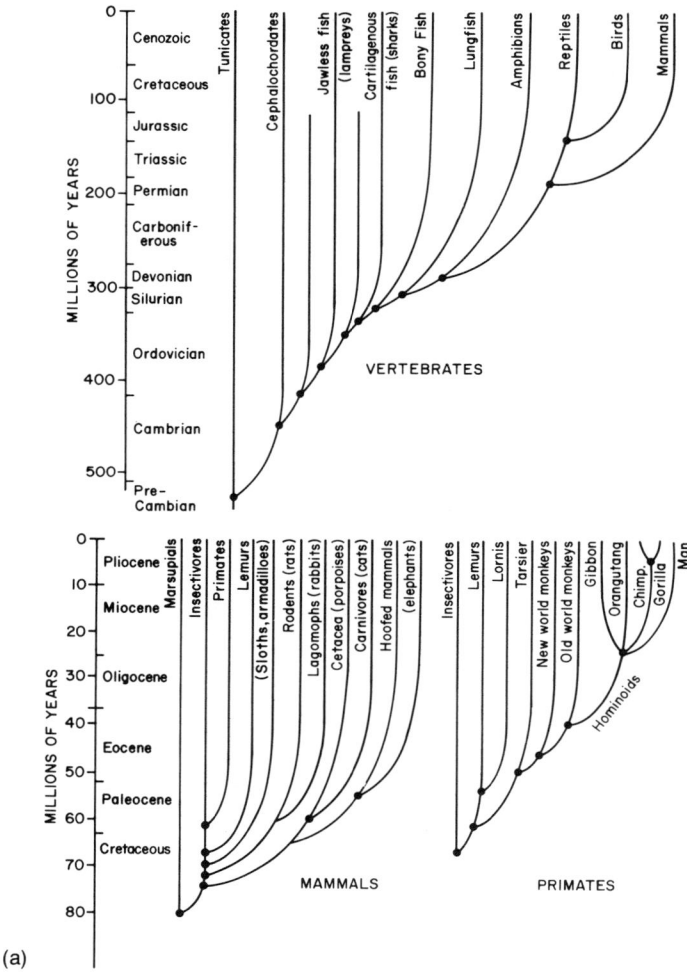

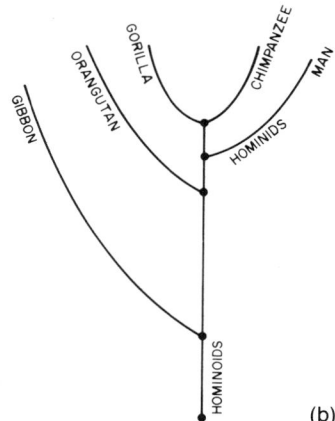

Figure I.2. (a) Simplified evolutionary trees of vertebrates, mammals, and primates. Specific examples of animal types are shown in brackets. (b) Revised evolutionary tree for the hominoids.

whether this hominid walked upright. The recently discovered Ngorora (Kenya) molar is probably of this genus.

Next we encounter a group of fossils that intervene in time between *Ramapithecus* and *Homo erectus.* Some of these belong to the genus *Australopithecus* (*A. boisei, A. africanus, A. robustus*), others are classified by some as *Homo* (*Homo habilis*).

The most complete hominid fossil yet found, "Lucy," is felt by its discoverer, Don Johanson, to belong to the genus *Australopithecus.* Richard Leakey's famous skull ER 1470 is probably best classified as *Homo* because of its exceptional cranial capacity (810 cc.).

It is clear that if these classifications are accurately dated, then two genera of hominids coexisted in Africa. If Leakey's recent *Homo erectus* find is correctly dated at from 1.5 to 1.8 million years old, then there is also overlap with yet a third genus. The Ndutu skull discovered by A. A. Mturi

TABLE 1.2 The Evolutionary Distance between Humans and Chimpanzees and Humans and Rhesus Monkeys.[a]

	Human/chimpanzee	*Human/monkey*	*Source*
DNA			
(nonreassociation)	2.5%	10.1%	Kohne, 1970
Hemoglobin			
(mutations)	1/579	15/287	Goodman *et al.,* 1972
Fibrinopeptides			
(mutations)	0/30	7/25	Doolittle and Mross, 1970
Carbonic anhydrase			
(immunological)	4 ID	50 ID	Wilson and Sarich, 1969
Carbonic anhydrase			
(mutations)	1/115	6/115	Tashian *et al.,* 1972
Albumin			
(immunological)	0	3.7%	Goodman, 1968
Albumin			
(immunological)	7 ID	35 ID	Wilson and Sarich, 1969
Transferrin			
(immunological)	0	3.7%	Goodman, 1968
Transferrin			
(immunological)	3 ID	30 ID	Wilson and Sarich, 1969
Gamma globulin			
(immunological)	.19%	3.4%	Goodman, 1968

[a]Although the units of measurement of evolutionary distance differ in the different studies, the distance between humans and chimpanzees is in all cases less than a quarter of the difference between humans and rhesus monkeys. (Some of the data are cited by S. L. Washburn, personal communication. Mutations minimum number of point mutations per number of shared codons; ID = immunological difference.)

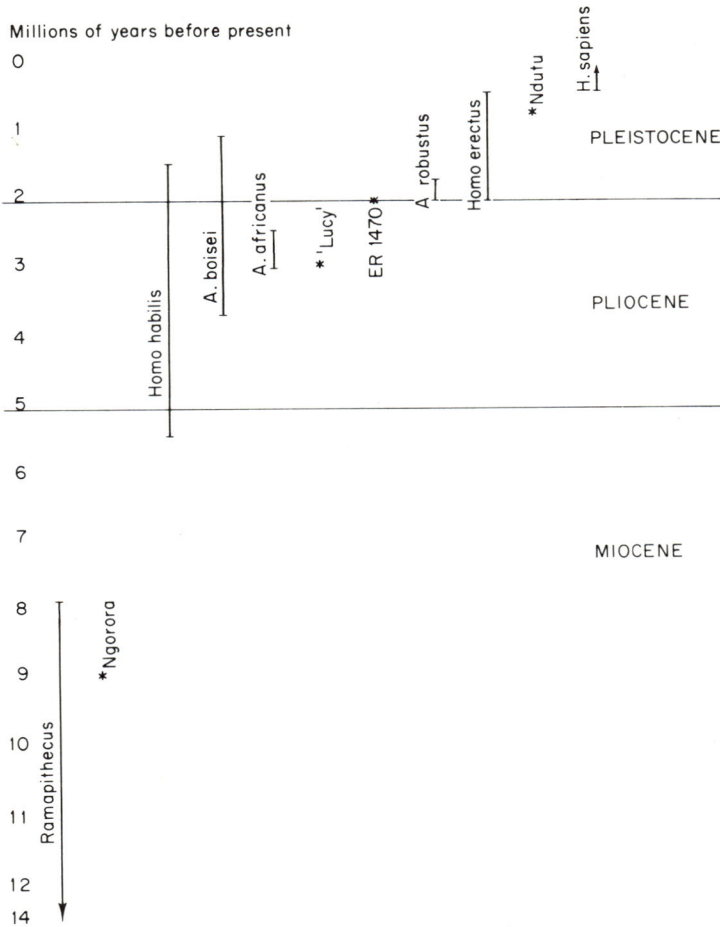

Figure 1.3. The fossil record of the hominids: A chronology.

in 1973 may represent a link between *Homo erectus* and *Homo sapiens* (see Campbell [1976] for a readable and up-to-date introduction to fossil man).

Thus, at some point perhaps 10 million years ago, portions of the common ancestral population of the pongids and hominids began their separate development. In both lineages there is a fossil record of this development. This record has been briefly reviewed for the hominid line; in the pongid line, a number of fossils found in Asia, Africa and Europe usually classified as belonging to the genus *Dryopithecus* provide a history of development since the Miocene. Besides this record, we can, of course, also study extant species in our attempt to reconstruct the evolutionary history of our ancestors. It is to the methods applicable to such a task, particularly as they relate to the evolution of such complex behaviors as communication systems, that we now turn.

THE CONCEPT OF BEHAVIORAL HOMOLOGY

As pointed out earlier, the discontinuity theory, first elaborated by Lenneberg (1967) and later supported in works by Chomsky (1972) and most recently Fodor *et al.* (1974), holds that language (i.e., essentially the universal aspects of human languages) is species-specific and that the structures that subserve it are task-specific. These specificities are logically independent, so that all possible combinations of them are imaginable and have been argued by philosophers and psychologists (see Dingwall, 1975). While certainly it is possible, it seems most unlikely, as S. Toulmin (1971) has noted, that language, regarded as a totality, suddenly arose in our hominid ancestors by some one-shot genetic saltation. It is equally unlikely that, given their genetic proximity to us, the Great Apes would evince no aspect of this complex behavior. What is much more likely is that such a behavior developed gradually over time by the process known as **mosaic evolution,** with structures subserving various aspects of the behavior not evolving at the same rate. The process of **preadaptation,** whereby some mutations and genotypes may become advantageous as an aspect of a behavior complex that did not prevail in the original selective situation, may also be involved.

As to evidence relevant to task-specificity, Atherton and Schwartz (1974) have suggested that:

1. the discovery of an organism of demonstrably inferior intelligence when compared with humans that can learn to speak any human language fluently
2. the discovery of an organism, perhaps from another planet, that, although superior in intelligence to man, nevertheless is incapable of acquiring human languages

Neither discovery seems likely. Much more probable is the discovery of an organism with intellectual abilities that approximate our own that is indeed capable of mastering some aspects of human language.

None of the questions relating to species-specificity and task-specificity can be answered without undertaking relevant comparisons among appropriate species of animals.

What are the appropriate animals to compare? This, of course, depends on one's aims. If one is interested in the phylogeny of a trait, as we are, then rather severe constraints obtain. Aristotle arranged animals according to their imagined complexity with man at the top. This classification is known as the *scala naturae* or the Great Chain of Being. Among vertebrates, the scale ascended from fish to amphibians, reptiles, birds, various mammals and, at the pinnacle, man. It was implied that there was a smooth continuity among these groups and that man was the inevitable goal of evolution. A glance at Figure 1.2 should convince the reader that comparisons of animals arranged in such a manner is meaningless if we are interested in phylogeny. No bony fish is ancestral to any amphibian, reptile, bird, or mammal. Rats and cats, whose behavior is often studied by psychologists, are not ancestral to the primates. Yet such comparisons, as Lenneberg (1967) quite correctly laments, characterize much of the research into the evolution of language. Hockett's design features (Hockett, 1959, 1960; Hockett & Altman, 1958; Hockett & Asher, 1964; Thorpe, 1972), for example, are nothing more than a logical analysis of communicative behaviors applied helter skelter throughout the animal kingdom without regard to the structures that subserve the behavior and without regard to phylogenetic proximity to man. As Hodos and Campbell (1969) point out in their detailed critique of the *scala naturae*, only data from living representatives of a common evolutionary lineage, supplemented by fossil evidence, where available, can provide a foundation for inferences about the phylogenetic development of behavior. The species that make up the *scala naturae* form a discontinuous sequence, as the phylogenetic trees in Figure 1.2 clearly indicate.

Further, evolution does not lead inevitably to man. Rather each species is maximally adapted for existence within its particular econiche (see also Hodos, 1970). Since we are interested in tracing the evolution of man's communicative behavior, the obvious animals to compare with man are, of course, living apes, as well as, perhaps, living representatives of the Old World Monkeys. Main emphasis will be on *Pan troglodytes* (the common chimpanzee), since this is the most extensively studied Great Ape. It is also our closest relative, as we have seen, in terms of biochemical evidence. However, on occasion, we shall consider data on other Great and Lesser Apes, as well as Old World Monkeys.

Having selected the animals for comparison, the next thing to decide is what the aim of such a comparison is to be and how best to carry it out. For our purposes, a reasonable objective would appear to be the determination of the presence or absence of homologies in communicative behavior. (A most crucial prior consideration, of course, is that such behavior be adequately defined—a task we shall take up at the beginning of the next section.)

Although the term **homology** was originally applied solely to structural characteristics, a number of ethologists and comparative psychologists, among others, have argued that the term can be fruitfully extended to behavior (see Atz, 1970; Campbell & Hodos, 1970; Hodos, 1976; and Masterton *et al.*, 1976). Behaviors that are similar in closely related species, that can be related to structures that show a high degree of concordance in a number of parameters, and that could—together with their structural correlates—be traced back to a common ancestor provide the most convincing examples of homology.

If a given complex behavior such as communication (in part or in toto) can be convincingly demonstrated to be nonhomologous with comparable behavior in closely related species, that is, species-specific, then it is necessary to provide some reasonable explanation of its evolution within a given lineage.

There are a number of guidelines (heuristics) that have been proposed by Hodos and others for the investigation of behavioral homologies. Some of the more important are listed below.

1. The most convincing examples of behavioral homology involve behaviors that are uniquely observed in closely related species.
2. Behavior, in order to be considered homologous, must be mediated by both peripheral and central structures that can be shown to be homologous. Very similar behaviors can be mediated by different structures and thus cannot be considered homologous. Thus, even though vocalization of marine and terrestrial animals are acoustically quite similar, they cannot be considered homologous, as they are mediated on the motor side by completely different peripheral structures.
3. One must avoid the circularity of employing behavior to establish taxonomies and then using such similarity in behavior as evidence of behavioral homology. The widest possible evidence for genetic relationships must be used.
4. In comparing acquired behavior across species, the maximum ability to perform the behavior should be the common reference point. Such evidence is important in establishing behavioral homologies, as the potential for efficient acquisition, storage, retrieval and utilization of information is set by the genotype. This heuristic is tied in with the concept of **potential variable capacity** advanced by Marshack (1976). It has important implications in the proper evaluation of human-like communicative behaviors in the Great Apes.
5. The ontogeny of behaviors, together with their mediating structures, can be an important clue in establishing behavioral homologies (see Campbell & Hodos, 1970; Scovel, 1972; and Lamendella, 1976).

Figure 1.4 provides a graphic representation of the basic concept of homology. Black dots indicate homologous features; circles and crosses, nonho-

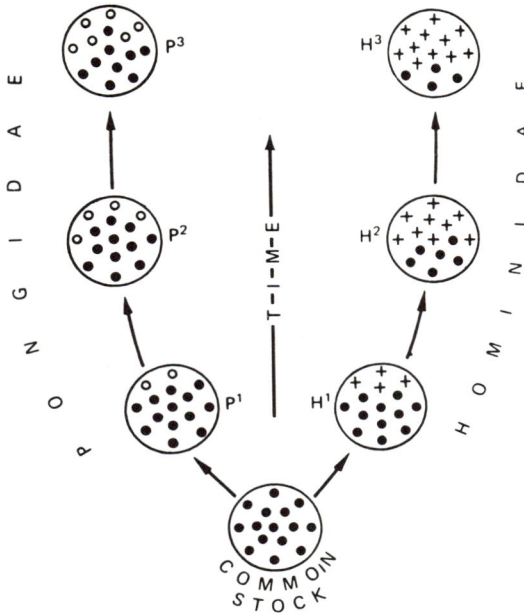

Figure 1.4. Diagram representing the divergence of two evolutionary sequences, the Pongidae (great apes) and the Hominidae (modern and extinct man). The two sequences inherit a common ancestry—characters of common inheritance (black circles). As the lines diverge, each one acquires its own distinctive features or characters of independent acquisition, those distinctive of the hominid sequence of evolution are represented by crosses and those of the pongid sequence by white circles.

mologous features developed after the period of common ancestry. Such features would, of course, be species-specific.

Besides homologous behaviors that have structural correlates traceable back to a common ancestor, there are also behaviors that, while similar, cannot be related to such ancestral structures. These are termed **behavioral homoplasies.** There are a number of processes which result in such behavioral homoplasies, among them **convergence, parallelism, mimicry, chance similarity,** and **analogy.** In the last section of this chapter, we shall consider a probable instance of convergence, that is, similarity in behavior in the absence of common ancestry. Although birds are not ancestral to man, there are striking similarities between vocal learning in man and in various species of altricial songbirds. In applying the term convergence, it is generally required that one demonstrate that the similarity in behavior arose through adaptation to similar ecological conditions.

It is the concept of behavioral homology that forms the organizing principle for the remaining sections of this chapter. As we have pointed out, in establishing behavioral homologies we must compare not only behaviors, but the structures that subserve such behaviors. Thus, we first turn to a study of behaviors linked to communication in primates. Following that, we examine structures that subserve such behaviors (both peripheral motor effectors and sensory receptors are involved, as well as central control and processing systems of the brain). Finally, we examine the ontogenesis of communicative behaviors and the structures that subserve such behaviors in both birds and primates. Before we can begin our search for behavioral homologies, we must first attempt to understand the complex system of behaviors which form the focus of our study.

EVOLUTION OF COMMUNICATIVE AND OTHER COMPLEX BEHAVIORS (BEHAVIORAL SYSTEMS)

> *. . . at the level of speech—in the sense of vocalized language—the contrasts between man and ape are manifestly qualitative. On a different level, let's say the ability to form concepts, or to combine various acts or subroutines into larger functional units, the differences appear to be matters of degree. Differences in the neural correlates of mental activity are even more probably of this sort.*
> [William A. Mason, 1976, p. 293]

An Attempt to Develop a Framework Suitable for the Description of Communication in Man as well as Other Species

Perhaps nothing has had a more deleterious effect upon investigations of the evolution of human communication systems than the terminology employed in the discussion of such systems. The use of terms such as **language** and **speech** not only serves to establish the uniqueness of human communication systems by verbal fiat, but also serves to engender confusion between a communication system (language) and one of its output modalities (speech). In addition, there is the use of **Language** (this useage has been distinguished by capitalization) to refer to the univeral aspects of human communication that many linguists believe form the basis of an innate universal grammar. Wherever the term **language** has been employed in this chapter, it is equivalent to the more cumbersome term **human communication systems.** The only virtue in the continued use of the former term lies in its brevity.

The model I propose for the general aspects of communication systems is schematized in Figure 1.5. Aspects I and II constitute the modes of conceptualization and of signification respectively. As will be noted, three symmetric transductions are proposed. The first (T_1) involves the capacity of the brain of an organism to produce and, if they impinge upon it, comprehend a variety of concepts, which may be either simple or complex. One cannot at present judge whether an organism is in command of a

ASPECT I.

BRAIN
$\uparrow$ T_1
CONCEPT (C)
$\uparrow$ T_2

ASPECT II.

NEUROSIGN (N_1, N_2)
$\uparrow$ T_3
INPUT/OUTPUT (I, O)

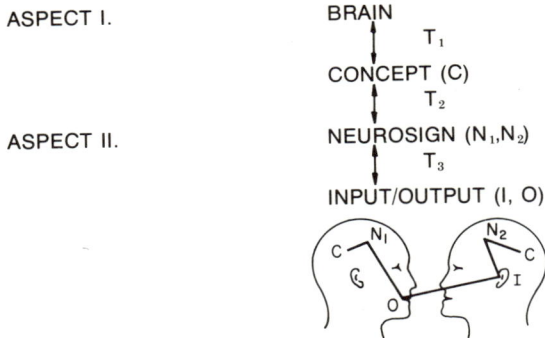

Figure 1.5. General aspects of communication systems.

particular concept unless it signals this fact in some manner. This involves linking the concept with a neurological state that mediates either its production or reception. The second transduction (T_2) has traditionally constituted the basic domain of theoretical linguistics: the linkage between an abstract conceptual structure and an equally abstract phonetic representation that is only imperfectly reflected in the various stages of its production or reception. Recent work by Sachs (1967), Bransford and Franks (1972), Kintsch (1974), and others has provided the first clear evidence of what conceptual structure might be like, while at the same time neuroscientists have demonstrated in EEG studies that what is being termed the **neurosign** is more than a theoretical construct (see Dingwall & Whitaker, 1974). On the other hand, the upshot of a decade of work in experimental psycholinguistics has made it abundantly clear that current linguistic theory fails to provide a viable model of either T_2 or its endpoints (see Watt, 1970, 1972, 1974; Dingwall & Shields, 1973). The third transduction (T_3) involves the processes of signal production and detection. It is this transduction, because of its relative accessability to study, about which the most is known, thanks to the efforts of physiologists, hearing and speech scientists, experimental phoneticians, and others interested in this aspect of communication (see Dingwall [1975] for further discussion).

Another barrier to the fruitful investigation of human communication systems has been the excessively narrow definition of such systems. Until very recently, linguists have been content to study language as an abstract structure totally removed from the organism that produces it and from the contexts within which it is produced. Insofar as input–output modalities have been considered, they have been regarded as exclusively auditory–vocal. This latter fact is clearly reflected in Hockett's design features (see Appendix), which are completely biased in this direction, although it is claimed they represent a general descriptive framework. Table 1.3 attempts to provide a more realistic account of the actual complexity of primate communication systems in terms of input modalities, contexts, and relevant

TABLE 1.3 Some Aspects of Primate Communication Systems

Input modality

Auditory	Visual	Tactile	Olfactory	Context	Knowledge
Prosodic features	Body posture	Grooming	Body odor	Physical	Knowledge of the
pitch	Body movement	Petting	Perfume	Social	communication system
pause	Hand gestures	Touching		Linguistic	Knowledge of the
loudness	Proximics	(Braille)			world (belief system)
tempo	Spatial orientation				Shared knowledge
Segmental features	Facial expression				of the communicators
vowels	gaze				
consonants	eye contact				
Voice qualifiers	blink				
Affective vocalization	brow movement				
laughter	Piloerection				
cries	Signs				
groans	Pictures				
Vegetative sounds	Writing				

knowledge. Obviously this table is incomplete in various ways, but at least it presents some idea of the multimodal nature of primate communication (see Abercrombie [1968], Hinde [1972], and Laver [1976] for further elaboration). Much of this information is processed simultaneously. If one system becomes partially or totally dysfunctional, then other systems may assume great importance. Alternative input–output modalities may be employed without altering informational content (e.g., writing, signing, braille, or pictures), only efficiency of encoding and decoding. One can define communication in such a way as to make it a unique characteristic of man, but one does so only by grossly misrepresenting its richness and complexity.

Finally, there has been a tendency, at least among linguists, to regard language as a unitary phenomenon that is acquired as a whole in phylogeny or ontogeny and is lost as a whole in pathology. Nothing could be further from the truth. Language is characterized by a vast conglomerate of skills that are acquired and lost in a mosaic fashion. It is necessary to emphasize this obvious point because of the tendency to speak of the presence or absence of language in this or that fossil hominid or living nonhuman primate. Rather than relying on preconceived ideas as to what constitutes language, the Gardners (1971, 1974) have done well in turning to the same techniques in evaluating language skills in chimpanzees as psycholinguists have been forced to employ in evaluating the emergence of language in children. In this way, the striking similarities in the communicative behaviors of the two species have been revealed. As noted earlier, it is highly improbable that a behavior as complex as human communication emerged full-blown at some point in hominid evolution. As in language acquisition, what we should expect is the gradual, mosaic emergence of communicative behaviors that approximate those of modern man.

One might define a maximally efficient communication system as one that is capable of transmitting the greatest amount of information in the least amount of time with the least ambiguity and the greatest intelligibility. It is obvious that certain trade-offs are involved in the emergence of such a desirable system. The simplest iconic systems imaginable are highly inefficient in the above sense, but require minimal processing and storage capacities. As one moves towards more complex systems involving arbitrary signalling units, concatenation, and hierarchical structure, then greatly increased processing and storage capacities are required.

Just as in the evolution of nervous systems, where older structures are not lost, but integrated into newer structures that appear later in phylogeny, so it often is with complex behaviors that such structures controls. A redundancy (as reflected in Table 1.3) and complexity increase, phylogenetically older behaviors are not totally lost. This is undoubtedly the main reason why paralinguistic behaviors in the Great Apes and man almost totally overlap, although some aspects of linguistic behaviors do not (see the Appendix). It should also be pointed out that input–output modalities do not mature at the same rate in ontogeny, nor need they arise at the same point in phylogeny. This observation is of crucial importance in evaluating the role of gesture versus speech in the evolution of language.

In summary, it is essential in conducting a comparative study of communication systems to keep in mind not only the end-points in Figure 1.5 (e.g., what concepts are available to the organism), but also the nature of the various encoding and decoding processes represented by T_1, T_2, and T_3. Some animal communication systems may be relatively simple in terms of input–output. This is not the case in primates, where a complex, multimodal system is involved (Table 1.3). Finally, systems also differ in their encoding and decoding efficiency. The means by which such efficiencies are effected offers still another object for comparison (see Dingwall [1978] for a more detailed discussion of human communicative behavior).

Naturalistic Studies of the Great Apes

> *A most surprizing Creature is brought over in the* Speaker, *just arrived from* Carolina, *that was taken in a Wood at* Guinea; *it is a Female about four Foot high, shaped in every Part like a Woman excepting its head, which nearly resembles the Ape: She walks upright, sits down to her Food, which is chiefly Greens, and feeds herself with her Hands as a human Creature. She is very fond of a Boy on board, and is observed always sorrowful at his Absence. She is cloathed with a thin Silk Vestment, and shews a great Discontent at the opening of her Gown to discover her Sex. She is the Female of the Creature, which the* Angolans *call Chimpanzee, or the Mockman.*
>
> [Reynolds, 1967, pp. 50–51]

The above quotation from the *London Magazine* describing the arrival of a chimpanzee in England in 1738 is perhaps not untypical of the naive observer's tendency to indulge in fancy when confronted with his closest relatives among primates. T. H. Huxley (1863), in the first chapter of his book mentioned earlier, gives an excellent account of what was known of the "man-like apes" in his day. Not all was fancy. There had been careful anatomical studies by Tyson in 1699 and Camper in 1779 that greatly clarified the similarities and differences between the Great Apes and man. Descriptions by such early travelers and naturalists as Battell, Buffon, and Savage, although containing some inaccuracies, are not totally inconsistent with what is known today. Still, it is only in relatively recent times that we have begun to amass truly accurate and detailed descriptions of the life of the Great Apes in the wild (see Schaller, 1963; Fossey, 1970; Bourne & Cohen, 1975 for the gorilla; Mackinnon, 1974; and Galdikas-Brindamour, 1975 for the orangutan; Yerkes, 1943; Lawick-Goodall 1965, 1968a, 1968b, 1971, 1973, 1975, 1976; Lawick-Goodall & Hamburg, 1974; Kortlandt, 1962; and Teleki, 1974 for the chimpanzee as well as general works such as DeVore, 1965; Reynolds, 1967; Altman, 1967; Napier, 1976; Yerkes & Yerkes, 1929; Menzel, 1973; Wilson, 1975; Tuttle, 1975; and Bourne, 1977). The picture that emerges from these studies is, if anything, more astonishing than any of the fanciful tales of the past. If one constructs a list of man's putatively unique behavior patterns, one would find on comparison with these studies that almost without exception these have precursors in the behavior of the Great Apes. In the following account we shall focus on the behavior of the chimpanzee. This account should not be thought of necessarily as generalizing to the other Great Apes, as there are considerable differences—some of which will be noted as we proceed.

GENERAL COMPLEX BEHAVIORS

Tool-use and construction. It is now well known that the ability to make and use tools is by no means unique to man. Even insects have this ability. Ants have recently been shown by researchers at the University of Maryland to use leaves for transportation of jelly left outside their nests. Birds may use pieces of paper to draw food into their cages. Otters use rocks to crack open abalone shells. But, as Lawick-Goodall has demonstrated in great detail, it is the chimpanzee that has developed this skill to the greatest extent, with the exception of man. They too use rocks to crack open shells. They use chewed leaves as "sponges" to sop up water from hollows in trees, to wipe up blood while eating meat, or to clean themselves. Twigs from which the leaves have been removed and blades of grass are used in collecting termites (see Figure 1.6). [Interestingly, quite similar techniques are employed by natives in the same region, who also enjoy termites (Teleki, 1974).] Sticks are used to open boxes, to poke at possibly dangerous objects, and as weapons. Stones and other objects are often hurled with a high degree of accuracy at foes (see Figure 1.6). The use of tools appears to be learned largely by imitation, a topic we shall return to later.

Cooperative Hunting and Food-sharing. If man cannot be truly considered *Homo faber,* perhaps he may at least be looked upon as the first true hunter among the primates. This has also proved not to be the case. Chimpanzees, unlike gorillas and orangs, have a definite taste for meat, hunting young primates as well as other animals. These hunts are often cooperative: When the prey is sighted, one chimpanzee will go after it while

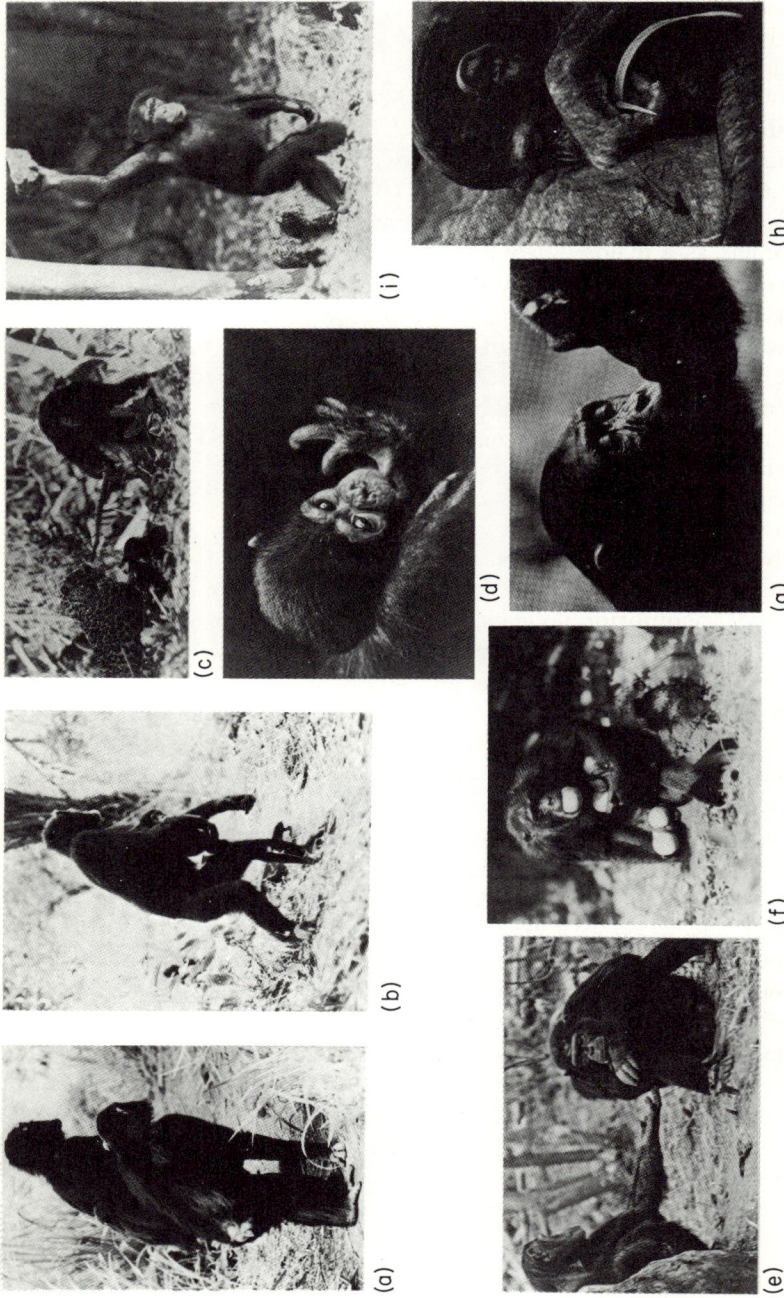

Figure 1.6. Some bodily postures and movements of chimpanzees. (a) Startled by sudden noise (note arm around back). (b) Mother walking upright with infant. (c) Using a stick to prod stuffed leopard. (d) Infant sucking thumb. (e) Begging for food with outstretched hand. (f) Walking upright when forelimbs are occupied. (g) Greeting with a kiss. (h) Angling for termites. (i) Juvenile about to hurl a rock.

24

others block off possible escape routes. Food-sharing is quite common among chimps. In fact the cries evoked by the discovery of food might be regarded as a somewhat indirect form of sharing. While sharing may occur in regard to other foods, particularly between a mother and her young, the main instances of this behavior observed by Lawick-Goodall have been in connection with meat-eating. Here begging with outstretched hands (see Figure 1.6) may often be rewarded with a partially chewed piece of the catch or, on occasion, an even larger portion thereof. Chimpanzees appear to regard brains as a major delicacy, something which appears also to have been true of our hominid ancestors (see Campbell, 1976).

Nest Construction. The construction of nests out of branches (sometimes with roofs) may foreshadow the early shelters of our ancestors. Such nests are usually constructed anew each night and are not besmirched with feces. Young chimpanzees up to 5 or 6 years of age sleep with their mothers.

Territoriality. Chimpanzees live in loose associations of about forty individuals. It has recently been discovered that groups of males often patrol the borders of their community's territory, attacking and even killing chimps from other communities that chance to wander within its borders. As in hunting, these attacks are often cooperative in nature.[7]

Bipedal Locomotion. Walking upright is not unusual in chimpanzees (see Figure 1.6), particularly when peering over high grass or when the arms are engaged in carrying fruit or other items. It is not, however, the natural mode of locomotion (as the *London Magazine* quotation implies). The natural mode involves walking on all fours, using the knuckles of the hands. This mode of locomotion is extremely difficult for humans, in part because of their decreased arm length.

Social Organization. The social ties in chimpanzee bands differ from those in most human communities. The strongest bonds are between a mother and her offspring and between siblings. Except at the time of conception, the father is nowhere in evidence. Sexual relations between males and females are almost completely unrestricted, except that there may be something like an incest taboo preventing males from mating with their mothers. Adults of the same sex may form "friendships" and forage together. Dominance in the community depends on the animal's sex and age.

The above is but the beginning of a long list of precursors and pressures tending plausibly in the hominid direction (see particularly Lawick-Goodall & Hamburg [1974] for a detailed discussion of how such factors might figure in the evolution of human behavior). In approaching the evolution of

[7] Exploring Human Nature Newsletter 2 (1975).

human communicative behavior specifically, it must be remembered that we are undoubtedly dealing with a very complex interaction of factors. All of the above tendencies may have been channeled in the hominid direction by some environmental change, such as a shift in habitat from woodland to savanna. This does appear to have occurred early in hominid evolution. Note how this change alone triggers further changes for which tendencies are already in evidence.

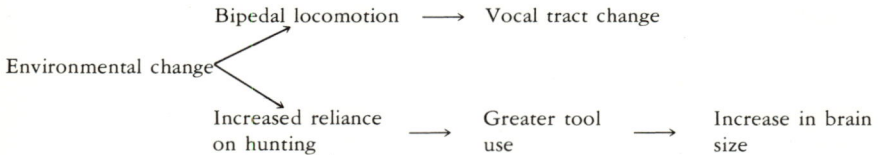

Bipedal locomotion $\longrightarrow$ Vocal tract change

Environmental change

Increased reliance $\longrightarrow$ Greater tool $\longrightarrow$ Increase in brain
on hunting   use   size

If cooperative behaviors, which are also already in evidence, result in increasing pressure for a more efficient form of communication, then the preadaptive change in vocal tract configuration, coupled with increased brain size allowing for greater storage capacity and complex information processing, are at hand to form the substrate for such an improved system (see Figure 1.19 for an elaboration of this interactive model).

COMMUNICATIVE BEHAVIOR

As documented in Table 1.3, primate communication in both the Great Apes and man involves a complex, partially redundant, multichannel system. Visual, tactile, olfactory, and auditory input modalities are involved. For the Great Apes, the last of these is probably the least important. Since the members of a group are well acquainted with each other, the modes of communication may be subtle indeed and there is little reason to believe that they are at this point fully understood (see Menzel, 1971).

Figure 1.6 clearly shows the remarkable similarity of many gestures employed by chimpanzees to those seen in humans. Lawick-Goodall has observed that in contexts of fear or apprehension chimpanzees touch or pat each other on the back, hold hands, hug, or otherwise seek contact with one another. After separation, kissing, embracing, and patting has been observed. A chimpanzee may bow in submission to a stronger rival, who then reaches out to touch him as a sign this gesture has been accepted. Threat postures involve upraised arms, the brandishing of sticks, and the throwing of objects. Begging with outstretched palm, tickling, pinching, kicking, and scratching all resemble these same gestures in man. A great amount of time is spent by chimpanzees in grooming one another. It appears that this is less important as a means of ridding each other of bits of dried skin and dirt as it is a means of extended contact. Lawick-Goodall suggests that his behavior may be retained as petting in human beings! Modern therapies involving a great deal of touching may simply represent a return to more primitive means of contact.

Facial expressions in primates have received considerable attention since the time of Darwin (see Darwin, 1972; Ekman, 1973; Andrew, 1963, 1965; and Van Hooff, 1971). The methodology followed by Darwin (see Chevalier-Skolnikoff, 1972) is very much like that advocated here, namely, a correlation of facial expressions not only with the contexts in which they occur, but also with the facial musculature that effects them and the central neural control centers involved. In terms of musculature, Huber (1931) found that there has been a substantial reduction of ear musculature in the Great Apes and man. Two facial muscles in man, the **risoris,** which pulls the mouth corners laterally, and the **mentalis,** which pushes the lower lip out, appear to be without homologue in the apes. There is a finer interlacing of muscles around the lips, which Huber suggests may have developed in connection with speech. As far as central control systems are concerned, we shall see later that facial expression and vocalization appear to be very closely related neurologically in nonhuman primates.

Figure 1.7 presents some of the more common facial expressions observed in chimpanzees. On the basis of the contexts in which they occur, as well as the peripheral and central structures involved, Chevalier-Skolnikoff (1972) and Jolly (1972) suggest the homologies listed in Table 1.4. Most investigators believe that the human smile and laugh have different origins, as this table suggests. In fact, in many societies, the smile is still more closely connected with apprehension and discomfort than humor or enjoyment.

Vocalization in the Great Apes consists of various grunts, barks, screams, hoots and roars. These are described by Schaller (1963) for the gorilla and by the Reynoldses (1965) and Lawick-Goodall (see publications cited earlier on p. 23) for the chimpanzee (see Table 1.5). Of these two species, the chimpanzee is decidedly the more vocal. In neither, does the number of distinguishable calls exceed 30. Most calls allow for some variation in loudness, frequency, etc. which appears to reflect the intensity of the state that elicits them. In both apes and monkeys, vocalizations are invariably tied to various emotional contexts such as threats, aggression, fear, pain, pleasure, feeding, separation, etc.

Such calls are clearly not homologous with human speech with which they differ in at least the following ways:

1. They are limited in number.
2. They are tied to a particular time and place.
3. They appear to be triggered by only a small set of emotional stimuli.

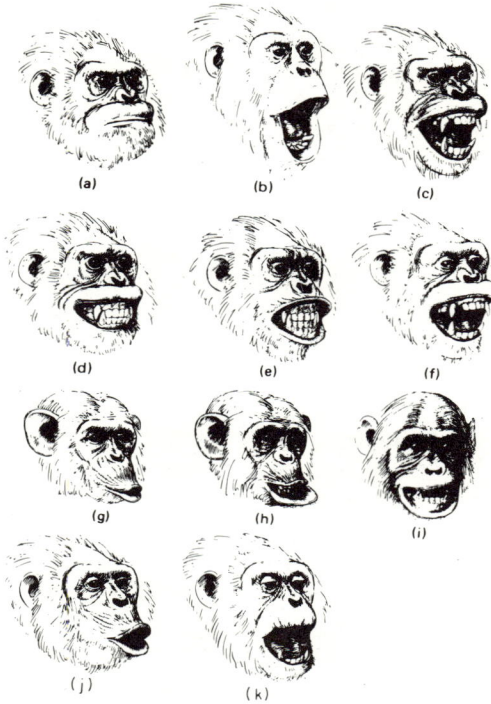

Figure 1.7. Some facial expressions of chimpanzees: (a) "Glare"; anger, type 1. (b) "Waa bark"; anger, type 2. (c) "Scream calls'; fear-anger (d) "Silent bared-teeth"; "type 1, horizontal bared-teeth"; submission. (e) "Silent bared-teeth"; "type 2, vertical bared-teeth"; fear-affection(?). (f) "Silent bared-teeth"; "type 3, open-mouth bared-teeth"; affection. (g) "Pout face"; desiring-frustration (?). (h) "Whimper face"; frustration-sadness (?), type 1, or type 1–2 transition (infant). (i) "Cry face"; frustration-sadness, type 2 (infant). (j) "Hoot face"; excitement-affection (?). (k) "Play face"; playfulness. **Note**—These drawings are presented for illustrative purposes only. They are diagrammatic and do not claim to precisely depict actual expressions of emotion. They are drawn after photographs and descriptions from van Hooff (1971) and van Lawick-Goodall (1968a, b). All expressions were drawn from the same angle in order to facilitate comparisons.

4. There is some evidence that they are the product of an essentially closed genetic program (see Mayr, 1974).
5. Finally, they do not evince what Hockett (1960) has termed **duality of patterning,** that is, they differ from one another as gestalts, and are not composed of recombinable, meaningless components.

These vocalizations resemble a component of human paralanguage termed **affective vocalization** (see Table 1.3).

In sum, it should be evident that nonhuman primate communication in the wild is not homologous with human speech, but rather with certain

TABLE 1.4 Possibly Homologous Facial Expressions in Chimpanzee and Man[a]

Chimpanzee	Man
(a) ———————————→	Angry face with compressed lips
(b)	
(c) ———————————→	Angry face with bared teeth
(d) ⎫	
(e) ⎬———————————→	Smile
(f) ⎭	
(g) ———————————→	Pout, begging fact (infant)
(h) ———————————→	Sad face (adult)
(i) ———————————→	Crying face (child)
(j)	
(k) ———————————→	Laughter

[a]Letters refer to facial expressions shown in Figure 1.7.

TABLE 1.5 Chimpanzee Vocalizations

Description of sound	Typical circumstances of emission
loud barks	finding food
scream	when attacked (fright)
wraaa call	alarm
pant-hoots	arrival at food source
	joining another group
whimpering	after attack
squeaks	fright
grunts	feeding, grooming, close-range contact calls
pant-grunts	approaching superior after threat or attack

aspects of human paralanguage. This shows up clearly when one compares these three communication systems in terms of Hockett's design features (see Appendix). Note the almost complete overlap of columns (1) and (2) in terms of feature values (14 out of 16 features identical). Comparison with column (6), on the other hand, shows only 2 out of 16 features identical. It would appear that speech that is articulated (i.e., evinces duality of patterning), as opposed to holistic (gestalt-like), is peculiar to the hominid line and overlies an older paralinguistic system that is a homologous communication system in the apes and man. That this is indeed the case will become increasingly clear as our investigation progresses. Note that in making this observation we are speaking only in terms of input–output modalities; other aspects of general communication systems depicted in Figure 1.5 have yet to be dealt with.[8]

[8] After this manuscript was completed, Marler and Tenaza (1977) published a comprehensive comparative study of the signaling behavior of apes with special reference to vocalization which should be consulted for additional information on the behavior discussed in this section.

Experimental Studies of the Great Apes

GENERAL COMPLEX BEHAVIORS

From the very outset, one of the prime objectives of experimental studies involving the Great Apes was the determination of the extent of their higher mental functions: learning, cognition, intelligence (see Yerkes & Learned, 1925; Yerkes & Yerkes , 1929; Köhler, 1951; Nissen, 1946; Rumbaugh, 1970, 1971; and Rumbaugh & Gill, 1973). The majority of these studies were conducted under laboratory conditions. A fair amount of data, however, is also available on apes raised in the investigators' own homes (see Kohts, 1935; Hayes, 1951; Hayes & Hayes, 1951; Hayes & Nissen, 1971; Kellogg, 1933, 1968; and Temerlin, 1975). A major purpose of these latter studies was to provide a comparison of the development of human children and apes being raised in identical environments. This aspect of these studies will be reviewed in the final section of this chapter, which deals with ontogenesis.

It would be impossible to survey all of the literature on the higher mental functions of the Great Apes. What will be attempted here is to provide the reader with a "feel" for the types of tasks involved and the abilities exhibited.

First of all, a number of caveats about such studies should be noted. We must not forget the lesson learned earlier concerning the so-called **scala naturae**. Hodos (1970) has noted that if one measures the development of learning set across taxa, one finds that pigeons do as well as monkeys and minks as well as chimpanzees. Only when examined within closely related species do we find similar rates of learning. Thus among primates, New World Monkeys tend to all perform at low rates; Old World Monkeys at intermediate rates; and the hominoids at the highest rates (see also Rumbaugh, 1970). Even among closely related species there may be great differences in attention, motivation, and the like. Such differences probably account for any variations in skills observed between chimps, orangs, and gorillas. Finally, evidence clearly shows that results will differ depending on the environment in which the animal has been reared. For example, the Hayeses presented many of their tasks both to their home-raised chimp, Viki, and to laboratory chimps at the nearby Yerkes Laboratories. In every instance, the latter chimps did worse.

Let us begin with self-recognition. Gallup (1970) has shown that chimpanzees clearly recognized themselves in a mirror, inspecting various parts of their bodies and worrying over dye marks placed on their faces by the experimenter. Macaques failed to demonstrate this behavior, continuing to regard the image in the mirror as another monkey.

Symbolic play has been observed in home-raised chimps by both the Hayeses and the Gardners. For example, Washoe, the Gardners' chimp, after being bathed several times, was observed washing her doll in the bathtub.

The ability to recognize photographs and drawings, whether in color or in black and white, is marked in chimpanzees, as we shall see in a number of different contexts below. Their artistic abilities, however, leave much to be desired, with the possible exception of their "architectural" talents as displayed in their constructions with blocks (see Bourne, 1971).

Numerous examples of insight learning have been documented by Köhler (1951) as well as Hayes and Nissen (1971). Boxes are stacked up in order to reach a reward. Poles are fitted together in order to reach a desired object. As those who have raised chimps at home have learned to their dismay, they have the ability to open almost any kind of latch or lock.

Viki, the Hayeses' "daughter," was able to perform at the level of a precounting child in matching cards with the same number of dots arranged in different ways. She did poorly when the number of dots was large or there were only slight differences between cards (see Hayes and Nissen 1971). Ferster (1964) has demonstrated that chimpanzees can be taught to count objects using the binary number system. The number of trials required to accomplish this was immense however (170,000 trials in all).

Rensch and Döhl (1968) have shown that a chimpanzee can learn to solve quite complicated maze problems. It is interesting that chimpanzees, like human subjects, appear to think their way through the maze before starting a problem.

Lenneberg (1971) suggested several experiments that might provide insight into whether apes evince language or not. One of them was relational in nature: Its object was to discover whether blocks might be interpreted as tables when surrounded by smaller blocks, but as chairs when surrounding a larger block. To my knowledge no one has performed this particular test on chimpanzees that have learned a symbolic communication system. Nevertheless, results of a transposition study performed by Gonzales *et al.* (1954) suggest chimpanzees might have little difficulty. Chimpanzees were shown in this study to be able to select one of three boxes, not in terms of absolute size, but in terms of relative size compared to other boxes.

The Hayes have been able to demonstrate Viki's remarkable ability in categorizing objects in various ways. Thus, she was able to distinguish between such classes as animals versus inanimate objects, males versus females, children versus adults, complete versus incomplete drawings, and the like. She was able to correctly sort objects differing in various ways, for example, paperclips versus nails, black buttons versus white buttons, spoons versus forks. Although she was able to sort items in terms of function, it appears that form was the more salient dimension to her. Thus, in sorting buttons and coins, buttons without holes in them were placed with the coins. In sorting pictures representing humans versus other animals, she correctly placed the picture of her father, Bokar, in the animal pile; a picture of herself, however, was placed unhesitatingly in the human pile!

Because of its putative relation to language, the investigation of cross-modal perception in nonhuman primates has assumed great importance. Geschwind (1965, 1970) originally suggested the idea that the ability to form cross-modal ties between two nonlimbic modalities (e.g., visual–auditory or tactile–auditory) was a crucial factor in the development of naming in particular and language in general. This theory has gained wide currency in anthropology, particularly through the writings of Lancaster (1968, 1975; Washburn & Lancaster, 1971). At the time this theory was advanced, experimental evidence indicated that the ability to form such cross-modal associations was unique to man (see Ettlinger & Blakemore, 1960). Since that time, numerous experiments demonstrating haptic–visual and visual–haptic transfer in apes (Davenport *et al.*, 1970, 1971, 1973, 1975; Davenport, 1976) and in monkeys (Cowey & Weiskrantz, 1975) have been performed. Transfer has also been demonstrated between auditory and visual labels for objects (Premack, 1976; Fouts *et al.*, 1976). Davenport (1976) reports, however, that he has not been able to train chimpanzees to match long and short pulses of sound to long and short flashes of light. Then again, a similar task appears to be impossible for humans (Cole *et al.*, 1961).

It is doubtful that cross-modal transfer plays more than a peripheral role in the learning of lexical items. As our model of communication (Figure 1.5) shows, language involves a linkage between simple and complex concepts and input–output modalities. This section has clearly demonstrated that the Great Apes can form such linkages. Many of the concepts they have learned have no visual counterparts. What Geschwind's model appears to amount to is a purely referential theory of meaning, which was long ago recognized as untenable. Furthermore, the idea that naming forms the basis of language is without justification. A dictionary of a language is rather unhelpful if one does not know how to put together the items it contains to signal complex meanings.

HUMAN-LIKE COMMUNICATIVE BEHAVIORS

In 1661, Samuel Pepys was afforded the opportunity to inspect what appears to have been a chimpanzee that had just arrived aboard ship from

"Guiny." Afterwards, he noted in his diary that the creature seemed to be able to understand much English and expressed the opinion that it could be taught to speak or make signs. Likewise, Lord Monboddo, relying on Tyson's comparative anatomical studies, felt that an ape should most certainly be capable of language. Indeed, in light of their remarkable intellectual abilities, which have just been surveyed, the two gentlemen's confidence does not seem to be unjustified. The experiments relating to this question are conveniently reviewed in terms of input–output modalities.

Auditory–Vocal Input–Output Modality. All experimenters who have worked with chimpanzees report evidence of auditory language processing. Kellogg (1968) notes that Gua, the chimpanzee he raised in his household, could respond reliably to 58 phrases; the Hayeses calculated that Viki responded to about 50 (Hayes, 1951). As we shall see later, chimpanzees can also transfer from auditory to signed responses (Fouts *et al.*, 1976).

On the other hand, there is but little evidence that the Great Apes can vocalize voluntarily or, for that matter, even suppress spontaneous vocalization. Thus, a chimp that may have managed to purloin quite cleverly some favored food invariably gives itself away by the utterance of noisy food grunts. Furthermore, the Great Apes, while possessing great abilities to imitate in other modalities, show little or no ability to imitate sounds.

This is not to say there has been no success along these lines. Witmer (1909) managed to train a chimpanzee to utter *mama* on appropriate occasions. As in all other reported experiments of this type, the vowel sounds were reported to be breathy, that is, probably whispered. Furness (1916) achieved even greater success teaching an orangutan two words: *papa* and *cup*. An idea of the difficulty involved in accomplishing this feat may be gleaned from Furness' own account of how the latter word was taught.

> The next word I attempted to teach her to say was "cup." (Let me say that by this time she understood almost everything that it was necessary for me to say such as "Open your mouth," "Stick out your tongue," etc., and she was perfectly gentle and occasionally seemed quite interested.) The first move in teaching her to say cup was to push her tongue back in her throat as if she were to make the sound "ka." This was done by means of a bone spatula with which I pressed lightly on the center of her tongue. When I saw that she had taken a full breath I placed my finger over her nose to make her try to breathe through her mouth. The spatula was then quickly withdrawn and inevitably she made the sound "ka." All the while facing her I held my mouth open with my tongue in the same position as hers so that her observation, curiosity, and powers of imitation might aid her, and I said *ka* with her emphatically as I released her tongue. After several lessons of, perhaps, fifteen minutes of this sort of training each day she would draw back her tongue to the position even before the spatula had touched it, but she would not say *ka* unless I placed my finger over her nose. The next advance was that she herself placed my finger over her nose and then

said *ka* without any use of the spatula; then she found that in default of my finger her own would answer the purpose and I could get her to make this sound any time I asked her to. It was comparatively easy from this to teach her to say '*kap*' by means of closing her lips with my fingers the instant she said *ka*. At the same time I showed her the cup that she drank out of and I repeated the word several times as I touched it to her lips. After a few lessons when I showed her the cup and asked "What is this?" she would say cup very plainly. Once when ill at night she leaned out of her hammock and said "cup, cup, cup," which I naturally understood to mean that she was thirsty and which proved to be the case. I think this showed fairly conclusively that there was a glimmering idea of the connection of the word with the object and with her desire [pp. 284–285].

This account is remarkably similar to Cathy Hayes's description of Viki learning the same word (K. Hayes, 1950; C. Hayes, 1951). Indeed, it is the Hayeses who had the greatest success of all in teaching vocal language to a chimpanzee: four words after 6½ years!

The harsh conclusion reached by Harlow *et al.* (1972) that any one observing the film of Viki's efforts must admit that "chimpanzees cannot speak, and no chimpanzee ever will speak, regardless of the training technique" is certainly not far off the mark. Still, these experiments, as well as those conducted by Yerkes and Learned (1925) with completely negative results, are highly instructive. They focus attention on what I would claim to be the only **qualitative** difference in the communication systems of the apes and man. The ape appears capable of some auditory processing, but is virtually unable to bring his articulation under auditory control. That some success, however meager, has been demonstrated may possibly be taken as an indication that our common ancestor with the apes was not totally incapable of moving in the direction of articulate speech. It would be a mistake to regard the ability to produce articulate speech as a paltry difference, a small step in evolution. As we shall see, it is clear even in light of what little is known today that articulate speech, coupled perhaps with other aspects of an efficient communication system, constitutes a quantum jump in man's neural organization compared to his primate relatives. On the other hand, it would be equally mistaken to read into the evolutionary development more than is there. What appears to be involved is a change in input–output abilities, with perhaps a concomitant increase in efficiency, not a qualitative change in the character of communication in general. This should be clearer after examining the communicative potential in nonhuman primates using an alternate input–output modality.

Visual–Manual Input–Output Modality. We have noted that as long ago as 1661 it had been suggested that, if apes could not be taught to speak, perhaps they could be taught to express themselves by means of manual gestures. We have already seen considerable evidence for such a mode of communication in the wild. The imitative abilities of nonhuman primates in terms of gestures and postures are well established. Parker (1974), who has done careful studies of manipulative ability, finds that the pongids outrank monkeys in grasping objects and applying manipulated objects to the body or to other objects. The use of gestures to convey meanings has also been observed in home-raised chimps (see Kellogg 1968). It was the realization that the film of Viki's efforts at vocal communication could be understood without sound—in terms of gestures alone—that initially encouraged the Gardners to undertake their research in teaching American Sign Language (ASL) to chimpanzees. After their considerable success with Washoe, a number of research projects employing the visual–manual modality sprang up. Pertinent aspects of these are presented in Table 1.6. In the results column of that table, only the productive vocabulary of the subjects is provided. As in the case of children acquiring their first language, recognition vocabulary may often be as much as twice as large as productive vocabulary and may not overlap that vocabulary in toto. Also, it might be pointed out that the stringent requirements for evidence of productive acquisition undoubtedly underestimates the chimp's abilities, particularly in comparison with language acquisition studies of children, where such requirements seldom hold.

Although the aims, training procedures, and communication systems differ considerably from one of these projects to another, the results of language training are strikingly similar. We shall therefore review these in general terms below (see Fleming, 1974a, 1974b; Linden, 1974; Watt, 1974; Symposium, 1975; and Mounin, 1976, for general discussions of this research).

Vocabulary. Each project has provided considerable evidence of the Great Apes' naming ability. Although there are differences among chimps in the time required to learn signs and there are particular signs that take longer to learn than others, no chimp tested so far lacks the ability to learn a visual–manual language (Fouts, 1973). Also, in the few cases where other species have been tested (an orang by Fouts [1975b] and a gorilla by Patterson [1978]), learning has been clearly demonstrated.

The Gardners require that a sign be observed in at least one appropriate and spontaneous occurrence each day for 15 consecutive days for it to be counted part of their chimp's productive vocabulary. In testing they employ a double-blind procedure, with two "blind" experimenters recording Washoe's responses to slides of objects back-projected on a screen neither experimenter can see. Typically, accuracy is 80–90% correct. Naming errors quite often involve substitutions within categories, for example, replacement of *brush* with *comb*. Signs learned in one situation are appropriately generalized to other cases. For example, the sign *open* may be learned in the context of doors, but is generalized to boxes, Coke bottles,

TABLE 1.6 Major Studies of the Great Apes' Communicative Abilities (Visual–Manual Input–Output Modality)

Projects: Principal investigator and representative publications	Name, species, age (at onset of study), and sex of subjects	Communication system	General results
1. Beatrice and Allen Gardner (1969, 1971, 1974a, 1974b, 1975a, 1975b)	Washoe (chimp., f., 8–14 months)	ASL	160 signs; considerable syntactic ability
	Moja and Pili (chimps., f., 1 day)	ASL	15 and 13 signs respectively; first two-sign combinations
2. Ann and David Premack (1970, 1971a, 1971b, 1972, 1976a, 1976b)	Sarah (chimp., f., 6 yrs.)	Plastic symbols	130 signs; considerable cognitive and syntactic abilities
	Work started with two new chimps: Elizabeth (f., 5 yrs.) and Peony (f., 5 yrs.)		
3. Roger Fouts (1972, 1973a, 1973b, 1974a, 1974b, 1975a, 1975b, 1976a, 1976b, In press)	Washoe (chimp., f., 33–39 months) plus numerous other chimps and one orangutan.	ASL	Varying sign vocabularies and syntactic abilities (see text)
4. Duane Rumbaugh (1973, 1974a, 1974b, 1976, 1977)	Lana (chimp., f., 2 yrs)	Yerkish	73 lexigrams plus considerable syntactic ability
5. Maurice Temerlin (1975)	Lucy (chimp., f., 1 month)	ASL	102 signs; considerable syntactic ability
6. H. Terrace (1976, n.d.)	Nim (chimp., m., 1 week)	ASL	45 signs; considerable syntactic ability
7. P. Patterson (1978)	Koko (gorilla, f., 12 months)	ASL	375 signs; considerable syntactic ability

and the like. Where overgeneralization occurs, it is of the type frequently observed in children learning their first language. Thus, Washoe applied the sign for *baby* appropriately to human infants, but also to pictures and miniature statues of animals.

Since cross-modal transfer has been evoked to account for naming ability, the evidence from these studies certainly supports its existence in the Great Apes. Further transfer between auditory and signed stimuli has been demonstrated by Fouts *et al.* (1976). Thus a chimp was able to relate English words to their referents reliably, learn signs for each of the words in the absence of their referents and then apply these signs correctly.

Clear evidence for the chimp's equation of the symbol and its referent was provided by Premack (1972), who showed that both an actual apple and the plastic symbol for apple (a blue triangle) were characterized in terms of identical features by Sarah, that is, both were red, both had a stem, and so forth.

Syntax. Spontaneous combination of signs was first noted in the tenth month of their project by the Gardners. It is somewhat easier to determine that signs are being used in combination in ASL than in a spoken language because of the typical posture of the hands following transmission of a sign combination. Hands and arms are moved from the signing space to come to rest on a nearby object or the lower body. Three years into their project, the Gardners had recorded 294 different two-sign combinations and 245 different combinations of three signs or more. Upon analysis these sign combinations were shown to display the same types of semantic elements that Roger Brown (1973) postulates for Stage I in child language development.

In the projects of Premack and Rumbaugh, strict ordering of elements is required from the very outset of training. In ASL, order is more tied to the context than in spoken English. Still, order is adhered to when it is crucial to the meaning. Thus, it is possible to sign: ROGER TICKLE LUCY as in Figure 1.8. But it is also possible to sign the converse: *LUCY TICKLE ROGER.* When this was first attempted, Lucy paused to think the proposition over and then proceeded to do as she was told. In some facets of syntax, Washoe demonstrates greater ability than her human counterparts. The Gardners report that Washoe makes fewer reversals of word order and that she performs at a higher level of accuracy (90 versus 50% correct) in matching reversible strings (such as *cat bit dog* versus *dog bit cat*) to pictures (see Linden, 1974, pp. 247–248).

Coining of new signs and sign combinations has been observed on numerous occasions. For example, one chimp made up a sign to refer to her leash, for which no sign had been provided her. Lucy first labeled a radish *food* until she chanced to bite into it, whereupon it was labeled as *cry hurt food.*

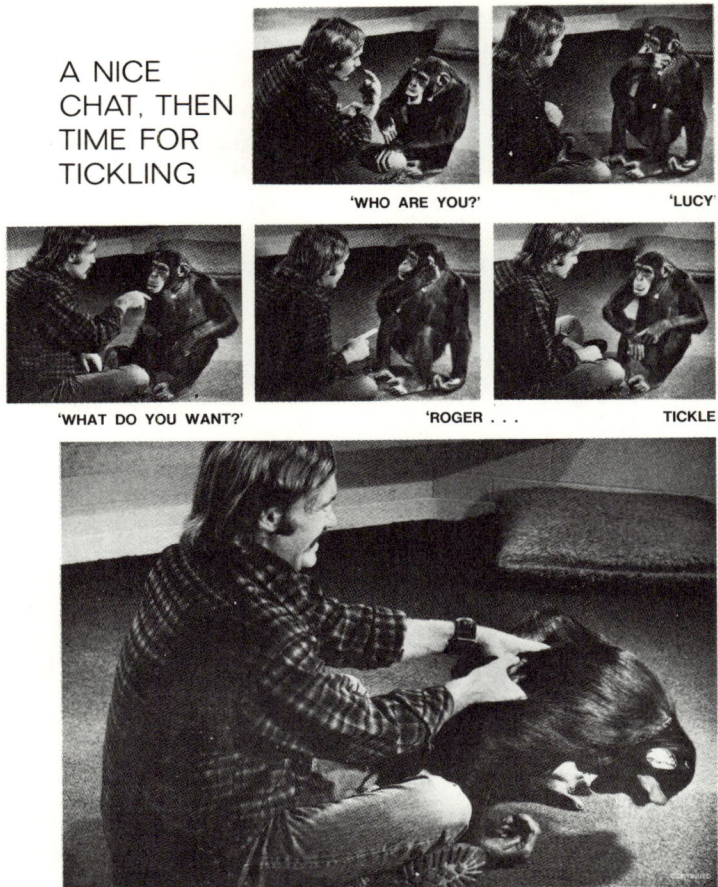

A NICE
CHAT, THEN
TIME FOR
TICKLING

'WHO ARE YOU?'   'LUCY'

'WHAT DO YOU WANT?'   'ROGER . . .   TICKLE

Figure 1.8. An example of a conversation in American Sign Language between Roger Fouts and the chimpanzee, Lucy.

Premack has demonstrated Sarah's ability to master structures which are conceptually quite complex. Thus, she is not only able to use symbols for negation and interrogative appropriately but is also able to demonstrate knowledge of conditional structures such as: *Sarah take apple ⊃ Mary give Sarah chocolate* (as in symbolic logic, a single symbol is used for the if–then relation). This is a structure that is acquired quite late by children, presumably because of its cognitive complexity, since syntactically it is less complex in many languages than structures regularly acquired earlier by the child (see Slobin, 1971).

A salient characteristic of the syntax of natural language is that it is organized hierarchically, that is, various groups of words in a sentence are more closely related than others and function as units (constituents). One feature of so-called *wh*-questions is that they require different constituents of sentences as answers. Thus, if there is a red lamp on the table, the *wh*-question *what is on the table?* elicits one constituent (*a red lamp*) while the question *where is the lamp?* elicits another (*on the table*). The Gardners (1975b) were able to show that Washoe was capable of answering such questions appropriately 84% of the time. Once again this result seems to be better than children at comparable stages of development.

Conversation. It is sometimes claimed by critics (e.g., Mounin, 1976) that chimps do not initiate conversations. This is clearly not the case. Mandel and Fouts (1975) note that one chimp, Lucy, initiated 77% of the 267 ASL conversations they analyzed. Miles (1976) notes that two-thirds of Ally's conversations were initiated by him. The research by Rumbaugh also supports this finding. Griffin (1976) has suggested that conversations with animals may lead to important insight into their mental life unattainable via traditional ethological techniques. Such insight has frequently been gained in exchanges with chimps. Thus it is now possible to query a chimp directly concerning the identity of its reflection in a mirror instead of resorting to the indirect methods of Gallup (1970) mentioned earlier. In the instances reported in the literature, chimps correctly respond by signing their names or pointing to themselves. It has been possible to observe prevarication in our closest relatives. Thus, Lucy, upon being interrogated as to who was responsible for besmirching a rug, implicated a number of other possible miscreants before admitting that she was the one responsible.

The existence of spontaneous conversation raises the possibility of communication among the Great Apes. Intraspecific teaching and communicative behaviors has already been observed in signing chimps. Roger Fouts is currently investigating such behavior from a number of different standpoints, including the possibility that a mother might be induced to teach her infant sign language.

The following interchange between human and chimp (Rumbaugh & Gill, 1976) provides as good an example as any of the level of communicative ability attained by nonhuman primates.

Tim had entered the anteroom with a bowl of monkey chow. Lana had asked that it be loaded into the machine; however, the conditions of the test called for Tim *not* to comply, to load cabbage for vending instead, and to declare that chow (which she had requested) was in the machine. Although Lana might have asked the machine to vend "chow," she did not—appropriate to the fact that cabbage, and not monkey chow, was in the vendor. She said:

Lana:	Please machine give piece of cabbage.	16:53
	? you (Tim) put chow in machine. (5 times)	16:54–16:55

Tim: (lying) Chow in machine. (In response to each of the 5
        requests.)
Lana: ? Chow in machine.   16:57
Tim: (still lying) Yes.   16:57
Lana: No chow in machine. (which was true)   16:57
Tim: ? What in machine. (repeat once)   16:57 & 16:58
Lana: Cabbage in machine. (which was true)   16:59
Tim: Yes cabbage in machine.   16:59
Lana: ? You move cabbage out-of machine.   17:00
Tim: Yes. (Whereupon he removed the cabbage and put in the   17:01
        monkey chow.)
Lana: Please machine give piece of chow. (Repeatedly until all was   17:01
        obtained.)

Conclusion: Lana discerned what had, in fact, been loaded in the machine, did not concur with Tim's assertion that it was "chow," asked that he remove it, and then asked for "chow" when it was loaded for vending [p. 575].

Although some have expressed doubts about the level of communicative abilities displayed in these experiments (see Bronowski & Bellugi, 1970; Lenneberg, 1970, 1971; Brown, 1973; Fodor *et al.*, 1974; and Mounin, 1976), it seems to me that they follow quite naturally from the studies reviewed above demonstrating the considerable cognitive capacities of the Great Apes. It is only to those that have decided a priori that species-specificity and task-specificity characterize human communication systems as a whole that these results are unexpected (cf. Appendix for a comparison of pongid and human ASL communication in terms of Hockett's design features).

A NOTE ON THE GESTURAL ORIGIN OF LANGUAGE

In a number of publications, Gordon Hewes (1973a, 1973b, 1973c, 1976) has offered support for the view of some antiquity (see Stam, 1976) that the most primitive hominid communication system utilized the visual–manual input–output modality for propositional transfer of information. It is not claimed that this was the sole modality employed (all modalities listed in Table 1.3 were operative)—only that this modality was the first to come under completely volitional control. This view is not implausible in terms of available evidence.

Comparative studies have demonstrated that volitional control of gestures exists throughout the primate order. It is in this modality that learning by imitation takes place. The studies we have just reviewed documenting human-like communication via this modality clearly support the potential for such communication in our common ancestor. On the other hand, there is little or no evidence for volitional control of the vocal tract musculature or for imitation using this output modality. Indeed, as we shall see, the vocal tract in nonhuman primates and man is only fractionally homologous.

As documented by Hewes (1973b), gestures are widely employed in situations where speech will not serve. This is true not only under noisy conditions or when unknown languages provide a barrier but also in cases of pathology. The use of a gestural language is, of course, best known among the deaf, but has also been demonstrated to be a possible mode of communication with feral children (Itard, 1962), autistic children (Offir, 1976) and in cases of aphasia (Critchley, 1975).

In language ontogenesis in humans, as we shall see, gesture combined with visual and auditory processing preceeds articulate speech. Deaf children and chimps also begin signing long before hearing children utter their first words (the Gardners, 1975a and Dale, 1976). This may be due to the fact that the neocortical components of the pyramidal system involved in hand-arm movements matures earlier than the areas involved in speech (see Lamendella 1977). There is some evidence that gestural systems of communication are invented spontaneously by isolated children (Kroeber, (1917) as well as the deaf (Goldin-Meadow & Feldman, 1975).

As far as central control is concerned, there is considerable evidence that both the production and processing of gestures is subserved by quite different neural substrates from speech (cf. discussion of cerebral lateralization later; also McKeever, 1976; Geschwind, 1965).

It seems quite reasonable to assume that the first communication of propositions would be via an input–output modality which was already in place. We have seen some possible precursors for speech in the studies reviewed on p. 33ff.). But these are rudimentary at best. The complexity of the peripheral and central control structures required for speech make it quite likely that their development was of a mosaic character and involved a considerable span of time.

EVOLUTION OF THE PRIMATE VOCAL TRACT AND EAR (PERIPHERAL STRUCTURES)

> *Among the primates, only man has the capacity of using the organ of voice to convey thoughts in the form of speech.*
> [Jozef Jordan, 1971, p. 97]

The role played by peripheral structures (the vocal tract and ear) in the evolution of speech has been a subject of much dispute in the past and continues to be today. Thus, in the eighteenth century Lord Monboddo felt that in the light of Tyson's comparative work chimpanzees had all the anatomical features necessary for speech. However, in the same century, Pieter Camper's anatomical and behavioral research on orangutans led him to declare that this closely related species totally lacked the physical apparatus for articulate speech. This dispute is carried on today by such noted scholars as Wind (1976), who sides with Lord Monboddo and Kelemen (1948), working on chimpanzees, who sides with Camper.

In regard to the ear's capacity for auditory and linguistic processing, there has been less dispute historically. It has generally been felt that animals such as cats and dogs, not to mention nonhuman primates (see Samuel Pepys's view mentioned earlier), were able to process human language to some extent.

In this section we shall examine what light, if any, recent research can throw on these questions.

The Vocal Tract

PAN-HOMO COMPARISON

For those who imagine that increased complexity of function inevitably leads to increased complexity in structure, it must come as a shock to discover that comparison of the vocal tracts of anthropoid apes and man yields evidence of considerable simplification in structure in the hominid line.

The comparative work of a number of investigators (Kelemen, 1948, 1949, 1958, 1964, 1969; Fink, 1963, 1975; Starck & Schneider, 1960; Negus, 1940, 1949; Jordan, 1971; and Wind, 1970, 1975) allows us to document the numerous anatomical and physiological differences that exist between the chimpanzee and the human vocal tract. Some of these are clear even in the grossly simplified representation in Figure 1.9. Vocalization in humans involves an energy source provided by the lungs that excites the vocal folds of the larynx producing a buzz-like sound. This sound is then molded in various ways by a number of resonators, two of which, the pharyngeal and oral cavities, can be altered in shape by so-called articulators. This complex chain of events is diagrammed in Figure 1.10 (see Lieberman [1975b] for a brief summary of the physiology and acoustics of speech).

Returning to Figure 1.9, one of the most striking and potentially important differences that one observes is the position of the larynx. In the chimpanzee, the larynx is positioned quite high with its superior margin at the level of the second cervical vertebra. In contrast, in humans the superior margin is, on the average, at C_3 in women and C_4 in men. Figure 1.11 shows that the position of the larynx in man is the culmination of a gradual process of descent in the primate order as a whole. The apes thus have a lower larynx position than the monkeys.

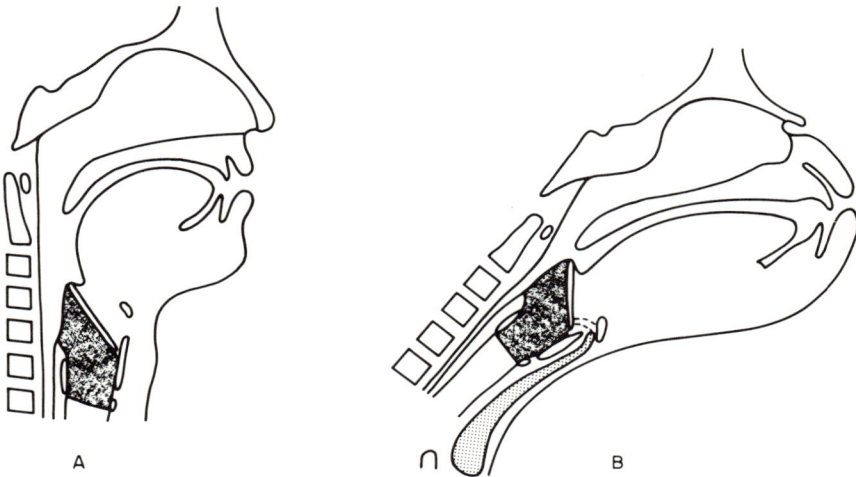

Figure 1.9. Scheme of the resonant tube in sagittal section in man (A) and chimpanzee (B). The black field is the laryngeal cavity, and the dotted field the laryngeal sac.

As a result of the descent of the larynx, the epiglottis no longer interacts with the soft palate to allow the oral cavity to be closed off while breathing. This is true in man and adult chimpanzees, where Jordan (1971) found the two structures are separated by a distance of some 4–5 mm. This has certain disadvantages in that it diminishes the acuity of smell when food is in the mouth. The epiglottis, which is high and wider in its upper portion in the chimpanzee, is capable of sealing off the inlet to the larynx while swallowing; this is no longer the case in man.

Many of the changes in the relations among the structures of the vocal tract may be the result of a change in posture (see Du Brul, 1958, 1976, 1977). We have already observed a tendency toward upright posture in chimpanzees. This tendency increased in the hominid line: Even as early as the Australopithecines, pelvic bones indicate upright posture and locomotion as the norm. One can see what effect this would have on the vocal tract

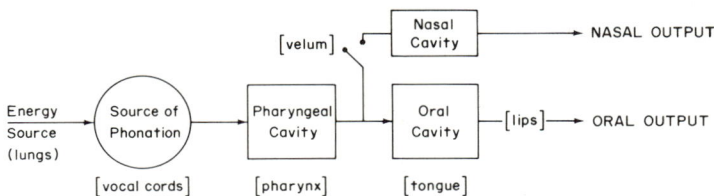

Figure 1.10. The basic components of the human vocal tract. (Boxes represent resonators; square brackets enclose articulators.)

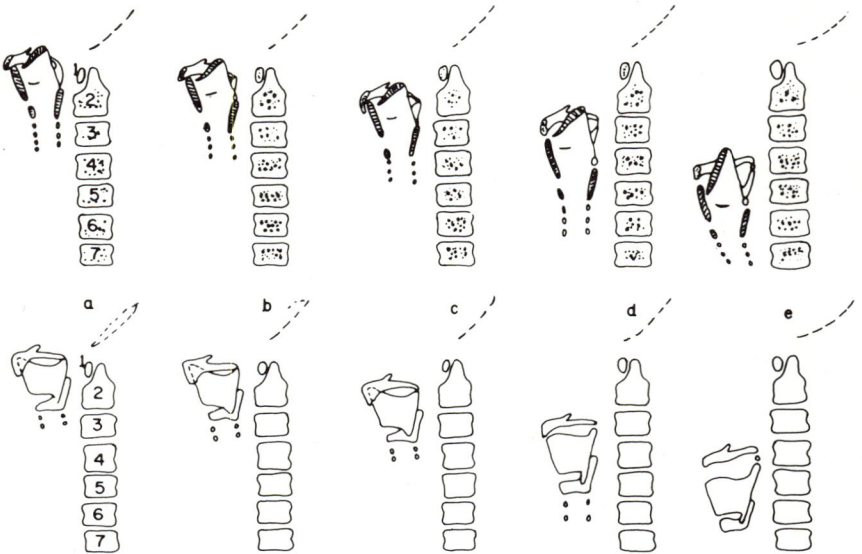

Figure 1.11. Station of hyoid bone and larynx in primates relative to cervical vertebrae. From left to right: *a*, lemur; *b*, Platyrrhina; *c*, Cercopithecidae, Ateles; *d*, Anthropomorpha; *e*, Homo. The interrupted line represents squamous occipital bone.

of a chimpanzee by aligning the spinal column of the chimpanzee in Figure 1.9 to match that of man. If the head is bent downward so the animal looks straight ahead rather then upward and the foramen magnum and the condyles are shifted forward to allow for better balance of the head on the spinal column, it is not too difficult to see how one would arrive at the vocal tract configuration of man. The tongue, which does not change in mass, is bent downward so that its posterior one-third becomes the anterior wall of the now greatly enlarged pharyngeal cavity. The larynx descends further down the throat with the descent of the tongue and the advance of the foramen magnum and the vocal tract assumes the inverted L-shape characteristic of man.

There have been other changes in the facial region. There has been a gradual recession of the jaws in the hominid line, a definitive chin has developed and the so-called simian shelf at the base of the jaw has disappeared, allowing for greater tongue mobility. Despite claims to the contrary (Koenigsmark, 1962; Leaky, 1960), the so-called **genial tubercles** to which the genioglossus muscle attaches in man cannot serve as evidence of articulate speech, since they are often lacking in quite articulate present-day humans (see Hooton, 1931; and Du Brul & Reed, 1960).

The tongue in nonhuman primates is flatter and thinner than in man. It is supplied with muscle spindles that may play an important role in feedback during articulation in humans (Bowman, 1971; Smith, 1973) and is capable of assuming a large number of positions (see Leyton & Sherrington, 1971). Nevertheless, according to Bastian (1965) and others, the tongue remains relatively immobile during the production of calls. If this is true, it is the locus of the qualitative distinction between man and nonhuman primates in articulate speech mentioned earlier and deserves careful study using both cineradiography and electromyography.

Examination of Figure 1.9 reveals another major difference, namely, the presence of the laryngeal air sac in the chimpanzee. These sacs are present in all Great Apes. They are most prominent in the orangutan, where they are clearly visible as large pouches at the front of the neck. In the chimpanzee, they may develop on either the left or right sides or both. They are connected to the laryngeal ventricles via a structure known as the **appendix**. Their precise function is in doubt. Kelemen (1948, 1969) holds that they may be inflated during inhalation or exhalation and provide an air source independent of the lungs. It is his view that air from the sacs can vibrate an appendage to the true vocal cords called the **labium vocale,** which, in conjunction with the ventricular folds, forms a glottis totally lacking in man.

Yerkes and Learned (1925) noted that chimpanzees, unlike man, are able to produce double tones. This is possible in Kelemen's view because the vocal folds close at different levels in front and behind the vocal processes.

There are numerous other differences in the structure of the larynx in the chimpanzee compared to that in man. The thyrohyoid membrane is shorter. The cricoid is funnel-shaped rather than round. There is an internal cricothyroid muscle lacking in man. The hyoid bone is larger and its corpus is hollowed-out and cupped. The true and false vocal cords can be articulated separately in the chimpanzee. Finally, the sharp, cusp-like edges of the vocal folds, which probably play an important role in preventing air from entering the lungs during brachiation, are not present in man.

Both Kelemen and Jordan agree that the chimpanzee vocalizes during both exhalation and inhalation. The latter pulmonic air-stream mechanism is not employed in normal speech in human beings (Ladefoged, 1971).

This catalogue of anatomical and physiological differences clearly indicates that the vocal tract structures in the chimpanzee are at best fractionally homologous with those in man in terms of their role in vocalization. As we shall see later, lack of homology is even clearer when the neural systems subserving these structures are examined.

LIEBERMAN'S THEORY OF THE EVOLUTION OF SPEECH

A most interesting theory concerning the evolution of efficiency in communication in hominids has been advanced recently by Philip Lieberman in a number of publications (Lieberman, 1971a, 1971b, 1971c, 1972a, 1972b, 1973a, 1973b, 1974, 1975a, 1975b, 1976). First of all, Lieberman (1972b) performed an acoustic analysis of the vocalization of human infants and various nonhuman primates and compared his results with similar analyses of adult human vocalization. He finds that the vocalization of nonhuman primates and infants are quite similar and differ from those of human adults. Infants and nonhuman primates do not appear to move their tongues when vocalizing. The output of their larynges is less periodic and they appear incapable of producing certain vocalic sounds such as [i u a].

If one compares the vocal tract of an infant with that of a nonhuman primate, one finds many similarities. Perhaps most striking is the high position of the larynx, which gradually descends in the human child recapitulating roughly the sequence in Figure 1.11 (see Negus, 1949, p. 28; Bosma, 1975). This high positioning of the larynx, which greatly decreases the size of the pharyngeal cavity, accounts for the absence of the vowel sounds [i u a] in Lieberman's view.

Next Lieberman, aided by an anatomist from Yale University, Dr. Edmund Crelin, set out to reconstruct the vocal tracts of various hominid fossils, including Australopithecines, several "classic" Neanderthals, several intermediary fossils often classified as Neanderthal (e.g., Broken Hill and Es-Skhūl) and Cro-Magnon man. These reconstructions could then be compared with the vocal tracts of human infants and adults as well as nonhuman primates.

Having available the size and shape of the various vocal tracts, Lieberman then proceeded to determine, via computer modeling, their phonetic capabilities. It was discovered that human infants, nonhuman primates such as the chimpanzee, Australopithecus and the "classic" Neanderthals typified by the La Chapelle-aux-Saints skull exhibited deficient phonetic inventories when compared with the other fossil hominids and modern man. In particular, none was able to produce the so-called point vowels [i u a].

The central element in Lieberman's theory is the importance that he attaches to these point vowels. After all, even if one accepts his fossil reconstructions and the validity of his computer modeling, what difference does it make that several nonhuman and fossil hominid vocal tracts are incapable of producing these sounds? Following Stevens (1972), Lieberman holds that these vowels are crucial for efficient vocal communication. They are presumed to be stable acoustically so that sloppy articulation does not distort them as easily as other vowels. They also have a normalizing effect in that they allow the hearer to estimate the size of different vocal tracts. This is important because Lieberman subscribes to the motor theory of speech perception, which postulates that covert articulation mediates speech perception. Citing work that demonstrates property detectors in various species matched to their vocal output, Lieberman seems to imply that the human auditory system might be similarly matched to the vocalization that can be produced by the human vocal tract. (This possibility will be taken up in some detail in the next section.) The important role attributed to these vowels may gain support from the fact that they appear to be **phonetically** present in all human languages.

It is important to stress that Lieberman is not claiming that communication via the auditory–vocal channel would be impossible in the absence of these vowels—only that it would be less efficient in the terms discussed earlier. This lack of efficiency, he speculates, may account for Neanderthal man losing out in the struggle for existence to Cro-Magnon man.

These then are the essential points of Lieberman's theory. To what extent is it valid? In evolutionary terms, it is certainly quite feasible. We have stressed several times the gradual, mosaic type of development that would be expected in a system as complex as communication. This is exactly what Lieberman envisions. However, there are numerous aspects of Lieberman's assumptions and method which can be criticized.

Although it appears to be true that the point vowels exist in all languages, a fact that surely requires explanation,[9] it may not be the case, as Gay (1974) points out, that these vowels evince the acoustic stability under articulatory variability that Stevens assumes. Still more damaging for the theory is a series of studies by researchers at Haskins Laboratories (Shankweiler *et al.*, 1975; Verbrugge *et al.*, 1974) that fail to support the putative role of the point vowels in normalization. In the Verbrugge *et al.* study, 15 vowels were presented in a /h＿＿d/ context. When no precursors were presented to the subjects, errors averaged 13%. With the same vowels in context preceded by the precursors: /kip/, /kap/, /kup/, errors averaged 12%. The difference between these results is not significant. In fact, the whole assumption that one needs to know the size of a given vocal tract in order to perceive speech sounds accurately is questionable in light of the very considerable evidence against the motor theory of speech perception.

---

[9] It should be noted that there are in fact some languages that lack at least two of the point vowels, for example, Cheyenne lacks [i] and [u] (cf. Petter, 1952). This, however, is irrelevant, since when Lieberman states (Lieberman, 1975b, p. 81) that the point vowels occur in all languages, he really means that at least one of them must occur (cf. Lieberman, 1975b, p. 113). But is this claim really compatible with his theory, since only [i] and [u] as well as [y] and [w]—to which we are told these vowels are respectively equivalent functionally (the meaning of *functional* is not made clear)—are determinate (see Lieberman, 1975b, p. 79)?

How is it, for example, that the infants (and probably the nonhuman primates) that Lieberman studied who cannot produce speech can nevertheless process it (see Eimas, 1975)?[10] The point vowel theory also seems to assume that fossil hominids necessarily processed speech in the same manner as modern man. But it is unreasonable to maintain that auditory processing has remained constant and only the vocal tract has evolved.

Although a given computer model of a vocal tract fails to produce certain sounds, it does not necessarily follow that the owner of the vocal tract in question could not produce these sounds. Various parameters may be involved that are not taken into consideration in the computer program. Jordan (1971) has done acoustic analyses of chimpanzee vocalizations that indicate that at least two of the point vowels are regularly produced. The orangutan studied by Furness (1916) and the Hayeses' chimpanzee, Viki, were both able to produce velar consonants that Lieberman's modeling indicates are impossible. Furthermore, humans with gross deformities of the vocal tract (see LeMay, 1975) and those with major portions of the tract, such as the larynx or tongue, removed (see Drachman, 1969) are capable of producing comprehensible speech. Finally, some birds are capable of producing good approximations of human speech sounds even though their vocal apparatus differs radically from that of humans.

A number of researchers have questioned Lieberman and Crelin's reconstruction of the Neanderthal vocal tract. The choice of the La Chapelle-aux-Saints skull as the basis of the reconstruction was probably ill-advised, as this specimen is not only deformed by pathology in life (tooth loss and severe osteoarthritis), but has been severely deformed in the fossilization process. Although it is not too clear from Lieberman's discussion how the position of the hyoid bone was determined for Neanderthal man, it appears that it was a kind of triangulation, using the inclination of the styloid process to determine the angle of the stylohyoid ligament and the genial tubercles to determine the angulation of the geniohyoid muscle. Du Brul (1977) notes that accurate determination of angulation using what remains of the styloid process is impossible, as the anterior portion of this process—which is absent in the fossil—varies in length and angulation in modern man. It is this portion to which the stylohyoid ligament is attached. The same strictures apply in regard to the genial tubercles, which may give little if any hint of the course followed by the geniohyoid muscle (see Falk, 1975). If the hyoid is positioned as high as indicated by Lieberman and Crelin (see Figure

---

[10] In a work which appeared after this chapter was completed, Lieberman seems to have modified his views on the motor theory rather drastically (see Lieberman, 1977, p. 124). He now appears to hold a view of speech perception based on modifiable neural property detectors. With such a change in position, it is difficult to see how Lieberman can continue to support his point vowel theory as outlined in this section.

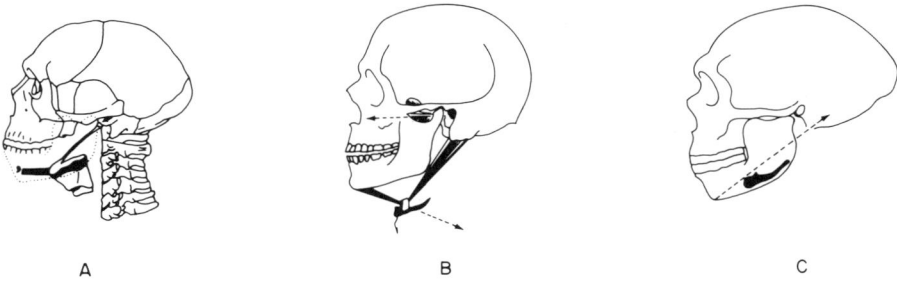

Figure 1.12. The position of the hyoid bone as reconstructed by Lieberman and Crelin for the La Chapelle-aux-Saints fossil (A and C) and its position in modern man (B). Note in (B) that the anterior and posterior bellies of the digastric are joined by a cable-like tendon sliding through the fibrous sling anchored to the stabilized hyoid bone. If either belly contracts, or if both contract together, the resultant action on the chin will pull down and backward as indicated by the lower dashed arrow. In (A) and (C), with the hyoid bone located within the body of the mandible, the digastrics can only pull the jaw up and back into the depth of the glenoid fossa, as indicated by the dashed arrow in (C). (No attempt has been made to re-draw the three illustrations to the same scale.)

1.12A), then it would appear that the digastric muscles, which function in a pulley-like fashion in conjunction with the hyoid bone to open the jaw (see Figure 1.12B), would simply have the effect of pulling the jaw backwards (see Figure 1.12C) without opening it (see Du Brul, 1975, 1977). This would explain the Neanderthal's lack of efficient speech: He couldn't open his mouth! Indeed, all the data available on human and chimp newborns (see Bosma, 1975; and Falk, 1975) indicate a hyoid position well below the mandible. In adult chimpanzees part of the anterior portion of the hyoid is located at the level of the gonial angle (Falk, 1975).

While Lieberman's postulation of a less efficient communication system in Neanderthal man and earlier hominid fossils strikes one as quite reasonable, it is clear that the evidence he has offered in support of his theory is far from convincing (see Dingwall, 1977).

The Ear

PAN-HOMO COMPARISON

Unlike the vocal tract, the structure of the chimpanzee ear does not differ markedly from that of man. House *et al.* (1964) found only slight differences in the angle of the tympanic membrane and in the slope of the auditory canal. The oval and round windows, as well as the cochlea, occupy positions similar to those in man. The number of coils and fine structure of the Organ of Corti were found to be identical to those in human beings. The innervation is also identical.

The auditory thresholds of chimpanzees are very similar to man's, but are generally below his except at 4,096 Hz. Chimpanzees do evince a greater sensitivity to higher frequencies than man. Actually, this upper limit is intermediate between man and monkeys. Temporal discrimination is not different from man's, but sound localization appears to be far superior. A summary of the auditory characteristics of chimpanzees and humans is presented in Table 1.7.

EVIDENCE FOR NEUROLOGICAL FEATURE DETECTORS

Neurological feature detectors may be defined as organizational configurations of the sensory nervous system that are highly sensitive to certain parameters of complex stimuli (Abbs & Sussman, 1971). Evidence of such detectors in the auditory and visual systems of a wide range of animals has been collected. Thus, for example, Wollberg and Newman (1972) have recently demonstrated that the auditory cortex of the squirrel monkey may be crucially involved in the analysis of species-typical vocalizations.

There is now a considerable body of evidence that such feature detectors may exist in human infants and adults for various parameters of speech. These detectors appear to be in part pretuned to process sounds in a linguistic manner. Thus, infants evince the same type of categorical perception of sounds along the voice onset time and place of articulation continua as do adults (see Eimas [1975] for a review of these studies).

Given this evidence for specialized speech detectors in man, it seems only natural to investigate the auditory processing of nonhuman primates to discover what parallels exist. First of all, it is clear from a number of studies that not only primates, but animals as distinct from man as chinchillas (see

TABLE 1.7   Auditory Characteristics of Humans and Chimpanzees

Characteristic	Man	Chimpanzee	Source
Upper limit (Hz)	22,600–23,700	26,000–33,000	Elder, 1935
	20,000	33,300	Spector, 1956
	16,949–20,630	24,470	Farrer and Prim, 1965
Lower limit (Hz)	20	—	Spector, 1956
Absolute threshold[a]	−8 db. (3–4000 Hz)	−14 db. (2048 Hz)	Elder, 1934
	20 db. (16,000 Hz)	−4 db. (16,000 Hz)	Spector, 1956
	46 db. (64 Hz)	38 db. (100 Hz)	Spector, 1956
Temporal discrimination	estimated to be the same as the chimpanzee	108 from 138 beats per minute	Bierans de Haan, 1951

[a]Sound pressure level (.0002 dynes/cm²).

Kuhl & Miller, 1975; Burdick & Miller, 1975), can discriminate human speech sounds reliably. Dewson and Cowey (1969) taught monkeys (*Macaca*) to discriminate two human vowel sound /i/ an /u/ even in the presence of masking noise. They have found that discrimination is retained even when the stimuli are presented by different speakers. (This is true also of chinchillas.)

Sinnott *et al.* (1975) showed that monkeys *(Macaca)* evince the so-called Lombard response, which is the experimental observation that we raise our voice in masking noise and there is a law-like relation between voice level and masking noise level. That the monkeys show this response indicates that they are sensitive to feedback from their own voice.

Sinnott (1974) and Sinnott *et al.* (1974) showed that Old World Monkeys (*Macaca* and *Cercopithecus*) could learn to discriminate between the human speech sounds /ba/ and /da/ whether spoken or synthesized. However, when several synthetic speech sounds were equally spaced along a continuum between /ba/ and /da/ and presented for discrimination, the monkeys failed to demonstrate categorical perception.

Morse and Snowden (1975) found a somewhat similar effect. Using EKG as a measure, they presented stimuli from the place of articulation continuum /bæ—dæ—gæ/ to eight rhesus monkeys. Each subject received a between–category, a within–category, and a no–shift stimulus in counterbalanced order. Their results suggest that monkeys are better able to discriminate between two stimuli that fall in separate human perceptual categories than between two acoustically different stimuli within such a category. Still, the within–category condition differed reliably from the control (no shift) condition.

Pisoni (1971) has demonstrated that under certain conditions requiring minimal memory load, human subjects can make within–category discriminations. This finding has led to the hypothesis that human beings possess both an auditory and phonetic short term memory. Speech sounds are briefly stored in auditory memory before being passed on to phonetic memory upon processing. In a recent paper, Morse (1976) tentatively suggests that rhesus monkeys' within–category discrimination may mean they lack a phonetic short term memory.

Using an avoidance task, Waters and Wilson (1976) obtained a result very similar to Morse and Snowden's on the voice onset time continuum. The rhesus monkeys performed very much better when the stimuli were from two different human categories, but within–category discrimination was possible.

In sum, it appears that monkeys can discriminate human speech sounds, but not in the manner of human subjects. While they show a tendency towards categorical perception, this tendency is not as pronounced as in human beings. There is also some evidence, as we have seen, of the ability to use auditory feedback volitionally. Unfortunately, similar experiments have yet to be performed on the Great Apes.

EVOLUTION OF THE BRAIN (CENTRAL CONTROL AND PROCESSING SYSTEMS)

> *All brains of primates seem to be models of each other. In fact, no new structure* per se *is found in man's brain that is not found in the brain of other primates.*
> [Charles Noback & Norman Moskowitz, 1963, p. 133]

The reader who has followed the discussion thus far and has weighed the evidence for and against behavioral homologies is in a good position to predict what might be found in regard to the evolution of the brain in hominoids. We have seen that there is a considerable degree of overlap between man's affective communication system and the Great Apes' communicative behavior in the wild. This overlap extends to the peripheral structures that subserve this communication system as well. Study of general complex behaviors in the wild, as well as in the laboratory and home, indicates that we are dealing with quantitative rather than qualitative differences. This seems true as well of the human-like communicative behaviors that Great Apes have been shown capable of. However, when we turn to the auditory–vocal input–output modality involved in nonaffective communication, we find considerable evidence supporting lack of homology. This evidence is perhaps somewhat stronger in the case of motor control of the vocal tract for speech than in the case of auditory processing of speech sounds.

What might this lead us to expect in terms of the evolution of the brain in the hominid line? At least two trends are likely: (1) an elaboration of extant structures concerned with higher mental functions (learning, general cognition, memory) and (2) reorganization of the brain to accommodate a nonaffective, volitional auditory–vocal input–output modality. Both these changes will lead to an increase in relative brain size. This increase will probably be heightened by the need for additional storage and information processing capacity that is entailed by a more efficient communication system.

Two basic procedures have been employed in the comparative study of the primate brain: one, descriptive or anatomical; the other, experimental or physiological. In seeking to determine whether our expectations regarding the evolution of the hominid brain are met, we shall survery each of these sources in turn.

Descriptive Procedures

The grossest measure of elaboration in neural structures is brain weight or volume. This measure alone will not do, however, since the brains of many large animals are considerably larger than man's. An adult male beaked whale (*Ziphius cavirostris*), for example, may have a brain weight of 2940 gm—more than twice that of modern man. What we have overlooked is that the brain is the control system for the body and that it makes sense to assume that the larger the body mass, the larger the organ that controls it. Empirical investigations have shown that there is indeed a relationship between brain size (in fact, organ size in general) and body size. When we measure the relation of brain weight to body weight in a large number of mammals, however, the result that emerges is still counterintuitive. While the whale now ranks well below man, several small-sized mammals, such as the tree shrew and squirrel monkey, are found to outrank him. This is so because the ratio of brain–body size decreases with increasing body size. What is needed is a reference point with which to compare brain weights for a given species. Thus, Stephan's (1972) **Index of Progression** compares the brain weights of primates with those of basal insectivores of the same body weight. Jerison's (1973, 1975a, 1975b, 1976) **Encephalization Quotient** employs the brain weight of an average living mammal as a reference point. Following the maxim that the most revealing comparisons are those conducted among closely related species, I prefer Passingham's use of the pongids as a reference point (see Figure 1.13). When this is done, we see that all fossil hominids greatly exceed the expected values for pongids of equal body weight (cf. Passingham & Ettlinger, 1975, pp. 255–257).

It has become customary to point out that brain size is obviously not related to the capacity for language, because nanocephalic dwarfs with brain–body weight ratios within the chimpanzee range have language (Lenneberg, 1967). Passingham and Ettlinger (1974), however, have shown that Lenneberg's calculation of brain weight for the hypothetic dwarf he lists is misleading, since it makes unwarranted assumptions concerning the growth rate of brains in this population. When one plots the brain–body weight ratio for one of the cases for which these measures are available (Seckel, 1960), it turns out that such a dwarf has a cranial capacity 1.7 times larger than that expected for a pongid of the same body weight (Figure 1.13, Point D). It should be pointed out that neither the language abilities nor the intelligence levels of these dwarfs is normal. Seckel (1960) notes that while their IQs may range from 90 to 70 around the age of three, they drop to 50 and below after that time. Many had much smaller vocabularies than the chimpanzee Washoe. Perhaps such cases can be regarded as providing some evidence, however meager, for the degree of encephalization minimally required to subserve speech.

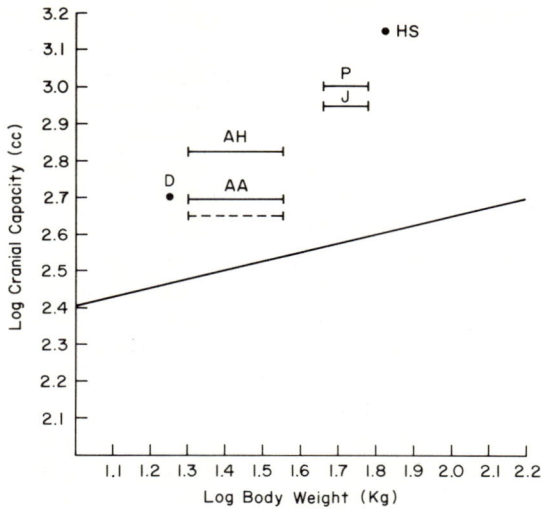

Figure 1.13. Regression line for cranial capacity on body weight for the pongids. Log cranial capacity = 2.17 + 0.24 × log body weight (kg). Data for pongids from A. H. Schultz (personal communication). D = Dwarf, AA = *Australopithecus africanus*, AH = *Australopithecus habilis*, J = *Homo erectus erectus* (Java), P = *Homo erectus pekinensis* (Peking), HS = *Homo sapiens sapiens*. Continuous line for AA is for cranial capacity as estimated by Tobias (1971); dotted line is for cranial capacity as estimated by Holloway (1972a).

Jerison (1976) has recently attempted to provide Rubicon values in terms of brain capacity for language competence. Using Luria's data on language deficits following traumatic lesions in various areas of the cortex, he postulates that 50% of the volume of both hemispheres is involved in language. This works out to around 240 ml for modern man. If this amount is added to the "language–incompetent" pongid, he will become "language–competent." If this amount is subtracted from a "language–competent" human, he then sinks to the "language–incompetent" level. This reasoning suggests that total brain volumes of 1000 ml or above are required for language. Brain volumes of 600 ml or below are a definite indication of language incompetence. Between these two values is a 400 ml gray area (pun unintended!). Jerison concludes on this basis that the Australopithecines and Habilines (*Homo habilis*) both lacked language.

This type of exercise is questionable for any number of reasons. Most obvious is that pongids are language competent to some extent. Without any additional brain tissue they are capable of mastering symbolic communication to some degree, as was seen. The nanocephalic dwarf is also language–competent to some degree and is even capable, unlike the pongid, of using the vocal–auditory channel, yet he evinces a brain size no larger than Australopithecus, who, according to Jerison, is language–incompetent. There are, of course, large variations in brain size within species and it has been widely assumed that differences as large as 1000 cc have no effect on cognitive abilities. As Passingham and Ettlinger (1974) point out, the evidence upon which to base this conclusion simply does not exist. Even if one accepts the concept that just adding neural mass would be sufficient to induce a completely human communication system in pongids (which I do not), it seems rash to base one's estimate on just one source of evidence, namely, the effects of traumatic lesions. Furthermore, as we shall see, it is incorrect to assume that it is just the neocortex that is involved in human language. Finally, one wonders why it is necessary to postulate an increase in mass in both hemispheres. Since it appears—from split brain, hemispherectomy and hemidecorticate studies—that the dominant hemisphere is probably capable of subserving language by itself, why not assume that this is the minimal mass required for language? Whatever reorganization took place in the minor hemisphere may constitute a separate phenomenon in terms of evolution.

If, as postulated at the beginning of this section, there are indeed two components in hominid encephalization, a quantitative component roughly related to intelligence and a qualitative component related to use of the vocal–auditory channel, it would be nice if we could somehow separate their contribution to brain mass. This might be possible if we adopt the suggestion of Passingham (1975b) that a comparison of brain to medulla volumes provides insight into the amount of central processing that exists over and above that employed for receiving information and executing commands. These purely sensory and motor capacities would be represented by medulla volume. Passingham demonstrates a high correlation between this measure and measures such as learning set in various animals. (The mean neocortex–medulla ratio for man is 104.6, versus a mean of 47.8 for chimpanzees and gorillas.) One wonders whether, if this measure were calculated for a nanocephalic dwarf, the significant difference in encephalization between him and the pongid line would disappear.

One can also calculate relative changes in various components of the hominid brain vis-à-vis nonhuman primates. In order to be able to evaluate what such componential changes might mean in terms of human communication systems, it may be helpful to consider the neurological systems that underlie our earlier more general analysis of human communication systems (refer back to Figure 1.5 and Table 1.3). These systems are presented in Table 1.8 in a manner that aids comparison with our earlier analyses. One thing that is immediately evident from this table is the vast number of pathways and regions of the brain that may play a role in human communi-

TABLE 1.8 **Neurological Systems Underlying Human Communication Systems**[a]

Peripheral systems	Transduction systems	Central control and processing systems
Receptors	*Transmitter (afferent)*	*Lower-order integrator*
auditory	auditory pathways	limbic system
visual	visual pathways	reticular formation
ʻtactile and kinesthetic	pathways for touch, pressure	cerebellum
	and kinesthesis	basal ganglia
		brain stem
	Transmitter (efferent)	*Higher-order integrator*
	pyramidal system	cerebral hemispheres
	extrapyramidal system	thalamus
	cranial nerves	
Effectors	*Sensors (feedback mechanisms)*	
respiratory	auditory	
phonatory	tactile–kinesthetic	
resonatory	visual	
articulatory		
manual		
facial		
postural		

[a]Adapted from Mysak (1976).

cation. By comparing relative development of these various systems with those in nonhuman primates, we may be able to gain some insight into what sorts of changes were involved.

In Figures 1.14 and 1.15, Passingham (1975) documents some of these regional changes. The most striking advance is in neocortex. This increase in neocortex is characteristic of the entire primate order, but it appears that selection pressures in this direction have been greatest in man. Since the neocortex figures prominently in most aspects of language, part or even all of this increase may be explained by the evolution of human communication.

As Jerison (1976b) quite correctly notes, "There is, perhaps, no motor system that requires finer controls than that of the voice box and its associated organs, and in which the context of motions involves so many interactions [p. 379]." Speech represents the ultimate in that tendency towards elaboration of structures dealing with fine movements and their co-ordination, which Tilney (1928) termed **neokinesis.** This same tendency has more recently been investigated in some detail by Noback and Moskowitz (1963). It is in clear evidence in Figures 1.14 and 1.15. Within the neocortex, we see a far greater increase in agranular cortex, which includes the motor and premotor areas, than in koniocortex, which includes most of

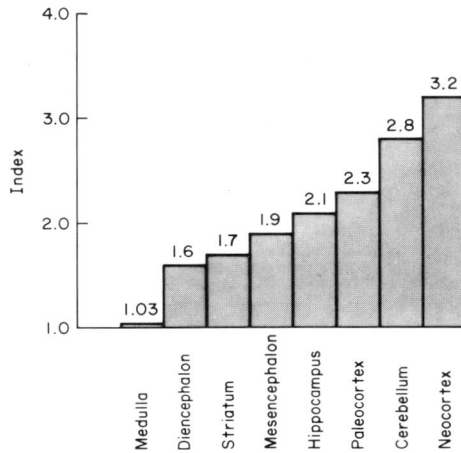

Figure 1.14. Indices showing the change in size of each area of man's brain compared with the values predicted for nonhuman primates of the same body weight. Data from Stephan *et al.* (1970). Least-squares regression lines were fitted to the data for body weight and brain area in the nonhuman primates. The index is the obtained value divided by the predicted value.

the primary sensory areas. Of structures figuring in the motor control of speech, it is the cerebellum that has increased most dramatically in size. There have also been increases in the diencephalon and striatum (basal ganglia), but to a considerably less extent. Noting that the cerebellum begins its relative growth expansion later in fetal life than the cerebral hemispheres do, Noback and Moskowitz (1963) speculate that cerebellar expansion may also be a relatively late phenomenon in hominid phylogeny. The importance of this observation will become clearer when we discuss the possible role of the cerebellum in the process of automatization.

It will be noted in Figure 1.15 that there has also been a considerable increase in eulaminate cortex, which includes the association areas felt by many to play an important role in speech and language.

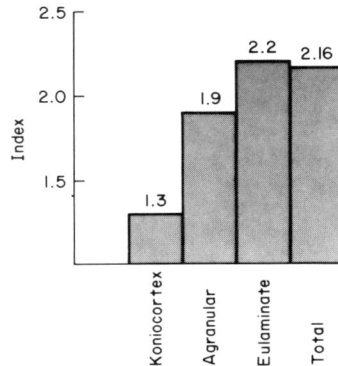

Figure 1.15. Indices showing the change in each area of the neocortex of man compared with the values predicted for nonhuman primates of the same body weight. Data from Shariff (1953). The values used for body weight are given in the text. Least-squares regression lines were fitted to the data for body weight and brain area in the nonhuman primates. The relations obtained were log koniocortex (cm³) = 1.02 + 0.51 × log body weight (gm); log agranular cortex (cm³) = 0.32 + 0.75 × log body weight (gm); log eulaminate cortex (cm³) = 0.71 + 0.83 × log body weight (gm); log neocortex (cm³) = 1.04 + 0.78 × log body weight (gm). The index is the obtained value divided by the predicted value. The indices for eulaminate cortex, agranular cortex, and toal neocortex are significant ($df = 36, p < .05$).

One of these areas figures prominently in Geschwind's theory of language evolution, which has already been introduced in connection with our discussion of cross–modal perception. Geschwind states, following Flechsig, that there are four zones in the brain that mature early in terms of myelination. These so-called primordial zones that man shares with nonhuman primates include the limbic system, the auditory and visual cortexes, and the motor-sensory strip. Adjacent to each of these zones, separating them from each other, are association cortexes. Geschwind maintains that there are no direct interconnections between the primordial zones; rather, there are connections to the neighboring association areas and long fiber tracts from these areas link up the primary zones.

Basic to Geschwind's theory is that in nonhuman primates the only associations that can be formed in learning be between each of the primary, neocortical areas and the limbic system as shown in part (2) of Figure 1.16. Direct transfer of learning from one modality to another without limbic mediation is presumed to be unique to man (see Figure 1.16, part 1). The area of the brain assumed to be most important in such nonlimbic cross–modal association is the angular gyrus. This area—which is presumably most developed in man—forms the nexus for the modalities of vision, audition, and somesthesis and is held to be the anatomical basis for language.

We have already seen that recent experiments with nonhuman primates demonstrate that cross–modal transfer is possible. Object-naming is clearly also not beyond their capabilities. It is not only from a behavioral standpoint that Geschwind's theory is questionable, but from an anatomical standpoint as well. The idea that the so-called primordial areas are not connected by long association fibers appears to be erroneous. Several studies on rhesus monkeys have shown direct connections between these areas across the corpus callosum (see C. G. B. Campbell, 1976, for a summary). Further, Pandya and Kuypers (1969) show the kinds of convergence of projections from different modalities in the inferior parietal lobule in the rhesus that Geschwind assumes are unique to man. Lastly, the angular gyrus is well-developed in the chimpanzee and on cytoarchitectural grounds there is no reason to doubt its homology with the same area in man (see Passingham, 1973).

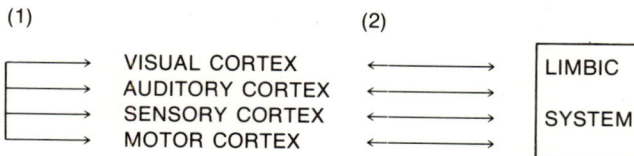

(1)   (2)

```
 ┌──────→   VISUAL CORTEX        ←────────→   ┌──────────┐
 ├──────→   AUDITORY CORTEX      ←────────→   │ LIMBIC   │
 ├──────→   SENSORY CORTEX       ←────────→   │          │
 └──────→   MOTOR CORTEX         ←────────→   │ SYSTEM   │
                                              └──────────┘
```

Figure 1.16.   Putative associations among primordial zones in man (1) and nonhuman primates (2).

Geschwind, in a number of publications (Geschwind & Levitsky, 1968; Geschwind, 1971) has called attention to the marked asymmetry between the two cerebral hemispheres of man involving the **planum temporale.** This area, which lies behind Heschl's gyrus and thus forms part of Wernicke's auditory speech area, is larger in the left (usually dominant) hemisphere of a significant percentage of the brains examined. Recently both Witelson and Pallie (1973) and Wada *et al.* (1975) have confirmed Geschwind's findings and have further demonstrated this asymmetry is also found in neonates. Wada *et al.* (1975) also studied the brains of 20 rhesus monkeys and 11 baboons and failed to find such an asymmetry. Asymmetries do appear to exist, however, in the Great Apes, particularly the orangutan and chimpanzee (LeMay & Geschwind, 1975; Yeni-Komshian & Benson, 1975). LeMay (1975, 1976; LeMay & Calebras, 1972) has argued that the endocast of the La Chapelle-aux-Saints skull shows a fissural pattern similar to that in modern man and the Great Apes. If this is so, it constitutes the first evidence of such an asymmetry in fossil man (but see Holloway's [1976] comments). These asymmetries constitute one more addition to our long list of similarities between the Great Apes and man. If the so-called principle of proper mass (see Jerison, 1973) can be said to apply, then these asymmetries in the Great Apes may indicate a preadaptation, possibly in the auditory realm, towards the type of input–output modality that characterizes human communication.

Bonin and Bailey (1961) note that the area in the chimpanzee brain corresponding to the motor speech area of Broca in man is hard to make out. Further, they note that the large cells in the third and fifth layers of this area in man are to be found only in the third layer of what appears to be the corresponding area in *Pan* (see Sarnat & Netsky [1974] as well as Whitaker & Selnes [1974]). One of many confusing points on this classical speech area is Wada *et al.*'s (1975) finding that the frontal operculum is larger on the **right** in both adults and infants they measured.

Jerzy Konorski (1967, p. 244) claims that the **arcuate fasciculus,** the bundle of nerve fibers that connects the auditory speech area with Broca's area, is lacking in the chimpanzee and that it is for this reason that imitation of sounds is not observed in this species (or other nonhuman primates, for that matter). This does indeed appear to be the case from Bailey *et al.*'s article (Bailey *et al.*, 1943) but Geschwind (1965; Millikan & Darley, 1967, pp. 17–18) disputes this, stating that the staining technique employed by Bailey *et al.* is incapable of delimiting the pathway followed by the tract in question. Pandya and Kuypers (1969) have delimited tracts running from the superior temporal gyrus to pre-motor areas in monkeys. The lack of imitation of sounds in nonhuman primates is noteworthy, but its anatomical basis remains obscure.

EXPERIMENTAL PROCEDURES

Evidence from a wide variety of sources, including clinical studies of aphasia, various neurosurgical procedures, electrical stimulation of the brain, pharmacological deactivation, event-related potentials, and dichotic listening all points to a striking characteristic of the human brain: cerebral lateralization of function (see Dingwall & Whitaker, 1971). As Teuber (1974) points out, there are at least three major questions relating to this characteristic which must be resolved. We would like to know **what** are the specific functions that reside in each hemisphere; **how** the commissures between the hemispheres transfer information and maintain functional asymmetry; and **whence** lateralization arises in ontogeny and phylogeny. None of these questions has been given a definitive answer, but we have learned immense amounts about each.

The simplest and in many ways most appealing answer to the **what** of cerebral dominance is to consider it the ultimate expression of neokinesis (fine motor control). In a number of articles Kimura (1973, 1976; Kimura & Archibald, 1974) has indeed argued that speech is only a derivative of lateralization for motor function, particularly lateralization involving the forelimbs. She links this view to Hewes's gestural theory of language evolution discussed earlier.

Unfortunately this view of lateralization is untenable for a number of reasons. First, it totally neglects evidence involving receptive disorders that clearly indicates that while the **what** of cerebral dominance includes speech, it is not exhausted by it (see Levy 1974). Secondly, neither movement copying nor limb apraxia is significantly correlated with aphasia, as Kimura's own data demonstrate.[11] Furthermore, Sussman and MacNeilage (1975) have failed to find dominance effects for the hand in their pursuit auditory tracking task. In this task subjects are required to match the pitch of a continuously varying pure tone presented to one ear with a second tone presented to the other ear and controlled by movements either of parts of the articulatory system (tongue, jaw) or the hand. As pointed out earlier, those without spoken language (the Great Apes, autistic children, global aphasics) may still be able to communicate using the manual–visual input–output modality. Third, the dominant hemisphere control that Kimura finds for movement copying may be due to a short-term memory effect having

---

[11] In fact Hugo Liepmann who provided us with the most detailed classification of the apraxias postulated that the hemisphere that is dominant for handedness is the repository of learned motor skills. Since handedness alone is a poor predictor of language dominance, it should follow that some might evince language and motor learning in different hemispheres. This does appear to be the case (cf. Geschwind [1975] for an insightful discussion of the apraxias).

nothing to do with movement per se. Finally, in deaf signers, finger spelling and ASL may be differentially affected by dominant hemisphere damage. In a case discussed by Battison and Padden (1974), both writing and finger-spelling were severely disturbed, but ASL remained virtually intact. Initial experiments dealing with the processing of signs have generally failed to find lateralization of this function (see McKeever *et al.*, 1976). In light of the above points, it is my contention that gesture and speech are not intimately related in the manner suggested by Kimura and that only the latter is lateralized. Note that this conclusion is in no way damaging to Hewes's position. It simply indicates that lateralization was not a necessary condition for a communication system based on gesture.

A more tenable set of answers to the **what** and **whence** of lateralization has been proposed by Levy (1969, 1972, 1974, 1976). She has proposed a genetic model that involves two genes, each with two alleles, controlling handedness and hemispheric dominance respectively. This model fits the data on the relationship between these two variables quite well. As to the **what** of lateralization, Levy adduces considerable experimental support for the view that the dominant hemisphere is involved in analytic functions, while the minor hemisphere processes in gestalt terms. Thus, for example, the minor hemisphere is normally superior in matching objects presented in its visual field to pictures. However, if the task involves matching objects to pictures whose names rhyme with the names of the objects, then the dominant hemisphere excels. The **whence** of lateralization in Levy's view lies in the incompatibility of the functions performed by the two hemi-spheres in man. If they were both represented in the same hemisphere, one or the other, or both, would be less efficient.

It is clear that the output modality of speech is lateralized. What of the rest of human communication? Studies of split brain patients with dominant left hemispheres clearly indicate that the minor hemisphere has considera-ble ability to process auditory or visually presented words, definitions as well as various syntactic constructions (see Zaidel, 1973). The same is true of patients in whom the dominant hemisphere has been pharmacologically deactivated (Wada *et al.*, 1975). Studies utilizing the dichotic listening technique show no interaction of semantic constraints, abstractness, or surface structure with right ear advantage (Borkowski *et al.*, 1965; Frankfur-ter & Honeck, 1973; Kimura, 1973; Herman, 1974). Using the same technique, investigators at Haskins Laboratories have uncovered degrees of encodedness in the processing of the speech signal itself, with stops being generally the most encoded speech sounds and vowels the least (Cutting 1972). In cases of hemispherectomy involving the dominant hemisphere, patients have demonstrated surprisingly good language comprehension and even some productive speech ability, albeit quite poor (see Moskovitch,

1973). Taken together, these findings make it difficult to maintain that human communication as a whole is lateralized in man. It may be that any aspect of human communication that can be processed in terms of a gestalt can, if need be, be dealt with by either hemisphere.

It may be worth considering the possibility that any communication system that lacks the efficiency of the auditory–vocal modality may not require lateralization because it can be processed in a holistic manner. It is interesting that writing systems invariably progress from an iconic, pictorial stage to an analytic stage involving duality of patterning. The early systems of symbolization discussed by Marshack (1976) appear to be basically iconic. Those systems with this characteristic that survive, for example Chinese characters, do not evince lateralization to the speech areas (Sasanuma, 1975). The processing of visual symbols by the Great Apes probably does not involve analysis of the type subserved by the dominant hemisphere (Healy, 1973). Vocalizations are undoubtedly processed in terms of unanalyzed gestalts. On this view, the **whence** of lateralization is a concomitant of the utilization of a new and more efficient input–output modality.

If this hypothesis is true, one would not expect to find lateralization of communicative functions in nonhuman primates and this appears to be the case. It is clear that handedness of the type evinced in humans does not exist in nonhuman primates (see Warren & Nonneman, 1976). Studies of chimpanzees have shown equal distribution of left and right handedness on tasks (Finch, 1941). As we shall see, electrical stimulation of the brain in either hemisphere is capable of producing vocalization. The only evidence so far for lateralization of any function has been reported by Dewson (see Yerkes Newsletter, Vol. 13.1, 1976). In a complex task involving the matching of sounds to colored buttons, it was found that rhesus monkeys with resection of the area on the left side homologous to Wernicke's area in man were unable to relearn a version of the task involving a delay of several seconds between the presentation of the sounds and the pressing of the buttons matching them. Right-side lesions failed to produce this result. This may point to lateralization for the short term memory of sounds, but it is unclear at present how this potentially important finding relates to the evolution of speech processing. We have seen that rhesus monkeys can differentiate human speech sounds, but not in the manner humans do. And further that they lack the asymmetry of Wernicke's area characteristic of man and the Great Apes. These latter animals would be more suitable subjects for testing lateralization of communicative function.

In investigating further the neural substrates of communication in man and nonhuman primates, it is useful to review the theory of localization proposed by Penfield and his coworkers (Penfield 1969; Penfield &

Roberts, 1959; Penfield & Rasmussen, 1968) for speech and language in the human brain. Their techniques of electrical stimulation and surgical excision are comparable to those used in investigations of nonhuman primates. Furthermore, Penfield's views on localization, while surely involving some oversimplification, receive considerable support from current research. He holds that speech and language involve two basic mechanisms: an **inborn motor articulation mechanism** that is bilaterally represented in the Rolandic and superior frontal areas of the neocortex, and an **ideational mechanism** that mediates the acquired elements of language. This latter mechanism, which is lateralized, consists of the "classical" anterior and posterior language areas plus part of the superior frontal area. The posterior area is the major language area; the anterior and superior frontal areas are secondary in that adult patients can recover speech when either one is destroyed. Penfield hypothesizes further that coordination of these ideational speech areas is carried out by a subcortical (centrencephalic) system involving parts of the thalamus. Finally, those areas of the temporal lobes not utilized for speech and language are usually involved in memory processes.

What evidence do we have for homologues of these neocortical speech and language areas in nonhuman primates? The only instances of vocalization from neocortical stimulation involve chimpanzees. Leyton and Sherrington (1917) report one instance of vocalization resulting from electrical stimulation of the larynx area of the motor strip. Since adduction of the vocal cords without vocalization was also observed in this general area, the "emission of sound," as it is described, may have resulted simply from the involuntary expulsion of air. Very elaborate movements of the jaw, lips, tongue, and larynx were also observed—all without accompanying vocalization. In one particularly interesting case, involving a very vociferous young male chimpanzee, stimulation of the lower motor strip produced movements of various parts of the vocal tract. However, stimulation of a field of cortex in front of this area failed to produce any movement of the vocal cords, larynx, lips, or tongue. This area corresponds to Broca's area and in man stimulation of it produces speech arrest. When this area was removed on the left side, no facial or other paralysis resulted and there was no impairment of vocalization (see also Grünbaum & Sherrington, 1903). Hines (1940) was able to produce vocalization in one chimpanzee, but could not reproduce the effect in the same animal or in another. The area involved did not coincide with the larynx area, but was dorsal to it in area 4. Dusser de Barenne *et al.* (1941) also report an instance of vocalization in the chimpanzee.

While movements of the vocal tract similar to those described in man and the Great Apes have been elicited in monkeys (Hast & Milojevic, 1966;

Hast *et al.*, 1974; Juergens, 1974), no instance of vocalization from stimulation of neocortical sites is recorded. Robinson (1967a) stimulated several
hundred neocortical sites in *Macaca mulatta* without ever eliciting any type
of sound. Juergens and Ploog (1970), working with squirrel monkeys,
report the same negative findings. Further, ablations of the homologues of
the language areas in monkeys, both unilaterally and bilaterally, fail to
produce any appreciable effects on vocalization (Kaada, 1951; Sutton *et al.*,
1974; Myers, 1969; Yamaguchi & Myers, in press). Myers (1976), however,
has produced marked effects on vocalization in rhesus monkeys by ablating
areas of cortex that he previously identified as controlling social behavior
and emotion. These areas include the prefrontal–orbitofrontal, the anterior
temporal, and the cingulate cortex. Of these three areas, it is the first that
produces the most lasting and devastating effects on vocalization. There is
thus no evidence for Penfield's ideational mechanism in nonhuman primates
and little evidence for a motor articulation mechanism at the neocortical
level. What evidence does exist of the latter applies only to the chimpanzee.

A number of studies of gibbons (Apfelbach, 1972), squirrel monkeys
(Ploog, 1967, 1968, 1969, 1970, 1975; Peters & Ploog, 1973; Juergens *et
al.*, 1967), and rhesus monkeys (Smith, 1941; Robinson, 1967a, 1967b,
1972, 1976; Myers, 1972, 1976; Yamaguchi & Myers, in press a, in press
b) clearly show that electrical stimulation of various structures other than
the neocortex can elicit almost the entire repertoire of species-typical calls.
These calls sound quite natural and are reacted to appropriately by other
members of the species. The sites of stimulation involved are quite diverse,
but, in general, they include portions of the limbic system, the thalamus,
and the midbrain. When we recall the set of emotional contexts with which
nonhuman primate vocalizations are tied as well as their reflexive nature, it
seems quite reasonable that this system of structures should be involved.

In man there is also evidence that parts of these structures figure in
communication (see Table 1.8). Brickner (1940) as well as Penfield and
Welsh (1951) have been able to evoke sounds through stimulation of the
mesial cortex just dorsal to the anterior cingulate. Schaltenbrand (1975) has
produced monosyllabic yells and exclamations from stimulation of the
ventral oral anterior nucleus of the thalamus and Forel's field. Such speech
tends to be automatic and not recalled by patients even though they are
conscious during stimulation. We now know that the role of the thalamus in
human communication is much more extensive than previously assumed
(see Ojemann, 1976). Both Robinson (1975) and Lamendella (1977) have
documented the continued involvement of the limbic system in human
communication.

We observe here in neurological terms a parallel to what has already
been observed in behavioral terms. Older structures are not lost, but are

integrated into newer structures and systems that emerge later in phylogeny. Thus all the structures that are implicated in nonhuman primate communication still play a role in human communication, but that role is subordinate and does not account for all of human communication. Furthermore, there is clear evidence of reorganization. First of all, most instances of stimulation involving these older areas in man result in arrest of speech, anomia rather than vocalization. Second, the vocalizations elicited in nonhuman primates cover almost the entire repertoire of their calls; the vocalizations in humans are, in contrast, limited to a few yells and exclamations. Finally, all the structures investigated in man appear to be lateralized for function, as at the neocortical level. In data from monkeys, sites eliciting vocalization are equally distributed in the left and right brain (see Drewe *et al.*, 1970).

While there is scant evidence that homologues of human speech and language areas in the neocortex play a role in the production of communicative behaviors in nonhuman primates, there is considerable evidence for their role in receptive behavior. Recording from single cells in the auditory cortex, a number of investigators (Newman & Wollberg, 1973a, 1973b; Wollberg & Newman, 1972; Miller *et al.*, 1972; Winter & Funkenstein, 1973) have reported differential responses evoked by species-typical calls. Ablation of primary auditory cortex in rhesus monkeys has been shown to result in an inability to relearn speech-sound discriminations (Dewson *et al.*, 1969). We have already seen that in certain complex tasks involving memory load there may even be lateralization of function in neocortical auditory areas in monkeys. Thus we have further evidence for some degree of preadaptation for human-like auditory processing. It is interesting to note that auditory processing is far in advance of volitional productive abilities in the ontogeny of speech and language in human children.

One final component is required for a maximally efficient communication system: automatization. This factor is involved in the learning of any complex motor behavior. As every pianist knows, learning a difficult passage is a slow, time-consuming process, but once it is accomplished the passage flows along flawlessly, allowing one to turn one's attention to such elements as phrasing and accentuation. Evarts (1973) has demonstrated that learned movements in monkeys may involve the establishment of some form of servo-loop resulting in latencies of the length usually associated with reflex behavior. The same sort of process is undoubtedly involved in speech production, where movements of at least 100 muscles must be coordinated with great precision and rapidity. A number of neurological explanations for automatization have been proposed. One which makes sense from a phylogenetic point of view has been advanced by Marr (Marr, 1969; Blomfeld & Marr, 1970). It is his view that the cerebellum constitutes a memorizing device for motor actions initially organized elsewhere. The cerebellum, via its feedback loops with the cortex (particularly the motor cortex), is influenced both by deep pyramidal cells, which code elemental movements, and by superficial pyramidal cells, which recognize the need for correction of current motor cortex output. If automatization is indeed one of the functions of the cerebellum, we may have an explanation for its great expansion, second only to the neocortex (see Figure 1.14), in the hominid line. Although automatization is probably required by many of man's skilled activities, such as tool-making, hunting, and the like, it is interesting to note that it is that area of the motor strip that subserves the vocal tract that projects to the phylogenetically newest region of the cerebellum (Whitaker, 1977).

We can summarize the discussion in this section by setting forth schematically some of the neurological components that play a role in primate communication systems. This is done in Figure 1.17. The first schema represents the affective, largely innate communication system exemplified by nonhuman primate communicative behavior in the wild as well as by portions of human paralanguage. The term **limbic system** is used here as a cover term for all of the structures that appear to be involved in such behavior. This schema accounts for production. Auditory processing appears to take place at the neocortical level, as was seen above.

The second schema represents the process underlying vocal learning and imitative behavior in certain species of birds. This convergent behavior will be discussed in the last section of this chapter. It is interesting to note that the aphasic syndrome termed "isolation of speech area" virtually reduces human communication to this system. The third schema is that involved in gestural learning and communication. Note that input is not confined to any particular modality. The final schema represents normal human communication. Note that none of the other systems is lost, but rather they are incorporated into this more elaborate network. Automatization plays a role in each of the systems with the exception of the first which is basically reflexive in nature.

ONTOGENY, PHYLOGENY, AND VOCAL LEARNING

> *If the imitative tendency of the parrot could be coupled with the quality of intelligence of the chimpanzee, the latter undoubtedly could speak.*
>
> [R. Yerkes & A. Yerkes, 1929, p. 53]

There are at least three reasons for studying the ontogeny of a behavior in order to gain insight into its phylogeny. First, by attending to the effects

I. GENERAL EXTERNAL————→RECEPTORS
    STIMULUS
                              ↓
                            LIMBIC————→MOTOR————→OUTPUT (Affective in all modes)
                            SYSTEM   SYSTEM
AFFECTIVE COMMUNICATION   ↑
SYSTEM   PARTICULAR
                            INTERNAL *Examples:* Nonhuman primate com-
                            STIMULUS munication in the wild, portions of
                                      human paralanguage

II. PARTICULAR EXTER-→RECEPTOR——→⎰ NEOCORTEX (partial) ⎱
    NAL STIMULUS   ⎱ STRIATUM   ⎰——→MOTOR→OUTPUT (Vocal mode)
                                                          SYSTEM
                                                             ↕
                                                       SUBCORTICAL
                                                       MOTOR LEARNING
                                                       (Vocal–auditory mode)

    VOCAL LEARNING AND
    IMITATION SYSTEM
                                                       Examples: "Isolation of Speech Area"
                                                       syndrome in humans, avian
                                                       vocal learning, and imitation

                              GENERAL INTER-
                              NAL STIMULUS
                                    ↓
III. GENERAL EXTERNAL————→RECEPTORS————→NEOCORTEX→MOTOR————→OUTPUT(Gestural–
     STIMULUS   SYSTEM   auditory, visual,
                                                       ↑   tactile mode)
                                                  SUBCORTICAL
     VOLITIONAL GESTURAL   MOTOR LEARNING
     COMMUNICATION SYSTEM   (Gestural–auditory, visual,
                                                   tactile mode)

                                                   Example: Primate manual communi-
                                                   cation systems

                              GENERAL INTERNAL
                              STIMULUS
                                    ↓
IV. GENERAL EXTERNAL ——→ RECEPTORS ——→NEOCORTEX
     STIMULUS   ↓   ↓
                            LIMBIC ———→ MOTOR ————————→ OUTPUT (Volitional and
                            SYSTEM   SYSTEM   affective in all modes)
HUMAN COMMUNICATION   ↑   ↑
SYSTEMS   PARTICULAR   SUBCORTICAL
                            INTERNAL   MOTOR LEARNING
                            STIMULUS   (All modes)
                                          Example: Normal human communication

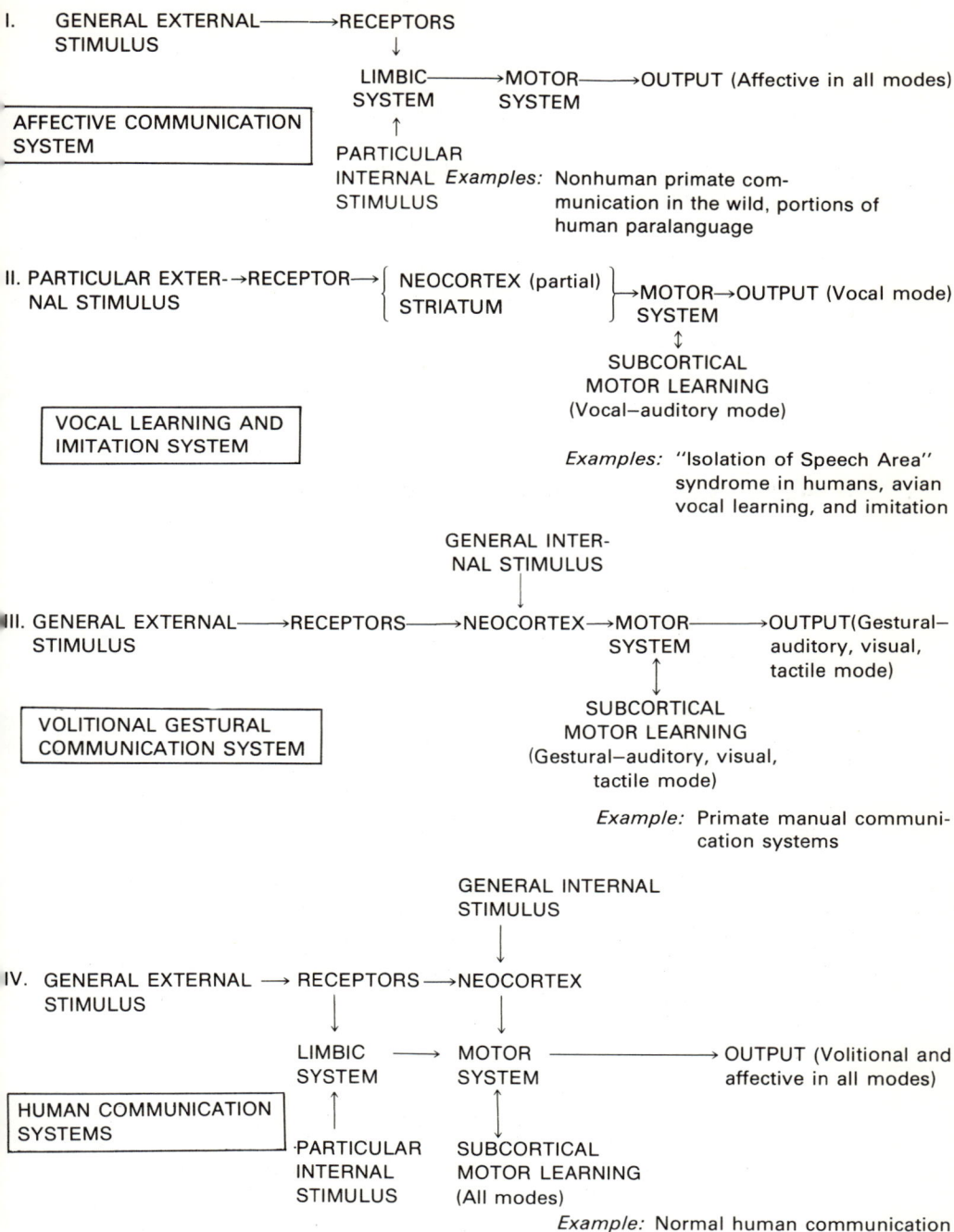

Figure 1.17. Neurological components of primate communication systems.

of isolation, deafening and the like, one can begin to distinguish those aspects of a behavior which are part of an open (as opposed to a closed) genetic program (Mayr, 1974). Second, as Hodos and Campbell (1970) point out, developmental patterns, insofar as they are part of a closed genetic program, can be used as evidence for behavioral homology. Third, by examining ontogeny we may be able to gain additional understanding of the development of the nonhomologous features we have observed in adults. In the last part of this section, we shall study vocal learning in various species of songbirds. In undertaking such a study we are not interested in discovering behavioral homologies, since by definition they cannot exist in species without a common ancestor. Rather we are interested in the mechanisms underlying such strikingly similar behaviors as vocal learning in man and songbird.

Ontogenesis of Communication Systems in Primates

Table 1.9 provides an overview of various milestones connected with the development of communicative behavior in human children and chimpanzees. One thing that immediately strikes us is the rapid maturation of the chimpanzee in every characteristic vis-à-vis the human child. It takes the child a full year to attain a percentage of adult brain size comparable to that which the chimp evinces at birth. However, the chimp's brain does not continue to develop for as long or at the rate of man's. By 9 months, the human brain has doubled in size; by 3 years, it has tripled (see Passingham, 1975). The chimp's motor abilities and musculature develop much more rapidly than the child's. It would appear that, up to the age of 3, its mental abilities do not lag far behind those of the child (Kellogg, 1968).

One major difference in development is clear immediately and is to be expected in light of our previous findings: lack of early vocalizations paralleling crying, cooing, babbling, and the like in the child. These initially reflexive behaviors, which undoubtedly play an important role in vocal learning, are lacking in the chimpanzee. On the other hand, species-typical affective vocalizations have been reported by every investigator who has raised a chimp in a home setting. This strongly suggests that these vocalizations are part of a closed genetic program, that is, little or no vocal learning is involved.

More and more developmental psycholinguists are becoming aware of the early emergence of a rather elaborate paralanguage system preceding articulate speech in children (see Dore *et al.*, 1976; Carter, 1975). This type of development was insightfully described by Darwin (1877) over a century ago, using his own child as a subject. What is involved is essentially the following stages leading up to one-word utterances:

  I. affective crying
  II. differentiated crying
 III. gesture + vocalization ('proto-words')
 IV. voluntary gestures + vocalization + intonation
  V. first words + voluntary gestures + vocalization + intonation

Darwin (1877) sums up this sequence of events as follows:

> the wants of an infant are at first made intelligible by instinctive cries, which after a
> time are modified in part unconsciously, and in part, as I believe, voluntarily as a
> means of communication,—by the unconscious expression of the features,—by ges-
> tures and in a marked manner by different intonations,—lastly by words of a general
> nature invented by himself, then of a more precise nature imitated from those which
> he hears; and these latter are acquired at a wonderfully quick rate.

It is in this essentially affective, paralinguistic system that we find, as we
might expect, homologies in communicative behavior between child and
chimpanzee. It is doubtful that the nonhuman primate ever brings his
vocalizations under any degree of volitional control, but such control is
exactly what we see developing gradually in the child (see Lamendella
[1977] for a discussion of neurological maturation paralleling the emergence of this paralinguistic system in the child).

  In the shared manual–visual modality, a number of similarities in development have been observed. Both the Gardners (1971, 1974a, 1974b)
and Miles (1975, 1976) have concluded from investigations of the signing
behavior of chimpanzees that, in terms of generalization of signs, semantic
relations expressed, sign order, and function of utterances, there are no
major differences from the communicative behavior of children during
Brown's Stage I of language acquisition and probably even beyond. The
same sorts of simplification of signs, overextensions within the same semantic field, and creative usage have been observed in both species. The
differences one sees here are surely quantitative (see also Hewes, 1973a).

Vocal Learning in Man and Birds

  Darwin (1871) was well aware, as was Yerkes (see the opening quotation), of the similarities of birdsong to speech in humans. He notes that it is
the songs rather than alarm cries that involve vocal learning and goes on to
quote Daines Barrington to the effect that the first attempts at song "may be
compared to the imperfect endeavour in a child to babble." Following his
unfortunate wont of accepting anecdotal accounts uncritically, Darwin was
led to believe that some birds (parrots) could not only imitate human
speech, but could use it appropriately. He quotes an Admiral Sulivan whose

TABLE 1.9 Selected Development Milestones for Human Child Compared with Chimpanzee[a]

	Human child			Chimpanzee	
Age	Characteristic behavior	Percentage of adult brain size	Age	Characteristic behavior	Percentage of adult brain size
Birth	Totally dependent on mother for food, transport and protection. Exhibits grasp reflex.	25	Birth	Totally dependent on mother for first 6 months for food, transport and protection. Exhibits strong grasp reflex, is quite strong compared to human infant.	65
	Vocalization: consists of crying (according to P. Lieberman, there is a total lack of supralaryngeal maneuvers and only gross laryngeal maneuvers). Crying may be distinguished from discomfort and vegetative sounds (Stark et al., 1975)			**Vocalization:** consists of repeated 'oo oo' sounds which burst into a scream under stress. No vocal indications of need for food, burping, dry diapers.	
3 months	**Vocalization:** crying + cooing	35	3 months	Moja and Pili started to make recognizable ASL signs.	70
6 months	**Vocalization:** crying + cooing + babbling. Sits up unsupported.	45	6 months	First attempt at walking (steady locomotion only around 3 years) Moja has 15 signs; Pili, 13. First two-sign combination occur in Moja.	70
8 months	First ASL signs produced by deaf children	50			
9 months	Can respond correctly to 68 spoken phrases.	60	9 months	Can respond correctly to 58 spoken phrases	70
1 year	**Vocalization:** gesture + protowords. Stands upright and walks unsupported. First sign combinations produced by deaf children; as many as 100 signs may be mastered.		1 year	Runs upright and on all fours.	70
15 months	Normal child has a vocabulary of around 10 words				

Age	%		Age	%	
18 months		First 3 sign combinations in deaf children.	18 months		Solves three hole form board; can draw straight line or scribble on imitation; can build block towers; feed self with spoon; open doors; wave bye, bye; turn pages of picture book; plays with toys; imitates adult activities; is extremely hyperactive; has only one spoken word used frequently; responds to many commands
2 years	70	First two-word utterances; Runs upright. Has vocabulary of about 200 words.	2 years	75	Engages in social activities with conspecifics
			4 years	85	Makes and uses tools to obtain food and drink. Begins to vocalize using sounds to express fear, excitement, anticipation of food and pleasure during grooming. Weaning process complete.
5 years		Vocabulary of 1500 words. Still has not mastered all aspects of phonology or syntax.			
			9 years	100	Spends long periods away from mother if male (female is dependent even longer) Puberty occurs between 7–10 years of age.
12–14 years	100	Puberty.	12–13 years		Full social maturity.

[a] Developmental information on chimps in the wild is mainly from Lawick-Goodall (1971) and Campbell (1976). Such information for home-raised chimps is mainly from Kellogg (1968), Hayes (1951), and the Gardners (1975a). It should be cautioned that age is a poor predictor of language development in human beings and presumably in other primates as well. Thus the ages given here are at best approximate.

African parrot correctly called guests and members of his household by name and appropriately used such salutations as *good morning* and *good night*.

Despite the questionable nature of these latter observations, the earlier ones concerning the analogies between birdsong and speech are well-founded (see Marler, 1970, 1975, 1976; Nottebohm, 1971, 1972, 1975; Petrinovich, 1972). There is a distinct possibility that some of the lacunae that exist in our understanding of the development of human vocal learning may be at least partially filled by the study of this behavior in birds and perhaps other species (such as porpoises and seals) that also evince it. For example, we are not certain of the role played by babbling in the development of human speech. It seems clear that it is initially a reflexive form of behavior, not shaped by external stimuli as some behaviorists have claimed (see Dingwall, 1975; Olney & Scholnick, 1975). It may be that it involves a form of vocal play similar to the stalking and pouncing we find so delightful in kittens. Such practice may be necessary in mastering the complex coordination of muscles required to produce speech. I know of only one case where early practice of this sort was interferred with and in which later motor control of speech was highly abnormal (Sonies, personal communication). Mattingly (1973) has suggested that the child may be engaging in a kind of vocal tract mapping, perhaps providing (via various feedback mechanisms) the ability to approximate sounds produced by more mature vocal tracts having very different characteristics from his own. It is true, as Darwin points out, that a form of immature song, perhaps similar to babbling, termed **subsong** exists in some species of songbirds. If a bird such as the chaffinch is deafened before the onset of the complex variety of this subsong, his song is more aberrant than if deafened after such a subsong has been produced (Nottebohm, 1975). We have already noted the lack of any form of vocal play in the Great Apes.

Not all species of birds acquire their species-typical vocalizations through vocal learning. Domestic chickens, turkeys, and ring doves do not require a conspecific model for their calls to develop, nor does deafening result in abnormal vocalization. These species also evince no early subsong stage.

From the scant evidence available, this also appears to be the pattern in nonhuman primates. Species-typical vocalizations appear in isolates and deafening has no effect on vocalization in infants or adults, save a compensatory increase in loudness indicating the presence of feedback (Talmage-Riggs *et al.*, 1972; also Ristau cited by Marler, 1975, pp. 32–33). This is, of course, not the pattern in human beings, in whom both early deafening and isolation have disastrous effects on the development of speech (see Fry, 1966; Fromkin *et al.*., 1974). Once again it is the human pattern that one finds in altricial songbirds, such as the chaffinch or white-crowned sparrow.

In these species, as we have seen, there is subsong. As in humans, deafening at various stages in development has differential effects. To explain these effects, Konishi (1965) has advanced the concept of the auditory template. In some species, such as the song sparrow, the template alone suffices for development of song as long as auditory feedback is available. In other species, such as the chaffinch and white-crowned sparrow, the template must be modified by exposure to a conspecific model. If such species are brought up in isolation or are exposed to songs of other species that their template rejects, they develop an abnormal song that presumably represents the content of the unmodified template. Vocal learning in these species takes place during a critical period and consists of two stages. During the first, the template exists in the form of a memory pattern, which must be practiced with auditory feedback if a normal song is to develop. Deafening at any stage before this motor practice takes place results in an abnormal song. After such practice, a process termed **crystallization** occurs and deafening no longer affects vocalization. At this stage the template has been transformed from an auditory memory to a learned motor pattern. I would suggest that this process involves what we have termed automatization. This template hypothesis as it applies to white-crowned sparrows is schematized in Figure 1.18.

We have already noted evidence for neurological feature detectors in human infants and adults (Eimas, 1975). These detectors, like templates, may aid the child in filtering out nonspeech from speech sounds. They also appear to be modifiable, as Eimas and his colleagues have shown using an inhibition paradigm. There is evidence for this at the cortical level as well. Thus, Van Lancker and Fromkin (1973), utilizing the dichotic listening paradigm, demonstrated lateralization for pitch distinctions in speakers of Thai (where such distinctions play a role), but they find no evidence of a right ear effect for such distinctions in speakers of English (where they do not play a linguistic role; see also Wood *et al.* [1971]). As in birds, the effect of deafening at various developmental stages differ in human beings. It is also increasingly clear that there is a critical period, ending around puberty, after which learning a language with native accent is difficult if not impossible (Krashen, 1975; Oyama, 1976). This finding extends to dialects, which have also been found in songbirds (Marler & Tamura, 1964). It is felt by some (Hill, 1972, 1974) that the existence of such dialect differences in birds and humans may serve as an isolating mechanism. This would lead to a population structure consisting of relatively small, largely endogamous demes with little cross-breeding—a structure that many feel favors extremely rapid evolution and great adaptive flexibility.

The parallels in vocal learning do not end here. They extend also to neurological control systems. Nottebohm (1971, 1972) has shown that in

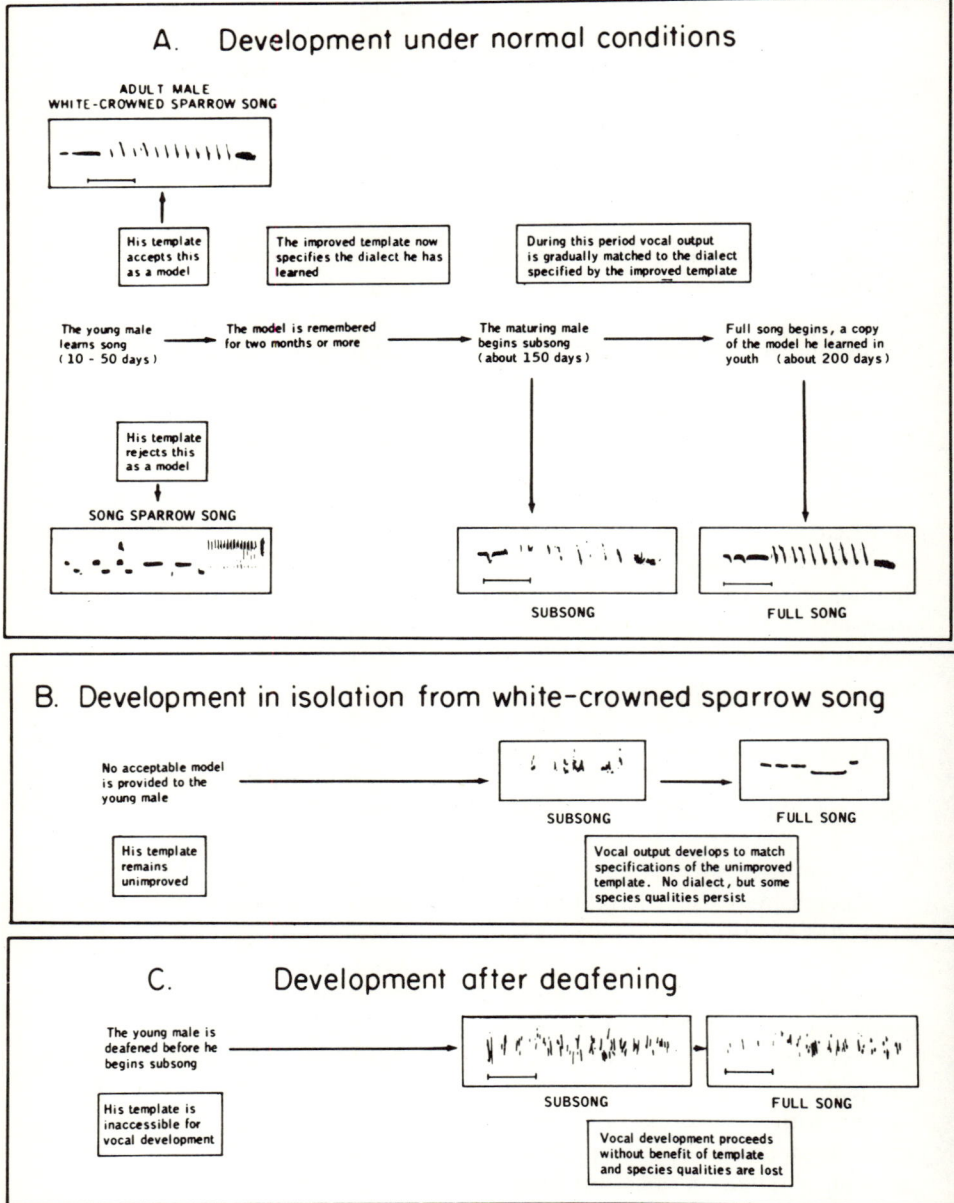

Figure 1.18. A diagrammatic representation of the 'template' hypothesis for song learning in white-crowned sparrows, as applied to development (A) in a normal male, (B) in a social isolate, and (C) after early deafening.

chaffinches, canaries, and white-crowned sparrows the left hypoglossal nerve controls two-thirds of all the sounds that make up songs. If this nerve is sectioned in adults after crystallization, the results are irreversible. Before vocal learning has begun, there is a degree of plasticity—as in humans—allowing for control by the right hypoglossus. There is also evidence that lateralization of function extends to the brain in some species (Nottebohm *et al.*, 1976). In canaries and zebra finches, the central control areas are significantly larger in males than in females. It is, of course, the males that sing (Nottebohm & Arnold, 1976).

Phylogeny of Vocal Learning in Primates

The discussion of the ontogeny of communicative behavior in humans and nonhuman primates and the study of the convergent phenomenon of vocal learning in songbirds gives us a great deal of insight into what might be involved in the phylogeny of speech in primates.

There had to be a shift from a closed to a largely open genetic program for the development of vocal communication. In ontogeny this required the ability to sort out appropriate from inappropriate models for imitation. The auditory processing side of this ability appears to exist to some extent in nonhuman primates, but not the ability to use an auditory model to shape vocalization (imitation). It appears that some form of vocal tract mapping is required in the acquisition of auditorily guided systems of vocal communication. This had to develop, as it is lacking in nonhuman primates.

Vocal learning had to become tied to a critical period (possibly based on hormonal regulation) during which the shift from a purely auditory to a proprioceptive–motor template occurs. This process we have termed automatization. Furth (1975) holds that a similar critical period for the acquisition of visual–manual communication systems does not exist. This appears supported by the roughly identical abilities of the Great Apes of very different ages to learn language-like communication using this modality.

Cortical control of communication had to develop, separating vocalization from its intimate tie with emotional states (limbic vocalization). Along with cortical control, lateralization of function had to occur, perhaps because of a new model of information processing involving duality of patterning and hence analysis. Vocal learning probably favored, as in birds, increased periods of immaturity. Development of dialects may have served as an isolating mechanism with various adaptive benefits.

Finally, it might be pointed out that vocal learning can be regarded as a separate system (as represented in Figure 1.17, Schema II) that could in principle emerge separately in phylogeny. It is not intimately tied to intelligence or cognition per se. Both primates and birds are intelligent, but only some species of the latter have developed such a system, while only the former are capable of language-like communication. In humans, vocal learning can be isolated from other faculties in pathology, as the "isolation of speech area" syndrome clearly shows (see Whitaker, 1976).

CONCLUSIONS

> *Our reverence for the nobility of manhood will not be lessened by the knowledge that Man is, in substance and in structure, one with the brutes; for, he alone possesses the marvellous endowment of intelligible and rational speech, whereby, in the secular period of his existence, he has slowly accumulated and organized the experience which is almost wholly lost with the cessation of every individual life in other animals; so that, now, he stands raised upon it as on a mountain top, far above the level of his humble fellows, and transfigured from his grosser nature by reflecting, here and there, a ray from the infinite source of truth.*
>
> [T. H. Huxley, 1863, p. 132]

This chapter has had two major aims: First, to convince the reader that a comparative investigation of closely and even, where warranted, distantly related species can prove instructive to those engaged in the study of human behavior, and, second, to attempt to provide an answer to the question of how human communication systems, in all their complexity, evolved. In this final section, we shall first survey, in outline form, the findings of our investigation and then, using these findings, construct a probable course for the evolution of human communication systems within the framework of behavioral homology that has formed the organizing principle of this chapter. Lest the reader has felt degraded by comparison with such "brutes" as the Great Apes, I offer by way of solace the words of T. H. Huxley in the opening quotation.

Summary of Findings

1. In terms of anatomical, physiological, and biochemical evidence, the Great Apes are more closely related to man than to other nonhuman primates. It is thus within the hominoid lineage that we are most likely to discover convincing behavioral homologies relevant to the evolution of human communication systems.

2. While there is certainly a quantitative difference between the higher mental functions in man and the Great Apes, there does not appear to be any evidence for a qualitative difference.

3. It would seem from studies of the apes' communicative behavior in the wild that man shares with them in large measure that portion of the human communication systems termed paralanguage.

4. Using the visual–manual input–output modality, the Great Apes are capable of acquiring a communication system sharing many of the properties of human language.

5. The vocal tract structures of man and chimpanzee are at best fractionally homologous in terms of their role in vocalization.

6. While the structure of the ear in chimpanzees and man is quite similar, there are clear differences in perceptual abilities. Chimpanzees evince hearing that is more sensitive at higher frequency levels. While monkeys clearly can discriminate human speech sounds, they appear to do so in a manner different from humans. The tendency they show towards categorical perception is much less pronounced than in humans. There is some evidence of the use of auditory feedback.

7. The cranial capacity of modern man is 3.4 times as great as that of a pongid with the same body weight. The greatest expansion has occurred in the neocortex and cerebellum. Eulaminate and agranular cortex has increased more than koniocortex.

8. While there is some evidence for lack of a homologue to Broca's area in the chimpanzee, the angular gyrus and an asymmetric temporal auditory region clearly exist in this species. The presence of a pathway homologous to the arcuate fasciculus is unresolved, but seems likely.

9. There is no experimental evidence for involvement of the "classical" anterior and posterior language regions in productive communication in monkeys or chimps.

10. There is some, albeit meager, evidence of a neocortical articulatory mechanism in chimpanzees, but none in monkeys.

11. The auditory cortex of monkeys is involved in processing species-specific sounds and human speech sounds. There is even evidence of possible lateralization in tasks involving short term memory for sounds.

12. Virtually the entire vocal repertoire of two species of monkeys and one species of ape can be elicited by electrical stimulation of structures within the limbic system, thalamus, and midbrain.

13. A comparative study of developmental milestones leading to communicative behavior in children and chimpanzees reveals similarities only within the paralinguistic stage preceding the emergence of speech and within language-like communicative behaviors employing the visual–manual input–output modality. Motor precursors of speech are lacking in the chimpanzee. Unlike humans, isolation and deafening leaves vocalization unaffected.

14. Vocal learning in certain species of songbirds is much more similar

to this behavior in humans both developmentally and otherwise than the ontogenesis of vocalization in nonhuman primates. where this behavior appears to be largely predetermined.

The Evolutionary Course of Human Communication Systems

Figure 1.19 sets forth a probable course for the evolution of human communication systems consistent with the findings of this chapter and known processes of evolution. This course stresses the complex interaction of factors touched on earlier. Tendencies that have been observed in the Great Apes towards bipedalism, hunting, imitation, voluntary vocalization, cross-modal transfer, auditory processing of speech-like sounds, and cerebral asymmetry are presumed to be channeled in the hominid direction in part by a shift in habitat from woodland to savanna. As stressed many times in our discussion, it appears most likely that a system as complex as human communication evolved in a mosaic fashion. Thus we do not have an

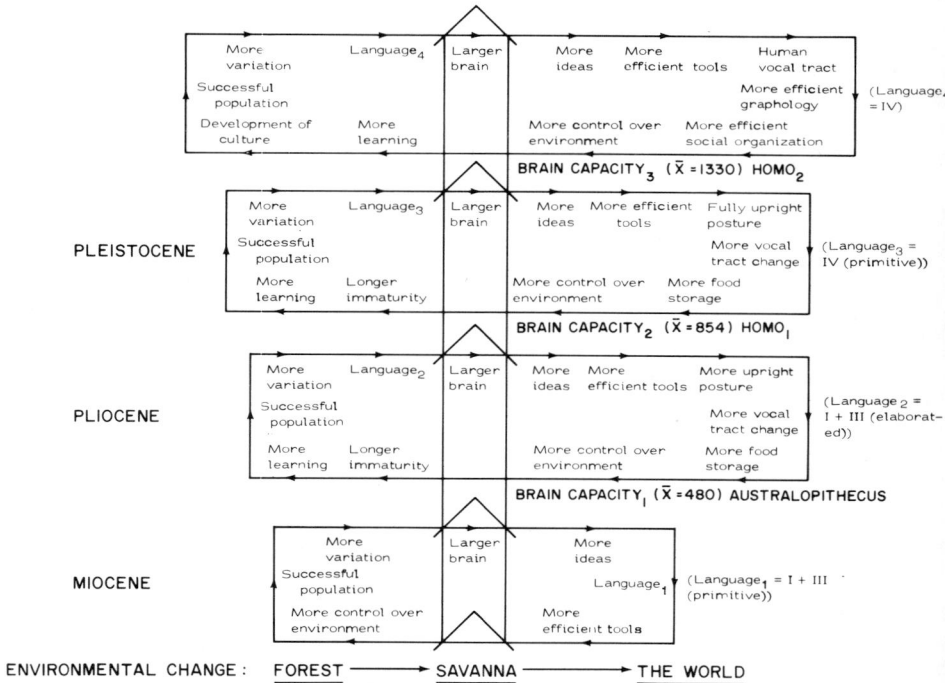

Figure 1.19. Feedback relationships among various factors relevant to the evolution of human communication systems.

instantaneous shift to language as we know it today in the hominid line. Rather some parts of the system developed before others. It is probable that propositional communication began with the utilization of an input–output modality already in place in the common ancestor. Thus, Language$_1$ and Language$_2$ are assumed to make use of neurological components I and III (see Figure 1.17) before shifting gradually to IV. Efficiency in the use of the auditory–vocal input–output modality developed gradually and was probably one of the selective pressures for longer immaturity in order to facilitate vocal learning. Reorganization of the brain, an increase in storage and information processing capacity entailed by an ever more efficient communication system, and continued growth in higher mental function led to a rapid expansion of brain size within the hominid line. The only qualitative difference between man and his closest nonhuman relatives lies in the development of vocal learning. It would be a mistake to regard the shift from a system such as Language$_2$ to Language$_3$ as a small step in evolutionary terms. Human speech represents a mode of information transfer more exquisite and more complex than that encountered anywhere else in the animal kingdom—one that no machine yet constructed by man in all his ingenuity begins to duplicate.

APPENDIX: COMPARISON OF VARIOUS COMMUNICATION SYSTEMS IN BIRDS, PONGIDS, AND HUMANS IN TERMS OF HOCKETT'S DESIGN FEATURES

Although there are many limitations to Hockett's design feature analysis of communication systems (some of which we have discussed above), it may prove enlightening by way of summary to apply the model to the communication systems employed by the species discussed and compared in this chapter. The first thing that strikes one is the extreme difficulty in determining in many instances whether a feature applies or not. Is "learnability" a factor in pongid communication in the wild? I doubt it, but I am unaware of any real evidence other than a few anecdotal accounts. Is ASL as used by the Great Apes characterized by "duality of patterning"? Again my guess would be "no," but I know of no experiments with the Great Apes on the model of those that appear to support this feature for ASL as employed by humans. On present evidence, one simply cannot definitively assign feature values in many cases.

With these considerable reservations about the correctness of feature assignments in mind, one can compare similarities and differences among systems. The matrix on page 81 has the number of differences between the various systems as cell values.

TABLE 1.10 Comparison of Various Communication Systems in Birds, Pongids, and Humans in Terms of Hockett's Design Features

	(1) Human paralanguage	(2) Pongid communication in the wild	(3) Pongid ASL communication	(4) Human ASL communication	(5) Avian communication	(6) Human vocal communication
1. Vocal-auditory Channel	Partial	Partial	No	No	Yes	Yes
2. Broadcast transmission + Directional Reception	Partial	Partial	No	No	Yes	Yes
3. Rapid Fading	Yes	Yes	Yes	Yes	Yes	Yes
4. Interchangeability	Yes	Yes	Yes	Yes	Yes (if same sex)	Yes (?)
5. Complete Feedback	Partial	Partial	Yes (?)	Partial	Yes	Yes
6. Specialization	Partial	Partial	Yes	Yes	Yes	Yes
7. Semanticity	Yes (?)	Yes (?)	Yes	Yes	Yes	Yes
8. Arbitrary	Partial	Partial	Yes (?)	Yes (?)	Yes	Yes
9. Discreteness	Partial	Partial	Yes (?)	Yes (?)	Yes	Yes (?)
10. Displacement	Partial	Partial	Yes	Yes	Yes (in space)	Yes
11. Openness	Yes (?)	Yes (?)	Yes	Yes	No	Yes
12. Tradition	Partial	Partial	Yes	Yes	Yes (in some species)	Partial
13. Duality of Patterning	No	No	No (?)	Yes	No (?)	Yes
14. Prevarication	Yes	No	Yes	Yes	No	Yes
15. Reflectiveness	No	No	Yes	Yes	No	Yes
16. Learnability	Partial	No (?)	Yes	Yes	Partial (in some species)	Yes

	(1)	(2)	(3)	(4)	(5)	(6)
(1)	—	2	13	12	14	13
(2)	—	—	14	13	13	14
(3)	—	—	—	2	12	7
(4)	—	—	—	—	13	6
(5)	—	—	—	—	—	9

One can see that there is considerable overlap between human paralanguage (1 in Table 1.10) and pongid communication in the wild (2) and between pongid (3) and human (4) ASL communication. The overlap between these two systems and human vocal communication (6), of course, lies generally in features not having to do with the vocal–auditory channel, whereas the overlap between avian communication (5) and human vocal communication involves these features almost exclusively. These findings are quite in line with what we would expect from our discussion of these systems.

ACKNOWLEDGMENTS

Discussions with a number of colleagues were most helpful in preparing this chapter—particularly those with William Hodos, E. Lloyd Du Brul, and Philip Lieberman. I want to thank especially John Lamendella for a long and careful critique of this chapter. I have not always followed the advice of my mentors and for such errors as exist I assume full responsibility.

REFERENCES

Aarsleff, H. 1967. *The study of language in England, 1780–1860.* Princeton: Princeton University Press.

Aarsleff, H. 1976. A survey of language-origins theory since the Renaissance. *Annals of the New York Academy of Sciences, 280,* 4–13.

Abbs, J., & Sussman, H. 1971. Neurophysiological feature detectors and speech perception: A discussion of theoretical implications. *Journal of Speech and Hearing Research, 14,* 23–36.

Abercrombie, D. 1968. Paralanguage. *British Journal of Disorders of Communication, 3,* 55–59.

Altmann, S. A. (Ed.). 1967. *Social communication among primates.* Chicago: University of Chicago Press.

Andrew, R. J. 1963. The origin and evolution of the calls and facial expressions of the primates. *Behavior, 20,* 1–109.

Andrew, R. J. 1965. The origins of facial expressions. *Scientific American, 213*(4), 88–94.

Apfelbach, R. 1972. Electrically elicited vocalizations in the gibbon *Hylobates lar (Hylobatidae)* and their behavioral significance. *Zeitschrift für Tierpsychologie, 30,* 420–430.

Atherton, M., & Schwartz, S. 1974. Linguistic innateness and its evidence. *Journal of Philosophy, 71,* 155–168.

Atz, J. W. 1970. The application of the idea of homology to behavior. In L. Aronson *et al.* (Eds.), *Development and evolution of behavior.* San Francisco: W. H. Freeman.

Avers, C. J. 1974. *Evolution.* New York: Harper & Row.

Bailey, P., von Bonin, G., Garol, H. W., & McCulloch, W. S. 1943. Long association fibers in cerebral hemisphere of monkey and chimpanzee. *Journal of Neurophysiology, 6,* 129–134.

Bastian, J. 1965. Primate signaling systems and human languages. In I. DeVore (Ed.), *Primate behavior: Field studies of monkeys and apes*. New York: Holt.

Battison, R., & Padden, C. 1974. *Sign language aphasia: A case study*. Paper presented at the 49th Annual Meeting of the Linguistic Society of America, New York.

Bender, M. L. 1973. Linguistic indeterminacy: Why you cannot reconstruct 'proto-human.' *Language Sciences, 26,* 7–12.

Blomfield, S., & Marr, D. 1970. How the cerebellum may be used. *Nature, 227,* 1224–1228.

Bolinger, D. 1975. The origin of language. *Aspects of language,* 306–325. New York: Harcourt.

Bonin, G. von, & Bailey, P. 1961. *Pattern of the cerebral isocortex. Primatologia II (10).* Basel: S. Karger.

Borkowski, J., Spreen, O., & Stutz, J. 1965. Ear preference and abstractness in dichotic listening. *Psychonomic Science, 3,* 547–548.

Borst, Arno. 1957–1961. *Der turmbau von babel.* Stuttgart: A. Hiersemann.

Bosma, J. F. 1975. Anatomic and physiologic development of the speech apparatus. In D. Tower (Ed.), *The nervous system* (vol. 3). New York: Raven.

Bourne, G. H. 1971. *The ape people.* New York: Putnam.

Bourne, G., & Cohen, M. 1975. *The gentle giants: The gorilla story.* New York: Putnam.

Bourne, G. H. (Ed.). 1977. *Progress in ape research.* New York: Academic Press.

Bowman, J. P. 1971. *The muscle spindle and neural control of the tongue.* Springfield, Illinois: C. C. Thomas.

Bransford, J., & Franks, J. 1972. The abstraction of linguistic ideas: A review. *Cognition, 1,* 211–249.

Brickner, R. 1940. A human cortical area producing repetitive phenomena when stimulated. *Journal of Neurophysiology, 3,* 128–130.

Bronowski, J., & Bellugi, U. 1970. Language, name and concept. *Science, 168,* 669–673.

Brown, R. 1973. *A first language: The early stages.* Cambridge: Harvard University Press.

Burdick, C. and Miller, J. 1975. Speech perception by the chinchilla: Discrimination of sustained /a/ an /i/. *Journal of the Acoustical Society of America, 58,* 415–427.

Byles, R. H. 1976. Different rates in the evolution of proteins and phenotypes. *Annual Review of Anthropology, 5,* 69–91.

Campbell, C. B. G., 1976. Brain evolution in the order primates. In R. B. Masterton, M. E. Bitterman, B. G. Campbell, & N. Hotten (Eds.), *Evolution of brain and behavior in vertebrates.* New York: Wiley.

Campbell, C. B. G., & Hodos, W. 1970. The concept of homology and the evolution of the nervous system. *Brain Behavior and Evolution, 3,* 353–367.

Campbell, B. G. 1972. Conceptual progress in physical anthropology: Fossil man. *Annual Review of Anthropology, 1,* 27–54.

Campbell, B. G. (Ed.). 1976. *Humankind emerging.* Boston: Little, Brown.

Carter, A. 1975. The transformation of sensorimotor morphemes into words: A case study of the development of 'more' and 'mine'. *Journal of Child Language, 2,* 233–250.

Chevalier-Skolnikoff, S. 1972. Facial expression of emotion in nonhuman primates. In P. Ekman (Ed.), *Darwin and facial expression.* New York: Academic Press.

Chomsky, N. 1972. *Language and mind.* New York: Harcourt.

Cole, M., Chorover, S. L., & Ettlinger, G. 1961. Cross-modal transfer in man. *Nature, 191,* 1225–1226.

Cowey, A., & Weiskrantz, L. 1975. Demonstration of cross-modal matching in rhesus monkeys, *Macaca mulatta. Neuropsychologia, 13,* 117–120.

Critchley, M. 1960. The evolution of man's capacity for language. In S. Tax (Ed.), *Evolution after Darwin* (Vol. 2). Chicago: University of Chicago Press.

Critchley, M. 1975. *Silent language.* London: Butterworths.

Cutting, J. E. 1972. A parallel between encodedness and the magnitude of the right ear effect. (Haskins Laboratories).

Dale, P. S. 1976. *Language development.* New York: Holt.

Darwin, C. 1859. *The origin of species.* New York: Atheneum.

Darwin, C. 1871. *The descent of man.* London: John Murray.

Darwin, C. 1872. *The expression of the emotions in man and animals.* (Chicago: University of Chicago Press. 1965.)

Darwin, C. 1877. A biographical sketch of an infant. *Mind, 2,* 285–294.

Davenport, R. 1976. Cross-modal perception in apes. *Annals of the New York Academy of Sciences, 280,* 143–149.

Davenport, R., & Rogers, C. 1970. Intermodal equivalence of stimuli in apes. *Science, 168,* 279–280.

Davenport, R., & Rogers, C. 1971. Perception of photographs by apes. *Behavior, 39,* 318–320.

Davenport, R., Rogers, C. M., & Russell, I. S. 1973. Cross modal perception in apes. *Neuropsychologia, 11,* 21–28.

Davenport, R., Rogers, C. M., & Russell, I. S. 1975. Cross-modal perception in apes: Altered visual cues and delay. *Neuropsychologia, 13,* 229–235.

DeVore, I. (Ed.). 1965. *Primate behavior.* New York: Holt.

Dewson, J., & Cowey, A. 1969. Discrimination of auditory sequences by monkeys. *Nature, 222,* 695–697.

Dewson, J., Pribram, K., & Lynch, F. C. 1969. Effects of ablations of temporal cortex upon speech sound discrimination in the monkey. *Experimental Neurology, 24,* 579–591.

Diamond, A. S. 1959. *The history and origin of language.* London: Methuen.

Dingwall, W. O. 1975. The species-specificity of speech. In *Developmental psycholinguistics: Theory and applications* Washington, D. C.: Georgetown University Press.

Dingwall, W. O. 1977. Review: On the origins of language (Lieberman). *Lingua, 43,* 280–292.

Dingwall, W. O. 1978. Human communicative behavior: A biological model. *Die Neureren Sprachen, 314,* 269–299.

Dingwall, W. O., & Shields, J. L. 1973. *From utterance to gist: Four experimental studies of what's in between.* Unpublished manuscript.

Dingwall, W. O., & Whitaker, H. A. 1974. Neurolinguistics. *Annual Review of Anthropology, 3,* 323–356.

Dore, J. *et al.* 1976. Transitional phenomena in early language acquisition. *Journal of Child Language, 3,* 13–28.

Drachman, G. 1969. Adaption in the speech tract. In R. Binnick *et al.* (Eds.), *Papers from the 5th regional meeting of the Chicago linguistic society.* Chicago: University of Chicago Press.

Drewe, E. A., Ettlinger, G., Milner, A. D., & Passingham, R. E. 1970. A comparative review of the results of neurophysiological research on man and monkey. *Cortex, 6,* 129–163.

Du Brul, E. L. 1958. *Evolution of the speech apparatus.* Springfield, Ill.: C. C. Thomas.

Du Brul, E. L. 1976. Biomechanics of speech sounds. *Annals of the New York Academy of Sciences, 280,* 631–642.

Du Brul, E. L. 1977. Origin of the speech apparatus. *Brain and Language, 4,* 365–381.

Du Brul, E. L., & Reed, C. A. 1960. Skeletal evidence of speech? *American Journal of Physical Antrhopology, 18,* 153–156.

Dusser de Barenne, J., Garol, H. W., & McCulloch, W. S. 1941. The 'motor' cortex of the chimpanzee. *Journal of Neurophysiology, 4,* 287–303.

Eimas, P. D. 1975. Speech perception in early infancy. In L. B. Cohen & P. Salapatek (Eds.), *Infant perception.* New York: Academic Press.

Ekman, P. (Ed.). *Darwin and facial expression.* New York: Academic Press.

Ettlinger, G., & Blakemore, C. B. 1960. Cross-modal transfer in the monkey. *Neuropsychologia,* 7, 41–47.

Evarts, E. V. 1973. Motor cortex reflexes associated with learned movement. *Science, 179,* 501–503.

Falk, D. 1975. Comparative anatomy of the larynx in man and the chimpanzee: Implications for language in Neanderthal. *American Journal of Physical Anthropology, 43,* 123–132.

Ferster, C. B. 1964. Arithmetic behavior in chimpanzees. *Scientific American* (May), *210,* 98–106.

Finch, G. 1941. Chimpanzee handedness. *Science, 94,* 117–118.

Fink, B. R. 1963. Larynx and speech as determinants in the evolution of man. *Perspectives in Biology and Medicine, 7,* 85–93.

Fink, B. R. 1975. *The human larynx: A functional study.* New York: Raven.

Fleming, J. 1974a. The state of the apes. *Psychology Today, 7*(8), 31–38; 43–44; 46; 49–50.

Fleming, J. 1974b. *The ABC's of chimp language.* Del Mar, California: Psychology Today. (Psychology Today Interview Cassettes).

Fodor, J., Bever, T., & Garrett, M. 1974. *The psychology of language.* New York: McGraw–Hill.

Fossey, D. 1970. Making friends with mountain gorillas. *National Geographic, 137,* 48–67.

Fouts, R. S. 1972. Use of guidance in teaching sign language to a chimpanzee. *Journal of Comparative and Physological Psychology, 80,* 515–522.

Fouts, R. S. 1973. Acquisition and testing of gestural signs in four young chimpanzees. *Science, 180,* 978–980.

Fouts, R. S. 1974a. Language: Origins, definitions and chimpanzees. *Journal of Human Evolution, 3,* 475–482.

Fouts, R. S. 1974b. Talking with chimpanzees. *Science Year,* 34–49. Chicago: Field Enterprises.

Fouts, R. S. 1975a. Communication with chimpanzees. In I. Eible–Eibesfeldt & G. Kurth (Eds.), *Hominisation und verhalten.* Stuttgart: Gustav Fischer Verlag.

Fouts, R. S. 1975b. Capacities for language in great apes. In R. H. Tuttle (Ed.), *Socioecology and Psychology of Primates.* The Hague: Mouton.

Fouts, R. S. and Couch, J. 1976. Cultural evolution of learned language in chimpanzees. In M. Hahn & E. Simmel (Eds.), *Communicative behavior and evolution.* New York: Academic Press.

Fouts, R. S., Mellgren, R., & Lemmon, W. 1973. *American Sign Language in the chimpanzee: Chimpanzee to chimpanzee communication.* Paper presented at the Midwestern Psychological Association Meeting, Chicago.

Fouts, R. S., Chown, B., & Goodin, L. 1976. Transfer of signed responses in American Sign Language from vocal English to physical object stimuli by a chimpanzee *(Pan). Learning and Motivation, 7,* 458–475.

Fouts, R. S. In press. Artificial and human language acquisition in the chimpanzee. In D. Hamburg & J. Goddall (Eds.), *Perspectives on human evolution.* Berkeley: Staples Press/W. A. Benjamin.

Frankfurter, A., & Honeck, R. 1973. Ear differences in the recall of monaurally presented sentences. *Quarterly Journal of Experimental Psychology, 25,* 138–146.

Fromkin, V., Krashen, S., Curtiss, S., Rigler, D., & Rigler, M. 1974. The development of languages in Genie: A case of language acquisition beyond the 'critical period'. *Brain and Language, 1,* 81–107.

Fry, D. B. 1966. The development of the phonological system in the normal and the deaf child. In F. Smith & G. Miller (Eds.), *The Genesis of Language.* Cambridge: MIT Press. Pp. 187–206.

Furness, W. H. 1916. Observations on the mentality of chimpanzees and orangutans. *Proceedings of the American Philosophical Society, 55,* 281–290.

Furth, H. 1975. On the nature of language from the perspective of research with profoundly deaf children. *Annals of the New York Academy of Sciences, 263,* 70–75.

Galdikas-Brindamour, B. 1975. Orangutans, Indonesia's "People of the forest". *National Geographic, 148,* 444–473.

Gallup, G. G. 1970. Chimpanzees: Self-recognition. *Science, 167,* 86–87.

Gardner, R., & Gardner, B. 1969. Teaching sign language to a chimpanzee. *Science, 165,* 664–672.

Gardner, B., & Gardner, R. 1971. Two-way communication with an infant chimpanzee. In A. Schrier and F. Stollnitz (Eds.), *Behavior of nonhuman primates.* New York: Academic Press.

Gardner, B., & Gardner, R. 1974a. Comparing the early utterances of child and chimpanzee. In A. Pick (Ed.), *Minnesota symposium on child psychology* (Vol. 8). Minneapolis: University of Minnesota Press.

Gardner, R., & Gardner, B. 1974b. Review: A first language: The early stages (Brown). *American Journal of Psychology, 87,* 729–757.

Gardner, R., & Gardner, B. 1975a. Early signs of language in child and chimpanzee. *Science, 187,* 752–753.

Gardner, B., & Gardner, R. 1975b. Evidence for sentence constituents in the early utterances of child and chimpanzee. *Journal of Experimental Psychology, 104,* 244–267.

Gay, T. 1974. A cinefluorographic study of vowel production. *Journal of Phonetics, 2,* 255–266.

Geschwind, N. 1964. The development of the brain and the evolution of language. *Monograph Series on Languages and Linguistics, 17,* 155–169.

Geschwind, N. 1965. Disconnexion syndromes in animals and man. *Brain, 88,* 237–294; 585–644.

Geschwind, N. 1970. Intermodal equivalence of stimuli in apes. *Science, 168,* 1249.

Geschwind, N. 1975. The apraxias: Neural mechanisms of disorders of learned movement. *American Scientist, 63,* 188–195.

Gill, T., & Rumbaugh, D. 1974. Mastery of naming skills by a chimpanzee. *Journal of Human Evolution, 3,* 483–492.

Goldin-Meadow, S., & Feldman, H. 1975. The creation of a communication system: A study of deaf children of hearing parents. *Sign Language Studies, 8,* 225–234.

Gonzales, R. C., Geutry, G. V., Bitterman, M. E. 1954. Relational discrimination of intermediate size in the chimpanzee. *Journal of Comparative and Physiological Psychology, 47,* 385–388.

Goodman, M. 1968. Evolution of the catarrhine primates at the macromolecular level. *Primates in Medicine, 1,* 10–26.

Goodman, M. 1972. Evolving primate genes and proteins. In A. B. Chiarelli (Ed.), *Comparative genetics in monkeys, apes and man.* New York: Academic Press.

Goodman, M. 1974. Biochemical evidence on hominid phylogeny. *Annual Review of Anthropology, 3,* 203–228.

Gray, J., & Wise, C. 1959. *The bases of speech.* New York: Harper.

Griffin, D. R. 1976. *The question of animal awareness: Evolution continuity of mental experience.* New York: Rockefeller University Press.

Grünbaum, A., & Sherington, C. 1903. Observations on the physiology of the cerebral cortex of the anthropoid apes. *Proceedings of the Royal Society (London), 72,* 152–155.

Harlow, H., Gluck, J. P. & Suomi, S. J. 1972. Generalization of behavioral data between nonhuman and human animals. *American Psychologist, 27,* 709–716.

Harnad, S. R., Steklis, H. D., & Lancaster, J. (Eds.). 1976. Origins and evolution of language and speech. *Annals of the New York Academy of Sciences, 280.*

Hast, M., & Milojevic, B. 1966. The response of the vocal folds to electrical stimulation of the inferior frontal cortex of the squirrel monkey. *Acta Otolaryngologica, 61,* 196–204.

Hast, M., Fischer, J. M., Wetzel, A. B., & Thompson, V. E. 1974. Cortical motor representations of the laryngeal muscles in *Macaca mulatta. Brain Research, 73,* 229–240.

Hayes, K. 1950. Vocalization and speech in chimpanzees. *American Psychologist, 5,* 275–276.

Hayes, C. 1951. *The ape in our house.* New York: Harper.

Hayes, K., & Hayes, C. 1951. The intellectual development of a home-raised chimpanzee. *Proceedings of the American Philosophical Society, 95,* 105–109.

Hayes, K., & Nissen, C. 1971. Higher mental functions of a home-raised chimpanzee. In A. Schrier & F. Stollnitz (Eds.), *Behavior of nonhuman primates.* New York: Academic Press.

Healy, A. F. 1973. Can chimpanzees learn a phonemic language? *Journal of Psycholinguistic Research, 2,* 167–170.

Herman, S. 1974. *The right ear advantage for the processing of linguistic stimuli* (Natural language studies No. 14). Ann Arbor: Phonetics Laboratory, University of Michigan.

Hewes, G. 1973a. Pongid capacity for language acquisition. *Symposia of the Fourth International Congress of Primatology. 1,* 124–143. Basel: S. Karger.

Hewes, G. 1973b. Primate communication and the gestural origin of language. *Current Anthropology, 14,* 5–24.

Hewes, G. 1973c. An explicit formulation of the relationship between tool-using, tool-making and the emergence of language. *Visible Language, 7,* 101–127.

Hewes, G. 1974. Abridged bibliography on the origin of language. In R. Wescott (Ed.), *Language origins.* Silver Spring, Md.: Linstok Press.

Hewes, G. 1975. *Language origins: A bibliography.* The Hague: Mouton.

Hewes, G. 1976. The current status of the gestural theory of language origin. *Annals of the New York Academy of Sciences, 280,* 482–504.

Hill, Jane. 1972. On the evolutionary foundations of language. *American Anthropologist, 74,* 308–317.

Hill, Jane. 1974. Possible continuity theories of language. *Language, 50,* 134–150.

Hinde, R. A. (Ed.). 1972. *Non-verbal communication.* New York: Cambridge University Press.

Hines, M. 1940. Movements elicited from precentral gyrus of adult chimpanzees by stimulation with sine wave currents. *Journal of Neurophysiology, 3,* 442–466.

Hockett, C. F. 1957. The terminology of historical linguistics. *Studies in Linguistics, 12,* 57–73.

Hockett, C. F. 1959. Animal "languages" and human language. *Human Biology, 31,* 32–39.

Hockett, C. F. 1960. The origin of speech. *Scientific American, 203,* 89–96.

Hockett, C. F., & Altmann, S. A. 1958. A note on design features. In T. A. Sebeok (Ed.), *Animal communication.* Bloomington: Indiana University Press.

Hockett, C. F., & Ascher, R. 1964. The human revolution. *Current Anthropology, 5,* 135–168.

Hodos, W. 1970. Evolutionary interpretation of neural and behavioral studies of living vertebrates. In F. Schmitt (Ed.), *The neurosciences, Second study program.* New York: The Rockefeller University Press.

Hodos, W. 1976. The concept of homology and the evolution of behavior. In R. B. Masterton, M. E. Bitterman, B. G. Campbell, & N. Hotton (Eds.), *Evolution, brain and behavior: Persistent problems.* New York: Wiley.

Hodos, W., & Campbell, C. B. G. 1969. *Scala naturae:* Why there is no theory in comparative psychology. *Psychological Review, 76,* 337–350.

Hoepp, G. 1970. *Evolution der sprache und vernunft.* New York: Springer-Verlag.

Holloway, R. L. 1976. Paleoneurological evidence for language origins. *Annals of the New York Academy of Sciences, 280,* 330–348.

Hooton, E. A. 1931. *Up from the ape.* New York: Macmillan.

House, E. *et al.* 1964. The ear of the chimpanzee (Technical Report No. 64-1). Air Force Research Lab., Holoman Air Force Base, New Mexico.

Huber, E. 1931. *Evolution of facial musculature and facial expression.* Baltimore: Johns Hopkins University Press.

Hutchinson, P. 1974. *Evolution explained.* Vancouver: David and Charles.

Huxley, T. H. 1863. *Evidence as to man's place in nature.* London: Williams and Norgate.

Itard, J. 1962. *The wild boy of Aveyron.* New York: Appleton-Century-Crofts.

Jerison, H. 1973. *Evolution of the brain and intelligence.* New York: Academic Press.

Jerison, H. 1975a. Fossil evidence of the evolution of the human brain. *Annual Review of Anthropology, 4,* 27–58.

Jerison, H. 1975b. Joint review: Evolution of the brain and intelligence. *Current Anthropology, 16,* 403–426.

Jerison, H. 1976a. Paleoneurology and the evolution of mind. *Scientific American, 234*(1), 90–101.

Jerison, H. 1976b. Discussion paper: The paleoneurology of language. *Annals of the New York Academy of Sciences, 280,* 370–382.

Jordan, J. 1960. Quelques remarques sur la situation du larynx chex les lemuriens et les signes. *Acta Biologica et Medica* (Gdańsk), *4,* 39–51.

Jordan, J. 1971. Studies on the structure of the organ of voice and vocalization in chimpanzees. *Folia Morphologica* (Warsaw), *30,* 97–126; 222–248; 323–340.

Juergens, U. 1974. On the elicitability of vocalization from the cortical larynx area. *Brain Research, 81,* 564–566.

Juergens, U., & Ploog, D. 1970. Cerebral representation of vocalization in the squirrel monkey. *Experimental Brain Research, 10,* 532–554.

Juergens, U., Maurus, M., Ploog, D., & Winter, P. 1967. Vocalization in the squirrel monkey *(Saimiri sciureus)* elicited by brain stimulation. *Experimental Brain Research, 4,* 114–117.

Kaada, B. R. 1951. Somato-motor, autonomic and electro-cortical responses to electrical stimulation of 'rhinencephalic' and other structures in primates cat and dog. *Acta Physiologica Scandinavica, 24* (Supplement 83).

Kelemen, G. 1948. The anatomical basis of phonation in the chimpanzee. *Journal of Morphology, 82,* 229–259.

Kelemen, G. 1949. Structure and performance in animal language. *Acta Otolaryngologica, 50,* 740–744.

Kelemen, G. 1958. Physiology of phonation in primates. *Logos, 1,* 32–35.

Kelemen, G. 1964. Evolutionary sources of human language. *Folia Phoniatrica, 16,* 59–66.

Kelemen, G. 1969. Anatomy of the larynx and the anatomical basis of vocal performance. In G. H. Bourne (Ed.), *The chimpanzee.* Baltimore: University Park Press.

Kellogg, W. N. 1933. *The ape and the child.* New York: McGraw-Hill.

Kellogg, W. N. 1968a. Communication and language in the home-raised chimpanzee. *Science, 162,* 423–427.

Kellogg, W. N. 1968b. Chimpanzees in experimental homes. *Psychological Record, 18,* 489–498.

Kimura, D. 1973. The asymmetry of the human brain. *Scientific American, 228*(3), 70–78.

Kimura, D. 1976. The neural basis of language qua gesture. In H. Whitaker & H. A. Whitaker (Eds.), *Studies in neurolinguistics* (Vol. 2). New York: Academic Press.

Kimura, D., & Archibald, Y. 1974. Motor functions of the left hemisphere. *Brain, 97,* 337–350.

King, M.-C., & Wilson, A. C. Evolution at two levels in humans and chimpanzees. *Science, 188,* 107–116.

Kintsch, W. 1974. *The representation of meaning in memory.* New York: Wiley.

Kiparsky, P. 1976. Historical linguistics and the origin of language. *Annals of the New York Academy of Sciences, 280,* 97–103.

Köhler, W. 1951. *The mentality of apes.* New York: Humanities Press.

Koenigswald, G. H. R. von. 1962. *The evolution of man.* Ann Arbor: The University of Michigan Press.

Kohne, D. E. 1970. Evolution of higher organism DNA. *Quarterly Review of Biophysics, 33,* 327–375.

Kohts, N. 1935. *Infant ape and human child.* Moscow: Scientific Memoirs of the Museum Darwinianum.

Konishi, M. 1965. The role of auditory feedback in the control of vocalization in the White-Crowned Sparrow. *Zeitschrift für Tierpsychologie, 22*, 770–783.

Konorski, J. 1967. *Integrative activity of the brain.* Chicago: University of Chicago Press.

Kortlandt, A. 1962. Chimpanzees in the wild. *Scientific American, 206*(5), 128–138.

Krashen, S. D. 1975. The critical period for language acquisition and its possible bases. *Annals of the New York Academy of Sciences, 263,* 211–224.

Kroeber, A. 1917. The superorganic. *American Anthropologist, 19,* 163–213.

Kuhl, P., & Miller, J. 1975. Speech perception by the chinchilla: Voiced–voiceless distinction in alveolar plosive consonants. *Science, 190,* 69–72.

Ladefoged, P. 1971. *Preliminaries to linguistic phonetics.* Chicago: University of Chicago.

Lamendella, J. 1976. Relations between the ontogeny and phylogeny of language: A neo-recapitulationist view. *Annals of the New York Academy of Sciences, 280,* 396–412.

Lamendella, J. 1977. The limbic system in human communication. In H. Whitaker & H. A. Whitaker (Eds.), *Studies in neurolinguistics* (Vol. 3). New York: Academic Press.

Lancaster, Jane. 1968. Primate communication systems and the emergence of human language. In P. Jay (Ed.), *Primates.* New York: Holt.

Lancaster, Jane. 1975. *Primate behavior and the emergence of human culture.* New York: Holt.

Lawick-Goodall, J. van. 1965. New discoveries among Africa's chimpanzees. *National Geographic, 128*(6), 802–831.

Lawick-Goodall, J. van. 1968a. A preliminary report on expressive movements and communication in the Gombe Stream chimpanzees. In P. Jay (Ed.), *Primates.* New York: Holt.

Lawick-Goodall, J. van. 1968b. The behavior of free living chimpanzees in the Gombe Stream Reserve. *Animal Behavior Monographs, 1,* 163–311.

Lawick-Goodall, J. van 1971. *In the shadow of man.* Boston: Houghton Mifflin.

Lawick-Goodall, J. van. 1973. The behavior of chimpanzees in their natural habitat. *American Journal of Psychiatry, 130,* 1–12.

Lawick-Goodall, J. van. 1975. The chimpanzee. In V. Goodall (Ed.), *The quest for man.* New York: Praeger.

Lawick-Goodall, J. van. 1976. Continuities between chimpanzee and human behavior. In G. Isaac & E. McCown (Eds.), *Human origins.* Menlo Park, CA.: W. A. Benjamin.

Lawick-Goodall, J. van, & Hamburg, D. 1974. Chimpanzee behavior as a modal for the behavior of early man. In D. Hamburg & K. Brodie (Eds.), *American Handbook of Psychiatry* (Vol. 6). New York: Basic Books.

Laver, J. 1976. Language and nonverbal communication. In E. Carterette & M. Friedman (Eds.), *Handbook of perception,* (Vol. VII). New York: Academic Press.

Leakey, L. 1960. Man as organism. In S. Tax & C. Callender (Eds.), *Issues in evolution* (Vol. 3). Chicago: University of Chicago Press.

Lehmann, W. 1955. *Proto-Indo-European phonology.* Austin: University of Texas Press.

LeMay, M. 1975. The language capabilities of Neanderthal man. *American Journal of Physical Anthropology, 42,* 9–14.

LeMay, M. 1976. Morphological cerebral asymmetries of modern man, fossil man, and nonhuman primate. *Annals of the New York Academy of Sciences, 280,* 349–366.

LeMay, M., & Calebras, A. 1972. Human brain—morphologic differences in the hemispheres demonstrable by carotid arteriography. *New England Journal of Medicine, 287,* 168–170.

LeMay, M., & Geschwind, N. 1975. Hemispheric differences in the brains of Great Apes. *Brain Behavior and Evolution, 11,* 48–52.

Lenneberg, E. 1967. *Biological foundations of language.* New York: Wiley.

Lenneberg, E. 1970. A word between us. In J. Roslansky (Ed.), *Communication.* Amsterdam: North Holland.

Lenneberg, E. 1971a. Of language knowledge, apes and brains. *Journal of Psycholinguistic Research, 1,* 1–29.

Lenneberg, E. 1971b. Developments in biological linguistics. *Monograph Series on Languages and Linguistics, 24,* 199–209.

Levy, J. 1969. Possible basis for the evolution of lateral specialization of the human brain. *Nature, 224,* 614–615.

Levy, J. 1972. Lateral specialization of the human brain: Behavioral manifestations and possible evolutionary basis. In J. Kiger (Ed.), *The biology of behavior.* Corvallis: Oregon State University Press.

Levy, J. 1974. Psychobiological implications of bilateral asymmetry. In S. Dimond & J. Beaumont (Eds.), *Hemisphere function in the human brain.* New York: Wiley.

Levy, J. 1976. Evolution of language lateralization and cognitive function. *Annals of the New York Academy of Sciences, 280,* 810–820.

Leyton, A., & Sherrington, C. 1917. Observations on the excitable cortex of the chimpanzee, orangutan and gorilla. *Quarterly Journal of Experimental Physiology, 11,* 135–222.

Lieberman, P. 1971a. *The evolution of the human speech anatomy.* SR-28, 205–222 (Haskins Laboratories).

Lieberman, P. 1971b. On the evolution of human language. Haskins Laboratories Status Report on Speech Research, *SR-27,* 113–131.

Lieberman, P. 1972. *The speech of primates.* The Hague: Mouton.

Lieberman, P. 1973a. On the evolution of language: A unified view. *Cognition, 2,* 59–94.

Lieberman, P. 1973b. On the evolution of human language. In A. Anderson & P. Kiparsky (Eds.), *A Festschrift for M. Halle.* New York: Holt.

Lieberman, P. 1974. *The evolution of speech and language.* SR-37/38, 25–44. (Haskins Laboratories).

Lieberman, P. 1975a. More discussion of Neanderthal speech. *Linguistic Inquiry, 6,* 335–339.

Lieberman, P. 1975b. *On the origins of language.* New York: Macmillan.

Lieberman, P. 1976. Interactive models for evolution: Neural mechanisms, anatomy and behavior. *Annals of the New York Academy of Sciences, 280,* 660–672.

Lieberman, P. 1977. *Speech physiology and acoustic phonetics.* New York: Macmillan.

Lieberman, P., & Crelin, E. S. 1971. On the speech of Neanderthal man. *Linguistic Inquiry, 2,* 203–222.

Lieberman, P., Crelin, E. S., & Klatt, D. H. 1972. Phonetic ability and related anatomy of the newborn and adult human, Neanderthal man and the chimpanzee. *American Anthropologist, 74,* 287–307.

Linden, E. 1974. *Apes, men, and language.* New York: E. P. Dutton Co.

MacKinnon, John. 1974. *In search of the red ape.* New York: Ballantine Books.

Mandel, B., & Fouts, R. S. 1975. *Human–chimpanzee conversations in a social setting: Initiations/terminations.* Unpublished manuscript.

Marler, P. 1970. Birdsong and speech development: Could there be parallels? *American Scientist, 58,* 669–673.

Marler, P. 1975. On the origin of speech from animal sounds. In J. Kavanagh & J. Cutting (Eds.), *The role of speech in language.* Cambridge: MIT Press.

Marler, P. 1976. An ethological theory of the origin of vocal learning. *Annals of the New York Academy of Sciences, 280,* 386–395.

Marler, P., & Tamura, M. 1962. Song dialects in three populations of white-crowned sparrow. *Condor, 64,* 368–377.

Marler, P., & Tenaza, R. 1977. Signaling behavior of apes with special reference to vocalization. In T. Sebeok (Ed.), *How animals communicate.* Bloomington: Indiana University Press.

Marr, D. 1969. Theory of cerebellar cortex. *Journal of Physiology* (London), 202, 437–470.

Marshack, A. 1976. Implications of the paleolithic symbolic evidence for the origin of language. *American Scientist, 64,* 136–145.

Marx, Otto. 1967. The history of the biological basis of language. In E. Lenneberg (Ed.), *Biological foundations of language.* New York: Wiley.

Mason, W. A. 1976. Environmental models and mental modes: Representational processes in the Great Apes and man. *American Psychologist, 31,* 284–294.

Mason, W. A., & Lott, D. 1976. Ethology and comparative psychology. *Annual Review of Psychology, 27,* 129–154.

Masterton, R. B., Bitterman, M. E., Campbell, B. G., & Hotton, N. (Eds.). 1976a. *Evolution of brain and behavior in vertebrates.* New York: Wiley.

Masterton, R. B., Hodos, W., & Jerison, H. (Eds.). 1976b. *Evolution, brain, and behavior: Persistent problems.* New York: Wiley.

Mattingly, I. G. 1973. *Phonetic prerequisites for first-language acquisition.* SR-34, 65–69 (Haskins Laboratories).

Mayr, E. 1972. The nature of the Darwinian revolution. *Science, 176.* 981–989.

Mayr, E. 1974. Behavior programs and evolutionary strategies. *American Scientist, 62,* 650–659.

McKeever, W., Hoe-Mann, H. W., Florian, V. A., & Van Deventer, A. D. 1976. Evidence of minimal cerebral asymmetries for the processing of English words and American Sign Language in the congenitally deaf. *Neuropsychologia, 14,* 413–423.

Menzel, E. W. 1971. Communication about the environment in a group of young chimpanzees. *Folia Primat, 15,* 220–232.

Menzel, E. W. (Ed.). 1973. *Precultural primate behavior.* Basel: S. Karger.

Miles, L. W. 1975. *The use of sign language by two chimpanzees.* Unpublished manuscript.

Miles, L. W. 1976. Discussion paper: The communicative competence of child and chimpanzee. *Annals of the New York Academy of Sciences, 280,* 592–597.

Miller, J. M., Sutton, D., Pfingst, B., Ryan, A., & Beaton, R. 1972. Single cell activity in the auditory cortex of rhesus monkeys. *Science, 177,* 449–451.

Millikan, C. H., & Darley, F. L. (Eds.). 1967. *Brain mechanisms underlying speech and language.* New York: Grune & Stratton.

Moran, J., & Gode, A. (translators). 1966. *On the origin of language* (Essays by Rousseau and Herder). New York: Ungar.

Morse, P. A. 1976. Speech perception in the human infant and rhesus monkey. *Annals of the New York Academy of Sciences, 280,* 694–707.

Morse, P. A., & Snowden, C. 1975. An investigation of categorical speech discrimination by rhesus monkey. *Perception and Psychophysics, 17,* 9–15.

Moscovitch, M. 1973. Language and the cerebral hemispheres: Reaction-time studies and their implications for models of cerebral dominance. In P. Pliner *et al.* (Eds.), *Communication and affect.* New York: Academic Press.

Mounin, G. 1976. Language, communication, chimpanzees. *Current Anthropology, 17,* 1–24.

Murphy, R. 1973. Genetic correlates of behavior. In G. Bermant (Ed.), *Perspectives on animal behavior.* Glenview: Scott, Foresman.

Myers, R. E. 1969. Neurology of social communication in primates. *Proceedings of the Second International Congress on Primates, 3,* 1–9.

Myers, R. E. 1972. Role of prefrontal and anterior temporal cortex in social behavior and affect in monkeys. *Acta Neurobiologica Experimentica, 32,* 567–79.

Myers, R. E. 1976. Comparative neurology of vocalization and speech: Proof of a dichotomy. *Annals of the New York Academy of Sciences, 280,* 745–757.

Mysak, E. D. 1976. *Pathologies of speech systems.* Baltimore: Williams and Wilkins.

Napier, J. 1976. *Monkeys without tails.* New York: Taplinger.

Negus, V. E. 1940. *The mechanism of the larynx.* St. Louis: Mosby.

Negus, V. E. 1949. *The comparative anatomy and physiology of the larynx.* New York: Hafner.

Newman, J., & Wollberg, Z. 1973a. Response of single neurons in the auditory cortex of squirrel monkeys to variants of a single call type. *Experimental Neurology, 40,* 821–824.

Newman, J., & Wollberg, Z. 1973b. Multiple coding of species-specific vocalizations in the auditory cortex of squirrel monkeys. *Brain Research, 54,* 287–304.

Nissen, H. W. 1946. Primate psychology. In P. L. Harriman (Ed.), *Encyclopedia of psychology.* New York: Philosophical Library.

Noback, C. R., & Moskowitz, N. 1963. The primate nervous system: Functional and structural aspects in phylogeny. In J. Buettner-Janusch (Ed.), *Evolutionary and genetic biology of primates* (Vol. I). New York: Academic Press.

Nottebohm, F. 1971. Ontogeny of bird song. *Science, 167,* 950–56.

Nottebohm, F. 1971. Neural lateralization of vocal control in a passerine bird I. Song. *Journal of Experimental Zoology, 177,* 229–62.

Nottebohm, F. 1972a. Neural lateralization of vocal control in a passerine bird II. Subsong, calls, and a theory of vocal learning. *Journal of Experimental Zoology, 179,* 25–50.

Nottebohm, F. 1972b. The origins of vocal learning. *The American Naturalist, 106,* 116–140.

Nottebohm, F. 1975. A zoologist's view of some language phenomena with particular emphasis on vocal learning. In E. H. Lenneberg & E. Lenneberg (Eds.), *Foundations of language development.* New York: Academic Press.

Nottebohm, F. and Arnold, A. 1976. Sexual dimorphism in vocal control areas of the songbird brain. *Science, 194,* 211–213.

Nottebohm, F., Stokes, T. M., & Leonard, C. M. 1976. Central control of song in the canary, *Serinus canarius. Journal of Comparative Neurology, 165,* 457–486.

Offir, C. W. 1976. Visual speech: Their fingers do the talking. *Psychology Today, 10*(1), 72–78.

Ojemann, G. A. 1976. Subcortical language mechanisms. In H. Whitaker & H. A. Whitaker (Eds.), *Studies in neurolinguistics* (Vol. I). New York: Academic Press.

Olney, R., & Scholnick, E. 1975. Adult judgments of age and linguistic differences in infant vocalization. *Journal of Child Language, 3,* 145–155.

Oyama, S. 1976. A sensitive period for the acquisition of a nonnative phonological system. *Journal of Psycholing. Research, 5,* 261–283.

Pandya, D. N., & Kuypers, H. 1969. Cortico-cortical connections in the rhesus monkey. *Brain Research, 13,* 13–36.

Parker, C. E. 1974. The antecedents of man the manipulator. *Journal of Human Evolution, 3,* 493–500.

Passingham, R. E. 1973. Anatomical differences between the neocortex of man and other primates. *Brain Behavior Evolution, 7,* 337–59.

Passingham, R. E. 1975a. Changes in the size and organization of the brain in man and his ancestors. *Brain Behavior Evolution, 11,* 73–90.

Passingham, R. E. 1975b. The brain and intelligence. *Brain Behavior Evolution, 11,* 1–15.

Passingham, R. E., & Ettlinger, G. 1974. A comparison of cortical functions in man and other primates. *International Review of Neurobiology, 16,* 233–299.

Patterson, P. 1978. The gestures of a gorilla: Language acquisition in another pongid. *Brain and Language, 5,* 72–97.

Penfield, W. 1969. Consciousness, memory, and man's conditioned reflexes. *On the biology of learning,* ed. by K. Pribram, 127–168. New York: Harcourt, Brace and World.

Penfield, W., & Rasmussen, T. 1968. *The cerebral cortex of man.* New York: Hafner.

Penfield, W., & Roberts, L. 1959. *Speech and brain-mechanisms.* Princeton: Princeton University Press.

Penfield, W., & Welch, K. 1951. The supplementary motor area of the cerebral cortex. A clinical and experimental study. *Archives of Neurology and Psychiatry, 66,* 289–317.

Peters, M., & Ploog, D. 1973. Communication among primates. *Annual Review of Physiology, 35,* 221–242.

Petter, R. 1952. *Cheyenne grammar.* Newton, Kansas: Mennonite Publications Office.

Petrinovich, L. 1972. Psychological mechanisms in language development. In G. Newton & A. Riesen (Eds.), *Advances in psychobiology.* New York: Wiley-Interscience.

Pfeiffer, J. E. 1969. *The emergence of man.* New York: Harper & Row.

Ploog, D. 1967. The behavior of squirrel monkeys as revealed by sociometry, bioacoustics, and brain stimulation. In S. A. Altmann (Ed.), *Social communication among primates.* Chicago: University of Chicago Press.

Ploog, D. 1968. Kommunikationsprozesse bei Affen. *Homo, 19,* 151–165.

Ploog, D. 1969. Early communication processes in squirrel monkeys. In R. J. Robinson (Ed.), *Brain and early behavior.* New York: Academic Press.

Ploog, D. 1970. Social communication among animals. In F. Schmitt (Ed.), *The neurosciences, Second study program.* New York: The Rockefeller University Press.

Ploog, D. 1975. Vocal behavior and its 'localization' as a prerequisite for speech. In K. Zuelch, Creutzfeld, O., & Galbraith, G. C. (Eds.); *Cerebral localization.* New York: Springer-Verlag.

Premack, A., & Premack, D. 1972. Teaching language to an ape. *Scientific American, 227*(4), 92–99.

Premack, A. 1976. *Why chimps can read.* New York: Harper & Row.

Premack, D. 1970. A functional analysis of language. *Journal of Experimental Analysis of Behavior, 1,* 107–125.

Premack, D. 1971a. Language in chimpanzee? *Science, 172,* 808–822.

Premack, D. 1971b. On the assessment of language competence in the chimpanzee. In A. Schrier & F. Stollnitz (Eds.), *Behavior of nonhuman primates.* New York: Academic Press.

Premack, D. 1976. Language and intelligence in ape and man. *American Scientist, 64,* 674–683.

Premack, D. 1976. *Intelligence in ape and human.* New York: Wiley.

Prestrude, A. M. 1970. Sensory capacities of the chimpanzee: A review. *Psychological Bulletin, 74,* 47–67.

Pulgram, E. 1970. Homo loquens: An ethological view. *Lingua, 24,* 309–342.

Rensch, B., & Döhl, J. 1968. Wahlen zwischen swei überschaubaren Labyrinthwegen durch einen Schimpansen. *Zeitschrift für Tierpsychologie, 25,* 216–231.

Reynolds, V. 1967. *The apes.* New York: Harper & Row.

Reynolds, V., & Reynolds, F. 1965. Chimpanzees in the Budongo Forest. In I. DeVore (Ed.), *Primate behavior.* New York: Holt.

Robinson, B. W. 1967a. Vocalization evoked from forebrain in *Macaca mulatta. Physiology and Behavior, 2,* 345–54.

Robinson, B. W. 1967b. Neurological aspects of evoked vocalizations. In S. Altmann (Ed.), *Social communication among primates.* Chicago: University of Chicago Press.

Robinson, B. W. 1972. Anatomical and physiological contrasts between human and other primate vocalizations. In S. L. Washburn & P. Dolhinov (Eds.), *Perspectives on human evolution 2.* New York: Holt.

Robinson, B. W. 1976. Limbic influences on human speech. *Annals of the New York Academy of Sciences, 280,* 761–771.

Rose, S. 1973. *The conscious brain.* New York: Knopf.

Rumbaugh, D. 1970. Learning skills in anthropoids. In L. Rosenblum (Ed.), *Primate behavior.* New York: Academic Press.

Rumbaugh, D. 1971. Chimpanzee intelligence. In *The chimpanzee* (Vol. 4). Basel: S. Karger.

Rumbaugh, D. (Ed.). 1977. *Language learning by a chimpanzee: The Lana project.* New York: Academic Press.

Rumbaugh, D., & Gill, T. 1973. The learning skills of Great Apes. *Journal of Human Evolution, 2,* 171–179.

Rumbaugh, D., & Gill, T. 1976. Language and the acquisition of language-type skills by a chimpanzee *(Pan)*. *Annals of the New York Academy of Sciences, 280,* 90–123.

Rumbaugh, D., T. Gill, E. vonGlaserfeld, 1973. Reading and sentence completion by a chimpanzee. *Science, 182,* 731–733.

Rumbaugh, D., vonGlaserfeld, E., Warner, H., Pisani, P., & Gill, T. 1974. Lana (Chimpanzee) learning language: A progress report. *Brain and Language, 1,* 205–212.

Sachs, J. D. 1967. Recognition memory for syntactic and semantic aspects of connected discourse. *Perception and Psychophysics, 2,* 437–42.

Sarich, V. M. 1969. *The phylogeny of the cercopithecoidea.* (Cited by Washburn & Moore, 1974:189).

Sarich, V. M. 1974. Just how old is the hominid line? Yearbook of Physical Anthropology.

Sarnat, H., & Netsky, M. 1974. *Evolution of the nervous system.* N.Y.: Oxford U. Press.

Sasanuma, S. 1975. Kana and kanji processing in Japanese aphasics. *Brain and Language 2,* 369–383.

Schaller, G. 1963. *The mountain gorilla.* Chicago: U. of Chicago Press.

Schaltenbrand, G. 1975. The effects on speech and language of stereotactical stimulation in thalamus and corpus callosum. *Brain and Language, 2,* 70–77.

Schleicher, A. 1873. *Die Darwinische theorie und die sprachwissenschaft.* Weimar.

Scovel, T. 1972. Does language ontogeny recapitulate language phylogeny? *9th* Int. Congress of Linguists.

Seckel, H. 1960. *Bird-headed dwarfs.* Springfield, IU.: C. C Thomas.

Shankweiler, D. et al. 1975. Speech and the problem of perceptual constancy. SR-42/43, 117–145 (Haskins Labs.).

Sinnott, J. 1974. A comparison of speech sound discrimination in humans and monkeys. Unpublished Ph.D. dissertation. An Arbor: U. of Michigan.

Sinnott, J. *et al.* 1973, Regulation of voice amplitude by the monkey *(Macaca). J. Acoust. Soc. Am. 53,* 378.

Sinnott, J. *et al.* 1974. A comparison of speech sound discrimination in man and monkey. *Journal of the Acoustical Society of America, 55,* 462.

Smith, T. S. 1973. Review: The muscle spindle and neural ontrol of the tongue (Bowman). *J. of Phonetics 1,* 171–9.

Smith, W. K. 1941. Vocalization and other responses elicited by excitation of the *Regio cingularis* in the monkey. *American J. Physiol. 133,* 451–2.

Stam, J. 1976. *Inquiries into the origin of language: The fate of a question.* New York: Harper & Row.

Starck, D., & Schneider, R. 1960. Larynx. Primatalogia. In H. Hofer *et al.* (Eds.), *Handbook of primatology* (Vol. III, Part 2). Basel: S. Karger.

Stark, R., Rose, S. N., & McLagen, M. 1975. Features in infant sounds: The first eight weeks of life. *Journal of Child Language, 2,* 205–221.

Stephan, H. 1972. Evolution of primate brains: A comparative anatomical investigation. In R. Tuttle (Ed.), *The functional and evolutionary biology of primates.* Chicago: Aldine Atherton.

Stevens, K. N. 1972. The quantal nature of speech. In E. David & P. Denes (Eds.), *Human communication.* New York: McGraw-Hill.

Stevick, R. D. 1963. The biological model and historical linguistics. *Language, 39,* 159–169.

Stross, B. 1976. *The origin and evolution of language.* Dubuque: William C. Brown.

Sussman, H., & MacNeilage, P. 1975. Studies of hemispheric specialization for speech production. *Brain and Language, 2,* 131–151.

Sutton, D., Larson, E., & Lindeman, R. C. 1974. Neocortical and limbic lesion effects on primate phonation. *Brain Research, 71,* 61–75.

Symposium on language and communication. In R. Hutchins & M. Adler (Eds.), *The great ideas today.* Chicago: Encyclopedia Britannica.

Talmage-Riggs, G., P. Winter, W. Mayer. 1972. Effect of deafening on the vocal behavior of the Squirrel monkey (*Saimiri sciureus*). *Folia Primat, 17*, 404–420.

Tashian, R. E., Tanis, R. J., Ferrell, R. E., Stroup, S. K., & Goodman, M. Differential rates of evolution in the carbonic anhydrase isozymes of catarrhine primates. *Journal of Human Evolution, 1,* 545–552.

Teleki, G. 1974. Chimpanzee subsistence technology: Materials and skills. *Journal of Human Evolution, 3,* 575–594.

Temerlin, M. K. 1975. *Lucy: Growing up human, a chimpanzee daughter in a psychotherapist's family.* Palo Alto: Science and Behavior Books.

Terrace, H., & Bever, T. 1976. What might be learned from studying language in the chimpanzee? The importance of symbolizing oneself. *Annals of the New York Academy of Sciences, 280,* 579–588.

Terrace, H., & Bever, T. n.d. *Language in chimpanzees: Implications for understanding human language.* Unpublished manuscript.

Teuber, Hans-Lukas. 1974. Why two brains? In F. Schmitt & F. Worden (Eds.), *The neurosciences, Third study program.* Cambridge: MIT Press.

Thorpe, W. H. 1972. The comparison of vocal communication in animals and man. In R. A. Hinde (Ed.), *Non-verbal communication.* New York: Cambridge University Press.

Tilney, F. 1928. *The brain from ape to man.* New York: Hoeber.

Toulmin, S. 1971. Brain and language: A commentary. *Synthese, 22,* 369–95.

Tuttle, R. H. (Ed.). 1975. *Socioecology and psychology of primates.* The Hague: Mouton.

Tylor, Edward B. 1878. *Researches into the early history of mankind and the development of civilization.* New York:

van Hooff, J. 1971. *Aspects of the social behavior and communication in human and higher non-human primates.* Rotterdam: Author.

Van Lancker, D., & Fromkin, V. 1973. Hemispheric specialization for pitch and 'tone': Evidence from Thai. *Journal of Phonetics, 1,* 101–109.

Verbrugge, R. et al. 1974. What information enables a listener to mapa talker's vowel space? *Haskins Laboratories Research Reports, SR-37/38,* 199–208.

Wada, J., Clark, R., & Hamm, A. 1975. Cerebral hemispheric asymmetry in humans. *Archives of Neurology, 32,* 239–246.

Warren, J., & Nonneman, A. 1976. The search for cerebral dominance in monkeys. *Annals of the New York Academy of Sciences, 280,* 732–744.

Washburn, S., & Lancaster, J. 1971. On evolution and the origin of language. *Current Anthropology, 12,* 384–386.

Washburn, S., & Moore, R. 1974. *Ape into man.* Boston: Little, Brown.

Waters, R. S., & Wilson, W. A. 1976. Speech perception by rhesus monkeys: The voicing distinction in synthesized labial and velar consonants. *Perception and Psychophysics, 19,* 285–289.

Watt, W. C. 1970. On two hypotheses concerning psycholinguistics. In J. R. Hayes (Ed.), *Cognition and the development of language.* New York: Wiley.

Watt, W. C. 1972. *Competing economy criteria* (Social Sciences Working Papers No. 5). Irvine: University of California.

Watt, W. C. 1974a. Mentalism in linguistics, II. *Glossa, 8,* 3–40.

Watt, W. C. 1974b. Review: Behavior of non-human primates (Schrier and Stollnitz (eds.)). *Behavioral Science, 19.* 70–75.

Wescott, R. W. (Ed.). 1974. *Language origins.* Silver Spring, Md.: Linstok Press.

Wescott, R. W. 1967. The evolution of language: Reopening a closed subject. *Studies in Linguistics, 19,* 67–81.

Whalen, R. E. 1971. The concept of instinct. In J. L. McGaugh (Ed.), *Psychogiology.* New York: Academic Press.

Whitaker, H. 1976. A case of the isolation of the language function. In H. Whitaker & H. A. Whitaker (Eds.), *Studies in neurolinguistics* (Vol. 2). New York: Academic Press.

Whitaker, H. A. Forthcoming. Speech production. In O. Dingwall & H. A. Whitaker (Eds.), *Language and the brain*. Stamford, Conn.: Greylock.

Whitaker, H. A., & Selnes, O. 1975. Broca's area: A problem in language-brain relationships. *Linguistics, 154/155*, 91–103.

Wilson, E. O. 1975. *Sociobiology*. Cambridge: Harvard University Press.

Wilson, A. C., & Sarich, V. M. 1969. A molecular time scale for human evolution. *Proceedings of the National Academy of Sciences, 63*, 1088–1093.

Wind, J. 1970. *On the phylogeny and the ontogeny of the human larynx: A morphological and functional study*. Groningen: Wolters-Noordhoff Pub.

Wind, J. 1975. Neanderthal speech. *ORL, 37*, 58.

Wind, J. 1976. Phylogeny of the human vocal tract. *Annals of the New York Academy of Sciences, 280*, 612–630.

Winter, P., & Funkenstein, H. 1973. The effect of species-specific vocalization on the discharge of auditory cortical cells in the awake squirrel monkey. *Experimental Brain Research, 18*, 489–504.

Witelson, S., & Pallie, W. 1973. Left hemisphere specialization for language in the newborn. *Brain 96*, 641–646.

Witmer, L. 1909. A monkey with a mind. *Psychological Clinic* (Philadelphia), *3*, 179–205.

Wollberg, Z., & Newman, J. 1972. Auditory cortex of squirrel monkey: Response patterns of single cells to species-specific vocalizations. *Science, 175*, 212–214.

Wood, C., Goff, W. R., Day, P. S. 1971. Hemispheric differences in auditory evoked potentials during phonemic and pitch discrimination. *Science, 173*, 1248–1251.

Yamaguchi, S., & Myers, R. E. In press (a). Cortical mechanisms underlying vocalization in rhesus monkey: Prefrontal-orbito-frontal, anterior temporal and cingulate cortex. *Neuropsychologia*.

Yamaguchi, S., & Myers, R. E. In press (b). Effects of 'speech' area lesions on vocalization in monkey. *Brain Research*.

Yeni-Komshian, G. and Benson, D. 1975. Anatomical study of cerebral asymmetry in humans, chimpanzees and rhesus monkeys. *Science, 192*, 387–389.

Yerkes, Robert M. 1943. *Chimpanzees*. New Haven: Yale University Press.

Yerkes, R., & Learned, B. 1925. *Chimpanzee intelligence and its vocal expression*. Baltimore: Williams and Wilkins.

Yerkes, R., & Yerkes, A. 1929. *The great apes*. New Haven: Yale University Press.

Zaidel, E. 1973. *Linguistic competence and related functions in the right cerebral hemisphere of man following commissurotomy and hemispherectomy*. Unpublished doctoral dissertation, California Institute of Technology.

2

The Neural Control of Eye Movements in Acquired and Developmental Reading Disorders[1]

Francis J. Pirozzolo

MINNEAPOLIS VETERANS
ADMINISTRATION HOSPITAL

Keith Rayner

UNIVERSITY OF MASSACHUSETTS

INTRODUCTION

In recent years dyslexia has become an area of vital interest in neuropsychology. Given this interest in reading disability, it is natural that researchers should be concerned with the relationship of reading eye movements to reading difficulties. Although there once was a great deal of research on eye movements in reading (see Tinker, 1958) and differences between good and poor readers, very few of these studies dealt directly with dyslexics. More recent studies dealing with eye movements in reading (see Rayner & McConkie, 1976) have tended to focus upon skilled reading. However, we believe that there are some important implications which can be drawn from the reading eye movement research and clinical observations of eye movement disorders that are particularly relevant to dyslexia.

One of the major problems in the study of dyslexia, of course, is the lack of a universally acceptable definition. There is great variation in the defi-

[1] Preparation of this chapter was supported by Grant BNS76-05017 from the National Science Foundation to Keith Rayner.

nitions which investigators choose to apply to dyslexics. Some studies have used "dyslexic" children who are 6 months below grade level in reading (e.g., Sobotka & May, 1977), while others argue for distinctions between those children who are low achievers in reading (backward readers) and those children who have a very specific reading retardation (Rutter & Yule, 1975). Even more controversial is the issue of etiology, with almost as many hypotheses as there are investigators. Surprisingly, there is even little agreement on the signs and symptoms of dyslexia.

For our present purposes, we shall refer to developmental dyslexia as a specific reading disability in which the child has normal intelligence and is at least 2 years behind expected grade level in reading, has normal sensory acuity, and is without neurological damage and emotional problems. Thus, we exclude from our definition readers who are slow learners (i.e., they have low IQs) and who are poor readers (i.e., they are behind grade level in reading, but not significantly so).

We will here review the characteristics of the normal reader's eye movements during reading, abnormal eye movements and the relationship of different types of dyslexia to eye movement patterns. With regard to the latter point, we will suggest that faulty eye movements in dyslexics (such as right-to-left scanning) are not the cause of dyslexia. We will demonstrate instead that only a small proportion of dyslexics manifest such oculomotor scanning problems and that evidence of other spatial problems in these children strongly suggests that it is the spatial mechanism which guides the eye, rather than the oculomotor mechanism itself, that is the causal factor.

We will also review in rather broad strokes the types of eye movement disorders that result from lesions of the central nervous system and attempt to illustrate how these abnormalities affect reading. Eye movement data from two patients with eye movement disorders will be presented and it will be shown that disordered efferent oculomotor control causes a severe and insuperable problem in understanding connected text. In addition, functional adaptations which compensate for the oculomotor deficiency, such as head and neck movements, are manifested by these two patients when reading or visual tracking tasks are required.

Finally, we will attempt to show that although dyslexics do not have the same reading eye movement pattern as normal readers, the variance is not attributable to an oculomotor disorder. We agree with recent evidence which suggests that at least two separate dyslexia syndromes exist. Eye movement monitoring during reading indicates that the eye movement phenomena that typify one form of dyslexia reflect difficulty in auditory-linguistic processing, while the eye movement phenomena in a small minority of cases reflect a difficulty in spatial processing.

Saccadic Eye Movement Control Mechanisms

During reading the eyes make a series of saccadic eye movements, generally in a left-to-right direction. The term saccade is used to distinguish this rapid, jerky type of eye movement, separated by fixational pauses, from pursuit or smooth tracking movements in which the eyes move slowly, maintaining fixation on a moving target or on a stationary point while the head moves. Cumming (1976) points out that saccadic eye movements and pursuit movements are different types of movement, serve different functions, and are initiated by different control systems. Another distinction is that saccades are under voluntary control, while relative movement between the head and a stimulus is usually necessary for pursuit movements. However, both types of eye movement are produced by the same extraocular muscles.

Although eye position is also regulated by the vestibular apparatus, the visual cortex is responsible for the continuous visual regulation of eye position. The cortical saccadic control mechanisms involved in the programming of eye movements are poorly understood at the present time. While pursuit movements seem to be represented cortically in the occipito–parietal association area, saccades are represented in the frontal eye field, located in the posterior end of the middle frontal gyrus. The frontal eye field (Brodmann's Area 8) was an early discovery that was often marshaled as evidence in favor of the localization theory of brain function. Penfield and Boldrey (1937) demonstrated that electrical stimulation in Area 8 resulted in contraversive eye movements. Further evidence of the function of this area comes from experiments which have found that Area 8 neurons fire 150–200 msec before saccadic eye movements—approximately the amount of time necessary to program and launch a voluntary saccade (Barlow & Ciganek, 1969). Although there is conflicting evidence that suggests that the neurons of the frontal eye field do not fire prior to saccadic eye movements but during the movement (Bizzi, 1968), clinical evidence would seem to support the suggestion that Area 8 mediates coordinated saccadic eye movements (Luria, 1966).

In addition to the evidence for frontal eye movement control, there is a small class of cells in Area 7 of the parietal lobe which appear to be saccade neurons. These neurons have also been observed to discharge up to 150 msec before visually evoked saccadic eye movements, but not before spontaneous saccades (Lynch, Mountcastle, Talbot, & Yin, 1977). The pathway which connects Area 7 with the brain stem oculomotor mechanisms has not been conclusively established, although it has been suggested that the abundant cortico-cortical fibers between the inferior parietal lobule and the frontal eye field carry efferent information before it is projected to the brain stem.

Other control mechanisms involved in the saccadic eye movement pathway are part of a complex extrapyramidal projection system. The major fiber pathway which begins in Area 8 descends via the internal capsule and globus pallidus to the ventrolateral thalamus, courses through the midbrain reticular formation and finally decussates at the pontine level. This sophisticated system requires additional vestibular information, which it receives from the cerebellum. The role of the cerebellum in saccadic eye movements is to provide precise information about the amplitude of the movements which is accomplished by correcting and regulating the duration of the saccades. The importance of the cerebellum in computing the displacement of the target and integrating visual and vestibular information is greatly underestimated (Kornhuber, 1973). The eye movement behavior of our patient MBO, which will be presented shortly as Case Report 1, will clearly show how important cerebellar function is to the saccadic system.

Three cranial nerves, the oculomotor (III), trochlear (IV), and abducens (VI), form the final common pathway for all movements of the eyes. The oculomotor nerve innervates many of the extraocular muscles and these muscles can trigger eye movements in all directions except outward. While eye movements are important components of an information processing theory of reading, it is clear that reading can be achieved in the absence of eye movements. For instance, several cases of congenital ophthalmoplegia (Moebius syndrome) have been reported in the clinical neurological literature and despite mild reductions in intelligence and the inability to make lateral or medial eye movements, some of these children are able to function at age level in reading (e.g., Stebbins, Emmel, Heriot, & Rockowitz, 1975).

Eye Movements during Reading

The saccadic eye movements that occur during reading last roughly 20–40 msec (depending upon the distance moved) and cover an average of about 8 character spaces, or about 2° of visual angle. Since the fovea, the area of high visual acuity, is relatively small (1–2° of visual angle), eye movements serve the function of bringing a region of text into the fovea for detailed analysis. Between each saccade there is a period of time during which the eye is relatively still in a fixation. It is during these fixation periods that information is processed to higher centers in the brain. The average fixation duration is generally between 200–250 msec. While these figures (200–250 msec for fixation duration and 8 character spaces for saccade length) are usually cited as stable indices of eye movements during reading, it is important to note that there is a great deal of variability in these measures both within and between subjects (Rayner & McConkie, 1976). Thus, although the mean saccade length of a given reader may be 8 character spaces, data show that saccades frequently range in length from 2–18 character spaces. Although the mean fixation duration may be 200 msec, the actual data values typically range from 100 to over 500 msec. The third major aspect of eye movements during reading is regressions. Regressions are right-to-left movements and constitute about 10–15% of normal, skilled readers' saccades.

Developmental studies indicate that there is a steady progression, from first grade to fourth or fifth grade, in which mean saccade lengths increase and mean fixation durations decrease. By fourth or fifth grade, average fixation durations and average saccade lengths are comparable to college-age readers. Number of regressions continues to decrease, however, through high-school age. In terms of differences between good and poor readers of the same age, it has generally been found that poor readers make shorter saccades, have longer fixation durations, and make more regressions than their more skilled peers.

Two important facts about eye movements which have been learned from experiments not involving reading (see Rayner, 1978a) are first, that the latency for a saccade is 125–250 msec depending upon the task and second, that the saccade is a ballistic movement and once programmed cannot be redirected. Information from the text is not picked up during the saccade due to partial visual suppression. The speed with which the eye (100–600 per second) moves across the text during a saccade is so great. that only blur would be perceived if it were not for this suppression.

Given that information is processed during the fixation and that the saccade is a ballistic movement, it is necessary to specify what guides a reader's eye movements. Many researchers have concluded that since the latency for a saccade is so brief, readers do not have time to program precisely where to direct their eye. Thus, these researchers have concluded that eye movements are under strictly oculomotor and physiological control. Interestingly, many researchers concerned with differences between good and poor readers have adopted the implicit assumption that eye movements are not determined by cognitive processing. That is, they have traditionally assumed that a major difference between good and poor readers is that good readers make smooth, rhythmical eye movements over the text while the poor readers do not. Thus, numerous studies were conducted to train poor readers to make rhythmical eye movements. Tinker (1958) concluded that these studies were largely ineffective and that eye movements reflect a symptom rather than a cause of reading problems. It is also important to note that these eye training experiments seemed to be based on erroneous assumptions since, as we have noted, good readers are also highly variable in their eye movement behavior and regressions in most instances aid comprehension instead of hindering it.

A great deal of recent evidence seems to support the idea that eye movements are made on a nonrandom basis. Rayner (1978b) found that the latency period for a saccade to parafoveally presented words was 30–100 msec shorter than the subject's mean fixation duration in reading. Rayner and McConkie (1976) found that although the probability of fixating a word is a linear function of word length, the probability of fixating on a letter within a word of a given length is a curvilinear relationship in which short words and long words do not receive as much attention as words four to eight characters long. Abrams and Zuber (1972) found that readers tend not to fixate on blank areas inserted in text. Rayner (1975a) demonstrated that there are fewer fixations in the region between sentences than would be expected if eye movements were made on a random basis; that is, on the last letters of one sentence, the period and spaces between, and the function word beginning the next sentence. O'Regan (1975) has reported that the length of the word to the right of the fixated word influences the next saccade. That is, if the word is longer, the eye tends to jump further. O'Regan also found that the word *the* is skipped more frequently than could be expected by chance. All these data indicate that eye movements are not made on a random basis. Also, since there is no correlation between the duration of a fixation and the preceding or following saccade, Rayner and McConkie (1976) have argued that these two components of eye behavior (saccade length and fixation duration) are not under the control of a single mechanism and that they represent independent aspects of eye behavior, which must be accounted for separately.

An issue closely related to the question of eye guidance in reading concerns the extent to which eye movements reflect the processing of central cognitive mechanisms. Many researchers have assumed that since the fixation durations are relatively brief and that the process of converting the printed symbols into some semantic representation is relatively slow, that eye movements cannot reflect cognitive processes. According to this assumption, the meaning is obtained only after the eye has moved on to a new area. While this is still very much an open issue, some recent data suggests that fixation durations reflect cognitive events. It has been known for some time that readers make shorter saccades and have longer fixation durations when reading difficult text (Tinker, 1958). More recently, a number of studies have shown a relationship between frequency of fixation and/or length of fixation and syntactic and semantic variables (Klein & Kurkowski, 1974; Rayner, 1977; Wanat, 1971). In addition, Rayner (1975a) and Pynte (1974) have shown that the duration of the fixation can be influenced by information acquired during the fixation itself. Rayner found that when subjects fixated on a nonword inserted in the text that fixation durations were increased considerably. Thus, there is growing evidence that fixation durations are influenced by characteristics of the text that the subject is looking at during a particular fixation.

Another question is very important to understanding the characteristics of eye movements during reading: From how wide an area is a reader able to get useful information during a fixation? In the past a number of techniques have been used to investigate this question. These techniques have ranged from tachistoscopic exposures of words and letter strings in the periphery to simply counting the number of fixations per line and dividing them into the number of character spaces on the line. However, Sperling (1960) has demonstrated that what subjects can report from a tachistoscopic array does not coincide with what was actually seen. Furthermore, the display pattern of a page of text is considerably more complex than single words or letter strings presented in the periphery. The method of dividing the number of fixations into the number of character spaces is problematic because it assumes that there is no overlap of information on successive fixations (an assumption that is clearly false as recent research has shown). More recently, investigators (Bouma & deVoogd, 1974; Newman, 1966) have used a method in which the subject is asked to maintain fixation as the text is passed from right to left in front of his eyes. But such a method inhibits normal eye movements that are important in determining where to look in reading, as we indicated earlier. Also, given the great variability within subjects in terms of saccade lengths, the capability of the subject to determine where he wants to look next seems very important. Thus none of these methods are problem-free.

A recent series of experiments using a novel technique that involved the subject controlling the characteristics of the display has provided data concerning the perceptual span in a more valid situation. These experiments involved monitoring the reader's eye position as he read text displayed on a cathode ray tube (CRT) of a computer. The signal from the eye movement sensors was fed into the computer, which therefore had moment-to-moment information about the location of the reader's gaze. Display changes in the text were then made contingent upon the location of the gaze. On the basis of these experiments (McConkie & Rayner, 1975, 1976; Rayner, 1975b), it appears that readers get different types of information from different areas within a fixation in reading. Information falling on the fovea is processed for its semantic content, while information from parafoveal vision is limited to rather gross featural information, such as word length. There was no evidence that information 5° or more from fixation was useful to the reader. However, the information from parafoveal vision is probably used by the reader as he integrates information from one fixation to the next and as an aid for guiding the eye movement. The results also indicated that the perceptual span is asymmetric and more useful information is obtained from the right of the fixation than from the left for English readers.

Finally, we conclude this section with a note concerning the lack of vision during a saccade. As we noted earlier, when the eye goes into motion visual suppression occurs. However, the notion of saccadic suppression that is attributed to retinal blur cannot fully account for this phenomenon since the suppression begins some 30 msec or so prior to the launching of the saccade and lasts for a short period of time after the eye comes to rest. Whatever the cause of this suppression prior to and after the saccade, it serves a very useful purpose in that it reduces the effects of masking. That is, when the eye moves and fixates a new location there must be some masking that occurs as the pattern from one fixation overrides the patterns from another fixation. However, the suppression which occurs apparently reduces the masking effect so that we do not perceive any overlapping of successive images. The fact that eye movements occur at the rate of four or five per second also limits the detrimental effects of masking. If fixations were more frequent, the masking effects would probably make it difficult for us to see anything (Gilbert, 1959).

DISORDERS OF THE SACCADIC EYE MOVEMENT SYSTEM

In the discussion that follows we will review disturbances of saccadic eye movements that are caused by central nervous system dysfunctions and consider the role of eye movements in the reading problems which are observed in patients with these disturbances.

Experienced clinicians note that among the first complaints of many patients afflicted with eye movement disorders are problems in reading. Typically the patient reports that he has great difficulty reading and comprehending even short passages, that he fatigues rapidly when reading, that he experiences difficulty following consecutive words or lines of text, that he has difficulty maintaining a fixation, or that headaches occur after very brief periods of reading.

There are three types of saccadic eye movement disorders which are known to influence reading behavior: paralytic or slow saccades, which result from lesions involving the basal ganglia, brain stem, and cerebral cortex (Cogan, 1975); impaired saccadic initiation, which results from acquired and congenital apraxias involving the left and right parietal lobe; and dysmetric saccades, which result from lesions involving the cerebellum and cerebellar pathways.

Slow saccadic eye movements have been observed and rigorously studied in neurological disorders such as spinocerebellar degeneration and Huntington's chorea. These patients are unable to make rapid, high-velocity saccadic eye movements. Instead they make eye movements which have roughly the same velocity as pursuit eye movements. Although it has been suggested that the residual slow eye movements may be "voluntary smooth pursuits," it has been shown that these movements are, in fact, abnormally slow saccades initiated by a defective saccadic system (Zee, Optican, Cook, Robinson, & Engel, 1976; Pirozzolo, 1978a).

Starr (1967) has demonstrated the relationship between Huntington's chorea and the disruption of the saccadic eye movement system by showing that these patients retain normal pursuit eye movement behavior, but have greatly diminished saccadic velocities. Although Starr did not specify his patient's reading ability, he was able to show that the normal reading eye movement pattern, that is, several saccades per line proceeding from left to right and separated by fixation pauses of roughly a quarter of a second, was absent. Instead, reading was accomplished through a strategy using head movements and smooth following movements of the eyes.

Prechtl and Stemmer (1959) have demonstrated that many word recognition errors made by children with choreatic syndrome (each child was, in addition, a disabled reader) were correlated with instances of involuntary eye movements, thus showing a definite relationship between an information processing dysfunction and abnormal eye movements.

Several observations of patients with bilateral lesions affecting the parieto-occipital cortex have shown a relationship between disorders of oculomotor control and visual perceptual processing. Similarly, a congenital form of this disturbance exists with deficiencies identical to those observed in the acquired form of the disorder. Hecaen and Ajuriaguerra (1954), Cogan (1952, 1965), Robles (1966), and Smith and Holmes (1916) have shown a slowness and instability of fixation, as well as a spasmodic fixation once fixation is achieved, in these patients. Cogan (1952) and Robles (1966) both described patients with congenital oculomotor apraxia and reading disability. In each of these cases, the strategy of head movements was employed to compensate for the deficiency in initiating saccades.

Cerebellar disorders result in the incorrect programming of saccades and other coordinated neuromuscular activities. Zee *et al.* (1976) have presented two patients who show the symptoms of slow saccades and saccadic dysmetria. Unfortunately, the reading eye movements of their patients were not recorded, but it is likely that reading was impaired. Frank and Levinson (1973, 1976) have proposed that developmental dyslexics may suffer from a cerebellar–vestibular dysfunction (and not a cerebral dysfunction as commonly held). These investigators have found evidence of dysmetric dyslexia and dyspraxia in 97% of a clinical group of dyslexics. The characteristics of this group of disabled readers, however, were not discussed.

The case illustrations that follow strongly suggest that disorders of oculomotor control are responsible for the reading disturbances observed in patients with basal ganglia and cerebellar disorders. Both patients were referred to us because they reported having great difficulty in reading, while other cognitive abilities appeared to be relatively spared.

Case Report 1

MBO is a 57-year-old, right-handed man with the diagnosis of spino–cerebellar degeneration. This disorder began in 1965 and he has been admitted for hospitalization to the University of Rochester Medical Center twice recently for observation. A brief neuropsychological screening battery was administered to assess his general level of intellectual functioning. Mental status examination revealed him to be oriented for time and place, with good recent and long-term memory. Digit span and Wechsler Memory Scale test results indicated that his short-term memory function was intact. There was a slight slurring of speech, but other speech and language functions were well within normal limits.

Convergence was intact and there was a full range of extraocular movements. Horizontal saccadic movements of the eyes appeared to be very slow. Pursuit tracking was smooth and apparently accurate. While reading, it was noted that MBO made a series of compensatory head movements, perhaps in an attempt to bypass the saccadic system and allow the vestibulo-ocular reflex to bring the peripheral characters of the text into foveal vision. It was therefore necessary to immobilize the head to record the saccadic eye movements of this patient while reading.

The eye movement recording of MBO's eye movements during reading yielded two important observations. First, for all saccades during reading, there was a large increase in the time the eye was in flight, estimated to be five times the normal duration. The duration of saccadic movements for normal readers was 35 msec, compared to approximately 170 msec for MBO. This observation is in good agreement with other measures of slow saccades in spino–cerebellar degeneration (Zee *et al.*, 1976). Second, and also notable, were overshoots at the end of the line and hypometric return sweeps. MBO's final saccade on a line overshot the end of the line, in contrast to a normal reader's last fixation on a line of text, which is usually five or six character spaces from the end of the line. The final hypermetric saccade was then followed by a series of right-to-left saccades until MBO found the beginning of the next line of text. Although a small hypometric error in the return sweep can be observed in normals, this pattern was consistent and grossly evident throughout the eye movement record of MBO.

Comprehension questions were administered immediately following the test session and performance was dramatically poorer than expected from this patient's performance on other cognitive measures. These results indicate that the patient's performance is severely affected by cerebellar dysmetria and slow saccades and that the visual disorientation and the greatly increased time the eye is in movement results in inability to read on a level even remotely compatible with the subject's intellectual ability.

Case Report 2

SMM is a 24-year-old, right-handed woman who was first diagnosed as having juvenile Huntington's chorea 6 years prior to our study. Symptoms included unsteady gait, slow refixational eye movements, choreiform movements and progressive intellectual detioration. The patient's father had adult onset Huntington's chorea and her only sibling, an 18-year-old sister, suffered from the juvenile form of the disease since puberty. Neuropsychological testing revealed a full-scale WAIS score of 87 with a verbal IQ of 95 and a performance IQ of 79. Short-term memory was moderately defective, as indicated by results of the Wechsler Memory Scale, subtests of the WAIS, and Benton Visual Retention Test. The patient also reported having frequent spells of forgetfulness.

Administration of a reading test revealed very slow saccadic eye movements as well as some compensatory head movements (which were observed also in MBO). One other remarkable strategy was readily apparent in the eye movement record. At the end of each line of print the patient made an eyeblink and then began a series of slow right-to-left saccades until she found the first word on the next line. This eye blinking seems to be a compensatory mechanism used to terminate the fixation before beginning the leftward eye movement. This strategy was also observed in a patient with Huntington's chorea by Starr (1967). Saccadic eye movement velocities were estimated to be approximately one-third those of normal patients, an observation which is consistent with a report by Bachman, Butler, and McKhann (1977) of two patients with juvenile Huntington's chorea.

Reading comprehension level was measured during the neuropsychological evaluation and again after the eye movement recording session. Each estimate was at the fifth-grade level. Performance on these reading tests, as well as other measures of visual information processing ability, suggest that recognition of visual material is disrupted by abnormally slow refixational saccades.

ACQUIRED DYSLEXIA

Kussmaul (1884) provided the first modern systematic description of reading disorders that result from brain lesions. Word blindness was clinically differentiated from five other forms of aphasic disturbances and was attributed to lesions which involved the "center of visual word images." Dejerine (1892) introduced the notion that there are two different types of alexia: alexia with agraphia and pure word blindness. The first type of acquired alexia resulted from lesions in the angular gyrus while the second type (pure word blindness) resulted from lesions disconnecting the visual cortex from the angular gyrus and other language mechanisms.

Recent neurolinguistic studies of acquired reading disorders have suggested that three forms of reading impairment exist. Marshall and Newcombe (1973) have analyzed the predominant patterns of paralexias and delineated the following three neuropsychological syndromes.

1. Visual Dyslexia—a paralexia which involves the faulty recognition of letters and words which are orthographically similar. The portion of the word which is most severely affected depends upon the site of the lesion. Thus, the ends of the words are misread most often (Warrington & Zangwill, 1957) due to the predominance of left hemisphere lesions in acquired reading disorders, although the beginnings of words can also be affected in right hemisphere pathology (Kinsbourne & Warrington, 1962).
2. Surface Dyslexia—a paralexia involving the partial failure of the grapheme-to-phoneme translation. Luria (1947) had previously described two forms of this disturbance: the inability to remember the phonemes associated with each visual symbol and the inability to read strings of letters in the correct sequential pattern.
3. Deep Dyslexia—a paralexia involving the semantic or internal lexical structure of words. Although the occurrence of semantic dyslexia is very rare, several cases of dyslexics making errors which are within the same semantic field as the stimulus have been reported in the literature (Beringer & Stein, 1930; Lhermitte, Lecours, & Ouvry, 1967; Luria, 1947; Saffran, Schwartz, & Marin, 1976; Weigl & Bierwisch, 1970).

In a similar taxonomic analysis of reading errors, Hecaen (1967) has also identified three forms of acquired reading disorders: verbal alexia, literal alexia, and global alexia. The evidence that these disorders are separate clinical entities is not conclusive, however. In fact, there is some evidence that the pattern of reading errors changes with recovery of reading function. However, there is fairly general agreement that the two forms of acquired reading impairment which were described by Dejerine are separate neuropsychological syndromes. These two acquired dyslexias have also been called aphasic alexia (alexia with agraphia) and agnosic alexia (alexia without agraphia) in the neurological literature. The documentation of these disorders is plentiful, although there is some debate over the possible pathophysiological mechanisms involved.

One further set of observations (Benson, 1977) provides a compelling argument for a third form of alexia. While most authorities would agree that alexia is a posterior cerebral dysfunction, Benson's evidence suggests an anterior alexia. In oral reading his patients have great difficulty reading grammatical formatives and, as in spontaneous speech, lexical formatives are read rather normally. This form of alexia differs from the other two forms in that patients with this frontal reading disturbance have relatively little difficulty in comprehending meaningful content words. Benson identified four factors which are possible causes of this disturbance: gaze paresis, a verbal sequencing deficiency, agrammatism, and a selective dysnomia for letters.

Eye Movements and Acquired Dyslexia

Eye movement disturbances are certainly not responsible for the neurological syndrome of agnosic alexia (alexia without agraphia). Presumably this syndrome is a disorder of perceptual recognition and, although the patient may not be able to move his eyes promptly on command to the left or right, the classic word recognition defect is clearly due to a disconnection between the visual and language areas of the cerebral cortex and not to a defect in lateral scanning.

There have been a number of suggestions that alexics have faulty eye movements, as well as observations that oculomotor scanning is intact in these patients. Newcombe, Hiorns, Marshall, and Adams (1975), for instance, have presented a longitudinal case study of acquired dyslexia resulting from destruction of the left parietal region. Although the patient was slightly dysphasic, her most pronounced difficulties were in understanding what she had read. This comprehension problem is intimately related to anomia and reflects a disruption of the internal lexicon, a disorder almost invariably evident in cases of acquired dyslexia. An additional reading problem was noted during the later stages of recovery—the inability to make a return sweep to the next line of print. The authors suggest that an examination of the eye movements of this patient may reveal that a visuo-spatial disability continues to disrupt the reading process after the linguistic disturbance has cleared.

Ajax (1967) presents two cases of acquired dyslexia without agraphia. In both cases oculomotor responses were reported to be unaffected, that is, both patients were able to move their eyes promptly and correctly on command. Hartje (1972) reports evidence that oculomotor scanning is intact during reading in some aphasic alexics, and not in others.

We have observed cases of both aphasic and agnosic alexia in which reading eye movements were dissimilar to the normal reading patterns, which suggests that oculomotor scanning problems can occur in both forms of acquired dyslexia. The lateral scanning problem is not, however, the cause of the reading deficiency, but a symptom of a spatial disturbance. This suggestion is supported by Lawson's (1962) demonstration that attempting to train patients with unilateral visual neglect to make lateral left-to-right eye movements in reading does not necessarily affect their proficiency in reading.

With regard to the problem of spatial orientation, in which the inferior parietal lobe undoubtedly plays an important role, a comment on the possible pathophysiology is pertinent. It has been shown that occipito-frontal cortico–cortical connections are uniquely important in carrying out many tasks for which visual guidance is critical (Kuypers & Haaxsma, 1975). It would seem, therefore, that any deep lesion which destroys the white matter of the angular gyrus would interrupt the superior longitudinal fasciculus and would thus interfere with sensory–motor functions for visually guided behavior. Since the lesions responsible for each form of alexia can theoretically interrupt the association fibers connecting visual cortex with the precentral motor cortex and Area 8, it is reasonable to assume that an eye movement disturbance—faulty lateral scanning—can be caused by the brain lesion responsible for the reading impairment.

Benson's (1977) observations on the "third alexia" suggest that an eye movement disorder may be a significant factor in anterior alexia. Specifically, several patients with anterior aphasic lesions may also have a gaze paresis to the right. Further evidence suggesting an oculomotor scanning problem in the third alexia comes from observations noting that anterior aphasics move very slowly from word to word and from line to line. Posterior aphasics, on the other hand, appear to move rapidly across and down the page. This clinical observation augments the evidence for an eye movement disorder in anterior alexia.

Case Report 3

SB is a 56-year-old, right-handed female musician who was referred for neuropsychological evaluation after a cerebrovascular accident that resulted in anomic aphasia and a severe alexia with agraphia. Neuroradiological reports indicated a lesion in the inferior parietal area extending into the occipital cortex. Neurobehavioral symptoms include dyslexia, dysgraphia, anomia, topographic disorientation, and finger agnosia. Neurolinguistic testing showed a marked naming difficulty on visual, tactile and auditory confrontation. Further testing revealed above-average intellectual ability with a WAIS IQ of 112 and a Peabody Picture Vocabulary IQ of 106. Orientation for time and place was good, although there was confabulation in all oral communication when the patient became "blocked." Interviews conducted with SB and her daughter indicated that she was formerly a very able reader and had written several muscial scores and a number of operas. The patient was forced to discontinue her work as a musician because she could no longer read music fluently or complete an unfinished opera.

The eye movement record of this patient suggested that the patient may be looking at nearly every letter of the text in an attempt to understand the graphic symbols. There was no evidence of a disturbance in visual scanning either in this study of her eye movements or on neurological examination.

DEVELOPMENTAL DYSLEXIA

The relationship between adults who have sustained brain damage and have, as a result of these lesions, lost the ability to read and write and children who have exceptional difficulty in learning to read and write has come under close scrutiny in recent years. Children with reading disabilities bear at least a modest resemblance to the acquired dyslexic. Although no clinico–pathological data are yet available to suggest that this apparently congenital disability is associated with pathological brain anatomy, it seems reasonable to assume that the elusive causal mechanisms in developmental dyslexia may be related to the brain mechanisms which are structurally altered in acquired dyslexia. Reading disability, however, will most certainly arise from factors other than the neurogenic ones which we shall discuss here.

Geschwind (1965) speculated that the congenital failure of reading acquisition may be caused by the delayed development of the angular gyrus—probably bilaterally. Not surprisingly, the angular gyrus is one of the last areas in the human cerebral hemispheres to develop (Flechsig, 1901; Yakovlev & Lecours, 1967). Geschwind presented the interesting, but as yet unsupported, proposition that this late myelination may be related to the interrelated problems of color naming deficits, cross-modal associations, and developmental dyslexia.

The ability to name colors is dependent upon the ability to form non-limbic cross-modal associations between the visual and auditory modalities. Since the angular gyrus is neuroanatomically situated in an important pathway connecting the visual cortex with the auditory cortex, it is a uniquely important area for performing functions that require cross-modal associations (such as color-naming, object-naming, and the ability to comprehend written language).

Color-naming and object-naming are among the prereading skills which dyslexic readers do not acquire as readily as normal readers (Denckla, 1972a, 1972b; Denckla & Rudel, 1976). As with other symptoms of dyslexia, it is a curious coincidence that adult patients with lesions disconnecting the language and visual areas have great difficulty with color-naming and object-naming (Geschwind & Fusillo, 1966; Lhermitte & Beauvois, 1973; Oxbury, Oxbury, & Humphrey, 1969).

The developmental Gerstmann syndrome (Benson & Geschwind, 1970; Kinsbourne & Warrington, 1963; Pirozzolo & Rayner, 1978) resembles the deficiencies constituting the Gerstmann syndrome (Gerstmann, 1924) in adults with lesions of the inferior parietal lobe. The symptoms of finger agnosia, directional disorientation, dysgraphia, and dyscalculia have persistent occurrence in children with a specific form of reading disability. These children have severe problems performing spatial and constructional tasks and some investigators, such as Boder (1971), have speculated that this may be due to their inability to revisualize the perceptual Gestalts which make up words. These dyslexic children make reversals and other visual errors which involve faulty encoding of the visual aspects of the text. The directional difficulty that these readers experience may result in the inability to make successive saccades in a rightward direction. Reversals can be attributed to the high percentage of right-to-left saccades which feed new information into the language areas for processing before the preceding information is processed or masked. Although the localizing significance of this congenital spatial disorder is not yet known, it may be related to the hypothesis proposed by Geschwind that developmental dyslexia is associated with the late myelination of bilateral angular gyrus areas.

Although research on subtypes of developmental dyslexia should be carefully analyzed, it would appear that there is general agreement among researchers that at least two subgroups of developmental dyslexia can be identified (see Pirozzolo, 1978b). Kinsbourne and Warrington (1965) were among the first to suggest two subgroups: a language disorder dyslexia and a developmental Gerstmann syndrome. Based on behavioral descriptions of dyslexics, linguistic analyses of paralexic errors, and neuropsychological analyses of test profiles from the WISC-R and ITPA, Pirozzolo and Hess (1976) isolated two clinical groups of dyslexics who resemble the two groups identified by Kinsbourne and Warrington. One group had low verbal and high performance scores on the WISC-R scales, with commensurate low auditory–vocal channel and high visual–motor channel scores on the ITPA psycholinguistic profile. This group made predominantly more errors involving faulty grapheme-to-phoneme translations than any other type of misreading. The second group had high verbal and low performance WISC-R scores with high auditory–vocal and low visual–motor ITPA scores. This group of poor readers made predominantly more errors which involved the visual characteristics of text; that is, they made more frequent letter and word reversals and confusions than other types of paralexic errors. These results as well as those of Kinsbourne and Warrington would seem to corroborate Myklebust's (1965) suggestion that there are at least two dyslexic syndromes that reflect deficiencies in central auditory and visual processing.

Eye Movements and Developmental Dyslexia

There are numerous inferences in the neurological, psychological, and educational literature on reading disorders that have cited oculomotor disturbances as causative factors in dyslexia. Although there is a considerable amount of research on reading disturbances and an impressive number of recent studies devoted to eye movements during reading, there are very few studies which have examined the disabled reader's eye movements. Despite the paucity of information about relationships between eye movements and reading disability, suggestions that faulty eye movements are the cause of dyslexia, that dyslexics have restricted perceptual spans, or that dyslexics have poor lateral scanning strategies are plentiful in the literature. There is, in fact, very little conclusive data to support such claims.

Another serious flaw in the treatment of this topic is the assumption that reading disability is a single, homogeneous clinical entity. Preliminary evidence from several neuropsychological studies suggests that this is not the case. We shall consider this point further in our discussion of developmental dyslexia.

Dossetor and Papaioannou (1975) compared the saccadic latency time for dyslexic and normal readers. There were longer latencies to a target dot presented to the right of fixation for normals as compared to longer latencies to the left in dyslexics. The target dots were xenon lights that were flashed randomly 40° to the left or right of a central fixation point. On the basis of their study of saccadic reaction times, they suggested that dyslexics' impaired ability to read may be associated with a deficiency involving the cortical control centers for saccadic eye movement. Dossetor and Papaioannou did not, however, describe the characteristics of their dyslexic group, nor did they provide any convincing explanation of their results. The reaction times they reported were longer (dyslexics = 500 msec; normals = 400 msec) than that reported by other investigators. Baloh and Honrubia (1976), for instance, found the normal range for mean saccadic reaction time to be 142–230 msec, while Westheimer (1954) suggested an even shorter saccadic reaction time to visual signals. Furthermore, the asymmetry reported by Dossetor and Papaioannou conflicts with the results of similar studies conducted by Lesevre (1964, 1968, 1976). While she found that reaction times were longer for dyslexics than for normal readers, the latency for a movement to the right was shorter than for movement to the left in normal readers (see also Rayner, 1978a). Dyslexics showed no lateral asymmetry in saccadic reaction time. Lesevre also found that dyslexics did not show a consistent left-to-right scanning strategy and that they showed significantly more short pauses while reading text than normals.

Rubino and Minden (1973) examined the relationship between eye movements and reading ability and have concluded that deficiencies in eye movements are related to reading disability. From analyses of eye movement patterns while reading passages of text, they found that disabled readers were significantly slower in reading the material and that they made a greater number of fixations and regressions.

But this evidence is not compelling enough to suggest "an eye movement deficit" such as Rubino and Minden propose. The same pattern of eye movement behavior in reading is frequently seen in younger children who are learning to read. In a study of the developmental changes in reading eye movements, Buswell (1922) demonstrated that beginning readers made approximately 3 times as many fixations per line of print (18.6), 10 times as many regressions per line (5.1), and had fixation durations that were $2\frac{1}{2}$ times as long as college readers (660 msec). Similarly, Taylor (1965) showed that one-third of first grade readers' saccades are regressions, but college students make regressions at the rate of 15% of the total number of saccades. These observations suggest that once reading proficiency is attained, both regression frequency and fixation duration decrease. Buswell (1922) showed, however, that adults reading unfamiliar foreign language grammar texts regress as much as 50% of their saccades.

Zangwill and Blakemore (1972) reported a case study of an adult dyslexic who was able to identify words presented at very low thresholds in a tachistoscope. However, when reading, his eye movement pattern showed many right-to-left saccades. Zangwill and Blakemore suggested that the abnormal eye movement pattern was responsible for the subject's tendency to reverse words (for example, *saw* for *was*) during reading. Ciuffreda, Bahill, Kenyon, and Stark (1976) reported on the eye movement pattern of an adult dyslexic who showed the same right-to-left type of saccades as Zangwill and Blakemore's patient. On the other hand, other records of the eye movements of dyslexic patients (Ciuffreda *et al.*, 1976; Hallpike's records in Critchley, 1970) do not show abnormal right-to-left saccades. Rather, these patterns are consistent with Lesevre's finding that dyslexics do not show a consistent left-to-right pattern.

In the next sections of this chapter, we present case studies of dyslexic patients that are consistent with the patterns just described and we argue that the nature of the disability affects the characteristics of the eye movement patterns.

Case Report 4

BT, a 22-year-old, right-handed high school graduate, was referred to us for evaluation of his reading problem. He was the subject of a previous report (Pirozzolo, Rayner, & Whitaker, 1977). Neuropsychological testing revealed superior range visuo–spatial abilities on such measures as the WAIS Performance Scale, Raven Coloured Progressive Matrices, and the Money Road Map Test. Verbal skills, as assessed by the WAIS Verbal Scale, Peabody Picture Vocabulary Test, and other experimental tests of our own design, were at age-appropriate levels. Reading skills were measured by means of the Gray Oral Reading Test, Wide Range Achievement Test, and the Spache Reading Diagnostic Scales. Results of these tests indicated reading comprehension equal to the fifth-grade level. A linguistic analysis of reading errors made during the administration of these tests showed a large number of grapheme-to-phoneme correspondence errors and many errors involving grammatical function words. A comparison of the subject's eye movements while reading passages that fell within his comprehension range with eye movements of a graduate student of approximately the same age revealed no significant difference in terms of fixation duration, regression frequency, or number of fixations. There was no evidence at this level of an increased number of right-to-left saccades or any tendency to overshoot or undershoot the first word of the next line of print. While reading more difficult passages above his comprehension level, BT made a large number of fixations and short regressions within words. When he encountered an unfamiliar word in silent reading or one that he could not decode in oral reading, his attack was to move ahead to the next word or regress to the previous word to look for contextual cues to the meaning of the difficult word. Under oral reading conditions, we recorded places where BT had difficulty decoding and compared these to the eye movement record. After silent reading we questioned the subject on the places that he found most difficult and compared these with the eye movement record. We found that, in addition to using context as a cue for decoding and comprehension, BT would adopt an almost letter-by-letter strategy which is characteristic of children who are learning to read. This strategy is similar to that found in skilled readers who are reading very difficult, unfamiliar text.

Case Report 5

CB is a 21-year-old college student who was referred to us at the Developmental Disorders Clinic, University of Rochester Medical Center, because of reading and writing difficulties. She was diagnosed as having "developmental Gerstmann syndrome" and was the subject of a previous publication (Pirozzolo & Rayner, 1978). The developmental Gerstmann syndrome consists of several neurobehavioral symptoms, including difficulty with finger differentiation, right–left disorientation, dyscalculia, and a visuo–constructive disability. Neuropsychological testing revealed average range verbal abilities and somewhat lower spatial abilities. CB becomes easily frustrated with tasks that involve mental rotation, directional sense, or visuo–constructional ability. She has an unusual hand orientation when writing or drawing, in which she uses her left hand to write, beginning at the lower right-hand corner, proceeds in a right-to-left direction writing upside down and returns to the next line above the finished line so that the text is readable to an observer facing the subject.

CB's eye movement pattern often showed a large number of right-to-left saccades. At the end of a line, after completing a series of left-to-right saccades, she frequently dropped her eyes to the next line and began a series of right-to-left saccades. After three or four saccades toward the left, she corrected her pattern by moving to the left margin of the text and beginning a series of left-to-right eye movements. An analysis of the errors made in oral reading revealed that she often ended one line and then began reading the last words on the next line.

Immediately after the session in which her eye movements were recorded while reading text in its normal orientation, we presented text for her to read which was rotated 180°. She reported that she found it considerably easier to read a book when it was upside down, but had been encouraged not to do it by her school teachers. Her eye movement pattern with inverted text showed the "staircase pattern" typical of normal readers, except that the saccades were in a right-to-left manner, as opposed to the normal left-to-right. Her comprehension while reading the inverted text improved to the tenth-grade level, compared to sixth-grade level when the text was in normal orientation.

This patient's eye movement records are consistent with previous reports that the reverse staircase movement pattern and the inability to perform return sweeps in certain dyslexics may be due to an "irrepressible tendency" to scan text in a right-to-left direction (Gruber, 1962; Zangwill & Blakemore, 1972). An underlying spatial disorder that causes the disordered visual orientation (and the symptoms of finger agnosia, directional disorientation, dyscalculia, and dysgraphia) may be responsible for the persistent reading disability.

DISCUSSION

Five case reports have been presented to illustrate various forms of reading disability. The reading disturbances manifested by our first two patients resulted from progressive deterioration of the mechanisms that regulate saccadic eye movements. In patient 1, slow refixations were further complicated by abnormal overshooting and undershooting of targets. Dysmetria, although not demonstrable in the middle portion of a line of print because of the nature of the task, was apparent at the end of a line, where the patient consistently overshot the last word by several degrees and then undershot the first word of the next line by several more degrees. Problems in making the return sweep were also exhibited by patient 2 and by patient 5, although there are important differences in the dysfunction for each of these patients.

Patient 2 adopted a compensatory strategy for making a return sweep that is not explicable on the basis of what is known about the basal ganglia disorder and the eye movement system. Dysmetria, visual field defects and spasmodic fixation were not demonstrated in this patient and it seems unlikely that the eye blinks and short leftward saccades resulted from the disruption of the neural systems which regulate these functions. The return sweep abnormality in patient 5 is often observed in patients with spatial disorders and has been frequently linked to developmental dyslexia (e.g., Mosse & Daniels, 1959). This disturbance is probably associated with a congenital parietal lobe dysfunction that results in visual disorientation (Pirozzolo & Rayner, 1978).

Patients 3 and 4 are examples of acquired and developmental reading disorders caused by the involvement of the central language system. The reading eye movements in these patients reflect cognitive processing dysfunctions. Patient 3 and patient 4 represent, respectively, the most frequently encountered forms of acquired and developmental reading disturbances. On the basis of observations of these two examples of dyslexia, it is understandable that Gassel and Williams (1963) suggested that there is no evidence of a relationship between oculomotor dysfunctions and reading disability.

Despite the widespread interest in developmental reading disorders and the rapidly increasing number of neuropsychological experiments designed to reveal the causal mechanisms involved, remarkably little agreement exists on the symptomatology and etiology of dyslexia. Children who have exceptional difficulty learning to read and write in spite of normal intelligence, sensory acuity, and social adjustment remain an enigma to investigators trying to specify the pathophysiology that underlies dyslexia. Although the consensus favors a maturational lag in the brain mechanisms that are used in the reading process, the localization and lateralization of these dysfunctional structures have not been identified. Numerous studies have concluded that a left hemisphere dysfunction is the causal pathophysiology (Boder, 1971; Denckla & Rudel, 1976; Orton, 1937), but other explanations, such as a right hemisphere dysfunction (Yeni-Komshian, Isenberg, & Goldberg, 1975), a bilateral dysfunction (Geschwind, 1965) and a cerebellar–vestibular dysfunction (Frank & Levinson, 1976), have also been proposed.

A considerable amount of controversy has been generated by the assumption that dyslexics may differ from normal readers in certain visual processing and oculomotor abilities such as:

1. an increased number of fixations per line of text
2. an increased number of regressions
3. longer fixation durations
4. return sweep inaccuracies
5. periods of confusion with many short regressions and forward movements intermixed
6. shorter span of apprehension
7. a slower reaction time to respond to information presented outside the fovea

There is reason to believe that at least two subgroups of developmental dyslexia exist from studies which have compared the performance of large clinical groups of dyslexics on a variety of neuropsychological and educational tests (e.g., Boder, 1973; Kinsbourne & Warrington, 1965; Mattis, French, & Rapin, 1975; Pirozzolo, 1978c). Our evidence suggests that disabled readers with auditory–linguistic dyslexia (Pirozzolo, 1978b) have eye movement patterns that are similar to those of children just learning to read. In particular, these individuals show an increased number of fixations per line of text, longer fixation durations, and instances of short regressions and forward saccades intermixed. Disabled readers with visual–spatial dyslexia (Pirozzolo, 1978b), on the other hand, have eye movement patterns that are unlike those of normal readers of any age. Return sweep inaccuracies and frequent instances of right-to-left scanning are the most apparent oculomotor scanning disorders observed in the monitoring of the reading eye movements of disabled readers. It may be this group that has a shorter span of apprehension (Bouma & Legein, 1977) and slower reaction time to respond to information outside of foveal vision (Lesevre, 1964).

SUMMARY

The role of eye movements in the human information processing system is not clearly understood. During reading, the eyes make a series of very rapid movements in an attempt to bring visual information which is in the near periphery into the central foveal region, which has the best visual acuity. There is reason to believe that there is some visual feature analysis taking place outside of the fovea (Pirozzolo & Rayner, 1977; Rayner, 1975b), although semantic processing is limited to information which is in foveal vision. There is general agreement that eye position reflects a visual information acquisition stage, although there is some evidence to suggest that eye movements may reflect a later stage of processing; that is, that the direction of eye gaze reflects the laterality of the thought process (Kinsbourne, 1974).

We have attempted to specify the visual information which the normal reader apprehends during a single fixation pause and the various factors which affect the reader's pattern of eye movements. There is considerable variation among subjects and in individual subjects in oculomotor behavior. Nevertheless, the complexity of the reading task requires that oculomotor performance be efficient. Reading disturbances in the presence of oculomotor disorders have been discussed and we have argued that distinctions must be made between reading problems that are caused by poor oculomotor performance and clinical syndromes in which there are possible difficulties in oculomotor scanning that do not contribute to reading problems.

With regard to the connection between oculomotor behavior and developmental dyslexia, we have concluded that the apparent oculomotor "deficits" in auditory–linguistic dyslexia, such as increased fixation duration, and the increased number of fixations and short regressions must be regarded as resulting from the dyslexic disturbance. In the visual–spatial form of developmental dyslexia, we have argued that the oculomotor disorders (return sweep inaccuracies and the "irrepressible tendency" to scan text in a leftward direction) are caused by a dysfunctional spatial mechanism that guides the reader's eye movements.

ACKNOWLEDGMENTS

The authors would like to thank John Lott Brown and Ola Selnes for their comments on the manuscript. Appreciation is also expressed to David Goldblatt and Ira Shoulson for referring patients 1 and 2.

REFERENCES

Abrams, S. G., & Zuber, B. L. 1972. Some temporal characteristics of information processing during reading. *Reading Research Quarterly, 8,* 40–51.
Ajax, E. T. 1967. Dyslexia without agraphia. *Archives of Neurology, 17,* 645–652.
Bachman, D. S., Butler, I. S., & McKhann, G. M. 1977. Long term treatment of juvenile Huntington's chorea with dipropylacetic acid. *Neurology, 27,* 193–197.
Baloh, R. W., & Honrubia, V. 1976. Reaction time and accuracy of the saccadic eye movements of normal subjects in a moving-target task. *Aviation, Space and Environmental Medicine, 47,* 1165–1168.
Barlow, J. S., & Ciganek, L. 1969. Lambda responses in relation to visual evoked responses in man. *Electroencephalography and Clinical Neurophysiology, 26,* 183–192.
Benson, D. F. 1977. The third alexia. *Archives of Neurology, 34,* 327–331.
Benson, D. F., & Geschwind, N. 1970. The developmental Gerstmann syndrome. *Neurology, 20,* 203–208.
Beringer, K., & Stein, J. 1930. Analyse eines Fales von "reiner" Alexie. *Zeitschrift für die Gesamte Neurologie und Psychiatrie, 123,* 472–478.
Bizzi, E. 1968. Discharge of frontal eye field neurons during saccadic and following movements in unanesthetized monkeys. *Experimental Brain Research, 6,* 69–80.
Boder, E. 1971. Developmental dyslexia: Prevailing diagnostic concepts and a new diagnostic approach. In H. Myklebust (Ed.), *Progress in learning disabilities.* New York: Grune & Stratton.
Boder, E. 1973. Developmental dyslexia: A diagnostic approach based on three atypical reading spelling patterns. *Developmental Medicine and Child Neurology, 15,* 663–687.
Bouma, H., & deVoogd, A. H. 1974. On the control of eye saccades in reading. *Vision Research, 14,* 273–284.
Bouma, H., & Legein, C. P. 1977. Foveal and parafoveal recognition of letters and words by dyslexics and by average readers. *Neuropsychologia, 15,* 69–80.
Buswell, G. T. 1922. *Fundamental reading habits: A study of their development* (Supplemental Educational Monograph No. 21). Chicago: University of Chicago Press.
Cogan, D. G. 1952. A type of congenital ocular motor apraxia presenting jerky head movements. *Transactions of the American Academy of Ophthalmology and Otolaryngology, 56,* 853–862.
Cogan, D. G. 1965. Ophthalmic manifestations of bilateral non-occipital cerebral lesions. *British Journal of Ophthalmology, 49,* 281–297.
Cogan, D. G. 1975. An introduction to eye movements. In T. N. Chase (Ed.), *The nervous system: The clinical neurosciences.* New York: Raven.
Ciuffreda, K. J., Bahill, A. T., Kenyon, R. V., & Stark, L. 1976. Eye movements during reading: Case reports. *American Journal of Optometry and Physiological Optics, 53,* 389–395.
Critchley, M. 1970. *The dyslexic child.* London: Heinemann.
Cumming, G. D. 1976. Eye movements and visual perception. In E. C. Carterette & M. Friedman (Eds.), *Handbook of perception* (Vol. 8). New York: Academic Press.
Dejerine, J. 1892. Contribution a l'etude d'anatomie-pathologique et clinique des differentes varieties de cecite verbale. *Memoires de la societe de Biologie, 44,* 61–90.
Denckla, M. B. 1972a. Color naming deficits in dyslexic boys. *Cortex, 8,* 164–176.
Denckla, M. B. 1972b. Performance on color tasks in kindergarten children. *Cortex, 8,* 177–190.
Denckla, M. B., & Rudel, R. 1976. Names of object-drawings by dyslexic and other learning disabled children. *Brain and Language, 3,* 1–15.

Dossetor, D. G., & Papaioannou, J. 1975. Dyslexia and eye movements. *Language and Speech, 18,* 312–317.

Flechsig, P. 1901. Developmental (myelogenetic) localisation of the cerebral cortex in the human subject. *Lancet, ii,* 1027–1029.

Frank, J., & Levinson, H. 1973. Dysmetric dyslexia and dyspraxia. *Journal of the American Academy of Child Psychiatry, 12,* 690–701.

Frank, J., & Levinson, H. 1976. Compensatory mechanisms in C-V dysfunction, dysmetric dyslexia and dyspraxia. *Academic Therapy, 12,* 5–27.

Gassel, M. M., & Williams, D. 1963. Visual function in patients with homonymous hemianopia. *Brain, 86,* 1–36.

Gerstmann, J. 1924. Fingeragnoise: Eine umschriebene Storung der Orientung am eigenen Korper. *Weiner klinische Wochenschrift, 37,* 1010–1012.

Geschwind, N. 1965. Disconnexion syndromes in animals and man. *Brain, 88,* 237–294; 585–644.

Geschwind, N., & Fusillo, M. 1966. Color naming defects in association with alexia. *Archives of Neurology, 15,* 137–146.

Gilbert, L. C. 1959. Saccadic movements as a factor in visual perception in reading. *Journal of Educational Psychology, 50,* 15–19.

Gruber, E. 1962. Reading ability, binocular coordination and the opthalmograph. *Archives of opthalmology, 67,* 183–190.

Hartje, W. 1972. Reading disturbances in the presence of oculomotor disorders. *European Neurology, 7,* 249–264.

Hecaen, H. 1967. Aspects des troubles de la lecture (Alexies) au coirs des lesions cerebrales en foyer. *Word, 23,* 265–287.

Hecaen, H., & Ajuriaguerra, J. de. 1954. Balint's syndrome (psychic paralysis of visual fixation) and its minor forms. *Brain, 77,* 373–400.

Kinsbourne, M. 1974. Direction of gaze and distribution of cerebral thought processes. *Neuropsychologia, 12,* 279–281.

Kinsbourne, M., & Warrington, E. 1962. A variety of reading disability associated with right hemisphere lesions. *Journal of Neurology, Neurosurgery and Psychiatry, 25,* 339–344.

Kinsbourne, M., & Warrington, E. 1963. The developmental Gerstmann syndrome. *Archives of Neurology, 8,* 490–501.

Kinsbourne, M., & Warrington, E. 1965. Developmental factors in reading and writing backwardness. In J. Money (Ed.), *The disabled reader.* Baltimore: Johns Hopkins University Press.

Klein, G. A., & Kurkowski, F. 1974. Effects of task demands on relationships between eye movements and sentence complexity. *Perceptual and Motor Skills, 39,* 463–466.

Kornhuber, H. H. 1973. Cerebellar control of eye movements. *Advances in Oto-rhino-laryngology, 19,* 241–253.

Kussmaul, A. 1884. *Les troubles de la parole.* Paris: Bailliere.

Kuypers, H., & Haaxsma, R. 1975. Occipito-frontal connections, a possible sensory-motor link for visually-guided hand and finger movements. In K. J. Zulch, O. Creutzfeldt, & G. C. Galbraith (Eds.), *Cerebral localization,* Berlin: Springer-Verlag.

Lawson, I. R. 1962. Visual–spatial neglect in lesions of the right cerebral hemisphere. *Neurology, 12,* 23–33.

Lesevre, N. 1964. *Les mouvements oculaires d'exploration: Etude electrooculographique comparee d'enfants normaux et d'enfants dyslexiques.* Unpublished doctoral dissertation, University of Paris.

Lesevre, N. 1968. L'organisation du regard chez des enfants d'age scolaire, lecteurs normaux et dysleques. *Revue de Neuropsychiatrie Infantile, 16,* 323–349.

Lesevre, N. 1976. Mouvements oculaires d'exploration et lecture. *Bulletin d'audiophonologie, 2,* 39–109.

Lhermitte, J., & Beauvois, M. F. 1973. A visual-speech disconnexion syndrome: Report of a case with optic aphasia, agnosic alexia and color agnosia. *Brain, 96,* 695–714.

Lhermitte, J., Lecours, A. R., & Ouvry, B. 1967. Essai d'analyse structurale des paralexies et des paragraphies. *Acta Neurologica et Psychiatrica Belgica, 67* 1021–1044.

Luria, A. R. 1947. *Traumatic aphasia.* The Hague: Mouton.

Luria, A. R. 1966. *Higher cortical functions in man.* New York: Basic Books.

Lynch, J. C., Mountcastle, V. B., Talbot, W. H., & Yin, T. C. T. 1977. Parietal lobe mechanisms for directed visual attention. *Journal of Neurophysiology, 40,* 362–389.

Marshall, J. C., & Newcombe, F. 1973. Patterns of paralexia: A psycholinguistic approach. *Journal of Psycholinguistic Research, 2,* 177–200.

Mattis, S., French, J., & Rapin, I. 1975. Dyslexia in children and young adults: Three independent neuropsychological syndromes. *Developmental Medicine and Child Neurology, 17,* 150–163.

McConkie, G., & Rayner, K. 1975. The span of effective stimulus during a fixation in reading. *Perception and Psychophysics, 17,* 578–586.

McConkie, G., & Rayner, K. 1976. Asymmetry of the perceptual span in reading. *Bulletin of the Psychonomic Society, 8,* 365–368.

Mosse, H. L., & Daniels, C. R. 1959. Linear dyslexia. *American Journal of Psychotherapy, 13,* 826–841.

Myklebust, H. 1965. *Disorders of written language.* New York: Grune & Stratton.

Newcombe, F., Hiorns, R. W., Marshall, J. C., & Adams, C. B. T. 1975. Acquired dyslexia: Patterns of deficit and recovery. In CIBA Symposium 34, *Outcome of severe damage to the central nervous system.* Amsterdam: Elsevier.

Newman, E. G. 1966. Speed of reading when the span of letters is restricted. *American Journal of Psychology, 79,* 272–278.

O'Regan, J. K. 1975. *Structural and contextual constraints on eye movements in reading.* Unpublished doctoral dissertation, University of Cambridge.

Orton, S. T. 1937. *Reading, writing and speech problems in children.* New York: Norton.

Oxbury, J. M., Oxbury, S. M., & Humphrey, N. K. 1969. Varieties of color anomia. *Brain, 92,* 847–860.

Penfield, W., & Boldrey, E. 1937. Somatic motor and sensory representation in the cerebral cortex of man as studied by electrical stimulation. *Brain, 60,* 389–443.

Pirozzolo, F. J. 1978a. Slow saccades. *Archives of Neurology, 35,* 618.

Pirozzolo, F. J. 1978b. *The neuropsychology of developmental reading disorders.* New York, Praeger.

Pirozzolo, F. J. 1978c. Cerebral asymmetries and reading acquisition. *Academic Therapy, 13,* 261–266.

Pirozzolo, F. J., & Hess, D. W. 1976. *A neuropsychological analysis of the ITPA: Two profiles of reading disability.* Paper presented to the New York State Orton Society Annual Convention, Rochester, New York.

Pirozzolo, F. J., & Rayner, K. 1977. Hemispheric specialization in reading and word recognition. *Brain and Language, 4,* 258–261.

Pirozzolo, F. J., & Rayner, K. 1978. Disorders of oculomotor scanning and graphic orientation in developmental Gerstmann syndrome. *Brain and Language, 5,* 119–126.

Pirozzolo, F. J., Rayner, K., & Whitaker, H. A. 1977. *Left hemisphere mechanisms in dyslexia: A neuropsychological case study.* Paper presented to the International Neuropsychological Society Fifth Annual Convention, Santa Fe, New Mexico.

Prechtl, H. F. R., & Stemmer, J. C. 1959. Ein choreatiformes Syndrom bei Kindern. *Weiner medinische Wochenschrift, 109,* 461–463.

Pynte, J. 1974. Readiness for pronunciation during the reading process. *Perception and Psychophysics, 16,* 110–112.

Rayner, K. 1975a. Parafoveal identification during a fixation in reading. *Acta Psychologica, 39,* 271–282.

Rayner, K. 1975b. The perceptual span and peripheral cues in reading. *Cognitive Psychology, 7,* 65–81.

Rayner, K. 1977. Visual attention in reading: Eye movements reflect cognitive processes. *Memory & Cognition,* **5,** 443–448.

Rayner, K. 1978a. Saccadic latencies for parafoveally presented words. *Bulletin of the Psychonomic Society.*

Rayner, K. 1978b. Eye movements in reading and information processing. *Psychological Bulletin,* 85, 618–660.

Rayner, K., & McConkie, G. 1976. What guides a reader's eye movements? *Vision Research, 16,* 829–837.

Robles, J. 1966. Congenital ocular motor apraxia in identical twins. *Archives of Ophthalmology, 75,* 746–749.

Rubino, C. A., & Minden, H. A. 1973. An analysis of eye-movements in children with a reading disability. *Cortex, 9,* 217–220.

Rutter, M., & Yule, W. 1975. The concept of specific reading retardation. *Journal of Child Psychology and Psychiatry, 16,* 161–197.

Saffran, E., Schwartz, M., & Marin, O. 1976. Semantic mechanisms in paralexia. *Brain and Language, 3,* 255–265.

Smith, S., & Holmes, G. 1916. A case of bilateral motor apraxia with disturbance of visual orientation. *British Medical Journal, i,* 437–441.

Sobotka, K. R., & May, J. G. 1977. Visual evoked potentials and reaction time in normal and dyslexic children. *Psychophysiology, 14,* 18–24.

Sperling, G. 1960. The information available in brief visual presentations. *Psychological Monographs, 74* (Whole No. 11).

Starr, A. 1967. A disorder of rapid eye movements in Huntington's chorea. *Brain, 90,* 545–564.

Stebbins, W., Emmel, A., Heriot, J. T., & Rockowitz, R. J. 1975. Congenital opthalmoplegia and school achievement: A case study. *Developmental Medicine and Child Neurology, 17,* 237–243.

Taylor, S. E. 1965. Eye movements in reading: Facts and fallacies. *American Educational Research Journal, 2,* 187–202.

Tinker, M. A. 1958. Recent studies of eye movements in reading. *Psychological Bulletin, 55,* 215–231.

Wanat, S. 1971. *Linguistic structure and visual attention in reading.* Newark, Delaware: International Reading Association.

Warrington, E., & Zangwill, O. 1957. A study of dyslexia. *Journal of Neurology, Neurosurgery and Psychiatry, 20,* 208–215.

Weigl, E., & Bierwisch, M. 1970. Neuropsychology and linguistics: Topics of common research. *Foundations of Language, 6,* 1–18.

Westheimer, G. 1954. Mechanisms of saccadic eye movement. *Journal of the Optical Society of America, 52,* 210–213.

Yakovlev, P. I., & Lecours, A. R. 1967. The myelogenetic cycles of regional maturation in the brain. In A. Minkowski (Ed.), *Regional development of the brain in early life.* Oxford: Blackwell.

Yeni-Komshian, G., Isenberg, D., & Goldberg, H. 1975. Cerebral dominance and reading disability: Left visual field deficit in poor readers. *Neuropsychologia, 13,* 83–94.

Zangwill, O. L., & Blakemore, C. 1972. Dyslexia: Reversal of eye movements during reading. *Neuropsychologia, 10,* 371–373.

Zee, D., Optican, L., Cook, J., Robinson, D., & Engel, W. K. 1976. Slow saccades in spinocerebellar degeneration. *Archives of Neurology, 33,* 243–251.

3

Structure in a Manual Communication System Developed Without a Conventional Language Model: Language Without a Helping Hand[1]

Susan Goldin-Meadow

THE UNIVERSITY OF CHICAGO

THE ROLE OF LINGUISTIC INPUT IN LANGUAGE DEVELOPMENT

What are the environmental constraints on language acquisition? Will language emerge under any external conditions (e.g., will a child learn language from a radio in a closet?), or are there statable limits on the flexibility of human language acquisition? Observations of natural language development in children do not usually bear directly on the question of flexibility, since most children acquire language under comparable conditions, namely, at an early age most children are exposed to the language of their culture as spoken by the adults around them. These conditions quite clearly suffice for language development in the child raised by human beings. At the other extreme, the lack of these conditions is correlated with an absence of language development: Children raised by wolves and bears

[1] This research was supported by grants from the Spencer Foundation through the University of Pennsylvania, and through the University of Chicago, and by funds from the Social Sciences Division of the University of Chicago. I was supported by the NICHHD Training Grant (HD 00337) and by an AAUW Fellowship during a portion of this work. Sections of this work were presented at the Conference on Sign Language and Neurolinguistics, Rochester, New York, 1976 and at SRCD, New Orleans, 1977.

125

do not spontaneously begin to speak (Brown, 1958; Lenneberg, 1967). Is it possible then that the **only** conditions which permit a child to develop language are those in which adults expose the child to data from a shared human language?

This study investigates human language learning flexibility with respect to one particular learning condition found in all natural language learning situations but in none of the feral situations: the role of linguistic input. It is obvious from the outset that young children exposed to different parent languages are able to learn these distinct languages readily. It seems quite clear then that, when available, linguistic input plays a significant role in language acquisition. But we can still wonder what the nature of that role is, and whether that role is or is not a necessary one.

Variations in Linguistic Input

The role of linguistic input in accounting for language acquisition has at times been minimized on the grounds that the speech the child hears, as it resembles adult-to-adult talk, is too unruly (containing false starts, mumbles, and ungrammatical sentences) for the young child to abstract language organization from it (Chomsky 1965). However, this argument is weakened by a closer examination of the speech that is actually addressed to children. Studies of speech to children have consistently shown that this speech (christened "motherese" by Newport, Gleitman, & Gleitman 1977) is actually far less garbled and complex than was originally supposed (Snow 1972; Farwell 1973; Phillips 1973; Newport 1976; see also Shatz & Gelman, 1973, and Sachs & Devin, 1973, for evidence that even young children can use this special kind of speech to yet younger children). "Motherese," therefore, cannot a priori be considered a poor language teaching device on the grounds of complexity. Nevertheless, it must be pointed out that apparently neat and orderly input to the child need not be the cause of neat and orderly output from the child. Indeed, orderly mother input is as likely to be a reflection, as a cause, of orderly child output.

To address the question of the actual effect of adult language input on child language output, one must in some systematic way vary the child's language input and subsequently observe the utterances of the child over the course of time. Studies which address this issue are of two types: those which concentrate on the natural range of variation in everyday speech to children, and those whose primary object is to extend the range of variation by manipulating linguistic inputs to children.

In a study of natural speech to children, Newport *et al.* (1977) correlated natural variation in mother speech with variation in the rate of child language development. Although it is admittedly difficult to prove cause and effect in a correlational study, Newport *et al.* found that language properties could be divided into two types along the dimension of responsiveness to input conditions: (1) those properties whose rate of acquisition is affected by the small natural variations in linguistic input (environment–sensitive properties such as the inflectional structure of English, for example, the verbal auxiliary and plural formation), and (2) those whose rate of acquisition is relatively impervious to the natural variation found in child language environments (environment–insensitive properties such as the items for expressing basic propositional structure). Thus, linguistic input appears to be selectively effective in shaping child output under natural language learning conditions.

There are, however, certain difficulties of interpretation associated with studies of mother speech in natural environments. Primarily, as Newport *et al.* point out, it is possible that all of the language properties they isolate are sensitive to some sort of variation in linguistic input, but that the range of variability in their samples of mother speech was too narrow to show such effects. In other words, all of the samples might have provided sufficient input to exceed a minimal amount of necessary input. Once beyond this threshold, variation in input might be inconsequential in predicting variability in acquisition. Thus, negative effects in studies of speech in natural environments can be interpreted only cautiously as noneffects of linguistic input.

Given the small amount of variation in natural speech to children, it would seem that we can determine the limits on human language learning flexibility only by increasing the range of variation in input. This can be done by providing either a richer or poorer linguistic environment than that found in nature. Some studies of the effects of input enrichment on language growth rates do exist. Nelson, Carskaddon, and Bonvillian (1973) have successfully used a manipulation technique of this sort. Specifically, they enriched the child's environment with expansions and recast sentences and observed the subsequent course of his language development. They found selected effects of input manipulation on a particular syntactic property, auxiliary growth. It is noteworthy that Newport *et al.* also hypothesized that the auxiliary was one of the environment–sensitive language properties.

Note, however, that while studies using enrichment techniques clearly provide interesting data on the positive effects of linguistic input on acquisition, these enrichment studies cannot bear on the threshold problem. After all, if the language that children naturally hear already provides the threshold amount of input necessary for certain language properties to develop, enrichment procedures obviously will not have a further effect on the development of those properties. Yet those same properties could still be sensitive to a reduction in linguistic input more drastic than ever observed in nature. Thus, as in studies of natural speech to children, negative effects in studies of speech in enriched language environments can also be interpreted only cautiously as noneffects of linguistic input.

The alternative approach to the flexibility question is to remove the linguistic input and observe the subsequent course of linguistic development. If there is some threshold amount of orderly linguistic input necessary for the child to develop certain language properties, these properties should not develop in a child lacking linguistic input. If, however, linguistic input is not necessary for the development of a certain property, we should expect this property to emerge ex nihilo in the communications of this child without input. Thus, in contrast to studies of speech in natural and enriched environments where noneffects of linguistic input must be inferred from negative results, in a deprivation study the **presence** of a particular property in a child's language is positive evidence for the noneffects of linguistic input.

Of course, radical deprivation manipulations of this sort cannot be performed deliberately, but some have nevertheless been performed inadvertently. We have already mentioned reports of children who have been brought up by animals (see Brown, 1958, for an account of this literature). Other children have been reared by human beings under inhumane conditions. For example, Rigler and Rigler (1975) studied a girl who had been isolated and confined to a small room with no freedom of movement and no human companionship for the first 13 years of her life. Under these circumstances of extreme linguistic, social, and sensory deprivation, language did not develop. However, it is obvious that these studies say little about the effect of linguistic isolation per se on language development: Language was only one of the many human factors missing in these circumstances.

The Study of Deaf Children of Hearing Parents

My approach to the problem of flexibility in language acquisition has been to study a population of children whose environments are entirely normal, save for the lack of significant input from conventional language models. The subjects were deaf children whose hearing losses prevented them from making use of the oral language environment around them. Moreover, these children were not exposed to a conventional manual language (such as Signed English or American Sign Language) by their hearing parents, but were instead educated by the "oral" method (i.e., extensive training to lipread and vocalize without audio feedback). At the time of the study, these subjects had benefitted very little, if at all, from their oral training. Thus, they were lacking usable input from conventional oral or manual language models. Our goal was to determine if these children, despite their deficient linguistic input, would nevertheless develop communication systems which resemble natural language.

Previous work on deaf children of hearing parents had indicated that a deaf child could use gestures to communicate without the benefit of a conventional language model. Deaf children who are orally trained have often been observed to gesture spontaneously to one another (Fant, 1972; Lenneberg, 1964; Moores, 1974; Tervoort, 1961). These gestures are referred to as "home signs." The existence of home signs suggests that linguistic input is not necessary for a child to begin to communicate with others.

Home signs, however, have not been previously studied as language systems. We therefore do not yet know if linguistic input is necessary for a child to communicate in a **structured** fashion. As a result, this analysis will focus on the structural aspects of deaf children's home signs. This heuristic leaves open the vexed question of whether or not home sign is a full-fledged natural language—it deals only with how similar to a language the home signs are. The direction of work has been to determine which linguistic properties found in natural languages can also be found in home sign. These structural properties can be presumed to be insensitive to the absence of conventional linguistic input.

The home signs of deaf subjects have both lexical and syntactic-semantic properties and comprise a language system in this sense (Goldin-Meadow & Feldman, 1977; Feldman, Goldin-Meadow, & Gleitman, 1978. Specifically, subjects were able to develop lexical signs to refer to objects, actions, and attributes. For example, one child swatted his fist in the air to describe the hitting action he and his mother used to knock block towers over. Several children held fists to their mouths and "chewed" to describe either the act of eating or edible items. Moreover, subjects also developed the ability to concatenate their signs into phrases that conveyed semantic relations among objects, actions, and attributes. For example, one child pointed at a block tower and then signed HIT (i.e., fist swat in air) to indicate that he had just hit the tower. In another example, the same child signed HIT, then pointed at his mother to request her to perform the hitting.

The home signs of deaf subjects also form a natural language system when developmental criteria are considered. In particular, in at least the early stages of acquisition, deaf children develop their sign system in a sequence comparable to the hearing child's pattern of acquiring spoken language (Goldin-Meadow & Feldman, 1975; Feldman *et al.*, 1978). The deaf children were at first limited to producing one sign at a time, just as the hearing child is limited at a certain period to producing only single words.

Moreover, deaf children produced their single signs in contexts comparable to the contexts in which the hearing child produced his single words (Bloom, 1973; Greenfield & Smith, 1976). The deaf children then progressed to a two-sign period, comparable to the hearing child's two-word period (Brown, 1973). During this time, the deaf children produced phrases that conveyed semantic relations and contained a substantial number of different lexical items. The present chapter concentrates primarily on semantic relation phrases produced during the deaf children's two-sign period. More specifically, it concentrates on the semantic content and the syntactic structure of these phrases.

Finally, there are preliminary data on the deaf children's next developmental period, the period during which they produced multi-sign phrases to convey conjoined relations. For example, during this time one child pointed at a picture of a bird beak, pointed at his own mouth, then pointed at the place where he was going to put the picture. The child had, in one phrase, commented on the mouth-like features of the bird beak picture as well as on its new location. Hearing children go through a comparable stage in which they conjoin and embed relations in one phrase (Brown, 1973).

Thus a deaf child with virtually no conventional linguistic input can develop a communication system which is language-like in many respects. In this chapter the ways in which semantic relations are conveyed in the communication systems developed by six deaf children of hearing parents are examined. First it is determined if semantic relations are conveyed in a structured fashion in these systems. Since semantic structure is found in the content of communications and syntactic structure is found in both the underlying and surface levels of these communications, it is then asked how these structures resemble those of child language in general. From there, the implications of the results of these inquiries for theories on the processes of language acquisition are explored.

METHOD

Subjects

The six deaf children in the study, four boys (Dennis, Chris, David, and Donald) and two girls (Kathy and Tracy),[2] were recruited by obtaining names of deaf children from private speech therapists and from oral schools for the deaf in the Philadelphia area. Each child's parents were contacted and permission was obtained to observe and videotape each child over a period of time. Although the children included in the study differed in age

---

[2] The names of the subjects have been changed.

TABLE 3.1 Subjects' Ages at Each Session in Years and Months

Subject	I	II	III	IV	V	VI	VII	VIII	IX	X	XI
				Sessions							
Dennis	2:2	2:3	2:4	2:6							
Kathy	1:5	1:6	1;9	1:10	2:0	2:2	2:3	2:5	2:8		
Chris	3:2	3:3	3:6								
Donald	2:5	2:5½	2:6½	2:7	2:8	2:10	3:0	3:11	4:0	4:2	4:6½
David	2:10	2:11	3:0	3:3	3:5	3:6	3:8	3:10			
Tracy	4:1	4:3									

(see Table 3.1), in number of siblings (from zero to four), in race, and in socio-economic background, they did share two characteristics necessary to be included in this study. First, none of the children could rely on oral language for communication. Second, none was exposed to any conventional sign language system.

Hearing abilities and oral language training. All of the children had received hearing evaluations at medical centers in the Philadelphia area. They were all judged congenitally deaf with no other physical or cognitive deficits. In one case, the cause of deafness was determined to be prenatal rubella; in the other five cases, the cause of deafness was unknown. The medical reports indicated that all the children had moderate to profound hearing losses, that is, losses of 31 to 100 dB. Five of the children wore hearing aids. The aid improved each child's hearing, but not sufficiently to allow the natural acquisition of oral language (i.e., acquisition without oral training). Dennis did not wear a hearing aid during the study, but did acquire an aid later.

Five of the children attended oral preschools. Dennis did not begin school until after we concluded our observations. Kathy, Chris, and Tracy all attended one oral preschool, while David and Donald attended another preschool in the Philadelphia area. At the time of our observations Kathy and Chris could neither read lips nor produce identifiable verbal words, although both produced sounds in what seemed like a haphazard fashion. Donald, David, and Tracy also verbalized haphazardly, but in addition they reliably produced verbal names in constrained situations for a very few objects, for example *horse*, and *bird*. None of the children was able to produce two concatenated verbal words (i.e., a verbal sentence).

Manual language training. The children received no formal training in a standard sign language either in school or at home, nor were they even exposed to standard sign languages in either environment. The children's parents knew neither American Sign Language nor Signed English. Even the older deaf siblings of two of the children knew no sign language. Kathy's sister, who was congenitally deaf, and Donald's sister, who was not, were both doing quite well in the oral program: they could lipread and speak relatively well, but knew no sign language. Donald's hearing siblings, one twin and two older children, were ignorant of sign language, as were David's and Dennis's older hearing siblings. Tracy and Chris had no siblings.

In sum, these deaf children had not been exposed to conventional sign language. However, some of the parents did gesture spontaneously to their children, although the preschools requested them not to. It is clear that the linguistic input these children received was radically reduced compared to the normal input. Whether it was zero is a question that cannot be answered, although it is further discussed later in this chapter. All that is, in fact, necessary to address a question of language learning flexibility is that linguistic input be greatly diminished with respect to the normal input. For these children this was clearly the case.

Procedure

Ideally, each child should have been observed under the same controlled conditions. However, some of the data were collected while developing a method of study. As a result, the testing circumstances were not as well controlled as they might have been. For example, the interval between observation sessions varied considerably both within and across children. Nevertheless, the data from these early sessions were included for several reasons. First, the early data often include valuable longitudinal information. In addition, the results do not seem to have been affected by the difference in the procedures used over the course of the study. For example, in the beginning of the study each child played with the same small set of toys. Over the course of the study, the set of toys was enlarged to give the child ample opportunity to converse about many topics. We were concerned that the changes in the toys might have produced spurious developmental changes in the child's language. That is, the children might have conversed about different relations as they got older simply because the toys changed in later interviews. However, even with the enlarged set of toys the younger children were less conversant than the older children. Thus, the variability in stimuli did not seem to have altered the results. Consequently, all of the data collected on each child are included and differences in data collection are overlooked.

The six deaf children were observed longitudinally over variable periods of time. The number of observation sessions varied from 2 to 11, with an interval between sessions of 6 to 10 weeks.[3] Each session was

---

[3] One major departure from this schedule occurred between Donald VII and VIII, a period

videotaped and lasted from 1 to 2 hours. Two female experimenters were present at all sessions; one experimenter taped while the second interacted with the child. Usually the child's mother, and occasionally a sibling, was also present during the sessions and interacted with the child. The sessions involved play with the child using a standard set of toys.

The goal when playing with the child was to elicit communication. Thus, a set of attractive and manipulable toys was present during each session. For the early part of the study, the set included the following toys: a zoo toy consisting of cages, plastic animals, and keys used to unlock the cages to free the animals; containers of Play-Doh; a Dapper Dan doll dressed in a cowboy outfit; two jars of bubble soap, one empty and one full; a frog that jumped when a bulb was squeezed; and a miniature school house, equipped with toy furniture and pupils.

Over the course of the study the set of toys grew to insure that the child had ample opportunity to communicate about varied topics. Dennis was the first subject and never played with the enlarged set of toys. All of the other children were observed playing with the enlarged set at least twice. The types of toys included in the enlarged set and the method of toy presentation were as follows:[4]

Transparent box. The child was shown several small toys in a transparent box (e.g., fork, merry-go-round, rabbit). Since the toys were visible but inaccessible, the child had to refer to them at a distance, without touching them.

Puzzles. The child was shown a puzzle that was then overturned to allow the child to reconstruct it. While the child was putting the puzzle together, the experimenter surreptitiously exchanged one puzzle piece for another of identical shape but different identity. For example, with the puzzle of a barefoot boy, we exchanged the boy's bare foot for a booted foot. On another trial, his hatless head was exchanged for a head with a hat. If the children showed some surprise at the novel pieces, other pieces were offered, all of which fit the puzzle but were not included in the original. This procedure was designed to elicit both comments on and requests for the puzzle pieces.

Action toys. The experimenter showed the child a series of mechanical toys that performed actions and a series of static toys that portrayed actions. For example, the set included a Santa Claus who swung on his trapeze when a button was pushed and a static Santa Claus frozen in the position of catching

---

of 11 months. We temporarily suspended visits to Donald because he was very uncooperative in sessions VI and VII.

[4] A complete list of the toy stimuli used in this study is found in Goldin-Meadow (1975) and Feldman (1975).

a ball. Some of the toy actors acted on toy objects (e.g., the dog hits a turtle, Santa pedals a bike, Mickey Mouse eats spaghetti with a fork); other toy actors performed objectless acts (e.g., Donald Duck walks, the frog jumps, the butterfly flies).

Static toys. These toys resembled the characters in the mechanical action toys. The child could either comment on the static toy's perceptual characteristics, or comment on the actions its "look-alike" toy performed. We often tried to force a choice between a static toy and its active likeness (e.g., Santa vs. Santa pedaling a bike) in order to encourage comments on either perceptual or action characteristics.

Difficult toy. This toy was difficult to operate and required that the player position a coin on a gun barrel and pull a trigger below. If done correctly, the coin shoots forward and lands in a bank. The toy was presented when both experimenters were with the child so that he had the opportunity to request one of the experimenters to initiate an action. In other words, the situation made it very likely that the child would specify the initiator (agent) of his choice.

Pictures. The toy set included colorful hand-drawn pictures of all of the individual parts of the action toys (e.g., a picture of Santa, a separate picture of his bike; a picture of Mickey Mouse, a picture of his spaghetti, a picture of his fork). The child could then comment on the role of each of the toy parts played in the total action (e.g., eater versus eaten). Furthermore, since one toy (e.g., Mickey Mouse) often played more than one actor role in the set of toys (e.g., walker, eater), the child could potentially comment on either or both of these roles. The pictures were presented before the toys and again after the toys to allow the child to comment on the individual parts before and after seeing them in action.

Picture book. When time, interest and patience permit, the experimenter either showed the child a picture book containing many examples of common and unusual objects and events or a family photograph album. The children were, in general, very responsive to pictures and photographs.

The set of toys thus incorporated several techniques to elicit communication. First and foremost, there was the appearance of new and exciting toys. Moreover, the set provided choices the children could make, changes that the children might not expect, and problems that the children might have with seemingly simple devices.

The videotapes of the play sessions were transcribed according to a system of coding categories. Since this coding system is crucial to the interpretation of the results, coding decisions and criteria are examined in detail in the next section (but see Feldman, Goldin-Meadow, & Gleitman [1978] for a more explicit account of the rationale behind the coding methodology).

THEORETICAL BASIS OF THE ANALYSIS AND DERIVATION OF CODING CATEGORIES

How does one begin a description of the deaf child's communication system? The problem lies, in some sense, in entering the system. After all, there is no established language model towards which the deaf child's system is developing. Consequently, there are no hints from a conventional system that might guide initial descriptions. As a result, the description procedure necessarily becomes a bootstrap operation. It begins with preliminary decisions on how to categorize the gestures produced by deaf subjects (e.g., how to isolate gestures from the stream of motor behavior, how to segment those gestures, how to describe them and assign them meanings).

The preliminary categories are based on two sources. The first is the descriptions of spoken language, particularly child language, and the growing number of descriptions of conventional sign languages. Second, and perhaps more importantly, is intuitions about the motoric forms and the semantic meanings of the gestures produced by deaf subjects.

Having established preliminary categories, these categories were used to transcribe the videotapes. The usefulness of these categories was tested in two ways. First, are the categories reliable? Reliability has been established between the experimenter and a second coder who was not at the original taping sessions. The agreement scores between these two coders are in general quite high, suggesting reliable categories. These scores will be presented separately later in the chapter when each coding category is described.

The second test of the categories is to ask if these particular categories result in coherent descriptions of the deaf child's communication system. These descriptions comprise the second half of the results section. The claim made here is that if a description based on these particular coding categories turns out to be coherent, this fact is partial evidence for the categories themselves. Consider the following example. Suppose we applied the semantic categories *PATIENT* and *ACT* to the deaf child's gestures. If we then discovered a pattern based on those categories (e.g., a sign-ordering rule following, say a *PATIENT–ACT* pattern), we have some evidence that those particular categories, patient and act, are part of the deaf child's communication system. The very existence of the pattern confirms the existence of the categories, since the former is formulated in terms of the latter.

There is, of course, the possibility that these patterns and categories are products of the experimenter's mind rather than the child's. However, this study is no more vulnerable to that possibility than are those investigating spoken child language. After all, adult experimenters may all be incapable of finding anything but language-like structure in a child's communication. Although this problem can never be completely avoided, the following assumption allows us to proceed: A coherent description of the deaf child's communications is more likely to be accurate (i.e., "true" of the child) than is an incoherent description. That is, if a category turns out to "make sense of," or organize, the child's communications (e.g., by forming the basic unit of a pattern), we are then justified in isolating that category as a unit of the system and in attributing that category to the child. In sum, the consistency of the results described later in this chapter justifies the establishment of the coding categories described herein.

Extracting Communicative Gestures from the Stream of Motor Behavior

The first task is to isolate communicative gestures from the stream of ongoing motor behavior. The problem is to discriminate acts that communicate indirectly (e.g., pushing a plate away, which indicates that the eater has had enough) from those acts whose sole purpose seems to be to communicate (e.g., a stop-like movement produced in order to suggest to the host that another helping is not necessary). Since we do not consider every nudge or facial expression produced by the deaf subjects to be a communicative gesture (no matter how much information is conveyed), we are forced to develop a procedure which isolates only those acts used for deliberate communication.

Lacking a generally accepted behavioral index of deliberate or intentional communication (see MacKay [1972] for an illuminating discussion of this problem), we have decided that a communicative gesture must meet both of the following criteria. First, the motion must be directed to another individual. This criterion is satisfied if the subject makes an attempt to establish eye contact with the communication partner (the criterion was strictly enforced unless there had been recent previous communication with eye contact such that the child could assume the continued attention of his partner). Second, the gesture must **not** be a direct motor act **on** the partner or on some relevant object. As an example, if the subject attempts to twist open a jar, he has not made a sign for "jar" or "open" even if in some sense he is, by this act, trying to get the experimeter to do something (i.e., to help him open the jar). But if the subject makes a twisting motion in the air, with his eyes first on the experimenter's eyes to establish contact, a communicative gesture has been made.

Once isolated, the gestures were recorded in terms of the three dimensions used in describing signs of American Sign Language (see Stokoe,

1960): the shape of the hand, the location of the hands with respect to places on the body or in space, and the movement of the hand or body.

Each videotaped session was transcribed either by one of the original experimenters or a trained research assistant. In order to establish reliability, a selected sample of videotape (the second reel of session VIII) of David, the most advanced subject, was transcribed by an experimenter who had been at the original taping session and by a trained coder who had not. Reliability scores were derived for both the isolation and description of gestures. In the videotape sample lasting approximately 45 min, 91%[5] of the gestures identified by either of the two coders were identified and similarly described by both coders (yielding 335 reliably coded gestures).

Segmenting Signs and Sign Phrases

Once having isolated gestures from the surrounding motor context, the next step is to determine the units appropriate for the system. There are two segmentation questions. First, are there grounds for dividing one long complicated gesture into word-like or **sign** units? Second, are there grounds for parsing sequences of these sign units into still larger organizations? That is, can these signs be said to be concatenated into sentence-like units which we call **phrases**? The criteria we use to divide gestures into sign units and phrase units are as follows.

DEFINING A SIGN

Distributional criteria (see Bloomfield, 1933; Harris, 1951) for sign segmentation were employed whenever possible. Specifically, a gesture was considered to be composed of two signs if each of those signs occurred separately in other communication contexts. However, distributional criteria alone were insufficient for segmenting signs, primarily because there was no corpus extensive enough for these purposes. Therefore, an intuitive criterion based on the motor organization of the gesture was also used. A single sign was a continuous, uninterrupted flow or a single motor unit. This motor flow, though difficult to describe (particularly without an established descriptive system of motor organization), was nevertheless easy to note, especially because of the change or break in the flow of movement preceding and following the sign. For example, suppose a child produces a twisting movement, then, breaking the twist, points to the table.

---

[5] Nods, head shakes and other gestures which were not used to refer to things and events, but served only a modulation function, were eliminated from this reliability calculation, since they are not included in the analyses in this study.

The twist movement is, in some unformalizable sense, self-contained, as is the pointing movement; these movements, therefore, comprise two units, which are called signs. The results described later in this chapter suggest that these segmentation criteria isolate sign units that feed into the structural description of the deaf child's communication system, that is, the criteria isolate units which seem to be appropriate for the system.

Reliability was established for assignment of sign boundaries in the following way: Within the set of gestures identified by both coders in the videotape sample, there were 335 sign boundary decisions to be made and there was 93% agreement between two coders on these decisions.

DEFINING A PHRASE

The most obvious determinant of phrase boundaries was timing: If two signs were uninterrupted by an appreciable time interval, they were candidates for being "within a phrase." However, these potential phrases then had to meet a second criterion in order to be considered a phrase: the return of hands to neutral signing space (i.e., the relaxation of the hands in front of the body that signals the end of a phrase). For example, if a child pointed to a toy and then, without bringing his hands to his chest or lap, pointed to the table, the two pointings were considered "within a phrase." The same two pointings, interrupted by a pause of the hands near the chest, would be classified as two isolated signs. This second criterion was initially used because "return to neutral position" marks sentence boundaries in American Sign Language (see Stokoe, 1960). We continue to use this criterion as well as the timing criterion because they seem to be valid for describing the deaf child's communication system. That is, when these criteria are used to define phrases, a coherent description of the system is produced.

Using these criteria, a reliability score for assignment of phrase boundaries was established as follows: In the gestures identified by both coders in the videotape sample, there were 327 decisions about sign concatenation into phrases to be made and there was 95% agreement between the two coders on these decisions.

Assigning Lexical Meanings to Signs

The subjects produced two types of signs differing in form.[6] **Deictic** signs were typically pointing gestures. These pointings maintained a constant kinesic form in all contexts and were used to single out objects,

---

[6] The child produced a third kind of sign, which served modulation functions. These sign markers (e.g., head nods and side-to-side headshakes) are notionally similar to words like *yes* and *no* in English. Markers are not considered in the analyses presented in this chapter.

people, places, and the like in the surroundings. In contrast, **characterizing** signs were stylized pantomimes whose iconic forms varied with the intended meaning of each sign. For example, a fist pounded in the air as someone was hammering, or two hands flapping in the presence of a pet bird both were considered characterizing signs. Reliability on classifying signs into these two sign types was quite high; the two coders agreed on 97% of the 327 classification decisions that could be made in the videotape sample.

Our next step was to assign lexical meanings to these sign types. The problems here are comparable to those that arise in assigning meanings to a hearing child's words. Consider an English-speaking child who utters the phrase *duck walk* as a toy Donald Duck waddles by. Adult listeners assume that since the child has used two distinct phonological forms, *duck* and *walk,* he intends to convey two different meanings, that is, to talk about two semantic aspects of the event in front of him, the feathered object and the walking action. Specifically, it is assumed that the child's *duck* refers to the **object** and that his *walk* refers to the **action** of that object. In a comparable leap of faith, when our deaf subjects produce the sign phrase "point–at–duck walking–motions," it is assumed that since the deaf child has used two distinct motor forms—the deictic point and the characterizing walking motions—he also intends to convey two different meanings about the event in front of him. Specifically, we assume that the deictic pointing at the duck refers to the **object** and the characterizing walking motions refer to the **action** of that object.

Note that in attributing lexical meanings to the hearing child, it is assumed that the child's particular lexical meanings for the words *duck* and *walk* coincide with adult meanings for these words. In general, we assume that nouns refer to objects, people, places, and the like and that verbs refer to actions, processes, and so forth. This decision, although difficult to justify (for discussion, see Braine, 1976), is bolstered by data from the child's language system taken as a whole. To the extent that the child has mastered other aspects of the adult system that are based on the noun–verb distinction, he can plausibly be said to have mastered the distinction in the instance of lexical meanings.

At this same stage of the lexical meaning assignment procedure for the deaf subjects, we have also to make assumptions. However, as there is no adult language model to guide us, the decision criteria behind the inferential assumptions for the deaf subjects must obviously differ from those for the hearing child. For the deaf children's gesture system, sign form is used as a basis for lexical assignment decisions. We assume, in general, that deictic signs (e.g., pointing at the duck) refer to objects, people, and places, and that characterizing signs (e.g., the walking motions in the air) refer to actions and attributes (see the following discussion). This decision is motivated and justified by a number of lines of argument that will be elaborated below.

GLOSSING DEICTIC SIGNS

The assumption in assigning lexical meanings to deictic signs was that the child's pointing sign was, in fact, intended to make reference, and that the referent of that deictic sign was a person, place, or thing (and not an action or an attribute). This assumption is motivated as follows. When pointings are included in analyses as noun-like lexical items, the deaf children's sign system looks remarkably similar, both semantically and syntactically, to the hearing child's early spoken language. Semantically, the referents of the deaf children's deictic signs can be described in terms of precisely those categories which can be used to describe the referents of the hearing child's nouns (see Feldman, Goldin-Meadow, & Gleitman, 1978). Syntactically, as will be shown later, deictic signs appear to play the same role in the deaf children's sign phrases as nouns play in the hearing child's spoken sentences. For these reasons, we feel justified in including pointing signs as noun-like lexical items in our analyses.

Note that these deictic signs, like pro-forms in English (e.g., *this* or *there*), effectively allow the child to make reference to any person, place, or thing in the present (remarkably, the deaf child appears to be incapable of taking full advantage of this latitude, and instead acquires only as limited a noun vocabulary as the hearing child at a comparable stage, see Feldman *et al.*, 1978). Further, as with the hearing child's pro-forms, context is essential for the interpretation of deaf children's deictic signs. In fact, using context as a guide, it turns out to be relatively easy to determine the referents of deictic signs reliably. In the 180 signs identified by both coders as deictics in the videotape sample, there was 93% agreement between the two coders on the lexical meanings of these signs.

It should be recognized that the relationship between the pointing sign and its referent is, at some level, quite different from the relationship between a word and its referent. The pointing sign, unlike a word, serves to direct a communication partner's gaze toward a particular person, place, or thing; thus, the sign explicitly specifies the location of its referent in a way a word (even a pro-form) never can. The pointing does not, however, specify **what** the object is, it merely indicates **where** the object is. That is, the pointing is "location-specific," but not "identity-specific," with respect to its referent. Single words, on the other hand, are often "identity-specific" (e.g., *cat* and *ball* serve to classify their respective referents into different sets) but not "location-specific," unless the word is accompanied by a pointing gesture.

GLOSSING CHARACTERIZING SIGNS

In contrast to their "location-specific" points, the deaf child's characterizing signs were "identity-specific." Recall that the characterizing sign is an iconic sign whose form is related to its referent by apparent physical similarity (e.g., a fist pounded in the air refers to the act of hammering). Through its iconicity the characterizing sign can specify the identity of its referent, but, like words and unlike pointing, the sign cannot specify its referent's location.

Using both sign form and context as a guide to lexical meaning assignment, it was easily established that subjects could gesture about actions with their characterizing signs. For example, one child held a fist near his mouth and made chewing movements while someone was eating lunch (*EAT*); another twisted his hand over an imaginary jar in order to request that his mother twist open the jar lid (*TWIST*). Similarly, sign form and context allowed us to establish that the children could gesture about perceptual attributes with their characterizing signs. For example, one child distinguished between a large and a small kangaroo by holding his flat palms parallel to each other and wide apart (*BIG*).

Occasionally, sign form and context did not lead to the same lexical meaning assignments. For example, one child gestured the characterizing twist to identify a picture of a jar, while another indicated round, stubby appendages on the head to identify Mickey Mouse's ears. Sign form suggests that the 'twist' sign refers to an action and that the 'round' sign refers to an attribute; context, however, suggests that the two signs are both nominals, referring to the jar and to the ears, respectively. The decision in these situations was to assume that the form of the sign gives its lexical meaning (i.e., *TWIST, ROUND*), and that context provides information about the way the sign is used (i.e., identification of an object in each instance).[7] Thus, in the example of the "twist" used with the picture of the jar, although the child is indeed identifying an object with his characterizing sign, he is nevertheless using an action feature to identify that object. It is, therefore, assumed that he is conveying an action characteristic of that object (i.e., that it can be **twisted** by someone, or that one can **twist** it). Consequently an action lexical meaning was assigned to the twisting sign. In general, we attribute to the child the lexical meaning related most closely to the form of the sign.

This assumption requires further justification. In conventional languages such as American Sign Language or English, signs and words are (metaphor aside) handed down to us ready-made. We as sign users or word

[7] See Feldman (1975) for further discussion of functional analyses of the deaf children's signs.

users may therefore not always be aware of the etymological history of a name, and thus may not realize, for example, that the sign for a girl in American Sign Language, "thumb drawn along the chin," was originally chosen because it represented the ribbon on a young girl's bonnet (Frishberg, 1975). Similarly, we may be quite surprised to discover the underlying justification for some common English words. (For example, skyscrapers are so named for their literally sky-scraping characteristics.) Names such as "girl" in Sign or "skyscraper" in English each has some nonarbitrary relationship to its respective referent. But how are we to know when to attribute knowledge of this relationship to an individual? After all, any given individual may or may not have had the "eureka" experience resulting in insight into a particular word's origin.

There is, however, one instance in which we can be quite confident that we are rightfully attributing such derivational knowledge to an individual: the instance when that individual is the inventor of the name. The first user of "skyscraper" was undoubtedly aware of the relationship between the celestial aspiring object and its name. Indeed, he selected the name to emphasize just that relationship. Similarly, on these grounds we feel justified in attributing to our deaf subjects knowledge of the relationship between action and attribute sign forms and their respective referents, precisely because these children are themselves the sign inventors. The young child himself chooses to identify, or name, if you will, a particular object in terms of either its action features or its perceptual attributes. Thus, at the very least, the child can be said to have noticed and to have explicitly communicated about those particular action and attribute features of the object. It is, therefore, these explicit action and attribute sign movements that we take to be the basis of the characterizing sign's lexical meaning (see Feldman *et al.*, 1978 for further discussion of this issue).

One consequence of this attention to sign form as the basis for lexical meanings is that we are able to extract more information from our deaf children's sign phrases than one could ever possibly hope to infer from an equally long string of a hearing child's words. For example, when the hearing child identifies an object by saying, *that ball* (glossed, 'that is a ball'), the adult listener might infer several things from the word *ball*: 'that is **round**', or 'that is **thrown**', or 'that **rolls**', or indeed any aspect at all of ballness, including some aspects which, though second nature to adult users of *ball*, may be totally foreign to the speaking child's experiences. Adults cannot possibly determine what, if anything, the speaking child means about the ball from these words alone. In contrast, the form of the deaf child's characterizing signs, if taken literally, allows us readily to discriminate among these several meanings. For example, the deaf child might point at the ball, then draw a circle in the air (the sign *ROUND*) to convey 'that is round'; or he might point at the ball, then make a throwing motion in the air (*THROW*) to convey 'that can be thrown by someone'; or he might point at the ball, then trace with his hand the forward motion of the ball as it would roll along the ground (*ROLL*) to convey 'that can roll'.

It is important to point out that the inferred lexical meanings of the deaf children's characterizing signs are almost always readily apparent. When sign form is taken literally to assign lexical meanings to characterizing signs, reliability is quite high: Within the set of gestures identified by both coders, there were 132 characterizing sign lexical decisions to be made and 94% of the time the two coders agreed on these lexical decisions.

For single signs in one–sign phrases, analyses went no further than assigning a lexical meaning to each sign. But for signs occurring in multisign phrases, analysis went one step beyond to assign relational meanings, in case–grammatical terms, both to the individual signs of each phrase and to the phrases themselves. Since this matter is more of a conclusion than a coding category, discussion of relational meaning assignment is postponed to the next section, where the domain of analysis for this study is also described.

CATEGORIZATIONS OF RELATIONAL MEANINGS

Defining the Domain of Analysis

The goal of this study is to investigate the particular semantic relations the deaf child conveys in his spontaneously generated communication system. In principle, semantic relations can be conveyed in a single sign or word unit. For example, the one-word utterance *yours* conveys the possession relation. However, a single word or sign, even in context, frequently does not provide enough information for an observer to determine the relation (see Bloom, 1973, for further discussion). For example, consider the child who says *rabbit* when a rabbit with very long ears hops by. In this situation, the observer can reasonably assume that the child wants to say something about the rabbit, but he is still faced with the problem of determining exactly what the child wants to say about the rabbit. That is, he cannot determine whether the child wants to talk about an attribute of the rabbit (e.g., the ears), or an action of the rabbit (e.g., hopping), or its existential rabbitness.

Since it is difficult to determine the particular relation conveyed by a single unit, we have limited the data base of this study to **multisign** phrases. Here the task of semantic identification is made easier as the additional signs in the phrase narrow down the field of possible interpretations. In the rabbit example, if the child were to say *rabbit hop*, the observer would be relatively certain that the child is referring to the action relation. Appendix A presents the number of phrases produced by each deaf child in each session, classified according to the number of signs per phrase. Only phrases containing two or more signs will be included in the data base of this study.

The data base therefore consists of multisign phrases that convey semantic relations, that is, multisign phrases that convey relationships between (or among) objects, actions, or attributes.[8] For example, several of the children produced the following phrase to comment on the action usually performed on a particular object:

(1) *drum picture—BEAT* ('one **beats drums**')[9]   [David, VIIIa, 5]

For this particular study, we describe only a segment of our collected data: those phrases which convey **one** relation. That is, we leave aside complex phrases conveying two or more relations. Phrase (2) is an example of a complex phrase that is excluded from the particular analyses presented in this chapter. David produced this four-sign phrase while looking at his sister after his mother gave him and his sister each a plastic knife:

(2) *knife₁–David—knife₂–sister* ('she/mother gave **knife₁** to **me/David;** she/mother gave **knife₂** to **you/sister**')   [David, IVa, 136]

David had, in effect, conjoined two transfer relations within one phrase and thus produced a complex phrase with two relations. In general, the children produced many more simple one-relation phrases than complex multi-relation phrases. Dennis, Kathy, Chris, Tracy, Donald, and David produced, respectively, 4, 11, 8, 10, 12, and 223 complex phrases, representing 10%, 17%, 14%, 12%, 7%, and 30% of all of the phrases they produced.[10]

---

[8] One type of multi-sign phrase is omitted here: repetition combinations that consist of one sign repeated. An example of a repetition combination occurs when the child points at a book and then, without breaking the flow of movement, points again at the same book. In general, there were very few repetition phrases. The children produced between 0 and 12 such phrases throughout the entire time of this study.

[9] The following conventions will be used in describing examples:

(1) The example should be read from left to right; the sign that occurs first in the temporal sequence is the first entry on the left.

(2) The referents of deictic signs are in lowercase letters (e.g., *drum*).

(3) Capitalized words (e.g., *BEAT*) are glosses for the referents of characterizing signs. A description of each sign is found either in Appendices B through G or in a footnote.

(4) The sentence in parentheses is an English gloss of the phrase. The boldface words stand for those referents that are explicitly signed in the phrase; the remaining words stand for referents that are omitted from the phrase and must be inferred from context.

(5) The information in brackets indicates the name of the child who produced the phrase (e.g., David), the session in which he produced the phrase (e.g., VIIIa), and the transcription number of the phrase (e.g., 5).

[10] Some of the children's phrases were uninterpretable, either because context was in-

In sum, the data base for this study consists of all of the multisign phrases conveying only one relation that were produced by our six subjects during the observation sessions. The relational categories used to classify these phrases are described in the next section, along with reliability scores for each category. Each phrase in the analysis was reviewed by two coders, and any disagreement between these coders was resolved by discussion. The few phrases for which agreement could not be reached were classified as uninterpretable.

Two Classes of Phrase Types: Action and Attribute

The deaf children in this study produced two basic classes of phrase types: actions and attributes. An action phrase is used to request the execution of an action, or to comment on an action that is being, has been, will be, or can be executed. Phrases (3) and (4) are examples of action phrases.

(3) *HIT–mother* ('**you/mother hit** blocks')   [David IVa 81]
(4) *MARCH–soldier* ('**he/soldier marches**')   [Chris III 117]

An attribute phrase is one which is used to comment on the perceptual characteristics of an object. Phrases (5), (6), and (7) are examples of attribute phrases.

(5) *elephant trunk picture–LONG* ('**elephant trunk** is **long**')
                                                          [Tracy I 141][11]
(6) *black train–black car* ('**black train** resembles **black car**')
                                                          [David IVa 40]
(7) *picture of soldier–soldier* ('**picture** resembles **soldier**')
                                                          [Donald IXa 97]

Reliability scores were established for classifying action and attribute phrases as follows: 66 such classification decisions were made in the videotape sample used to establish reliability and there was 96% agreement between two coders on these decisions.

The deaf child's action phrases can be profitably described in terms of semantic **elements** that combine to form semantic **relations**.[12] A description of these elements and relations follows.

---

sufficient to determine the child's intended meaning (if any), or because the videotaped picture was not clear enough to determine what the child was pointing at. Uninterpretable phrases ranged from 10–16% of the phrases the children produced.

[11] LONG = index finger slides down from nose in U-shaped curve.

[12] A complete list of all of the one-relation action phrases produced by each child can be found in Appendices B through G. A detailed description of the attribute phrases produced by the deaf children can be found in Goldin-Meadow (1975 and in forthcoming reports).

Semantic Elements: Predicates and Cases

Following Fillmore (1968) we isolate two types of semantic elements in the deaf child's action phrases: predicates and cases. Each phrase can be viewed as a miniature drama whose plot is given by the verb or **predicate** and whose players, in their various roles, are given by the **cases**. Each relation of a phrase may have only one predicate, but may have several cases. Since the data base is limited to phrases with one relation, it is limited to phrases with one predicate. Consider the following example of predicates and cases in the deaf child's communication system.

(8) *food–EAT–Susan* ('**you/Susan** will **eat food**')   [David Vb 130]

The characterizing sign *EAT* conveys the predicate of this phrase and the deictic signs *food* and *Susan* convey the cases.

The method of predicate and case assignment was an outgrowth of Bloom's (1970) "method of rich interpretation," in which semantic predicates and cases are assigned to words (or signs, in our study) by observing the phrase's relationship to ongoing events. For example, if the hearing child says *Mommy doll* while his mother is dressing the doll, Bloom would claim the child's intent was to communicate 'Mommy dresses doll.' *Mommy* then would be assigned an actor case in the sentence, while *doll* would be assigned a patient case; the act predicate *dresses* would be classified as unsaid, but implied by the context.

We follow Bloom in assigning to each sign within a phrase a semantic predicate or case according to its presumed function in the phrase. For example, if the deaf child pointed first at mother, then at the doll while mother was indeed dressing the doll, the actor case would be assigned to the first pointing (at mother) and the patient case to the second pointing (at the doll). But suppose the same two concatenated pointings were produced while the child handed the doll to the mother. The first pointing at mother is then assigned the recipient case, while the one at the doll remains the patient case.

Using this method of rich interpretation, it was determined that the predicates in the deaf child's action phrases were **acts** which were always conveyed by characterizing signs.[13] The cases in these action phrases were

---

[13] Since the data base is limited to phrases with one relation and therefore to phrases with one predicate, note that it is also limited to phrases with at most one characterizing sign. A characterizing sign identifies an object or action by specifically conveying a relational aspect of that object or action. For example, *THROW* (curved palm arcs forward in air) conveys the "throwability" of an object or the act of throwing. Thus, when two characterizing signs are concatenated, two relational aspects are necessarily conveyed and the phrase is then classified as a complex multi-relation phrase. For example, *THROW–GIVE*, meaning perhaps 'you **give** me that which can be **thrown** by someone,' or 'you **give** me that which I will **throw**,' is a complex phrase and is not included in the data base for this study.

patients, recipients, actors, and places, each of which was always conveyed by a deictic sign. Note that the decision to classify characterizing signs as act predicates and deictic signs as the various cases is a natural outgrowth of our lexical meaning assignments (see earlier for the details and justification behind these lexical decisions). Definitions of these predicates and cases, along with illustrations appear below (the defined element is set *boldface italic* in each example).

Act Predicate: The act that is carried out to effect a change of either state or location.

(9) *car–GO* ('car should **go** there') [David, VIIa, 169]
(10) *bubbles–BLOW* ('one **blows** bubbles') [Dennis, IV, 104]

Patient Case: The object or person which is acted upon or manipulated.

(11) *duck–TWIST* ('you/Susan **twist** duck') [David, Ia, 300]
(12) *cookie–GIVE* ('she/sister **give** cookie to me/David') [David, Ib, 46]

Recipient Case: The locus or person toward which someone or something moves, either by transporting himself/itself, or by being transferred by an actor.

(13) *duck–Susan* ('you/sister give **duck** to her/Susan') [David, Ib, 12]
(14) *hat–head* ('you/Susan put **hat** on mother's head') [Chris, II, 299]
(15) *David–garage* ('**I**/David go into garage') [David, VIa, 141]

Actor Case: The object or person which performs an action in order to change its own state or location, or to change the state or location of an external patient.

(16) *GO AROUND–Pinocchio* ('**Pinocchio** did **go around**')
[Donald, XIa, 116]
(17) *WALK–duck–WALK–duck* ('you/**duck** will **walk**') [Kathy, VIIa, 24]
(18) *SHOOT–Kathy* ('**I/Kathy** will **shoot** toy gun') [Kathy, VIIb, 114]
(19) *sister–napkin* ('you/**sister** put cookie on napkin') [David, Ib, 60]

Place Case: The locale where an action is carried out, but which is not the endpoint of a patient's or actor's change of location.

(20) *Susan+CHEW–kitchen+CHEW* ('you/**Susan** will **chew** lunch in **kitchen**') [David, IVa, 177]
(21) *track–PUT TOGETHER* ('you/Lisa **put together** blocks on **track**')
[David, Va, 158]

Animate versus inanimate cases. In the definition of the recipient case, inanimate and animate recipients are combined. That is, people and places are considered equivalent, in the sense that they are both endpoints of a relocation action. The justification for making no distinction between animate and inanimate recipients is on the following grounds.

1. Animate recipients and inanimate recipients function alike in the child's communication system. That is, we find that the same set of rules can describe phrases with either type of recipient. In some sense, then, there is no justification for dividing the category along the animate dimension.

2. In many languages, the same inflection or preposition is used for both dative (which includes our animate recipients) and spatial (our inanimate recipients) locatives (Anderson, 1971). Indeed, Kurylowicz (as reported by Anderson, 1971) states, about the origin of the dative in Indo-European, that "the dative is generally nothing less than an offshoot of the loc[ative] used with personal nouns."

Animacy is also an issue in our definition of the actor case. Usually an actor is animate, but not always. An actor must be **perceived** by the gesturer to have its own motivating force. In some situations, actor assignment was straightforward (e.g., *"HIT—mother"* meaning 'you/mother hit blocks'). In other situations, however, it was not so easy to decide if the child considered a particular object to be self-motivating. There were some inanimate objects (i.e., inanimate according to an adult's judgment) that a child might consider to be self-propelling and therefore animate (e.g., a picture of an airplane—do children think that airplanes fly themselves?— or a duck that walks, but only when its key is twisted). These ambiguous phrases were dealt with operationally, using the form of the child's characterizing sign as a guide.

1. An object was judged to be an **actor** if the characterizing sign conveying the act predicate in the phrase portrayed the action **of** the object. For example, the forward motion of the car in example (9) and the walking motion of the duck in example (17) classify both the car and the duck as actors.

2. An object was judged to be a **patient** if the characterizing sign for the act predicate portrayed an action that is done **on** the object. For example, the twisting motion the child might use to operate the duck in example (11) classifies the duck as a patient.

If the act predicate was not explicitly signed in the phrase in question, the phrase was considered ambiguous and not further classified. There were very few questionable phrases lacking explicit act predicates.

The inference that the child views certain inanimate objects as actors was supported by results. Inanimate actors (inanimate from an adult's point of view) functioned the same as animate ones in the child's system. That is, they could be described by the same set of rules as those actors the adult considered animate.[14]

Reliability scores were determined for assigning predicates and cases to action phrases as follows. In the reliability videotape sample, there were 115 decisions made on semantic element assignment and 97% agreement between the two coders on those decisions.

Semantic Relations:
Transfer, Transform, Transport, and Perform

The set of elements described in the preceding section comprises the units of the deaf child's semantic relations. A relation is defined in terms of sets of permissible elements. An element is permissible in a particular relation on two grounds. First, if (on some intuitive level) an element is a necessary component of a relation, it is potentially permissible in that relation. For example, the actor, patient, and act elements can be permissible in a phrase expressing an "eat" notion simply because a plausible account of the physical act of eating concept includes a doer (actor), a done-to (patient), and a chewing–swallowing–digesting action which relates the two (act). Eating cannot possibly occur without both an eater and an eaten. In contrast, only the actor and the act are permissible in a phrase expressing a "dance" notion simply because dancing requires that a doer (actor) perform a leg-moving, body-swaying motion (act), but certainly does not require that a done-to (patient), other than the dancer himself, be involved. Second, if an element is considered to be a necessary component of a particular relation and also can be found in the deaf child's sign repertoire, it is considered permissible in that relation. For example, the **source** case is intuitively part of the notion of transfer (I moved book from **table** to stool). However, the deaf children never produced explicit signs for the source case. Consequently, the source was not considered permissible in the deaf child's relations produced at this period.

Using these guidelines, four types of relations were isolated in the deaf child's phrases. Each relation is defined and illustrated below (the permissible elements are boldfaced in each definition).[15]

---

[14] Bloom, Lightbown, and Hood (1975), in their descriptions of hearing children learning English, appear to have made a similar coding decision with respect to inanimate actors (again, inanimate from an adult's point of view). In particular, they permit inanimate objects to be **actors**, as in the following example. Peter at time IV was watching the reels of a tape recorder and said, *tape go round.* Bloom *et al.* (1975:11) consider *tape* to be an **actor** and *go round* to be an **action.**

[15] Each of these relations can underlie phrases which express ongoing actions, potential actions, or completed actions.

Transfer relation: An act by an actor on a patient that results in the patient's transfer to a **recipient** (either a locus or person).

(22) *book–GIVE–David–book*[16] ('you/mother **give book** to *me/David*')

[David VIIb 88]

(23) *car–MOVE* ('you/Heidi **move car** to me/Dennis') [Dennis IVb 148]

Transform relation: An act by an actor on a patient which affects the state of that patient, either temporarily or permanently.

(24) *cookie–CHEW* ('I/David am **chewing cookie**')   [David Ib 22]

(25) *bubble wand–mother* ('**you**/mother blow **bubble wand**')

[Kathy Va 32]

Transport relation: An act by an actor which results in the actor's own relocation at a new **recipient** (either at a new locus, or near a new person).

(26) *balloon picture–GO UP* ('**balloon goes up** to sky')   [Donald XIa 64]

(27) *bridge–FALL* ('**bridge fell** to floor')   [David IVa 176]

Perform relation: An act by an actor which affects the actor's own state and not the state of an external patient.

(28) *lion picture–ROAR* ('**lions roar**')   [Tracy I 168]

(29) *father–[ss]–SLEEP* ('No. **he/father sleeps**')[17]   [David IVa 178]

Note in examples (22)–(27) that not all of the permissible elements have to be explicitly signed for coding a particular relation. The method of rich interpretation is used to determine relations. That is, the signs the child produces in context determine the relation he intends to convey. For example, consider a child who is watching a toy mouse eat spaghetti. The child points at the mouse and then produces the characterizing sign *EAT*. He has explicitly signed the actor case (the mouse) and the act predicate (eat). We infer from the context that he is conveying a transform relation and that he has omitted from his phrase the sign for the patient case (the spaghetti).

Reliability scores were determined for assigning relation types to phrases as follows. There was 94% agreement between two coders on the 51 relation assignment decisions made in the videotape sample.

In sum, the deaf children convey four different types of action relations in their sign phrases. The four relations are similar in that each relation permits a predicate, the act. The relations differ, however, with respect to the number and types of cases they permit. If we classify these relations according to number of permissible cases, we find that the deaf child conveys **three-case** relations (transfer), **two-case** relations (transform and

---

[16] Note that occasionally an element may be signed more than once in a phrase, as is "book" in example (22). These repetitions do not affect classification according to relation.

[17] [SS] = side-to-side headshake; the headshake marker is functioning anaphorically in this phrase and is negating the preceding phrase: roughly glossed, 'Father is not eating; he is sleeping.'

transport), and **one-case** relations (perform). If we now classify relations according to types of permissible cases, we find that the deaf child produces both **transitive** relations, relations permitting the patient case (transfer and transform), and **intransitive** relations, relations which exclude the patient (transport and perform). The significance of these two types of class-ifications will become apparent as we examine the children's phrases in the next sections.

STRUCTURE IN THE DEAF CHILD'S REPRESENTATION OF SEMANTIC RELATIONS

The coding categories used to describe the deaf child's communication system have passed our first test. The categories are reliable. We turn now to our second test of the categories: Do these categories result in a coherent description of the deaf child's communication system? We find that these categories do indeed yield a description of a **structured** communication system. We have isolated structure on several levels of analysis and each type of structure is found in natural spoken languages developed by hearing children. These examples of structure not only lend support to the categorization scheme, but, more importantly, suggest that a child in impoverished language learning conditions can develop a communication system that is structured in ways similar to natural languages.

Structure in Semantic Content

ACTION VERSUS ATTRIBUTE PHRASES

The deaf children in this study tended to produce action phrase types more often than attribute phrase types (see Table 3.2, which presents the proportions of action and attribute phrases produced by each child). Note that five of the six children in the study conformed to this pattern.

The cross-sectional data presented in Table 3.2 also suggest a developmental pattern. The younger children (Dennis, Kathy, and Chris, all under three years, 6 months throughout the study) produced proportionately fewer attribute phrases than the older children (David, Tracy, and Donald, all over three years, 6 months at some point in the study). On the basis of these cross-sectional data, the younger deaf child appears to be less likely to convey attribute phrases than the older deaf child. Longitudinal data support this inference. Two of the three children who did not produce either action or attribute phrases at the beginning of the study began to produce action phrases before attribute phrases. Kathy began action production in session II and attribute production in session VI; Donald began action

TABLE 3.2   Action and Attribute Phrases

Child	Action phrases	Attribute phrases	Static phrases[a]	Total one-relation phrases
Dennis	.87	.10	.03	31
Kathy	.86	.09	.05	42
Chris	.70	.26	.04	43
Donald	.63	.36	.01	145
David	.58	.37	.05	437
Tracy	.38	.57	.05	65

[a] These phrases could not be classified as either action or attribute phrases. A phrase was considered to be static if the phrase could potentially be a comment on the static location or possession of an object. For example, consider a child who points at a picture of his brother and then points out the door. The child could either be commenting on the fact that his brother went outside (an action) or on the fact that his brother is now outside (static location). Similarly, pointing at his own Halloween costume and then at himself could either be a comment on his having received the costume at one time (an action), or on his current possession of the costume (static possession). Because of such problems of interpretation, these phrases were classified separately. Note, however, that static phrases make up a small proportion of the total one-relation phrases produced by the children.

production in session II and attribute production in session VIII. However, Dennis did produce two attribute phrases in session I, but did not begin action production until session II. In general, then, the cross-sectional and longitudinal data suggest that the deaf child begins to convey action relations before attribute relations, but that, over time, attribute production does increase relative to action production.

ACTION RELATIONS: TRANSFER, TRANSFORM, TRANSPORT, PERFORM

Structure exists not only in the two classes of phrase types the children produced, but also in the types of action relations they produced. Table 3.3 presents the cross-sectional evidence for such structure: the proportions of transfer, transform, transport, and perform relations produced by each child throughout the study. The children produced transfer and transform relations (both transitive relations) more frequently than transport and perform relations (both intransitive relations).

In addition, longitudinal data suggest that intransitive production increases relative to transitive production over developmental time. Dennis, Kathy, and Donald all produced transitive phrases during session II, but Dennis did not begin intransitive production until session III, Kathy until session IV, and Donald until session IX. Even during session IX, only 17% of Donald's action phrases were intransitive, but later (in session XI) as many as 42% of his action phrases were intransitive. David produced transitive phrases during session I, but did not begin intransitive production

TABLE 3.3 Action Relation Phrases

	Transfer phrases	Transform phrases	Transport phrases	Perform phrases	Total action phrases
Dennis	.59	.37	.04	.00	27
Kathy	.53	.31	.08	.08	36
Chris	.57	.23	.07	.13	30
Donald	.48	.37	.09	.05	91
David	.38	.40	.15	.07	253
Tracy	.08	.56	.12	.24	25

until session III; during sessions III and IV David produced only one intransitive phrase per session (11% of his action phrases), but by sessions VII and VIII he was producing 23 and 19 such phrases, respectively (32% of his action phrases). The longitudinal data from the other two children do not bear directly on this developmental question, since both Chris and Tracy produced transitive and intransitive phrases during session I.

In sum, it appears that the deaf child conveys relations that permit patient cases (i.e., transitive relations) before he conveys relations which do not permit the patient (i.e., intransitive relations). Moreover, intransitive phrases become proportionately more frequent relative to transitive phrases as the child develops. Thus there is development in the relational typology of the deaf children's signing. Evidence for a division of transitive relations into transfer and transform and a division of intransitive relations into transport and perform will be presented later.

SEMANTIC ELEMENTS: CASES AND PREDICATES

We turn now to the semantic elements produced by the deaf children. By and large, the children tended to sign only two elements per phrase: Dennis, Kathy, Chris, Donald, David, and Tracy each produced 24, 31, 26, 82, 228, and 23 two-element phrases, representing 88%, 93%, 89%, 97%, 92%, and 96%, respectively, of each of their total action phrases.[18] Each

---

[18] Some action phrases could not be classified according to semantic elements. In particular, for some phrases, the imprecision of the pointing sign prevented determining which particular case the child intended to convey. For example, a child who wanted his mother to give him a toy might point toward his mother holding the toy and then produce the characterizing sign for GIVE (open palm with the palm up). From our vantage point, we could not determine whether the child meant 'that–GIVE' (patient–act) or 'you–GIVE' (actor–act). In fact, the child may have intended to incorporate both interpretations into his phrase. The percentages of such phrases ranged from 0 to 8% of the total action phrases produced by the children; these phrases are not included in the calculations of two-, three-, or four-element phrases, nor are they included in Table 3.4.

child produced some three-element phrases and David produced a few four-element phrases.

A look at the particular elements the children signed (see Table 3.4) shows that elements differed in frequency of occurrence. The **place** case was rarely produced in either two-element or three-element phrases. On the other hand, the **patient, recipient,** and **actor** cases and the **act** predicate were all produced frequently. Note, however, in the two-element phrases described in Table 3.4, that all of the three possible pairings of patients, recipients, and acts occurred fairly often, while the actor case occurred frequently only when concatenated with the act predicate.

The actor case is, thus, combined relatively infrequently with certain elements. The actor is, however, produced by all of the children at one time or another. We return to this problem of the infrequent actor in the next section where we show that the rare instances of actor production can in fact be predicted on the basis of a hypothetical underlying structure.

Underlying Structure

It was earlier suggested that the deaf child conveys four different types of action relations, each of which can be defined in terms of configurations of predicates and cases. The relations differ from one another with respect to the hypothetical number of cases they permit with each act predicate. Specifically, transfer relations are hypothesized to permit three cases, for example, I[actor] give[act] **book**[patient] to **mother**[recipient]. Transform and transport relations are hypothesized to permit two cases, for example, I[actor] eat[act] **apples**[patient], or I[actor] go[act] to **corner**[recipient].

TABLE 3.4 **Action Phrases with Two Signed Elements**[a]

	PA[b]	PR	AR	Actor A	Actor P	Actor R	Total action phrases
Dennis	.44	.22	.07	.00	.11	.04	27
Kathy	.36	.06	.18	.21	.09	.03	33
Chris	.41	.14	.17	.17	.00	.00	29
Donald	.50	.08	.17	.14	.04	.02	84[c]
David	.34	.18	.08	.22	.05	.02	248[c]
Tracy	.45	.00	.00	.38	.08	.00	24[c]

[a] This table includes all two-element action phrases regardless of the order of the elements in the phrase. For example, the column marked "PA" includes phrases in which patients precede acts, acts precede patients, patients and acts are signed simultaneously, and also phrases in which one or both elements are repeated. The proportions do not sum to 1.00 because from 5 to 10% of the phrases contained three elements and so are excluded here (see also footnote c.).

[b] P = Patient, A = Act, R = Recipient.

[c] David and Donald produced a few Act–Place phrases (3% and 2% of their action phrases, respectively) and Tracy produced one Actor–Place phrase (4% of her action phrases).

Perform relations are hypothesized to permit one case, for example, I[actor] dance[act]. Since not all of these elements need appear in the surface form of a given phrase, the definitions hypothesize an underlying structure for phrases that is often richer than the surface form of those phrases. We will now attempt to justify the particular configurations (i.e., three-case, two-case, one-case) hypothesized by showing how surface structure in the deaf child's phrases is systematically related to these underlying configurations.

The surface measure used to look at underlying configurations is production probability. Production probability is a measure of the child's propensity to sign explicitly an element in those phrases where the element is hypothetically applicable. For example, consider a phrase which conveys a transfer relation involving a boy (actor) giving (act) a ball (patient) to his dog (recipient). A child in the two-sign period is unable to sign explicitly in one phrase all of these four semantic elements: he is at this time limited to a two (or rarely three) sign output. The child is thus forced to include in his signed phrase some elements (for example, *ball–dog*) and exclude others (in this instance, *boy–GIVE*) which might have been thought equally likely to appear. Production probability for a given element represents the likelihood that that element will be included in the surface forms of those phrases in which the element is hypothetically permissible.

Production probability is determined for each semantic element by first classifying all of the deaf child's two-element phrases according to the relation conveyed by that phrase. This determination is made on the basis of linguistic and nonlinguistic evidence. For example, a phrase about giving books to mother is classified as transfer, a phrase about eating apples is classified as transform, a phrase about going to the corner is classified as transport, and a phrase about elephants dancing is classified as perform. Production probability for each element is then calculated separately for each relation hypothesized to have a different underlying configuration. For example, production probability for the actor case in phrases with three-case underlying configuration (transfer relations) would be the number of two-element transfer phrases with explicitly signed actors divided by the total number of two-element transfer phrases. Production probability for the actor case in phrases with two-case underlying configurations (transform and transport relations) would be the number of two-element transform and transport phrases with explicitly signed actors divided by the total number of two-element transform and transport phrases.

ACTOR PRODUCTION PROBABILITY

It might be expected that production probability for any particular element, in this instance, the actor, would be constant across all relation types. That is, a child would produce a sign for actors with some constant probability, irrespective of the type of action relation performed by that actor (e.g., giver, eater, goer, dancer).

The data in Figure 3.1 do not support these expectations. Each child's actor production probability in phrases with two explicitly signed elements is shown in that figure for each of the three configurations hypothesized to underlie the deaf child's four relation types. Note that actor production probability is not constant across the three types of configurations. Rather, for all six children, actor production probability appears to vary systematically with configuration type. Actor production is more likely in phrases with one-case underlying configurations (conveying perform relations) than in phrases with two-case underlying configurations (conveying transform and transport relations). Moreover, actor production is more likely in phrases with two-case underlying configurations than in phrases with three-case underlying configurations (conveying transfer relations).

To account for these data, it must be assumed that elements that do not appear in the surface forms of the deaf child's phrases can influence those which do. Furthermore, on the basis of these data, the deaf child possesses three different configurations of elements that underlie and therefore influence the surface structures of his phrases.

We are, in essence, hypothesizing that for a two-sign child there will be competition among underlying elements for the limited number of spaces in surface structure. According to this hypothesis, the total number of underlying elements should have some effect on the probability of any particular element appearing in surface structure. The fewer elements underlying, the better chance of any one element making it to the surface. Thus, phrases with small underlying configurations, such as the one-case perform relation phrases, should contain elements with relatively high production probabilities. As the underlying configurations of phrases increase in size, that is, as underlying configurations change from one-case to two-case to three-case, production probabilities should decrease accordingly. Figure 3.1 reveals that the likelihood of actor production decreases systematically with the hypothesized one-case, two-case, and three-case underlying configurations. To account for these facts of surface structure, we therefore attribute an abstract level of representation, called underlying structure, to the deaf child's sign system.

If correct about the competition hypothesis and about these three particular underlying configurations, we would also predict that in the child's longer phrases (i.e., in phrases with three explicitly signed elements) the same general pattern of actor production would emerge, but accompanied by an overall rise in level of actor production. Figure 3.2 summarizes the data in Figure 3.1 for phrases with **two** explicit elements and presents

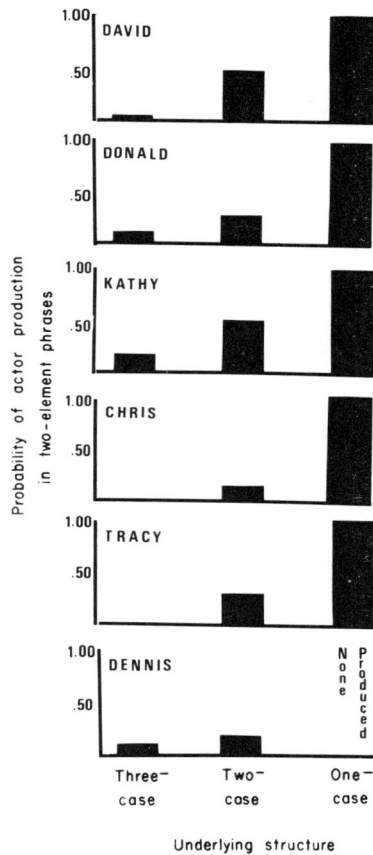

Figure 3.1 Actor production probability in two-element phrases as a function of underlying structures. Probabilities are based on the total number of two-element phrases of each structure type produced by each child; the totals for David are three-case = 88, two-case = 123, one-case = 17; for Donald 40, 37, 5; for Dennis 13, 11, 0; for Chris 14, 8, 4; for Kathy 16, 12, 3; and for Tracy 2, 15, 6.

comparable data on phrases with **three** explicit elements. Both predictions are verified. The production probability of actor cases does indeed rise with the inclusion of a third signed element in the phrase. Moreover, this overall increase conforms to the pattern found in two-element phrases with the expected increase in production probability in two-case phrases. With competition reduced, actors are always signed in three-element phrases with one-case and two-case underlying structures, but are still relatively unlikely in three-element phrases with three-case underlying structure.[19]

[19] It is almost, but not quite, a tautological outcome of the coding procedure that the actor is always explicitly signed in phrases hypothesized to have one-case underlying structures. Recall that one-sign phrases were excluded from the data base for this study. It would seem then that one-case relation phrases, which are hypothesized to permit only two elements (e.g., baby–sleep), could not be counted in this study unless these phrases contained both elements

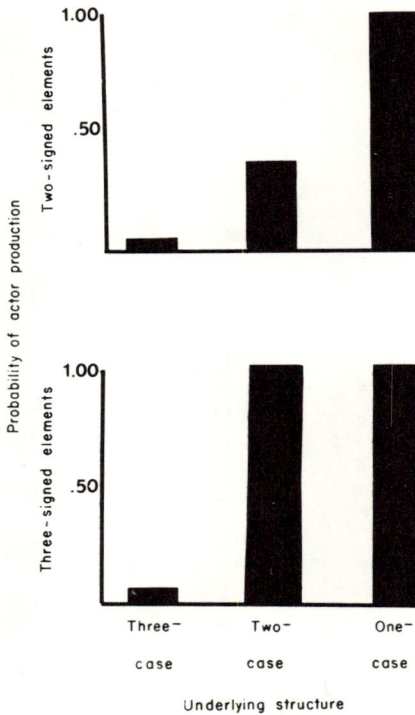

Figure 3.2 Actor production probability in two-element versus three-element phrases as a function of underlying structures. Probabilities are based on the total number of two- and three-element phrases of each structure type produced by all six children; the total for two-element phrases are three-case = 173, two-case = 206, one-case = 35; for three-element phrases 15, 12, 1.

ACT PRODUCTION PROBABILITY

The problem of underlying structure was investigated by examining the production probabilities of the actor case for two reasons. First, the actor was signed sometimes but not all the time, thereby providing the variability necessary for the phenomenon to become apparent. Second, the actor was hypothesized to be permissible in each of the four relations types, thereby allowing the competition phenomenon its greatest degree of expression.

---

explicitly signed. However, it it just possible, under this coding scheme, that a one-case phrase could have the actor (or act) omitted and also be included in the data base. This situation could have occurred if the optional **place** case were explicitly signed in a phrase conveying a perform relation. For example, the subject could have gestured "SLEEP-bed" or "baby-bed" as ways of indicating 'baby sleeps in bed.' But this never happened, so the appearance of both actor and act in one-case relations is 100% (see Figure 3.1 and Table 3.5). Given the dependence of this fact on the coding procedure, the importance of Figure 3.1 (and Table 3.5) centers particularly on the effects for two-case and three-case relations, as well as in the comparison of Figure 3.1 with Figure 3.2. In fact, it did turn out that a child produced the **place** case in three-sign phrases conveying one-case relations (see Figure 3.2). The surface form of such a phrase includes the **actor,** the **act,** and the **place** (e.g., David VIIIa 139: *elephant picture–DIVE–water picture,* a comment on a picture of an elephant diving while in a pool of water).

The act predicate is also hypothetically permissible in each of the four relations; moreover, the act is not always signed whenever it can be. Consequently, we now examine the probabilities of act production to see if these probabilities also reflect posited underlying configurations.

Table 3.5 presents the probabilities of act production in two-element phrases for each of the three underlying structures. Act production probability is higher across the board than actor production probability, but for four of the six children, it follows the same pattern. That is, act production is most likely in phrases with one-case underlying structure, less likely in phrases with two-case underlying structure, and least likely in phrases with three-case underlying structure.

Act production in three-element phrases is also consonant with our notions of underlying structure. A three-element phrase, in effect, raises the limit on surface structure, thereby reducing the competition in three-case underlying structures. Consequently, act production in three-element phrases should be quite high for all three underlying structures. The data verify these predictions. Analyzed across all six subjects, the probability of act production in three-element phrases was 1.00 for phrases with any of the three types of underlying structures.

PATIENT PRODUCTION PROBABILITY

Patient production probability provides further evidence of underlying structure. Since patients are not hypothesized to be permissible in phrases with one-case underlying structures, patient production is examined only in phrases with two-case and three-case underlying structures (see Table 3.6). The pattern is evident in five of the six children: Patient production is more likely in phrases with two-case underlying structure than in phrases with three-case underlying structure, reflecting the effect of competition from other cases in the latter instance.

TABLE 3.5 Act Production Probability[a]

	Three-case relations	Two-case relations	One-case relations
David	.47(88)[b]	.87(123)	1.00(17)
Donald	.75(40)	.94(37)	1.00(5)
Dennis	.46(13)	.73(11)	—(0)
Chris	.71(14)	1.00(8)	1.00(4)
Kathy	.81(16)	.75(12)	1.00(3)
Tracy	1.00(2)	.80(15)	1.00(6)

[a] The data base for this analysis includes action phrases in which two elements are explicitly signed.

[b] The numbers in parentheses represent the total number of phrases with three-case, two-case, and one-case underlying structures produced by each child during the study.

TABLE 3.6   Patient Production Probability[a]

	Three-case relations	Two-case relations
David	.78(88)[b]	.83(88)
Donald	.53(40)	.90(29)
Dennis	.85(13)	1.00(10)
Chris	.64(14)	1.00(7)
Kathy	.63(16)	.87(9)
Tracy	1.00(2)	.85(13)

[a] The data base for this analysis includes action phrases in which two elements are explicitly signed.

[b] The numbers in parentheses represent the total number of transitive phrases with three-case and two-case underlying structures produced by each child during the study.

In sum, we have found a systematic relation between the hypothesized underlying structures and the actual likelihood of actors, acts, and patients appearing in surface structure. The systematic relation itself constitutes evidence for the proposed underlying structures.

Surface Structure

PRODUCTION PROBABILITY AS A SURFACE MARKING DEVICE

We have shown in the previous section that the production probability for each case varies systematically with underlying structure. That is, each individual semantic case is progressively less likely to be signed as the number of elements in the underlying structure increases. However, it turns out that, across all underlying structures, certain cases are more likely than others to be signed when they can be signed. In fact, each of the three major cases in the deaf child's system appears to have a characteristic level of production probability.

Table 3.7 presents the conditional production probability of cases, that is, production probability for each case figured in terms of only those phrases which permit that case. It is apparent that, for all six children, the patient case is the most likely case to appear in the surface structure of any of the phrases in which it is permissible (i.e., in transfer and transform phrases). Moreover, for five of the six children the recipient case was the next most likely case to be signed when it could be, and the actor case was the least likely case to be signed when it could be. Thus, across all relation types, each of the three cases is characterized by an overall level of production probability: Patients have high production probability, recipients medium production probability, and actors low production probability.

In sum, the characteristic level of production probability associated with each case contributes to surface regularity in the deaf child's phrases. In this

TABLE 3.7 Conditional Production Probability of Cases[a]

	Patient	Recipient	Actor
Dennis	.91(23)[b]	.64(14)	.17(24)
Kathy	.68(25)	.47(19)	.35(31)
Chris	.76(21)	.60(15)	.19(26)[c]
Donald	.75(69)	.48(48)	.21(82)
David	.81(176)	.57(123)	.32(228)
Tracy	.87(15)	.00(4)	.52(23)

[a] The data base for the analysis includes action phrases in which two elements are explicitly signed.

[b] The numbers in parentheses represent the total number of phrases which permit patient, recipient, or actor cases produced by each child during the study.

sense, then, production probability level functions as a syntactic device which marks the deaf child's cases (see Feldman, Goldin-Meadow, & Gleitman [1978] for a more extensive discussion of production probability as a syntactic device).

SIGN ORDER AS A SURFACE MARKING DEVICE

We have just seen that production probability for a given element determines, at least in part, whether or not the deaf child will sign that element in the surface structure of his phrases. We now find that the surface forms of the deaf child's phrases are further determined by a second surface marking device, the ordering rule. Given that a certain element will appear in the surface structure of a phrase, ordering rules determine where in the phrase the element will tend to appear.

The deaf children expressed their action relations by following syntactic ordering rules: they tended to sign certain elements before others in their two-sign phrases. For example, when producing a two-sign phrase containing a patient and an act, the deaf child was more likely to produce the sign for the patient before the sign for the act.

Sign order data for the most frequent types of phrases (i.e., for phrases containing pairings of patients, recipients, and acts) can be found in Figure 3.3, which presents the number of two-sign phrases classified according to the order of each element in the phrase.[20] All children always produced **patients** before **recipients** in their two-sign phrases, for example, "book-mother," requesting that the book be given to mother. Not all the children

---

[20] All phrases containing pointings at pictures are excluded from this ordering analysis because the children tended to point at pictures before producing other signs. The pictures pointed at were most often facsimiles of objects playing the patient role; thus, we would have, perhaps artifactually, inflated patient-first orderings if these phrases were included. As a result, Tracy is not included in this analysis because she produced very few phrases conveying action semantic relations that did not contain points at pictures.

showed ordering tendencies for the remaining pairs of elements, but those children who did all showed them in the same direction (but see below). Certain of the children tended to produce **patients** before **acts,** as in the above example *drum–BEAT* (David $\chi^2 = 5.48, p < .04$; Dennis $\chi^2 = 7.36$, $p < .01$). In addition, some tended to produce **acts** before **recipients** (e.g., "GIVE-mother" again requesting transfer of an object to mother). David always followed this act-recipient ordering and Donald showed a strong tendency in the same direction ($\chi^2 = 10.28, p < .001$).

These tendencies of our deaf subjects to order elements in their two-sign phrases can be summarized with the following sign order rules:[21]

$$\text{Phrase} \longrightarrow \text{Patient} \begin{Bmatrix} \text{Act} \\ \text{Recipient} \end{Bmatrix}$$

$$\text{Phrase} \longrightarrow \text{Act–Recipient}$$

A more parsimonious description (i.e., fewer rules) of the same data would be:

(Choose any two elements maintaining order)
$$\text{Phrase} \longrightarrow \text{(Patient)(Act)(Recipient)}$$

In addition to indicating that the children structure their phrases, the presence of ordering rules based on predicates and cases is further evidence for the existence of the predicate and case categories themselves. That the children consistently order these categories suggests that, at some processing level, these categories exist for the children. The above order data document evidence for three categories: patients, recipients, and acts.

Although Chris did not appear to have a consistent order for patients and acts, closer inspection of his phrases revealed an ordering tendency completely unique to him. When Chris's patient/act phrases were divided into those conveying transfer relations (e.g., *book/GIVE*) versus those conveying transform relations (e.g., *cookie/EAT*), competing ordering tendencies emerged. Specifically, Chris tended to put patients before acts in transform phrases *(cookie–EAT)*, producing six patient–act transform phrases and only one act–patient transform phrase. However, he tended to put acts before patients in transfer phrases *(GIVE–book)*, producing four

---

[21] The following conventions are used in describing order rules:

1. → indicates that the symbol on the left can be rewritten as the symbol(s) on the right. The order of the symbols on the right must be maintained in the rewriting process.
2. {} indicates that either of the symbols in the braces, but not both, can be chosen in the process of rewriting.
3. ( ) indicates that the symbol in the parentheses is optional, that is, can be chosen or not in the rewriting process.

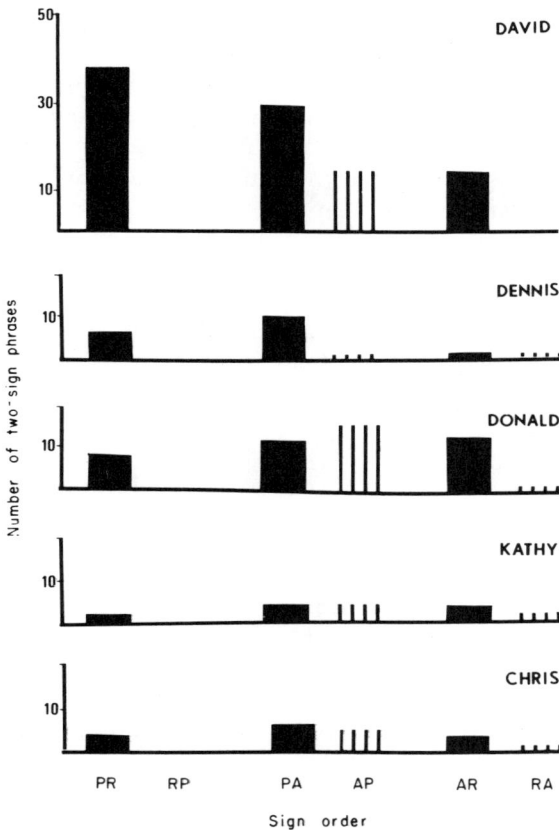

Figure 3.3 Number of two-sign phrases classified according to the order of each element in the phrase. P = patient, A = act, R = recipient.

act–patient transfer phrases and no patient–act transfer phrases. These two tendencies appear to be reliably different in Chris's system (probability < .05 by Fisher Exact Test). Moreover, these two sets of patient/act ordering rules distinguish between transfer and transform relations and provide further evidence for these two relational categories in Chris's system.

FORM-BASED ORDER RULES

An alternate description of at least some of the children's sign orders might be proposed. This description would be based not on the semantic element analysis presented above, but rather on an analysis of the **form** of the signs, that is, deictic signs versus characterizing signs. For example, a "characterizing first–deictic second" strategy might be proposed as an adequate, nonsemantic, description of two-sign action phrases.

One argument against such a form–based rule is the strength of the patient–recipient ordering tendency. Since both patients and recipients are deictic signs, a form-based rule would predict random ordering of these cases. However, as was shown in Figure 3.3, patients are consistently ordered before recipients.

Further, a form-based rule is not well supported by the overall ordering data. Table 3.8 presents the number of two-sign action phrases in which deictics occurred in first or in second position and the number of two-signs phrases in which characterizing signs occurred in either position. There is no essential difference in the number of phrases in which each type of sign occurred in first and second position for David, Chris, and Kathy. Thus, these children do not appear to have a general ordering strategy based on sign form.

The remaining two children provide at best only partial support for form-based rules. Dennis tended to put characterizing signs in second position ($\chi^2 = 6.23$, p < .02), a tendency that does, in fact, explain his patient–act orders. However, since Dennis produced only two act/recipient phrases, we cannot test the generality of this "deictic first-characterizing second" rule. For Dennis, we therefore cannot decide between a semantic-element and a sign-form analysis of his patient-act ordering rule.

In contrast to Dennis, Donald tended to put deictic signs in second position of his two-sign phrases ($\chi^2 = 4.70$, p < .05), and characterizing signs in first position ($\chi^2 = 7.04$, p < .01). Thus, Donald's act–recipient order can equally well be described as a "characterizing first–deictic second" order. However, if Donald were following such an order based on sign form, he should put his characterizing signs for acts before his deictic signs for patients (i.e., to have an act-patient order). In fact, he does not. Thus, even Donald's data provide no strong evidence for ordering rules based on sign form.

TABLE 3.8 Deictic and Characterizing Sign Orders in Two-Sign Phrases

	Deictic signs		Characterizing signs	
	In first position	*In second position*	*In first position*	*In second position*
Dennis	21	12	2	11
Kathy	13	15	10	10
Chris	10	15	12	7
Donald	22	39	29	12
David	90	91	40	39

In general, it appears that a semantic element analysis of the order data better describes the children's phrases. We therefore suggest that the predicate/case level is a more fruitful one on which to analyze sign orders in surface structure in these children's phrases.

ACTOR ORDER RULES

What is the surface position of the actor in the deaf children's two-sign phrases? Since the deaf children produced only a small number of phrases containing the actor case, we must be cautious in making any inferences about actor-ordering rules from these data. The data that do exist suggest that actors do **not** tend to occupy consistent positions when paired with other elements. Overall, actors are just as likely to occur in the first position in a two-sign phrase as in the second position. David produced 17 actor-first phrases versus 21 actor-second phrases; comparable figures for Kathy, Chris, Dennis, and Donald are respectively, 3 versus 4, 0 versus 3, 3 versus 1, and 3 versus 1. Although suggestive of nonorder, these data do not definitively decide the issue of actor ordering. This issue is taken up again in the next section, where the deaf child's actor category is reanalyzed.

Organizational Structure

Syntax can be defined as the principles of arrangement of word units in sentences; syntactic devices are then those devices which serve to produce these surface arrangements (Lyons, 1971; Gleason, 1961). The surface regularities of English, for example, are partially produced by two common syntactic devices: word order (e.g., *Jim hit Jules*, where the position preceding the verb often, but not always, marks the actor and the position following the verb tends to mark the patient), and prepositions (e.g., *I went to the store* where *to* marks the recipient role).

One important function of syntactic devices in natural adult languages is to distinguish among the various roles nouns can play in sentences. In the above example of a transitive sentence, the word order device distinguishes the actor role of the first noun (*Jim*) from the patient role of the second noun (*Jules*). When two nouns are present in the surface form of a sentence, as is generally the situation in transitive sentences, it is particularly important that the two noun roles be distinguishable on some grounds. When there is only one noun present in the surface form of a sentence, as in intransitive sentences (e.g., *elephants dance*), it is of course less crucial that the actor role of the single noun be marked.

In general, natural languages can be classified according to how they mark the single noun role (actor) of intransitive sentences with respect to the two noun roles (actor and patient) of transitive sentences. Specifically, certain languages, called ergative languages, mark intransitive actors like transitive patients, and mark transitive actors differently from both. In contrast, accusative languages mark intransitive actors like transitive actors, and mark patients differently from both (Fillmore, 1968).

It was shown in the previous section that, like natural languages, the deaf children's communication system has at least two syntactic devices that produce surface regularities: (1) production probability, which determines the likelihood of a case appearing in the surface level of a phrase, and (2) sign order, which determines the position of a case in the surface level of a phrase. In the next sections, it will be shown that the deaf subjects' communication system uses its two syntactic devices to mark the intransitive actor like the patient and to mark the transitive actor differently from both. Thus, the deaf children's sign system is ergative.

ERGATIVE VERSUS ACCUSATIVE LANGUAGES

To elaborate on the ergative pattern as it is found in natural languages, we may contrast ergative languages with English, a language which has an accusative case marking pattern. The hallmark of the distinction between ergative and accusative languages is the manner in which the intransitive actor is marked. Consider the intransitive phrase *You go to the corner.* In this phrase, the intransitive actor *you*, in some sense, has a double meaning. On the one hand, *you* refers to the **goer**, the **actor**, the **effector** of the going action. On the other hand, the *you* refers to the **gone**, the **patient**, the **affectee** of the going action. At the end of the action, *you* both *have gone* and *are gone*, and the decision to emphasize one aspect of the actor's condition over the other is somewhat arbitrary.

In English, we choose to emphasize the effector properties of the intransitive actor by marking it like other effectors. For example, the intransitive actor "you" in *You go to the corner* is marked just like the transitive actor "you" in *You eat grapes.* That is, both actors precede the verb. In contrast, ergative languages emphasize the **affectee** properties of the intransitive actor by marking it like other affectees (i.e., patients). Thus, the intransitive actor of a going relation (you) is marked just like the transitive patient of an eating relation (grapes). An English sentence following an ergative pattern might be, *Go you to the corner,* in which the "you" actually does seem to have an affected rather than effecting sense.

In sum, accusative languages highlight the effector properties of the intransitive actor by grouping it with transitive actors, while ergative languages highlight the affectee properties of the intransitive actor by grouping it with transitive patients. Below we provide evidence of ergativity in the deaf child's system by showing how the child's two syntactic devices, production probability and sign order, are each used to create an ergative case-marking pattern.

PRODUCTION PROBABILITIES

We have already characterized the patient as a case which is likely to be signed in a phrase, and the actor as a case **unlikely** to be signed. The next step is to reanalyze the actor case to determine production probabilities for intransitive actors versus transitive actors. Since it has previously been shown that production probabilities are not independent of underlying structure, we must select phrases which have similar underlying structures to compare production probabilities for the cases in question. Both transform and transport relations have two-case underlying structures and are therefore ideal for comparison. Recall that the transform relation permits actor, act, and patient elements (e.g., *he eats apples*); this relation is transitive. The transport relation permits actor, act, and recipient elements (e.g., *he goes there*) and is intransitive. Now we can compare production probabilities for the actor and patient cases in these two relation types.

If the deaf child's system were accusative, the production probabilities for both the intransitive and the transitive actor should be similar to each other, and should differ from the production probability for the patient. Alternatively, if the deaf child's system were ergative, the production probabilities for the intransitive actor and for the patient should be similar; moreover, this production probability should differ from the production probability for the transitive actor.

Table 3.9 presents the data. It is apparent that these deaf children marked intransitive actors like patients, and not like transitive actors, with respect to production probability. That is, the children were as likely to sign

TABLE 3.9 Actor and Patient Production Probabilities in Two-Case Relation Phrases (Transform and Transport)[a]

	Transitive actor	Intransitive actor	Patient
David	.28(88)[b]	.80(35)	.83(88)
Donald	.10(29)	.75(8)	.90(29)
Dennis	.20(10)	1.00(1)	1.00(10)
Chris	.00(7)	1.00(1)	1.00(7)
Kathy	.44(9)	.67(3)	.77(9)
Tracy	.30(13)	1.00(2)	.85(13)

[a] The data base for this analysis includes action phrases in which two elements are explicitly signed.

[b] The numbers in parentheses represent the total number of phrases with two-case underlying structures that permit transitive and intransitive actors and patients.

the intransitive actor case as they were to sign the patient case in their two-element phrases. In contrast, all of the six children were likely to omit the transitive actor case. Thus, the "you" in *You go to the corner* would be just as likely to be signed as the "grape" in *You eat grapes*; and both would be much more likely to be signed than the "you" in *You eat grapes*. With respect to production probability, then, the deaf children's system appears to emphasize the affectee (and not the effector) properties of the intransitive actor. That is, the system is ergative.[22]

SIGN ORDER

According to the ordering rule which describes the deaf children's phrases, the patient case tends to appear in the first position of two-sign phrases containing patients, acts, and recipients. Recall that there was no particular consistent ordering for actors. We now reanalyze the actor data to determine if there are consistent ordering tendencies for intransitive actors that are distinct from orderings for transitive actors.

According to the ergative hypothesis, if there are any ordering tendencies, intransitive actors should resemble patients and occupy first position,[23] whereas transitive actors should differ and, presumably, occupy second position. The fact that the deaf children produced very few actor phrases makes this analysis particularly tentative. Only David produced a sufficient number of actor phrases to be analyzed in this way. As predicted, David tended to sign intransitive actors in first position (10 phrases with the intransitive actor in first position versus 5 with the intransitive actor in second position) and transitive actors in second position (16 phrases with

[22] The fact that actor production probability differs in the two two-case relation phrases (transport and transform) raises the possibility that transport and transform relations should not both be described as having two-case underlying structures. However, the act predicate, hypothesized to be permissible in the underlying structure of both relations, was just as likely to occur in transport phrases (production probability = .88, analyzed over instances for all six children) as it was in transform phrases (.87). This similarity in production probability across the two types of relations is exactly what would be predicted if we assigned the same two-case underlying structure to each of the two relation types. Allowing this interpretation of transport and transform relations, the production probability data taken as a whole then suggest that the deaf child, in effect, has two different types of actors, transitive actors and intransitive actors. It is important to note that the original claim that surface structure varies systematically with underlying structure still holds even if the production probabilities for transitive and intransitive actors are considered separately. In particular, for transitive actors, production probability in three-case phrases was lower (.06) than production probability in two-case transform phrases (.21). For intransitive actors, production probability in two-case transport phrases was lower (.80) than production probability in one-case phrases (1.00).

[23] Note that intransitive actors and patients can never occur in the same phrase (e.g., one cannot say *I slept the apple*). Thus, both intransitive actors and patients could always occupy first position without conflicting with one another.

the transitive actor in second position versus 7 with the transitive actor in first position) (Fisher exact probability = .05). Thus, David would tend first to point at the actor, (you) and then sign *GO* (i.e., *you–GO*) in conveying *You go to the corner*, just as he would tend first to point at the grape before signing EAT (i.e., *grape–EAT*) in conveying *You eat grapes*. In contrast, David would be likely first to sign EAT and then point at the actor (you) (i.e., *EAT–you*) in conveying *You eat grapes*. These ordering differences suggest ergativity, especially as they tend to confirm the production probability data. Intransitive actors follow the same ordering tendency as patients, whereas transitive actors follow their own distinct ordering tendency.

In sum, the deaf children have developed syntactic techniques (i.e., production probabilities and sign orders) that mark, and therefore structure, a relationship among intransitive actors, transitive actors, and patients. Moreover, the children have structured this particular relationship in precisely the same way as some natural languages do (i.e., as in ergative languages, intransitive actors are syntactically marked like patients, and not like transitive actors).

Summary: A Patient-Based System

Structure in the deaf child's communication system has been described on four different levels. We now show that these structures taken together as a whole present a coherent picture of the deaf child's communication system. In particular, many aspects of the system described in previous sections appear to center around the patient role. The following facts about the deaf children's communication system demonstrate that the system is "patient-based."

Content. The deaf children conveyed transitive relations, that is, relations permitting the patient case, earlier in development than intransitive relations (relations excluding the patient). Thus, in terms of what they communicate, the children sign about actions on objects (or patients) before they sign about actions which involve no objects.

Production probability. The patient case had the highest conditional production probability of all of the elements in the deaf child's system. Thus, whenever the patient case could potentially be signed (which was quite often, since transitive relations were so frequent), the patient was very likely to be signed.

Ordering rules. The deaf children tended to sign the patient case in first position of their two-sign phrases. If "coming first" reflects psychological importance, as it might at this age, the patient case once again assumed a primary role.

Case grouping. The deaf children syntactically marked the intransitive actor like a patient, not like a transitive actor. Since a priori the intransitive actor can reasonably be categorized with either the transitive actor or with the patient, this demonstrated preference of the deaf child further substantiates the predominance of the patient case in his language system.

In sum, the relational concept "patient" appears to assume importance in many facets of the deaf child's communication system.

DISCUSSION

We have discovered that deaf children of hearing parents, though essentially deprived of all standardized linguistic input, can spontaneously develop a gestural communication system. Analysis reveals that the deaf child's communication system is language-like in many respects. Thus, our data suggest that a system which has language-like properties can be developed by a child under relatively impoverished language learning conditions.

We turn next to the demonstration that the deaf child's ability to create a communication system is in many ways comparable to the hearing child's ability to acquire spoken language from a linguistic model. In order to argue that data on the deaf child bear on the question of how the hearing child normally acquires language, both parallel structures and parallel development must be shown.

Comparison to the Acquisition of Conventional Languages

SEMANTIC CONTENT: ACTION AND ATTRIBUTE RELATIONS

Bloom, Lightbown, and Hood (1975) have reported that young hearing children learning English convey both action and attribute relations early in speech development, and furthermore that they convey action phrases earlier in development than attribute phrases. There is, in fact, widespread agreement that children learning conventional languages talk about both action and attribute relations early in development (Brown, 1973; Bowerman, 1973). Even children learning a conventional manual language (American Sign Language) appear to express both action and attribute relations early in their linguistic development (Newport & Ashbrook, 1977).

Bloom *et al.* have also shown that the hearing children in their study produced types of action relations that turn out to be comparable to our deaf children's action relation types. The hearing children produced transitive and intransitive locative action phrases (comparable to the deaf child's transfer and transport relations, respectively) and transitive and intransitive action phrases (comparable to the deaf child's transform and perform relations, respectively). However, Bloom *et al.* did not find, as was found with the deaf children, that the hearing children developed transitive relations prior to intransitive relations. In fact, there is no mention at all of a developmental difference between transitive and intransitive relations in any of the hearing child language literature. We return to this difference between the deaf and hearing groups in a later section.

Finally, there is great similarity between the deaf subject's and the hearing child's semantic elements. In particular, in the early stages of development, the hearing child produces words for both verbs and adjectives (Brown, 1973; Bloom, 1970), comparable to deaf subjects' signs for act and attribute predicates, respectively. Moreover, the hearing child frequently produces words for the patient, recipient, and actor cases (Brown, 1973) just as deaf subjects often produce signs for these cases. The similarities even extend to omissions: The hearing child infrequently produces words for the place case, or for the benefactive case (e.g., *I made the cake for her*), just as deaf children also infrequently produce signs for cases such as these. Thus, in terms of the content of communications, the hearing child and deaf subjects have much in common.

UNDERLYING STRUCTURE

There have been several different accounts of underlying structure in the literature of the hearing child's language acquisition. Antinucci and Parisi (1973) suggest that their hearing subject (Claudia) possesses underlying representations that are more complex than her surface forms. They attempt to demonstrate, through a simple prompting technique, that the various underlying elements of a particular relation can be brought to the surface. For example:

> Claudia: *Doll.*
> Mother: *What are you giving the doll?*
> Claudia: *Cookie.*

The child first mentions the recipient case and after prompting mentions the patient case. Similarly, in the next example, the child first mentions the act predicate, and then the act plus the recipient case:

> Claudia: *Give.*
> Mother: *Who to, to the doll or to Claudia?*
> Claudia: *Give Claudia.*

However, as Schlesinger (1974) and Braine (1976), among others, point out, these data do not convincingly argue for underlying structure. Claudia could well be attending to only one aspect of the situation at a time; her verbalization would then reflect only the aspect to which she is attending (i.e., the salient aspect) and not to the entire set of aspects which make up the relation. Prompting might merely prod the child to change the focus of her attention, and consequently, her verbalizations to another (and for her, not necessarily concurrent) aspect of the situation. Thus, prompting data such as these can never provide strong evidence that, for the purposes of communication, the child simultaneously considers all of the aspects of the relation (e.g., *mother–give–cookie–Claudia*) as part of a unified underlying structure.

However, more convincing evidence for underlying structure in the hearing child's oral language development is found in Bloom (1970) and Bloom, Miller, and Hood (1974). Bloom *et al.* (1974) show, through statistical analyses, that the constituents (or semantic elements in our terms) that appear in the surface forms of their children's utterances are not randomly selected. Rather, there appears to be systematic variation among the surface constituents. Furthermore, the analyses presented in Bloom (1970) suggest that at least some of this systematic variation is accounted for by underlying structure.

Bloom (1970) imputes to her hearing subjects an underlying structure that includes items that are not expressed in the children's surface forms. As evidence for this claim, Bloom notes that the hypothesized underlying items that are deleted from the surface forms of certain utterances did appear in the surface forms of other utterances at the same moment in development. When these items were missing from surface structure, they were missing because of an output constraint on the child's utterances (a maximum length, all of Bloom's subjects being at the "two-word" stage). For example, even though subject noun phrases appeared in the surface forms of the affirmative sentences uttered by these children, for example *mommy sock*, subject noun phrases did not appear in the children's negative sentences (which include the extra word *no* or *not*). Since the inclusion of the negative in a sentence involves producing one extra morpheme, one of the other underlying elements (e.g., the subject or the object of the sentence) must be deleted to reduce the sentence to the required length. The thrust of this argument is that the existence of underlying elements in the hearing child's language explains, at least to some extent, the regularities of their surface structure.

Further evidence for underlying structure in hearing children comes from reanalyzing these data in terms of the framework used to describe the deaf child's spontaneous sign system. Indeed, using our techniques we find

**TABLE 3.10 Patient and Act Production Probabilities in Phrases
Produced by Four Hearing Children**[a]

	Patient[b]		Act[c]	
	Three-case relations	Two-case relations	Three-case relations	Two-case relations
Gia	.68(88)[d]	.74(334)	.78(88)	.88(456)
Peter	.55(83)	.90(311)	.82(83)	.99(401)
Eric	.52(69)	.87(218)	.87(69)	.97(400)
Kathryn	.89(152)	.87(447)	.83(152)	.97(656)

[a] The data for this analysis are from Bloom *et al.* 1974 (from Table 5 for Gia II through VI; Table 7 for Peter IV through IX; Table 4 for Eric II through VI; and Table 6 for Kathryn I through IV).

[b] Termed *object* in Bloom *et al.* (1974).

[c] Termed *verb* in Bloom *et al.* (1974).

[d] The numbers in parentheses represent the total number of two-element (or two-constituent, in Bloom *et al.*'s terms) phrases with three-case and two-case underlying structures that permit either patient or act elements produced by each child throughout the study.

that the hearing child not only produces phrases with underlying structures, but he also shares particular underlying structures with deaf children.

Table 3.10 displays the data (from Bloom *et al.*, 1974) pertinent to this point. From it we can readily infer that the hearing children appear to have both three-case and two-case underlying structures.[24] The argument for the existence of these structures in the hearing child runs precisely parallel to that for the deaf child: The children studied by Bloom *et al.* were less likely to produce patients and acts in phrases with three-case underlying structures than in phrases with two-case underlying structure.[25] These findings are borne out in three of the four hearing children for the patient case (for the fourth child, the production probabilities are the same for both structures) and in four out of four children for the act predicate. Thus, by positing three-case and two-case underlying structures, we are able to explain, at least in part, the hearing child's patient and act production probabilities, just as for the deaf child.

SURFACE STRUCTURE: ORDERING RULES

Sign order was a predominant syntactic device used by the deaf children to convey their semantic relations. Word order seems to be a predominant

[24] Intransitive phrases (Agent–Action) that could have had one-case underlying structures were not included in the analyses presented in the Bloom *et al.* (1974).

[25] In Bloom *et al.*'s terminology, phrases with three-case underlying structure are agent–locative action–object–place phrases (comparable to our transfer phrases); their phrases with two-case underlying structure are agent–action–object phrases (comparable to our transform phrases) and mover–locative action–place and patient–locative action–place phrases (comparable to our transport phrases).

syntactic device used by hearing children to convey semantic relations early in their linguistic development. Other devices, for example inflectional endings or prepositions, are generally unavailable to the hearing child at this age.[26] The generality of this word order phenomenon in hearing children has led Slobin (1973) to postulate that a language-acquiring child is equipped with an elementary operating principle: Pay attention to the order of words and morphemes in the model language. Slobin might argue that Bloom's subjects (1970) tend to order actors before patients (e.g., *mommy sock*, where mommy is putting on the child's sock) precisely because, in English, actors tend to precede patients.

Obviously, our deaf population, lacking a conventional linguistic model, cannot avail itself of this hypothetical operating principle. It is striking that order exists in their phrases nevertheless. This finding suggests that the use of order as a syntactic device is an active strategy on the part of the child, with or without a linguistic model. Of course, when exposed to a linguistic model, a child will ultimately adopt a particular order influenced not only by his own inherent ordering strategy, but also by the particular orders found in the adult language which surrounds him. We take up this issue again in the following sections.

SURFACE STRUCTURE: CASE MARKING PATTERNS

Recall that the deaf subjects marked patients and intransitive actors alike in terms of ordering rules as well as production probabilities. Specifically, both patients and intransitive actors tended to occur in first position of two-sign phrases, and also tended to be explicitly signed whenever possible. These characteristics led us to label their spontaneous system as ergative. What can be said of the case marking patterns of young hearing children? Ultimately hearing children acquire the case marking patterns of their language models; that is, they eventually produce either an ergative or an accusative pattern depending upon which occurs in the adult tongue that surrounds them. But what of developmental stages along the way?

Following Slobin's operating principle, the hearing child's ordering rules for patients and actors should follow adult models, even from the earliest stages. Thus, the hearing child learning English, an accusative language, ought to group intransitive actors with transitive actors, at least with respect to ordering rules. The data on children learning English suggest that this is so: Both intransitive and transitive actors tend to precede the verb, in

---

[26] The issue has been raised that not **all** children may follow word-order rules in their early phrases (Brown, 1973; Bowerman, 1973). Further, there is some doubt that all those children who do use order have order rules based on the **same** categories (Braine, 1976). However, most of the data suggest that most children use word order to convey semantic relations most of the time.

contrast to the position of the patient case which tends to follow the verb (Braine, 1976; Bloom, 1970).

Although it is likely that the young child's **ordering** patterns are dictated by his linguistic model, it is far less reasonable to suppose that case **production probability** patterns are modeled in the same way. Case production probability, after all, is a phenomenon which is inherently dependent upon the young child's apparent length limitation. At early stages, children appear to be forced to choose between explicitly saying the patient or the actor, precisely because the child at this stage is limited to a two- or three-word sentence length. Adults, of course, have no such length constraints on their utterances, and even speakers of Motherese do not produce such abbreviated utterances as *mommy sock*.[27]

From these considerations, the young child might be predicted to be less influenced by his adult linguistic model in production probability patterns than in ordering patterns. The data, in fact, confirm this hypothesis. Young English learners, like deaf children and unlike adult English speakers, tend to group intransitive actors with patients with respect to production probabilities. Table 3.11 presents a reanalysis of the data presented in Bloom *et al.* (1974) for young speakers acquiring English at the two-word stage.[28] The patient (or object in Bloom *et al.*'s terminology) was as likely to be explicitly mentioned as the intransitive actor (or mover, or patient).[29] Furthermore, the transitive actor (or agent) was much less likely to be explicitly spoken than either the patient or the two intransitive actor cases.[30]

[27] In fact, English does permit the actor to be omitted in certain sentences, such as imperatives. However, to account for the pattern reported here, we would have to make the unlikely prediction that caretakers are far more likely to produce transitive imperatives (*Eat the peas*) than intransitive imperatives (*Go over there*).

[28] Note that only those phrases with two-case underlying structure are included in this reanalysis. Bloom *et al.*'s Agent-Action-Object phrases are transitive and are comparable to our transform phrases; their Mover-Locative Action-Place and Patient-Locative Action-Place phrases are intransitive and are comparable to our transport phrases.

[29] In Bloom *et al.*'s classification scheme, a patient in Patient-Locative Action-Place relations differs from an object in Agent-Locative Action-Object-Place relations in two ways: 1) patients precede verbs, *lamb go in there*, and objects follow verbs, *Gia away a lamb*; and 2) patients occur with verbs like *go* and *fall*, but objects occur with verbs like *put* and *away*.

[30] As can be seen in Table 3.11, Bloom *et al.* make a distinction between "movers" and "patients" in two-case transport relations: A mover transports itself (e.g., *I go down*) while a patient is transported (e.g., *lamb go in there*). This distinction is based on the experimenters' intuitions about the causes of movement, and may not reflect the child's views. Particularly since three of the four children appear to treat intransitive movers as patients (both transitive and intransitive) in terms of production probability, it might be hypothesized that the child makes no distinction between movers and patients and views movers more as "being affected by movement" than as "effecting" movement. However, Peter's data do not completely fit this ergative pattern (but note that neither do the data fit an accusative pattern). In terms of production probability, Peter appears to treat movers of intransitive relations (*I get down*) like

TABLE 3.11   Actor and Patient Production Probabilities in Two-Case Relation Phrases Produced by Four Hearing Children[a]

	Transitive actor[b]	Intrasitive actor[c]		Transitive patient[d]
Gia	.43(334)[e]	.74(77)	.75(45)	.74(334)
Eric	.14(218)	.89(65)	.67(117)	.87(218)
Kathryn	.17(447)	.50(111)	.70(98)	.87(447)
Peter	.10(311)	.76(34)	.11(56)	.90(311)

[a] The data for this analysis are from Bloom *et al.* (1974); specifically, from Tables 4, 5, 6 and 7.

[b] Termed *agent* in Bloom *et al.* (1974).

[c] The first column is Bloom *et al.*'s *mover*; the second is their *patient.*

[d] Termed *object* in Bloom *et al.* (1974).

[e] The numbers in parentheses represent the total number of two-element phrases with 2-case underlying structures which permit transitive and intransitive actors and patients, produced by each child throughout the study.

The grouping pattern seen in Table 3.11 is exactly what is found in the deaf child's sign phrases: Intransitive actors resemble transitive patients in terms of production probability, and differ from transitive actors.[31] Thus, where the linguistic model does not constrain the child, that is, in case production probabilities, the hearing child learning English seems to have ergative tendencies, as do our deaf subjects. However, where the linguistic model does provide a clear pattern, that is, in ordering rules, the English learning child exhibits the accusative tendencies of his model.

SUMMARY

In sum, the deaf subjects' communication system does indeed resemble that of the hearing child. These similarities at the relational level of analysis are evident despite differences in the two systems at the lexical level of analysis. Recall that, as we discussed earlier, the deaf children's signs and the

---

patients of transitive relations (*open drawer*), but not like patients of intransitive relations (*lamb go in there*).

[31] The data in Bloom *et al.* (1974) resemble our data on actor production: Their subjects were more likely to omit the actor than any other case. On the other hand, the data in Brown (1973), Bowerman (1973) and Braine (1976) appear on the surface to contradict our findings: The subjects they describe produce a large number of actor–act phrases. However, recall that the actor is expected to be frequent in intransitive relation phrases. Thus, these data do not necessarily mean that the actor has a high priority for these children, if their actor–act phrases are primarily intransitive. Bloom *et al.* have reanalyzed Bowerman's data and found that many of the actor–act phrases she reported are, in fact, intransitive. Moreover, may of the phrases reported by Braine also appear to be intransitive, although additional context is needed to make decisions about several of the phrases. Thus, the low priority of the actor may be a more general phenomenon than it appears at first analysis.

hearing child's words differ in terms of the referential information each conveys. Specifically, the deaf children's deictic pointing is "location-specific" and therefore differs from the hearing child's noun; moreover, the deaf children's characterizing sign is iconic and, in this respect, different from the hearing child's verb. In addition, the criteria for lexical meaning assignment differ in this study and in studies of hearing children: This study relies on sign form; child language researchers typically rely on the word's function in adult grammar.

Nevertheless, despite these differences in the criteria for lexical meaning assignment and in the nature of lexical items themselves, the same topics are conveyed and the same formal classes of structure convey them in both the deaf and hearing children's communication systems. Both systems have underlying structures, production probability syntactic devices, and sign order syntactic devices. Moreover, within each of these formal classes of structure, the deaf and hearing children have certain substantive structures in common. Both children's systems have the same particular configurations underlying the surface forms of their phrases (i.e., three-case, two-case underlying structures). In both systems the production probability syntactic device produces patient-based case markings. Interestingly, the one difference in substantive structures between the two systems is found in ordering rules: The deaf child without a conventional linguistic model has a patient-based ordering rule; the hearing child follows the ordering rules of his linguistic model, be they patient-based or not.

Data from our deaf children suggest that a child's early communication system, when uncontaminated by a conventional linguistic environment, will be patient-based: Both ordering rules and production probabilities give priority to the patient case over other cases. A linguistic model, when available, may override the patient-based ordering tendencies of the child with its own ordering regularities. However, when no guide is offered by the linguistic environment, as is the situation for production probability patterns, the patient-based tendencies of the child emerge with or without a conventional language model.

The similarities between the deaf children's and the hearing child's systems are of interest primarily because they suggest that the data from our deaf children may be relevant to questions of the processes and factors involved in normal language acquisition. The deaf children in and of themselves are of particular interest to acquisition questions because they appear to be developing a language-like system without the benefit of a conventional linguistic model. Because the nature of deaf children's input is central to any inferences about language acquisition drawn from this study, we turn next to the issue of input to the deaf children.

The Deaf Child's Sign Environment

Deaf children were included in this study only if they could not acquire oral language naturally and if they had no exposure to a conventional sign language. Thus, the sign system created by these subjects was developed without the benefit of such conventional systems. However, it is possible that the subjects' parents communicated with their children by unconsciously creating their own sign system (unconsciously, because the subjects' parents were committed to oral education) that was then imitated by our subjects. In fact, some mothers of the subjects did use gestures with their children. To determine whether the children or their caretakers first developed the system described here, we transcribed the gestures produced by the mothers of two of the subjects during the first four interviews. The same coding procedures were used for the mothers' gestures as for the children's and mother was compared to child in lexicon and sign phrases.

Lexicon. There were no obvious differences between mother and child in their tendencies to point to objects. Since pointing is common in all mother-child interactions, subjects may very well have learned to point from those around him. But deictic pointing is only a subset of the lexicon of this system. More revealing comparisons between mother and child emerge when characterizing signs and sign phrases are examined.

Both mothers produced some characterizing signs; over the course of four sessions they produced as many different types of characterizing signs as their children (see Table 3.12, Column 1). However, as can also be seen in the table, mother and child did not appear to have developed the same characterizing lexicon: only 25% of the characterizing signs produced by mother and child were common to both. Further evidence for the child's ability to develop characterizing signs on his own comes from the fact that the children invented iconic signs for stimulus toys and actions they had not previously seen.

TABLE 3.12 Mother–Child Comparison of Number of Characterizing Signs Produced during Sessions I–IV

				Tokens[b]			
	Types[a]			Alone		In phrases	
Subject	Child	Mother	In common	Child	Mother	Child	Mother
David	56	54	18	107	90	47	9
Dennis	25	23	5	50	58	18	3

[a] Number of different characterizing signs.
[b] Number of occurrences across types.

Sign phrases. The mothers also produced sign phrases conveying semantic relations, but they produced fewer such phrases than their children. Over the course of the four sessions under consideration, David and Dennis produced 127 and 42 such phrases, respectively, while their mothers produced only 43 and 13, respectively (see Table 3.13). Furthermore, the mothers began producing sign phrases at some time later than their children did. Both children produced a number of these sign phrases in Session I. But David's mother produced only 3 such phrases in Session I (compared to David's 27), and Dennis's mother did not begin production at all until Session II. Thus, there is no evidence that the children learned to produce sign phrases to express semantic relations by imitating their mothers' signs and there is some evidence to suggest that the children developed their sign phrases independently.

Finally, the children were more likely to integrate their characterizing signs into their sign phrases than were their mothers. The mothers produced as many characterizing signs in one-sign phrases as their children, but far fewer characterizing signs in multi-sign phrases (see Table 3.12, Columns 2 and 3). Consequently, these data suggest that the children did not learn to integrate their characterizing signs into their phrases by imitating their mothers' productions.

In general, the mothers' gestures were less explicit than their children's. For example, one of the deaf subjects might point to his sneakers and then to the stairs when he wants his sneakers put on the stairs. In contrast, his mother would be more likely to tilt the sneakers themselves toward the stairs in a global gesture incorporating the object. Thus, the mother–child comparison data now available suggest that the deaf child's system is certainly different from, and is possibly more advanced than, his mother's gestures. The data might be taken to suggest that, if anything, the mother is learning the sign system from her child, and not the reverse.

In sum, our deaf subjects develop their sign systems without the guidance and direction of a conventional language model. Moreover, they also seem to develop the system without the benefit of an ad hoc sign model.

TABLE 3.13 Number of Phrases Per Session Produced by Mother and Child

Session	David		Dennis	
	Child	Mother	Child	Mother
I	27	3	3	0
II	40	6	4	1
III	6	12	18	4
IV	54	22	17	8
Total	127	43	42	13

It is certain, in any case, that they develop such a system without the rich linguistic input the hearing child normally receives. Nevertheless, the deaf subjects' and the hearing child's communication systems are remarkably similar. We focus now on the implications of these similarities.

The Noneffects and Effects of Linguistic Input on Language Development

Analyses and comparisons up to this point support the following generalization: with or without a conventional language model, in words or in signs, children during the early stages of language acquisition communicate about the same conversational topics and use the same formal devices to structure these communications. We now discuss this generalization and whether or not such a generalization can be applied to the later stages of language development, first in terms of the semantics of communications, and then in terms of the formal structure of these communications.

SEMANTICS OF COMMUNICATIONS

As we might have expected, the young language-acquiring child does not appear to need a conventional language model to guide him in his choice of conversational topics. The young child, hearing or deaf, converses about attribute relations and several types of action relations (actions with and without effects on an object, actions with and without movement toward a new location). Moreover, in conversing about action relations, the young child signs or speaks explicitly about the central figures in these action relations; that is, those who act (actors), those who are acted upon (patients), and those who are acted toward (recipients). On the other hand, at this same moment in development, the child refrains from explicitly mentioning what are assumed to be the less central components of action relations, for example, the time and place of an action, the benefactor of an action, the instrument of an action, and the like.

Our results here receive support from those in the literature on linguistic environment. By correlating mother speech at time I with child acquisition rate from time I to time II, Newport *et al.* (1977) show that the development of basic propositional structure (specifically, the number of true verbs and noun phrases incorporated into each sentence) appears to proceed independently of variations in linguistic input. These aspects of propositional structure, which Newport *et al.* hypothesize to be insensitive to variations in linguistic environment, are found in the deaf subjects' signs (in semantic predicates and cases) and are developed without a linguistic environment. Taken together, these findings suggest that the semantic structure of early language appears to be due to predispositions of the child (most likely, predispositions to encode linguistically what he knows best), rather than to variations in the linguistic environment.

Although the basic semantic structure of communications appears relatively impervious to variations in linguistic input at the early stages of language development, it is not unreasonable to suppose that semantic structure becomes more sensitive to variations in linguistic input as language learning proceeds. Thus, we might reasonably expect certain gaps in semantics as our deaf subjects grow older. In fact, there is already some evidence that the deaf subjects' lack of a conventional language model has had effects on the semantics of their communications. Recall that there was a developmental delay in the appearance of intransitive relations (that is, actions without objects) in the deaf children's sign system. A comparable delay is not reported for the hearing child learning a conventional spoken language (Bloom *et al.*, 1975; Goldin-Meadow, Seligman, & Gelman, 1976), nor for the deaf child learning a conventional sign language (Newport & Ashbrook, 1977). We suggest that our deaf subjects' relatively late acquisition of intransitive relation phrases is due to the fact that intransitive signs are difficult to create in a manual modality. We recall that the subjects must create signs because they lack conventional linguistic input; they must create manual signs because they are deaf.

To elaborate on this hypothesis, in order to create a sign for the transitive act "hit," all the child need do is, literally, "pull back" from the object of the hitting action and perform the action in vacuo, removed from the object. Thus, in the HIT sign (closed fist swatted in air), the child's hand need represent nothing more than his hand pretending to act on an object. In contrast, to create a sign for the intransitive act "walk," the child can do either of two things: He can use his hand metaphorically, that is, his rhythmically moving fingers can stand for walking legs; or he can create a whole-body sign, for example, wiggle his entire body to simulate walking.

Impediments to both these inventions are readily apparent. In the first instance, the ability to allow the hand or fingers to stand for the walker, runner, or jumper, or other actors undoubtedly requires more cognitive sophistication than allowing the hand simply to represent the hand, as it would do in the iconic gesture for hitting. Alternatively, the clumsy whole-body sign for walking violates certain manual–visual constraints on sign systems—the sign extends beyond the circumscribed area around the face and upper chest where most signing in conventional sign languages occurs (Siple, 1973) and where most of these subjects' signing occurs as well. Thus, both options for inventing intransitive signs in the manual modality appear to have difficulties not found in transitive sign creation. Parenthetically, of the two options, it appears that the second poses fewer problems for the young children in this study, as the children's early intransitive signs were, in fact, whole-body signs (e.g., *WALK* = feet walk in place).

To summarize this hypothesis, the deaf child's semantics of communications may be affected by the absence of linguistic input simply because an absent input forces the child to invent symbols on his own. As pointed out in the preceding paragraph, this symbol creation process, which is carried out by the deaf child in the manual modality, may be particularly difficult to execute for intransitive relations.[32] Thus, at this point in the deaf subjects' development, the absence of linguistic input appears to have had some effect, albeit small (only a slight delay in the onset of one relation type), on the semantics of his communications.

THE FORMAL STRUCTURE OF COMMUNICATIONS

Not unexpectedly, the early stages of semantic development turned out to be essentially independent of variations in conventional linguistic input. It is rather more surprising to discover that the early development of a structured representation of these semantic contents is also independent of variations in conventional linguistic input. With or without a conventional language, the young child, hearing or deaf, uses formal devices to structure his communications. In particular, at the early stages of language development, both groups of children use at least two syntactic means—ordering devices and production probability devices—to structure the surface forms of their systems. Moreover, the underlying meanings of the child's early communications are also structured, and it is this structure that is systematically related to the surface features of the child's system (specifically, to the production probabilities of semantic elements). Thus, even without a conventional structured input, the child will produce a structured output in order to communicate.

Up to this point the role of linguistic input has been characterized negatively: A child need not be exposed to a conventional language model in order to develop a structured communication system. But what if the child is exposed to a conventional language model? What role does this

---

[32] An alternative hypothesis to account for the absence of intransitive phrases in the deaf children's sign system posits the effect of an absent linguistic input not on the child's ability to convey intransitive relations, but rather on his ability to conceptualize these relations. According to this "Whorfian" hypothesis, deaf subjects would communicate about intransitive relations later than the child learning a conventional language simply because the deaf children, lacking linguistic input, begin to conceive of these notions later than the conventional language learner does. Whichever of the two hypotheses turns out to be correct, the point to be stressed is that the absence of linguistic input does seem to have had some effect on deaf subjects' content of communications.

model then play in the process of language acquisition? Quite clearly, one function of a conventional language model is to shape the substantive rules of the child's language system. A child may come to the language learning situation with, for instance, a tendency to order symbols. But the substantive ordering rules which this child will eventually learn will be the rules of English if he hears English, Japanese if he hears Japanese, and so on.[33] We have shown here that without a conventional linguistic model the child's ordering rules will tend to be patient-based, as will the rest of his communication system. With a model, however, the ordering rules will follow the particular orders provided by that model. Thus, at the very least, conventional language models serve to separate English-speakers from Japanese-speakers from French-speakers, a worthwhile end from the point of view of the Tower of Babel.

There is additional evidence from the literature on linguistic environment that a conventional language model can have a substantial effect on the development of language structures. Newport *et al.* (1977) in their study of the effects of Motherese, have shown that the development of grammatical functors, such as nominal inflections and verb auxiliaries, is sensitive to variations in mother speech. Using a different technique (an enrichment manipulation), Nelson *et al.* (1973) found a similar result: Enriching a child's linguistic environment with expansions and recast sentences produces selected effects on that child's auxiliary growth. It is precisely these inflectional structures for which there is no evidence in our deaf children's signs. It may be that, for the development of these structures, the linguistic environment is absolutely necessary.

We have now outlined a set of linguistic structures whose acquisition appears to require a linguistic environment and a second set of structures whose acquisition appears independent of a linguistic environment. There may indeed be a middle ground. Some of the language structures whose invention is spontaneous at the early stages of language development may eventually lag in complexity behind those structures developed by children

---

[33] With no language model to provide conventional linguistic regularities, the deaf children must clearly find their ordering regularities elsewhere. One possibility is that they induce their sign orders from the manual modality. For example, the deaf child may induce his patient–recipient sign ordering tendency from his motoric acts on the world. If the child wishes to transfer an object from one location to another, he must first situate the object and then move it to its new location; in other words, the **object** (or patient) occurs before the **location** (or recipient) in the child's manual motor action patterns. McNeill (1974) has argued that motor action schemas of this sort play an important role in organizing a child's phrases even when that child communicates orally and has a language model. He maintains that the structure of the action schemas through which the young child represents his world gives structure to the utterances which the child uses to describe this world.

exposed to linguistic input. Such structures are not yet identified, but as it is unreasonable in the extreme to expect each deaf child on his own to create a language as sophisticated as American Sign Language, these deficiencies will surely appear. When they do, the opportunities for analysis of the cognitive–linguistic interface will become readily apparent.

SUMMARY AND CONCLUSIONS

The sign system developed by the deaf children in this study resembles other child languages in many respects. This resemblance is of particular interest because it is somewhat unexpected—unexpected because the deaf children had no conventional language models to guide their development, and because, having no conventional adult language to guide analyses, different assumptions were used in classification procedures than are usually made in other child language studies. Thus, when similarities exist in the descriptions of the children's systems, they are found despite our differences in assumptions, and despite the children's differences in language model input. The fact that the results have countered initial expectations has implications for studies and theories of language acquisition, implications that are summarized as follows.

Descriptive Categories

Since the methods of the study of language acquisition are for the most part interpretive, requiring inferences from both nonlinguistic and linguistic data (e.g., Bloom's method of rich interpretation), researchers are always open to the claim that descriptions of child language describe structure in the adult experimenter's head, not structure in the child's head. Although the results presented here cannot refute this claim, they make the claim less likely. In particular, we have changed some of the ground rules of the descriptive enterprise by changing some of the assumptions underlying classification procedures, yet the outcome of the enterprise remained unchanged. This consistency of description despite inconsistency of method lends validity to child language description in general, and validity to these descriptions in particular.

One outcome of this study, then, is the confirmation of certain descriptive findings already in the child language literature, as well as the introduction of new findings that can be explored more generally in child language studies. Specifically, these results support the use of a semantic analysis (with units such as relation types, cases, predicates, and the like) to describe child language. With respect to surface structure, we have found supporting evidence for syntactic ordering rules; moreover, we have found evidence for an additional syntactic marking device, production probability. With respect to underlying structure, the results support those previous studies that posited underlying structures in child language. The primary contribution of this study has been to suggest that patterns of the surface marking device (production probability) can be used as evidence for the existence of particular underlying structures. From an analysis of these data, we suggest that certain notions that underlie phrases (e.g., transfer, transform, transport, perform) appear to have a greater linguistic (and perhaps more generally cognitive) reality than was heretofore recognized. Finally, we have suggested that case markings (e.g., surface order markings, production probability markings) can be considered at a broader level to determine if children use their syntactic marking devices to systematically group cases according to particular patterns (e.g., accusative or ergative patterns).

The Flexible Process and Constrained Output of Language Learning

The fact that our deaf subjects had no conventional language yet still developed a language-like system allows some conjectures about the nature of language learning. Language learning is a flexible process with respect to linguistic input; that is, under widely varying input conditions, language acquisition still proceeds. There is evidence from other studies that language learning is flexible with respect to internal factors as well. For example, Lenneberg (1967) found that the order of acquisition of certain syntactic structures is the same, though slower, for feeble minded children as it is for normal children and that the language learning capacity early in life survives radical pathologies, such as organic damage to the speech centers in the brain. Thus, language learning appears to be relatively indifferent to individual differences in intelligence and relatively immune to early pathology. Indeed, to date few conditions, either external or internal, have been conclusively shown to be crucial for the learning of language.

This study has added to the evidence that the process of language acquisition is flexible with respect to certain environmental conditions. However, at the same time it calls attention to the fact that the output of this flexible process is remarkably constrained: All children, under vastly varying conditions, acquire the same formal language system during the early stages. Why should there be such consistency? The puzzle of language acquisition has been considered by some theorists (e.g., Chomsky, 1965; Fodor, Bever, & Garrett, 1974) to center around exactly this issue. Even if present, linguistic input, no matter how neat or messy, under-determines the child's output. That is, the language samples that the child hears support a very large number of different generalizations about the language that the child is acquiring. What then narrows down the field of possible generalizations for the child?

It may not be unreasonable to suppose that the child, hearing or deaf, brings to the language learning situation certain predispositions that narrow down the field of potential languages to be acquired. These predispositions need not be mysterious, particularly in the early stages of language acquisition. For example, the fact that the child has four semantic elements in the underlying structure of his phrases when he begins to talk or sign about transfer relations could merely reflect that child's four-part organization of transferrals (i.e., the giver, the given, the given-to, the giving-act) apart from language. Similarly, the child's low actor production probability might be an outgrowth of the child's own view of the communication setting. The child might think, as Greenfield and Smith (1976) have suggested, that the actor is more obvious from the context than the object acted upon (the patient), and therefore, for communicative economy, the child would be less likely to explicitly mention that actor in his here-and-now type of conversations. Of course, as underlying structure becomes less transparently related to surface structure, as in adult grammars, there may be less cause to attribute cognitive or social underpinnings such as these to language structures.

Whatever the explanations of the substantive structures constituting human language, the fact of structured early communication without structured conventional linguistic input is clearly demonstrated here. Even under adverse circumstances, the human child has the natural inclination and the capacity to develop a structured communication system. It is this capacity to make do under less than perfect conditions that allows us to conclude that humans are prepared for language learning, even when their linguistic environments are not prepared for them.

ACKNOWLEDGMENTS

I thank Heidi Feldman, Rochel Gelman, Henry Gleitman, Lila Gleitman, Janellen Huttenlocher, William Meadow, and Elissa Newport for their clarifying thoughts on nascent sign languages. Thanks also go to Rosalind Charney, Louise Cherry, and Martha McClintock for reading earlier versions of this manuscript, to Lisette Tefo, Barbara Gray, and Lorraine Stepneski for their help in transcribing videotapes, and to the children in the study and their families for their continued cooperation and friendship.

APPENDIX A: NUMBER OF PHRASES PRODUCED BY EACH CHILD CLASSIFIED ACCORDING TO LENGTH

Child and session	Number of signs per phrase								
	1	2	3	4	5	6	7	8	9+
David									
I	155	31	5						
II	101	40	7			1			
III	49	8							
IV	198	43	11	7	1		1		
V	265	110	45	22	7	6	1	2	3
VI	129	51	12	5	1	1			
VII	260	131	32	23	9	1	3		1
VIII	393	116	52	27	8	5	1	4	2
Total	1550	530	164	87	26	14	6	6	6
Donald									
I	10	2							
II	40	2							
III	6	1							
IV	34	3							
V	44	6							
VI	61	3	2						
VII	24	1							
VIII	128	27	4	2					
IX	288	52	15	2					
X	203	15							
XI	168	39	4	1					
Total	1006	151	25	5					
Kathy									
I	30								
II	64	1							
III	83	8	1						
IV	39	1							
V	72	8							
VI	93	13	4	3					
VII	113	10	1	2		1			
VIII	93	11	6						
IX	85	10	1						
Total	672	62	13	5		1			
Chris									
I	111	13	4	1					
II	129	18	1	1					
III	138	19	4	2					
Total	378	50	9	4					
Dennis									
I	68	3							
II	32	6							
III	118	14	4						
IV	72	17	1						
Total	290	40	5						
Tracy									
I	136	36	6	2					
II	212	31	8	1	1	1			
Total	348	67	14	3	1	1			

APPENDIX B1: DAVID'S ACTION PHRASES PRODUCED DURING SESSIONS I–VIII[34]

Transfer Phrases

PATIENT-ACT

Ib	46	*cookie–GIVE* (she/sister **give cookie** to me/David)[35]
	80	*cards–GIVE* (you/sister **give cards** to me/David)
	82	*GIVE–cards–GIVE* (she/sister **give cards** to me/David)
	167	*object–GIVE–object* (you/sister **give object** to me/David)
IIa	46	*Play-Doh–GIVE* (you/Heidi **give Play-Doh** to me/David)
b	35	*crown–GIVE* (you/sister **give crown** to me/David)
IVb	189	*hat–GIVE* (you/Susan **give hat** to me/David)
Va	74	*toys–PUSHAWAY* (I/David will **pushaway toys** to there)
b	70	*ball–GIVE–ball–GIVE* (you/Susan **give ball** me/David)
	112	*orange–ROLL* (you/Susan **roll orange** to here)
	142	*GIVE–lemon* (you/Susan **give lemon** to me/David)
VIa	142	*toybag–LIFTIN* (you/Grandma **liftin toybag** to carriage)
VIIa	18	*TRANSFER–letter* (I/David **transferred letter** here)
	29	*GIVE–that–GIVE* (you/Heidi **give that** to me/David)

---

[34] The phrases included in this and all the following appendices are organized according to relation type, and according to the explicitly signed semantic elements in the phrases irrespective of sign order.

[35] The transcription conventions used in this and all the following appendices are as follows:

1. Each phrase is identified according to the session number (e.g., I) and the tape reel (e.g., b) in which it occurred, and according to its number in the original transcription (e.g., 46).
2. The example should be read from left to right; the sign that occurs first in the temporal sequence is the first entry on the left.
3. The referents of deictic signs are in lower case italic letters (e.g., *cookie*).
4. Capitalized words (e.g., GIVE) are glosses for the referents of characterizing signs. A description of each sign is found in section 2 of each of the appendices, B through G.
5. The sentence in parentheses is an English gloss of the phrase. The boldface words stand for those referents which are explicitly signed in the phrase; the remaining words stand for referents which are omitted from the phrase and which must be inferred from context.
6. Markers, which have not been included in the analyses of this study, occur in some phrases and are shown in brackets in these appendices (e.g., [nod], [SS]). The following abbreviations are used:

SS	=	side-to-side headshake to indicate some form of negation.
nod	=	up and down head nod to indicate approval or affirmation.
MO	=	mouth opens wide to indicate surprise.
flip	=	two hands, held out at sides, flip from palm down to palm up to indicate doubt.
B reject	=	flat palm flapped in air to indicate rejection or disapproval.
naughty	=	fist with extended index finger waved diagonally in air to indicate disapproval.
tap	=	flat palm tapped on a person to attract attention.

    38 *GIVE–letter* (you/Heidi **give letter** to me/David)
   327 *mask–PUTON* (you/Mother **put mask** on face)
VIIIa 86 *piece–GIVE* (you/Heidi **give piece** to me/David)
   308 *toys–PUSHAWAY* (you/Heidi **pushaway toys** to there)
   336 *GIVE–GIVE–toy* (you/Heidi **give toy** to me/David)
   398 *ball–MOVE* (you/Heidi **move ball** to here)
  b 152 *motorcycle–GIVE–motorcycle* (you/Susan **give motorcycle** to me/David)
   207 *card–GIVE* (you/Susan **give cards** to me/David)
   212 *GIVE–cards* (you/Susan **give cards** to me/David)
   231 *cards–GIVE* (you/Susan **give cards** to me/David)

PATIENT–RECIPIENT

  Ib 12 *duck–Susan* (you/sister give **duck** to her/**Susan**)
   13 *duck–Susan* (you/sister give **duck** to her/**Susan**)
   55 *cookie–napkin* (you/sister put **cookie** on **napkin**)
   58 *cookie–napkin* (you/sister put **cookie** on **napkin**)
   59 *cookie–napkin* (you/sister put **cookie** on **napkin**)
   94 *bubbles–table* (you/mother put **bubbles** on **table**)
   95 *bubbles–table* (you/mother put **bubbles** on **table**)

  IIa 156 *hole–key–hole–key* (I/David put **key** in **hole**)
   159 *key–hole–key* (I/David put **key** in **hole**)
  b 19 *crown–head* (you/Susan put **crown** on my **head**)
   21 *crown–head* (you/Susan put **crown** on my **head**)
   23 *crown–David* (you/Susan give **crown** to me/**David**)
   31 *crown–David* (you/sister give **crown** to me/**David**)
IVb 205 *kitchen–knife–kitchen* (I/David will put **knife** in **kitchen**)
   289 *banana–Susan* (I/David will give **banana** to you/**Susan**)
   296 *banana–banana–sister* (I/David will give **banana** to her/**sister**)

  Va 1 *socked foot–shoes* (one puts **socked feet** into **shoes**)
   81 *track–here* (you/Lisa put **track here**)
   138 *hand–block* (you/Lisa put **hand** on **block**)
   139 *blocks–tower* (you/Lisa put **blocks** on **tower**)
  b 40 *ball–David* (you/Susan give **ball** to me/**David**)
   103 *ball–here* (you/Susan bounce **ball** to **here**)
   212 *here–here–glass–here* (you/mother put **glass here**)
   259 *floor–glass–floor* (I/David will move **glass** to **floor**)
  VIa 3 *paper–David* (you/sister give **paper** to me/**David**)
   6 *sister–paper* (can I/David give **paper** to her/**sister**?)
   40 *frog–floor* (you/Heidi put **frog** on **floor**)
   175 *man+boat* (I/David will put **man** in **boat**)
   176 *[SS]–man+boat* (I/David can't put **man** in **boat**)
   203 *foot–ground* (you/Heidi put doll's **foot** on **ground**)
  b 60 *pictures–sheet* (you/Heidi put **pictures** in **sheet**)
  VIIa 31 *toy–lap* (you/Heidi put **toy** in my **lap**)
   45 *bag–here* (you/Heidi put **bag here**)
   54 *toy–village* (you/Heidi put **toy** in **village**)
   260 *pieces–[flip]–puzzleboard pieces* (you/Heidi put **pieces** in **puzzleboard**)
VIIIa 23 *piece–puzzleboard* (I/David will put **piece** in **puzzleboard**)
   30 *piece–piece–puzzleboard* (I/David will put **piece** in **puzzleboard**)
   60 *hat–head* (one puts **hats** on **heads**)
   70 *piece–puzzleboard–[SS]* (I/David can't put **piece** in **puzzleboard**)
   71 *piece–puzzleboard–[flip]*(I/David can't put **piece** in **puzzleboard**)
   111 *juice–David* (she/mother gave **juice** to me/**David**)

395 *head–stem* (you/Heidi put **head** on **stem**)
435 *penny–gun* (you/Heidi put **penny** on **gun**)
438 *penny–gun* (you/Heidi put **penny** on **gun**)
b 36 *penny–slot–penny* (you/Heidi put **penny** in **slot**)

ACT–RECIPIENT

Ib 106 *GIVE–GIVE–David* (you/mother **give** bubbles to **me/David**)
  158 *box bottom–PUT–box bottom* (you/Susan **put** cover on **box bottom**)
IIIb 109 *GIVE–David* (you/brother **give** bubbles to **me/David**)
  132 *GIVE–David* (you/brother **give** Play-Doh to **me/David**)
IVa 7 *PUTIN–yellowpiece* (you/mother **put** cherry in **yellowpiece**)
  125 *PLACE–closet* (you/Heidi **place** coat in **closet**)
Va 225 *GIVE–David* (you/Lisa **give** stick to **me/David**)
b 96 *here–here–BOUNCE–here* (you/Susan **bounce** ball to **here**)
  98 *BOUNCE–here* (you/Susan **bounce** ball to **here**)
VIb 28 *GIVE+palm–GIVE* (you/Heidi **give** grape to my **palm**)
VIIb 2 *GIVE–David* (you/sister **give** mask to **me/David**)
  13 *GIVE–hole* (you/Heidi **give** key to **hole**)
  17 *GIVE–hole–[naughty]–GIVE* (you/Heidi **give** key to **hole**)
VIIIa 89 *GIVE–GIVE–here* (you/Heidi **give** piece **here**)
  354 *GIVE–David* (you/Heidi **give** bell to **me/David**)
  417 *GIVE–palm* (you/Heidi **give** penny to my **palm**)
b 42 *GIVE–palm* (you/Heidi **give** gum to my **palm**)

RECIPIENT–ACTOR

Ib 60 *sister–napkin* (**you/sister** put cookie on **napkin**)
VIIIb 245 *Susan–David* (**you/Susan** give motorcycle to **me/David**)

PATIENT–ACT–RECIPIENT

Vb 79 *crackers–GIVE–David–GIVE–crackers–GIVE* (you/mother **give crackers** to **me/David**)
  115 *cupcake–ROLL–here* (you/Susan **roll cupcake** to **here**)
VIIa 42 *object–MOVE–village–object* (you/Heidi **move object** here onto **village**)
b 88 *book–GIVE–David–book* (you/mother **give book** to **me/David**)
VIIIa 309 *toys–PUSHAWAY–there–toys* (you/Heidi **pushaway toys** to **there**)
  366 *mouse–there–MOVE* (you/Heidi **move mouse** to **there**)
b 40 *GIVE–gum–mouth* (you/Heidi **give gum** to my **mouth**)

PATIENT–RECIPIENT–ACTOR

VIIIb 261 *glass–David–glass–kitchen–glass* (**I/David** will transfer **glass** to **kitchen**)

Transform Phrases

PATIENT–ACT

Ia 300 *duck–TWIST* (you/Susan **twist duck**)
b 22 *cookie–CHEW* (I/David am **chewing cookie**)
  86 *bubbles–BLOW* (one **blows bubbles**)

IIa 117 *bubbles–PUFF* (can I/David **puff bubbles?**)
IVa 68 *BLOW–bubbles–[nod]* (can I/David **blow bubbles?**)
127 *can–TURNOVER* (you/sister **turnover can**)
128 *TURNOVER–can–TURNOVER* (you/sister **turnover can**)
Va 48 *PEDAL–bike picture* (one **pedals bicycles**)
54 *bike picture–PEDAL* (one **pedals bicycles**)
60 *ladder picture–CLIMB* (one **climbs ladders**)
62 *ladder picture–CLIMB* (one **climbs ladders**)
65 *ladder picture–CLIMB* (one **climbs ladders**)
73 *horse–RIDE–horse* (one **rides horses**)
76 *ice cream cone picture–LICK* (one **licks ice cream cones**)
140 *block–SETUP* (I/David will **setup blocks**)
179 *CLIMB–ladder* (one **climbs ladders**)
180 *ladder–ladder–CLIMB* (one **climbs ladders**)
205 *PEDAL–bike picture* (one **pedals bicycles**)
217 *lawnmower picture–PUSH* (one **pushes lawnmowers**)
b 170 *TILT–glass picture* (one **tilts glasses**)
178 *knife picture–MOVE BACK and FORTH* (one **moves back and forth knives**)
179 *SCOOP–SCOOP–spoon picture* (one **scoops spoons**)
180 *knife picture–MOVE BACK and FORTH* (one **moves back and forth knives**)
210 *EAT–orange* (one **eats oranges**)
VIa 25 *big kangaroo–CRADLE +[SS]–big kangaroo* (one doesn't **cradle big kangaroos**)
138 *door–RAISE–door–RAISE–door–RAISE* (you/Heidi **raise door**)
145 *OPEN–package* (you/Heidi **open package**)
146 *package–OPEN* (you/Heidi **open package**)
b 16 *foot–TWIST APART* (you/Heidi **twist apart** doll's **foot**)
61 *pictures–TAKE OUT–pictures* (you/Heidi **take out pictures**)
VIIa 95 *carrot picture–NIBBLE* (rabbit **nibbles carrot**)
315 *TAKEOFF–glasses–TAKE OFF–glasses–TAKE OFF–glasses* (you/Heidi **take off** your **glasses**)
322 *TAKE OFF–glasses* (you/Heidi **take off** your **glasses**)
b 3 *TAKE OFF–mask* (you/Heidi **take off** your **mask**)
4 *DEPRESS–key* (you/Heidi **depress key**)
5 *key–DEPRESS–key* (you/Heidi **depress key**)
29 *EAT–food–EAT–food–EAT* (one **eats food**)
42 *banana picture–EAT* (one **eats bananas**)
46 *LICK–ice cream picture* (one **licks ice cream cones**)
62 *grape–EAT* (one **eats grapes**)
80 *key picture–TWIST* (one **twists keys**)
100 *CRADLE–baby picture–CRADLE* (one **cradles babies**)
170 *CRADLE–baby picture* (one **cradles babies**)
VIIIa 5 *drum picture–BEAT* (one **beats drums**)
9 *drum picture–BEAT* (one **beats drums**)
48 *bangs–PUSHUP* (you/Susan **pushup** your **bangs**)
136 *toothbrush picture–MOVE BACK and FORTH* (one **moves back and forth toothbrush**)
145 *car picture–STEER–car picture* (one **steers cars**)
159 *shovel picture–SHOVEL UP and DOWN* (one **shovels up and down shovels**)
201 *HOLD and SPRAY–hose picture–HOLD and SPRAY* (one **holds and sprays hose**)
202 *ladder picture–CLIMB–ladder picture–CLIMB* (one **climbs ladders**)
223 *baby picture–CRADLE* (one **cradles babies**)
230 *icecream picture–LICK* (one **licks icecream cones**)
249 *motorcycle picture–REV–motorcycle picture–REV–motorcycle picture* (one **revs motorcycles**)
394 *ACTON–toy* (can I/David **acton toy?**)

b   11 *guitar–STRUM* (santa **strums guitar**)
     35 *lever–DEPRESS* (you/Heidi **depress lever**)
     63 *PEDAL–bike picture* (one **pedals bicycles**)
    176 *paddle picture–PADDLE* (one **paddles paddle**)
    222 *cards–PICKUP* (you/Susan **picked up cards**)

ACT–ACTOR

IVa 81 *HIT–mother* (**you/mother hit** blocks)
      97 *HIT–mother* (**you/mother hit** blocks)
  b 337 *mother–PATTYCAKE* (**you/mother pattycake** hands)
Va 171 *EAT–Lisa* (will **you/Lisa eat** lunch?)
  b 10 *EAT–Lisa* (**you/Lisa** will **eat** lunch)
     133 *EAT–Lisa* (**you/Lisa** will **eat** lunch)
     134 *EAT–Heidi* (**you/Heidi** will **eat** lunch)
     135 *EAT–Susan* (**you/Susan** will **eat** lunch)
     158 *bear picture–MOVE BACK and FORTH* (**bear moves back and forth** toothbrush)
     182 knife picture–*CUT* (**knives cut** food)
VIIIa 265 *David–DON* (**I/David** will **don** my vest)
     294 *TILT–David* (**I/David** will **tilt** glass)

PATIENT–ACTOR

Ia 299 *Susan–duck* (**you/Susan** fix **duck**)
IIb 11 *wand–David* (**I/David** will blow **wand**)
IVb 322 *David–hand* (can **I/David** pattycake your/mother's **hand**?)
Va 177 *bridge–Lisa* (**you/Lisa** knocked over **bridge**)
    216 *book–David* (**I/David** will open **book**)
    234 *toy–Heidi* + [*nod*] (**you/Heidi** pull **toy**)
  b 137 *food–Susan* (**you/Susan** will eat **food**)
VIIb   9 *Heidi–door* (**you/Heidi** open **door**)
VIIIa 412 *toy–Susan–toy* (**you/Susan** work **toy**)
     431 *toy–toy–Heidi* (**you/Heidi** work **toy**)
  b 20 *gum machine–Heidi* [*nod*] (**you/Heidi** work **gum machines**)
     31 *gum machine–Heidi* (**you/Heidi** work **gum machine**)
     122 *cowboy picture–straw picture* (**cowboy** sips **straw**)

ACT–PLACE

VIIb 35 *EAT–kitchen* (one **eats** food in the **kitchen**)
     53 *outside–PUSH* (will you/Daddy or I/David **push** lawnmower **outside?**)
Va 158 *track–PUT TOGETHER* (**you/Lisa put together** blocks on **track**)

PATIENT–ACT–ACTOR

Va 53 *car picture–STEER–David* (**I/David steer cars**)
    111 *car–STEER–car–STEER–Lisa* (**you/Lisa steer cars**)
  b 130 *food–EAT–Susan* (**you/Susan** will **eat food**)
VIIIa 150 *lawnmower picture–PUSH–David* (**I/David push lawnmower**)
  b 121 *cowboy picture–cup picture–TILT* (**cowboy tilts cup**)

ACT–ACTOR–PLACE

IVa 177 *Susan +CHEW–kitchen +CHEW* (**you/Susan** will **chew** lunch in **kitchen**)
Vb 156 *bear picture–basin picture–WASH* (**bear washes** face in **basin**)

PATIENT–ACT–ACTOR–PLACE

VIIIb 145 *SIP–cowboy picture–straw picture–SIP–cup picture* (**cowboy sips straw** in **cup**)
178 *paddle picture–David–downstairs–David–paddle picture–PADDLE–downstairs–David [flip+SS]*(**I/David paddle** the **paddle downstairs**)

Transport Phrases

ACT–ACTOR

Va 46 *truck–DRIVE* (**truck drives** to there)
109 *whistle–MOVE ALONG* (**whistle** should **move along** to here)
117 *MOVE ALONG–whistle* (**whistle** should **move along** to here)
176 *bridge–FALL* (**bridge fell** onto floor)
b 213 *glass–FALL–glass* (**glass** could **fall** onto floor)

VIa 87 *GO–baggage car picture* (**baggage car goes** to there)

VIIa 110 *people picture-GO* (**people go** into airplane)
112 *airplane picture–FLY UP* (**airplane flies up** to there)
113 *airplane picture–FLY UP* (**airplane flies up** to there)
115 *blimp picture–FLY UP* (**blimp flies up** to there)
116 *airplane picture–FLY UP* (**airplane flies up** to there)
117 *airplane picture–FLY UP* (**airplane flies up** to there)
119 *car picture–GO* (**car goes** to there)
120 *scooter picture–GO* (**scooter goes** to there)
145 *train picture–GO* (**train goes** to there)
146 *lawnmower picture–GO* (**lawnmower goes** to there)
169 *car–GO* (**car** should **go** to there)
333 *mother–COME* (**you/mother** should **come** to here)

VIIIa 146 *SLIDE–sled picture–SLIDE* (**sled slides** to there)
180 *oar picture–FALL* (**oar falls** to water)
181 *oar picture–FALL* (**oar falls** to water)
363 *MOVE ALONG+[SS]–mouse–MOVE ALONG* (**mouse** should not **move along** to here)
b 21 *gumball–MOVE ALONG* (**gumball** should **move along** to there)
23 *MOVE ALONG–gumball* (**gumball** should **move along** to there)
34 *MOVE ALONG–gumball* (**gumball** should **move along** to there)

ACT–RECIPIENT

VIIb 131 *GO AWAY–old house picture–GO AWAY–old house picture* (**we/family go away** to **old house**)
132 *old house picture–GO AWAY* (**we/family go away** to **old house**)
164 *old house picture–GO AWAY* (**we/family go away** to **old house**)

RECIPIENT–ACTOR

VIa 140 *us–garage+[SS]* (**us/Heidi and David** do not go into **garage**)
141 *[SS] David–garage* (No. **I/David** go into **garage**)

VIIIa 205 *cat picture–trampoline picture* (**cat** jumps to **trampoline**)

ACT–PLACE

VIIa 100 *ladder picture–GO UP* (one **goes up** there on **ladders**)
  b 69 *GO UP–ladder picture* (one **goes up** there on **ladders**)
VIIIa 167 *ladder picture–GO UP* (one **goes up** there on **ladders**)
     168 *ladder picture–GO UP* (one **goes up** there on **ladders**)

ACT–RECIPIENT–ACTOR

Vb 110 *banana–MOVE ALONG–here* (**banana** should **move along** to **here**)

ACT–ACTOR–PLACE

VIIIa 148 *FALL–leaf picture–outside–FALL* (**leaves fall** to ground **outside**)

Perform Phrases

ACT–ACTOR

IIIb   77 *WING–bird* (**bird wings**)
IVa 178 *father–[SS]–SLEEP* (No. **father sleeps**)
VIa 41 *frog–JUMP* (**frog jumps**)
    114 *merry-go-round picture–GO AROUND* (**merry-go-rounds go around**)
VIIa 98 *seesaw picture–RISE UP* (**seesaws rise up**)
    105 *bear picture–PULL UP* (**bear pulls up**)
    106 *merry-go-round picture–GO AROUND* (**merry-go-rounds go around**)
    114 *helicopter rudder picture–GO AROUND* (**helicopter rudders go around**)
    182 *WALK–mouse* (**mouse** should **walk**)
    254 *balloon picture–FLOAT* (**balloons float**)
VIIIa 11 *balloon picture–FLOAT* (**balloons float**)
     15 *balloon picture–FLOAT* (**balloons float**)
    105 *DANCE–elephant picture* (**elephant dances**)
    110 *balloon picture–FLOAT* (**balloons float**)
    172 *fish picture–SWIM* (**fish swim**)
    176 *fish picture–SWIM* (**fish swim**)
    238 *Indian picture–POWOW–Indian picture* (**Indians powow**)

ACT–ACTOR–PLACE

VIIIa 139 *water picture–DIVE–elephant picture–water picture* (**elephant dives** in the **water**)

APPENDIX B2: CHARACTERIZING SIGNS IN DAVID'S ACTION PHRASES PRODUCED DURING SESSIONS I–VIII

Gloss	Description[36]	Occurrences[37]
1. ACT ON	Two A hands, pull back toward self	VIII(1)
2. BEAT	Two A's beat in air	VIII(2)
3. BLOW	O at mouth with lips pursed, blow	I(1), IV(1)
4. BOUNCE	O moves in downward motion at a 45° angle, then moves up at a 135° angle	V(2)
5. CHEW	mouth opens and closes	I(1), IV(1)
6. CLIMB	Two A's climb up in air	V(4), VIII(1)
7. CRADLE	Two A's, arm folded across chest, rock arms from side to side	VI(1), VII(2), VIII(1)
8. CUT	B, palm perpendicular to floor, moves in back and forth motion	V(1)
9. DANCE	Down on all fours, two B palms dance on floor	VIII(1)
10. DEPRESS	G plunged downward	VII(2), VIII(1)
11. DIVE	Two 5's palms touching, tilt forward	VIII(1)
12. DON	Two A's arch forward from shoulders to chest	VIII(1)
13. DRIVE	A glides horizontally	V(1)
14. EAT	O at mouth, touching lips	V(7), VII(4)
15. FALL	B flops over	V(2), VIII(3)
16. FLOAT	B, palm down, rises vertically into the air	VII(1), VIII(3)
17. FLY UP	B rises into air at a 45° angle	VII(5)
18. GIVE	B, palm parallel or perpendicular to ground, arm extended slightly	I(5), II(2), III(2), IV(1), V(4), VI(1), VII(6), VIII(11)
19. GO	B, palm down, slides along	VI(1), VII(6)
20. GO AROUND	B, arm extended, goes around in jerky movements making a circle	VI(1), VII(2)
21. GO AWAY	B moves in an arc out to side	VII(3)
22. GO UP	G moves up into air	VII(2), VIII(2)
23. HIT	A swats in air	IV(2)
24. HOLD & SPRAY	Two A's, one on top of the other, move side to side	VIII(1)
25. JUMP	B, palm down, raises up in quick movement	VI(1)
26. LICK	A at mouth, tongue licks	V(1), VII(1), VIII(1)
27. LIFT IN	Two B's raise up, then move down toward object	VI(1)
28. MOVE	G or B moves back and forth in air	VII(2), VIII(2)

[36] The signs in this and all following appendices are described in terms of American Sign Language handshapes. The following abbreviations are used (Stokoe, Casterline, & Croneberg, 1965):

A = closed fist
B = flat palm
C = hand arcs in a semi-circle
D = extended index finger, other three fingers and thumb form small circle
G = fist with extended index finger
L = index finger and thumb in right angle
O = fingertips meet thumb forming a circle
5 = palm with fingers spread

[37] In this and all following appendices, Roman numerals indicate the sessions during which the sign was produced; the numbers in parentheses represent the total number of tokens of this sign produced during that session.

29. MOVE ALONG	G moves along path	V(3), VIII(4)
30. MOVE BACK & FORTH	A, palm down, moves horizontally back and forth	V(3), VIII(1)
31. NIBBLE	C at mouth, lips move very quickly in chewing motion	VII(1)
32. OPEN	O twists in take off motion	VI(2)
33. PADDLE	A, arm extended forward, moves quickly up and down	VIII(2)
34. PATTYCAKE	Two B's, palms vertical or perpendicular to ground, held in air	IV(1)
35. PEDAL	Pedal motion with legs	V(3), VIII(1)
36. PICK UP	C moves up and closes	VIII(1)
37. PLACE	B, palm down, move toward object	IV(1)
38. POW WOW	B taps open mouth several times	VIII(1)
39. PUFF	Puffs with mouth	II(1)
40. PULL UP	Two A's, palms down, both slide up, then jerk down	VII(1)
41. PUSH	Two A's, palms down, move horizontally back and forth	V(1), VII(1), VIII(1)
42. PUSH AWAY	B, palm perpendicular to the ground, push movement	V(1), VIII(2)
43. PUSH UP	G flicks up	VIII(1)
44. PUT	B, palm down, pat in air	I(1)
45. PUT IN	B, palm down, fingers tap toward object	IV(1)
46. PUT ON	C, palm facing object, moves toward object	VII(1)
47. PUT TOGETHER	Two O's, out to sides and arms separated, move forward and together	V(1)
48. RAISE	B, palm down, moves up	VI(1)
49. REV	Two A's, each out to the side at shoulder level, quickly turn under in place	VIII(1)
50. RIDE	Two A's, held together in front of trunk, body bobs up and down	V(1)
51. RISE UP	B, palm down, rises up slowly	VII(1)
52. ROLL	B, palm down, brushes along floor	V(2)
53. SCOOP	A, twists at wrist and moves up to mouth	V(1)
54. SET UP	O set down in air	V(1)
55. SHOVEL UP & DOWN	Two A's, one on top of the other, move together up and down	VIII(1)
56. SIP	O at mouth, suck in	VIII(1)
57. SLEEP	Two B's, palms touching, held at cheek and head tilted to one side	IV(1)
58. SLIDE	B, palm down, dips down, then up	VIII(1)
59. STEER	Two A's move in steering motion in air	V(2), VIII(1)
60. STRUM	B strums on chest	VIII(1)
61. SWIM	B, palm perpendicular to ground, wiggles in forward movement	VIII(2)
62. TAKE OFF	O jerks away from object	VII(3)
63. TAKE OUT	A twists in air	VI(1)
64. TILT	C tilts toward mouth	V(1), VIII(2)
65. TRANSFER	G, pointed downward, moves in air toward object	VII(1)
66. TURN OVER	G twist over	IV(2)
67. TWIST	D twists in air	I(1), VII(1)
68. TWIST APART	Two O's twist apart	VI(1)
69. WALK	A bobs on floor	VII(1)
70. WASH	Two B's, palms facing in, move in rubbing motion in air	V(1)
71. WING	Two B's, out to sides, flapping movement	III(2)

APPENDIX C1: DONALD'S ACTION PHRASES PRODUCED DURING SESSIONS I–XI

Transfer Phrases

PATIENT–ACT

II	71	*GIVE–jar* (you/Robin **give jar** to me/Don)
II	16	*wand–GIVE–wand* (you/brother **give wand** to me/Don)
IV	53	*object–GIVE* (you/Robin **give object** to me/Don)
Vb	29	*microphone–GIVE* (you/Heidi **give microphone** to me/Don)
	32	*microphone–GIVE* (you/Heidi **give microphone** to me/Don)
c	3	*GIVE–doll* (you/Heidi **give doll** to me/Don)
	7	*GIVE–candy bag* (you/brother **give candy bag** to me/Don)
	9	*GIVE–candy bag* (you/brother **give candy bag** to me/Don)
VI	101	*helicopter–GIVE* (you/Heidi **give helicopter** to me/Don)
VIIIa	17	*toy bag–GIVE* (you/Heidi **give toy bag** to me/Don)
IXb	120	*GIVE–penny* (you/Susan **give penny** onto gum machine)
	151	*GIVE–penny* (you/Susan **give penny** onto gum machine)
Xa	95	*GIVE–Mickey Mouse* (you/Heidi **give Mickey Mouse** to me/Don)
	124	*GIVE–bicycle* (you/Heidi **give bicycle** to me/Don)
b	57	*[MO+SS+flip] GIVE–other piece* (No. you/Heidi **give** other **piece** to me/Don)
	60	*puzzle piece [+nod]–GIVE* (Yes. you/Heidi **give** that **piece** to me/Don)
XIa	92	*GIVE+box [+SS]* (no. you/Heidi **give box to** me/Don)
	98	*GIVE–box* (you/Heidi **give box** to me/Don)

PATIENT–RECIPIENT

IV	44	*lid–can* (I/Don will put **lid** on **can**)
	65	*balloon–mouth* (you/Robin put **balloon** in your **mouth**)
IXa	103	*drum–bear* (you/Heidi put **drum** on **bear**)
	162	*toy head–stick* (you/Heidi put **toy head** on **stick**)
b	75	*penny–bottle* (you/Susan transfer **penny** to **bottle**)
Xb	22	*penny [+MO]–gun* (you/Heidi put **penny** on **gun**)
	81	*duck–table* (you/Heidi put **duck** on **table**)

ACT–RECIPIENT

Vc	5	*GIVE–Don* (you/brother **give** candy bag to **me/Don**)
VIII	53	*GIVE–puzzle board* (you/Susan **give** piece on **puzzle board**)
	54	*GIVE–puzzle board* (you/Susan **give** piece on **puzzle board**)
IXb	93	*GIVE–gun* (you/Susan **give** penny onto **gun**)
	122	*GIVE–gum machine* (you/Susan **give** penny onto **gum machine**)
	127	*gum machine–GIVE* (you/Susan **give** penny onto **gum machine**)
	129	*GIVE–gum machine* (you/Susan **give** penny onto **gum machine**)
	136	*GIVE–gum machine* (you/Heidi **give** penny onto **gum machine**)
	146	*GIVE–gum machine* (you/Heidi **give** penny onto **gum machine**)
	150	*GIVE–gum machine* (you/Heidi **give** penny onto **gum machine**)
Xa	9	*GIVE–puzzle board* (you/Heidi **give** puzzle piece onto **puzzle board**)
b	56	*GIVE–puzzle board* (you/Heidi **give** puzzle piece onto **puzzle board**)

PATIENT–ACTOR

IXb 186 *gum machine–Susan–gum machine* (**you/Susan** give **gum machine** to me/Don)

RECIPIENT–ACTOR

IXa 110 *[shrug]–Heidi's hand–bear* (**you/Heidi** put drum on **bear**)
  b 79 *Susan's hand–gun* (**you/Susan** put penny on **gun**)

PATIENT–ACT–RECIPIENT

IXb 82 *gun–penny–GIVE* (you/Susan **give penny** onto **gun**)

Transform Phrases

PATIENT–ACT

VIIIa 83 *TIE–laces* (you/Susan **tie** my **laces**)
    92 *horn picture–BLOW* (one **blows horns**)
    97 *drum picture–BEAT* (one **beats drums**)
  ɔ112 *food picture–EAT* (one **eats food**)
  113 *glass picture–TILT* (one **tilts glasses**)
  115 *birthday cake picture–EAT* (one **eats cakes**)
  171 *ice cream cone picture–EAT* (one **eats ice cream cones**)
IXa 38 *cat picture–PET* (one **pets cats**)
    48 *pants picture–DON* (bear **dons** his **pants**)
    88 *drum picture–BEAT* (soldier or bear **beats drum**)
    90 *gun picture–SHOOT* (man **shoots gun**)
    93 *cup picture–LIFTOFF* (one could **liftoff cup**)
  131 *[MO]+tape–TAKEOFF* (you/Heidi **takeoff tape**)
  132 *[MO]+tape–TAKEOFF* (you/Heidi **takeoff tape**)
  139 *STRUM–cello* (santa **strums cello**)
  b 41 *straw picture–SIP* (cowboy **sips straw**)
    85 *gun–SHOOT* (you/Susan **shoot gun**)
Xa 63 *BLOW–bubbles* (can I/Don **blow bubbles?**)
XIa 71 *guitar picture–STRUM* (one **strums guitars**)
    79 *SUCK–straw* (cowboy **sucks straw**)
  112 *knob–TWIST* (you/Heidi **twist knob**)
  145 *SQUEEZE–toy* (can I/Don **squeeze toy?**)
  156 *straw–SIP* (brother is **sipping straw**)
  b 55 *oxen picture–RIDE* (bear **rides oxen**)

ACT–ACTOR

VIIIa 150 *bear picture–WASH* (**bear washes** his face)

PATIENT–ACTOR

VIIIa 80 *Susan–laces* (**you/Susan** tie my **laces**)
IXb 193 *Don–gum machine* (**I/Don** will pick up **gum machine**)

ACT—PLACE

IXb 53 *cup picture—SIP—cup picture* (cowboy **sips** straw in **cup**)
    207 *cup picture—SIP* (cowboy **sips** straw in **cup**)

PATIENT—ACT—ACTOR

VIIIb 169 *animal picture—TILT—cup picture* (**animal** could **tilt cup**)

Transport Phrases

ACT—ACTOR

IXa 59 *rabbit picture +[MO]—GO UP—rabbit picture* (**rabbit goes up** to there on seesaw)
    80 *airplane picture—FLY UP* (**airplanes fly up** to there)
    81 *airplane picture—FLY UP* (**airplanes fly up** to there)
XIa 60 *GO—car picture* (**cars go** to there)
    64 *balloon picture—GO UP* (**balloon goes up** to there)
  b 206 *kite picture—GO UP* (**kite goes up** to there)

ACT—RECIPIENT

IXa 73 *MOVE—there* (you/Heidi **move** to **there**)
  b 135 *MOVE—gum machine* (you/Heidi **move** to **gum machine**)

Perform Phrases

ACT—ACTOR

IXa 57 *raccoon picture—TURN* (**raccoon turns**)
XIa 52 *WALK—duck picture* (**duck walks**)
    67 *butterfly picture—WING* (**butterfly wings**)
    116 *GO AROUND—Pinocchio* (**Pinocchio** did **go around**)
  b 200 *owl picture—WING* (**owls wing**)

APPENDIX C2: CHARACTERIZING SIGNS IN DONALD'S ACTION PHRASES PRODUCED DURING SESSIONS I–XI

Gloss	Description	Occurrences
1. BEAT	2 A's beat in air	VIII(1), IX(1)
2. BLOW	Index & thumb held at mouth, lips pucker, puff	VIII(1), X(1)
3. DON	B, palm up, scoops forward & up slightly	IX(1)
4. EAT	O at mouth, bobs in & out, bites (optional)	VIII(5)
5. FLY UP	G rises at 45° angle into air	IX(2)
6. GIVE	B, palm parallel or perpendicular to ground, arm extended slightly	I(2), II(1), III(1), IV(1), V(6), VI(1), VIII(2), IX(10), X(6)
7. GO	B, perpendicular to ground, moves sideways in air	XI(1)
8. GO AROUND	O circles in air	XI(1)
9. GO UP	G rises straight up in air	IX(1), XI(2)
10. LIFT OFF	A rises up at 45° angle, then down to ground	IX(1)
11. MOVE	B moves back & forth in air	IX(2)
12. PET	B strikes gently	IX(1)
13. RIDE	2 A's held together in front of body, bob up & down	XI(1)
14. SHOOT	L closes in air several times	IX(2)
15. SIP	Index & thumb held in air, or mouth, sucks in	IX(3), XI(1)
16. SQUEEZE	2 O's squeeze in air	XI(1)
17. STRUM	B strums in air	IX(1), XI(1)
18. SUCK	pucker lips, suck in	XI(1)
19. TAKE OFF	B, palm up, twists over in air	IX(2)
20. TIE	O moves down in air, then in small circles	VIII(1)
21. TILT	C tilts toward mouth	VIII(2)
22. TURN	C turns upside down in air	IX(1)
23. TWIST	B, palm down, parallel to ground, twists in air	XI(1)
24. WALK	2 B's walk in air	XI(1)
25. WASH	2 A's rub eyes	VIII(1)
26. WING	2 B's flap at sides, shoulder height	XI(2)

APPENDIX D1: KATHY'S ACTION PHRASES PRODUCED DURING SESSIONS I–IX

Transfer Phrases

PATIENT–ACT

IIIa 109 [*tap*]–*sandwich–GIVE* (you/Susan **give sandwich** to me/Kathy)

Va 61 *bubble jar–GIVE* (you/Heidi **give bubble jar** to me/Kathy)

VIa 77 *toy–GIVE* (you/Heidi **give toy** to me/Kathy)

VIIa 27 *GIVE–bag* (you/Heidi **give bag** to me/Kathy)
  48 *GIVE–toys* (you/Heidi **give toys** to me/Kathy)
  58 *GIVE–battery* (you/Heidi **give battery** to me/Kathy)
  b 97 *GIVE–candy bag* (you/mother **give candy bag** to me/Kathy)

PATIENT—RECIPIENT

IIIa 12 *keys—head* (you/mother put **keys** on your **head**)
VIIIb 25 *picture—table* (you/Heidi put **picture** on **table**)

ACT—RECIPIENT

Va 37 *GIVE—jar* (you/mother **give** wand to **jar**)
VIIa 56 *GIVE—battery case* (you/Heidi **give** battery to **battery case**)
VIIIa 20 *GIVE—puzzle board* (you/sister **give** piece to **puzzle board**)
23 *MOVE—puzzle board* (you/Heidi **move** piece to **puzzle board**)
66 *santa—MOVE* (you/sister **move** horse onto **santa**)

ACT—ACTOR

IVb 11 *Lisa's arm—GIVE* (**you/Lisa give** grape to me/Kathy)

PATIENT—ACTOR

IIa 4 *mother +dog* (**you/mother** threw **dog** onto floor)

PATIENT—ACT—RECIPIENT

VIIIb 58 *GIVE—piece—puzzle board* (you/Heidi **give piece** to **puzzle board**)
IXa 37 *MOVE—puzzle—Kathy* (you/sister **move puzzle** to me/Kathy)

Transform Phrases

PATIENT—ACT

III 41 *pea picture—CHEW* (one **chews peas**)
VIII 44 *key—[tap]—TWIST* (you/Susan **twist key**)
IXa 24 *drum picture—STRUM* (one **strums drums**)
54 *balloon string picture—HOLD* (one **holds balloon strings**)
58 *guitar picture—STRUM+[nod]* (one **strums guitars**)

ACT—ACTOR

VIIb 114 *SHOOT—Kathy* (**I/Kathy** will **shoot** gun)
IXa 66 *scissors picture—CUT[nod]* (**scissors cut** objects)

PATIENT—ACTOR

Va 32' *wand—mother* (**you/mother** blow **wand**)
32 *wand—mother* (**you/mother** blow **wand**)

Transport Phrases

ACT–RECIPIENT

VIIb 163 *television–MOVE* (you/Heidi **move** to **television**)

ACT–ACTOR

IVa 45 *toy–MOVE* (**toy** can **move** there)

RECIPIENT–ACTOR

VIIb 146 *Heidi's leg–chair* (**you/Heidi** sit down on **chair**)

Perform Phrases

ACT–ACTOR

VIIa 24 *WALK–duck–WALK–duck* (**you/duck** will **walk**)
        34 *WALK–mouse* (**you/mouse** will **walk**)
VIIIb 42 *object picture–SCAMPER* (**object scampers**)

APPENDIX D2: CHARACTERIZING SIGNS IN KATHY'S ACTION PHRASES PRODUCED DURING SESSIONS I–IX

Gloss	Description	Occurrences
1. CHEW	Mouth opens wide, tongue out touching upper lip	III(1)
2. CUT	Thumb & index finger form V and cut in air	XI(1)
3. DO	B palm flap toward actor	V(1)
4. GIVE	B extended to desired object	III(1), IV(2), V(1), VI(2), VII(5), VIII(2)
5. HOLD	A in air in hold position	IX(1)
6. MOVE	B or G moves back & forth in air	IV(1), VII(4), VIII(2), IX(1)
7. SCAMPER	5 finger crab walk	VIII(1)
8. SHOOT	O pulls back in air	VII(1)
9. STRUM	B strums on chest	XI(2)
10. TWIST	O twists in air	VIII(1)
11. WALK	2 B's flap alternately in air, then slap knees	VII(2)

APPENDIX E1: CHRIS'S ACTION PHRASES PRODUCED DURING SESSIONS I–III

Transfer Phrases

PATIENT–ACT

I   89 *GIVE–toy* (you/Heidi **give toy** to me/Chris)
     90 *GIVE–toy+[nod]* (you/Heidi **give toy** to me/Chris)
     93 *GIVE–toy+[nod]* (you/Heidi **give toy** to me/Chris)
   100 *GIVE–duck* (you/Heidi **give duck** to me/Chris)
   186 *toy–GIVE–toy* (you/Heidi **give toy** to me/Chris)

PATIENT–RECIPIENT

II 116 *floor–[nod]–santa toy* (you/Susan put **santa toy** on **floor**)
   299 *hat–mother's head* (you/Heidi put **hat** on mother's **head**)
   305 *motorcycles–hat* (I/Chris will put **motorcycles** in **hat**)
   306 *motorcycles–hat–motorcycles–hat* (I/Chris will put **motorcycles** in **hat**)

ACT–RECIPIENT

II 296 *mother–TRANSFER+[nod]* (you/Heidi **transfer** watch to **her/mother**)

III   5 *GIVE–table* (you/mother **give** drink to **table**)
     6 *GIVE–table* (you/mother **give** drink to **table**)
     9 *[B reject+SS] GIVE–Chris* (No. you/Heidi **give** my drink to **me/Chris**)
   50 *MOVE–table* (you/Heidi **move** soldier to **table**)

PATIENT–ACT–RECIPIENT

II 147 *box–TRANSFER–toys+[nod]* (you/Susan **transfer toys** to **box**)
III   20 *puzzle piece–MOVE–board–MOVE* (you/Heidi **move piece** to **board**)

Transform Phrases

PATIENT–ACT

I   99 *toy–LIFT OUT+[nod]* (you/Heidi **lift out toy**)

II 217 *pictures–LEAF THROUGH* (you/Heidi **leaf through pictures**)
   276 *package paper–TAKE OFF–[nod]* (you/Heidi **take off paper**)

IIIa 129 *string–PULL* (one can **pull string**)
   197 *PEDAL+[nod]–bicycle* (one or santa **pedals bicycles**)
   221 *video knob–TWIST* (Barbara **twisted video knob**)

b 24 *television knob–TWIST* (you/Heidi **twist television knob**)

Transport Phrases

ACT–ACTOR

I   74 *[nod]–water picture–SPRAY UPWARD* (**water spray upward** to house)

ACT–RECIPIENT–ACTOR

I   75 *SPRAY UPWARD–water picture–house picture* (**water spray upward** to **house**)

Perform Phrases

ACT–ACTOR

II   196 *CIRCLE–santa on bike* (**santa circles**)

III   28 *pinwheel picture–CIRCLE* (**pinwheels circle**)
     117 *MARCH–soldier* (**soldier marches**)
     222 *MARCH–soldier* (**soldier marches**)

APPENDIX E2: CHARACTERIZING SIGNS IN CHRIS'S ACTION PHRASES PRODUCED DURING SESSIONS I–III

Gloss	Description	Occurrences
1. CIRCLE	G circles in air	II(1), III(1)
2. GIVE	B arm extended	I(5), III(3)
3. LEAF THROUGH	G flicks up in air several times	II(1)
4. LIFT OUT	B, palm up, moves up & down in air	I(1)
5. MARCH	arms & legs stiffly move back & forth in air	III(2)
6. MOVE	B moves back & forth in air	III(2)
7. PEDAL	hands in handlebar position & feet circle in air	III(1)
8. PULL	Index & thumb pinch together & pull back in air	III(1)
9. SPRAY UPWARD	fist opens to 5 as hand rises	I(2)
10. TAKE OFF	O jabs up & down	II(1)
11. TRANSFER	G sweeps downward or sideways in air	II(2)
12. TWIST	5 or A twists in air	III(2)

APPENDIX F1: DENNIS'S ACTION PHRASES PRODUCED DURING SESSIONS I–IV

Transfer Phrases

PATIENT–ACT

II   28 *wand–GIVE* (you/Robin **give wand** to me/Dennis)

IVb 146 *car–GIVE* (you/Heidi **give car** to me/Dennis)
    148 *car–MOVE* (you/Heidi **move car** to me/Dennis)
     77 *clay–MOVE* (you/Heidi **move clay** to me/Dennis)

PATIENT–RECIPIENT

II   1 *key–hole* (I/Dennis will put **key** in **hole**)

IIIa 47 *mother's clay–floor* (you/mother put your **clay** on **floor**)
     127 *bubbles in jar₁–jar₂* (you/mother move **bubbles** to **jar₂**)
     161 *soda–Dennis* (you/mother give **soda** to **me/Dennis**)
   b 196 *clay–outside* (I/Dennis will put **clay outside**)
     197 *clay–outside* (I/Dennis will put **clay outside**)

ACT–RECIPIENT

IVa 71 *GIVE–empty* jar (you/mother **give** bubbles to **empty jar**)
  b 136 *car–GIVE* (you/mother **give** man to **car**)

PATIENT–ACTOR

IIIa 72 *mother–fruit* (**you/mother** give **fruit** to me/Dennis)

PATIENT–ACT–RECIPIENT

III 128 *bubbles in jar₁–jar₂–MOVE* (you/mother **move bubbles** to **jar₂**)
IV   70 *empty jar–MOVE–bubbles in full jar* (you/mother **move bubbles** to **empty jar**)

PATIENT–ACT–ACTOR

IIIa 71 *mother–fruit–GIVE* (**you/mother give fruit** to me/Dennis)

Transform Phrases

PATIENT–ACT

II   41 *wand–PUFF AT* (I/Dennis can **puff at wand**)
III 100 *jar–TWIST–jar–[flip]–jar* (you/Susan **twist jar**)
IV   4 *lid–PULL OFF* (you/Heidi **pull off lid**)
       6 *lid–TWIST OFF* (you/Heidi **twist off lid**)
      57 *nail–HAMMER* (you/mother **hammer nail**)
      87 *box–TAKE OUT* (you/Heidi **take out box**)
      88 *TAKE OUT–box* (you/Heidi **take out box**)
     104 *bubbles–BLOW* (one **blows bubbles**)

PATIENT–ACTOR

IIIa 60 *mother–fruit* (**you/mother** pick up other **fruit**)
      61 *mother–fruit* (**you/mother** pick up other **fruit**)

Transport Phrases

RECIPIENT–ACTOR

IIIa 36 *outside–Dennis–[nod]* (**I/Dennis** will go **outside**)

APPENDIX F2: CHARACTERIZING SIGNS IN DENNIS'S ACTION PHRASES PRODUCED DURING SESSIONS I–IV

Gloss	Description	Occurrences
1. BLOW	puffs in air	IV(1)
2. GIVE	B arm extended toward desired object	II(1), IV(3)
3. HAMMER	B moves up & down on object	IV(1)
4. PUFF AT	lips tight & loosen twice, verbalization	II(1)
5. PULL OFF	5 pulls back off object	IV(1)
6. MOVE	G moves back & forth	III(1), IV(3)
7. TAKE OUT	B palm up taps up & down on side of bag	IV(2)
8. TWIST	B, parallel to ground, twists over jar	III(1)
9. TWIST OFF	G flips over in air	IV(1)

APPENDIX G1: TRACY'S ACTION PHRASES PRODUCED DURING SESSIONS I–II

Transfer Phrases

PATIENT–ACT

IIa 139 *GIVE–soldier–GIVE* (you/Susan **give soldier** to me/Tracy)
  b 67 *cowboy–MOVE* (you/Heidi **move cowboy** to me/Tracy)

Transform Phrases

PATIENT–ACT

I   2 *HOLD–telephone–HOLD* (one **holds telephones**)
   18 *telephone picture–HOLD* (one **holds telephones**)
   19 *HOLD–telephone* (one **holds telephones**)
   92 *ladder picture–CLIMB–[flip]* (no one **climbs** this **ladder**)
 127 *baggage picture--LIFT* (one **lifts baggage**)
 151 *knife picture–MOVE BACK AND FORTH–knife picture–MOVE BACK AND FORTH* (one **moves back and forth knives**)
 155 *spoon picture–SCOOP TO MOUTH* (one **scoops to mouth spoon**)
 174 *toothbrush picture–MOVE BACK AND FORTH* (one **moves back and forth toothbrushes**)
II 42 *drum picture–BEAT* (one **beats drums**)

ACT–ACTOR

IIa 124 *Susan–TWIST* (**you/Susan twist** key)
  b 108 *dog–HIT* (**you/dog** did **hit** me/Tracy)

PATIENT–ACTOR

I 111 *horse picture–TRACY* (**I/Tracy** rode a **horse**)
IIb 109 *rear end–mother* (**you/mother** did hit my/Tracy's **rear end**)

Transport Phrases

ACT–ACTOR

I   123 *picture of pig–GO OUT* (**pig goes out** to there)

ACTOR–PLACE

II   91 *santa picture–chimney picture–santa picture–chimney picture–santa picture–chimney picture* (**santa** goes down to there in **chimney**)

ACT–ACTOR–PLACE

II   92 *santa picture–chimney picture–GO DOWN* (**santa goes down** to there in **chimney**)

Perform Phrases

ACT–ACTOR

I   168 *lion picture–ROAR* (**lions roar**)
    169 *lion picture–ROAR* (**lions roar**)
    171 *lion picture–ROAR* (**lions roar**)
    172 *lion picture–ROAR* (**lions roar**)
    219 *ferocious animal picture–ROAR* (**ferocious animals roar**)
    220 *octopus picture–WRIGGLE* (**octopuses wriggle**)

APPENDIX G2: CHARACTERIZING SIGNS IN TRACY'S ACTION PHRASES PRODUCED DURING SESSIONS I–II

Gloss	Description	Occurrences
1. BEAT	5 beats in air	II(1)
2. CLIMB	index & middle finger climb upward	I(1)
3. GIVE	B palm up, arm extended	II(1)
4. GO DOWN	5 palm down, moves vertically down in air	II(1)
5. GO OUT	G moves sideways in air several times	I(1)
6. HIT	B palm perpendicular to ground slaps in air	II(1)
7. HOLD	A held at ear	I(3)
8. LIFT	5 rises and lowers slightly in air, fingers wiggling	I(1)
9. MOVE	B moves back & forth	II(1)
10. MOVE BACK AND FORTH	A fist moves back & forth	I(2)
11. ROAR	5 palm facing out in claw position & roars	I(5)
12. SCOOP TO MOUTH	A moves to mouth	I(1)
13. TWIST	A twists in air	II(1)
14. WRIGGLE	5 fingers wiggle in air	I(1)

REFERENCES

Anderson, J. M. 1971. *The grammar of case: Towards a localist theory.* New York: Cambridge University Press.

Antinucci, F., & Parisi, D. 1973. Early Language Acquisition: A Model and Some Data. In C. A. Ferguson & D. I. Slobin (Eds.), *Studies of child language development.* New York: Holt.

Bloom, L. 1970. *Language development: Form and function in emerging grammars.* Cambridge, Mass.: MIT Press.

Bloom, L. 1973. *One word at a time.* The Hague: Mouton.

Bloom, L., Lightbown, P., & Hood, L. 1975. Structure and variation in child language. *Monographs of the Society for Research in Child Development, 40* (2, Serial No. 160).

Bloom, L., Miller, P., & Hood, L. 1974. Variation and reduction as aspects of competence in language development. In A. Pick (Ed.), *The 1974 Minnesota symposium on child psychology.* Minneapolis: University of Minnesota Press.

Bloomfield, L. 1933. *Language.* New York: Henry Holt.

Bowerman, M. 1973. *Early syntactic development: A cross-linguistic study with special reference to Finnish.* New York: Cambridge University Press.

Braine, M. D. S. 1976. Children's first word combinations. *Monographs of the Society for Research in Child Development, 41*(1).

Brown, R. 1958. *Words and things.* New York: The Free Press.

Brown, R. 1973. *A first language.* Cambridge, Mass.: Harvard University Press.

Chomsky, N. 1965. *Aspects of the theory of syntax.* Cambridge, Mass.: MIT Press.

Fant, L. J. 1972. *Ameslan: An introduction to American Sign Language.* Silver Spring, Md.: National Association of the Deaf.

Farwell, C. 1973. The language spoken to children. *Papers and Reports on Child Language Development (Stanford University), 5,* 31–62.

Feldman, H. 1975. *The spontaneous creation of a lexicon by deaf children of hearing parents, or, there is more to language than meets the ear.* Unpublished doctoral dissertation, University of Pennsylvania.

Feldman, H., Goldin-Meadow, S., & Gleitman, L. 1978. Beyond Herodotus: The creation of language by linguistically deprived deaf children. In A. Lock (Ed.), *Action, symbol and gesture: The emergence of language.* New York: Academic Press.

Fillmore, C. J. 1968. The case for case. In E. Bach & R. J. Harms (Eds.), *Universals in linguistic theory.* New York: Holt.

Fodor, J. A., Bever, T. G., & Garrett, M. 1974. *The psychology of language: An introduction to psycholinguistics and generative grammar.* New York: McGraw-Hill.

Gleason, H. A. 1961. *An introduction to descriptive linguistics* (revised edition). New York: Holt.

Goldin-Meadow, S. 1975. *The representation of semantic relations in a manual language created by deaf children of hearing parents: A language you can't dismiss out of hand.* Unpublished doctoral dissertation, University of Pennsylvania.

Goldin-Meadow, S., & Feldman, H. 1975. The creation of a communication system: A study of deaf children of hearing parents. *Sign Language Studies, 8,* 225–234.

Goldin-Meadow, S., & Feldman, H. 1977. The development of language-like communication without a language model. *Science, 197*(4301), 401–403.

Goldin-Meadow, S., Seligman, M. E. P., & Gelman, R. 1976. Language in the two-year old: Receptive and productive stages. *Cognition, 4,* 189–202.

Greenfield, P. M., & Smith, J. H. 1976. *The structure of communication in early language development.* New York: Academic Press.

Harris, Z. S. 1951. *Methods in structural linguistics.* Chicago: University of Chicago Press.

Lenneberg, E. H. 1964. The capacity for language acquisition. In J. A. Fodor & J. J. Katz (Eds.), *The structure of language: Readings in the philosophy of language.* Englewood Cliffs, N.J.: Prentice-Hall.

Lenneberg, E. H. 1967. *Biological foundations of language.* New York: Wiley.

Lyons, J. 1971. *Introduction to theoretical linguistics.* New York: Cambridge University Press.

MacKay, D. M. 1972. Formal analysis of communicative processes. In R. A. Hinde (Ed.), *Non-verbal communication.* New York: Cambridge University Press.

McNeill, D. 1974. *Semiotic extension.* Paper presented at the Loyola Symposium on Cognition, Chicago, Illinois.

Moores, D. F. 1974. Nonvocal Systems of Verbal Behavior. In R. L. Schiefelbusch & L. L. Lloyd (Eds.), *Language perspectives: Acquisition, retardation, and intervention.* Baltimore: University Park Press.

Nelson, K. E., Carskaddon, G., & Bonvillian, J. D. 1973. Syntax acquisition impact of experimental variation in adult verbal interaction with the child. *Child Development, 44,* 497–504.

Newport, E. L. 1976. Motherese: The speech of mothers to young children. In N. J. Castellan, D. B. Pisoni, & G. R. Potts (Eds.), *Cognitive theory: Vol. II.* Hillsdale, N.J.: Lawrence Earlbaum Association.

Newport, E. L., & Ashbrook, E. F. 1977. The emergence of semantic relations in ASL. *Papers and Reports on Child Language Development,* (Stanford University) *13*.

Newport, E. L., Gleitman, H., & Gleitman, L. R. 1977. Mother, I'd rather do it myself: Some effects and non-effects of maternal speech style. In C. A. Ferguson & C. E. Snow (Eds.), *Talking to children.* New York: Cambridge University Press.

Phillips, J. R. 1973. Syntax and vocabulary of mothers' speech to young children: Age and sex comparisons. *Child Development, 44,* 182–185.

Rigler, D., & Rigler, M. 1975. *Persistent effects of early experience.* Paper presented at Society for Research in Child Development Meeting, Denver.

Sachs, J., & Devin, J. 1976. Young children's use of age-appropriate speech styles in social interaction and role-playing. *Journal of Child Language, 3,* 81–98.

Schlesinger, I. M. 1974. Relational Concepts Underlying Language. In R. L. Schiefelbusch & L. L. Lloyd (Eds.), *Language perspectives: Acquisition, retardation, and intervention.* Baltimore, Md.: University Park Press.

Shatz, M., & Gelman, R. 1973. The development of communication skills: Modifications in the speech of young children as a function of listener. *Monographs of the Society for Research in Child Development, 38*(5).

Siple, P. 1973. *Constraints for a sign language from visual perception data.* Working paper, Salk Institute, La Jolla, California.

Slobin, D. I. 1973. Cognitive prerequisites for the development of grammar. In C. A. Ferguson & D. I. Slobin (Eds.), *Studies in child language development.* New York: Holt.

Snow, C. E. 1972. Mothers' speech to children learning language. *Child Development, 43,* 549–565.

Stokoe, Jr., W. C. 1960. Sign language structure: An outline of the visual communications systems. *Studies in Linguistics, Occasional Papers, No. 8.*

Stokoe, Jr., W. C., Casterline, D. C., & Croneberg, C. G. 1965. *A dictionary of American Sign Language on linguistic principles.* Washington, D.C.: Gallaudet College Press.

Tervoort, B. T. 1961. Esoteric symbolism in the communication behavior of young deaf children. *American Annals of the Deaf, 106*(5), 436–480.

4

Aphasic Dissolution and Language Acquisition[1]

Maureen Dennis

THE HOSPITAL FOR SICK CHILDREN, TORONTO

Carole Ann Wiegel-Crump

TROY UNIVERSITY, EUROPEAN DIVISION,
SOESTERBERG AND THE INTERNATIONAL
SCHOOL, AMSTERDAM

THE REGRESSION HYPOTHESIS

John Hughlings Jackson first formulated the regression hypothesis, which is the proposal that the language dissolution of adult aphasics can best be described as a relapse to an earlier stage of language development. Later researchers have been stimulated to search for parallels between the patterns of early language acquisition and those of adult aphasic breakdown, in the hope that such analogues would show whether the rules operating in the development of language are lawfully and linearly related to the processes of language breakdown. The issue is not whether there exists an absolute correspondence between adult dissolution and ontogenetic growth of language—Jackson himself admitted that any relationship must be relative—but whether there is enough in common to make the regression hypothesis a tenable account of language function.

The original conceptualization of the evolution–dissolution principle was that of a schematic or diagrammatic model to guide research into how behavioural functions were built up or broken down, acquired or lost. Jackson (1958b) took a cautious view of how the model might apply to actual aphasic conditions. He even cautioned those who might not understand his use of it as a heuristic device. "The reader . . . is asked, indeed, not

[1] Preparation of this chapter was supported by an Ontario Mental Health Foundation Research Scholarship to Maureen Dennis.

STUDIES IN NEUROLINGUISTICS, VOLUME 4

to accept any part of what may be inferred until he has convinced himself that the principles illustrated apply to actual cases of disease [p. 29]."

Jackson begins his discussion of regression in aphasia by noting the reduction from voluntary to automatic language, nonpropositional, or emotional utterances. He cites as his example swearing, which is automatic and emotional but not necessarily simple in form. The striking feature of aphasic speech for him was its automatic character, not necessarily its simplicity; he seems to have perceived the automatic–voluntary and simple–complex dimensions as at least partly orthogonal.

It is evident that he had no simple linear model relating dissolution to evolution. Development was perceived as global in a way that dissolution was not, so that "obviously, disease of a part of the nervous system could not be a reversal of the evolution of the whole . . . [1958a, p. 47]." Restricted aphasic conditions could not therefore be a mirror of the normal process of overall acquisition. Further, the very fact that dissolution was more local than evolution meant that the quality of aphasic performance would have to depend upon the workings of both impaired and intact language. "Evolution not being entirely reversed, some level of evolution is left. . . . [The aphasic's] positive mental symptoms are still the survivals of his fittest states [1958a, pp. 46–47]." Aphasic language, for Jackson, is the outcome of the interaction between "fit" and broken language systems.

There is, then, nothing in this original account of regression to suggest a simple mirror-image relationship between acquisition and dissolution. In its strong form, the hypothesis means just that; in a weaker cast, it only claims significant parallels between the two language processes. The aim of the present paper is to review the evidence for the two forms of the hypothesis, considering both the data itself and the logic by which the data were considered to be proper tests of the hypothesis.

The implications of the regression hypothesis should first be outlined. One is that, in aphasic dissolution, later acquired functions will be lost and earlier or simpler ones preserved. This should hold for either form of the hypothesis. The usual test of this claim is a demonstration of similar order of difficulty for a function in children and aphasics.

However, establishing rank order correlations does not constitute a test of the identity of immature and aphasic language systems (although it is of course congruent with this). One can readily construct a visual confrontation naming test in such a manner as to produce a perfect correlation between child and aphasic performance, with both groups passing certain items (e.g., dog, cat) and failing others (e.g., okapi, wildebeest, bunyip). Such data need mean no more than that stimulus dimensions like word frequency operate in both acquisition and dissolution; they cannot of themselves reveal whether naming had broken down in the aphasic along the same lines as it had developed in the child. It is not a sufficient test of regression, then, to show that children and aphasics are subject to common rules of language use.

A second implication of the hypothesis is that, since the aphasic is considered to be operating with a childlike or lower-level language system, he should make mistakes appropriate to the developmental stage to which he has regressed. To test this implication it is not sufficient to analyze only the end products of production or comprehension, because the final result may have been produced differently in the child and the aphasic. To establish that the same processes were used in each instance, what must be studied are the errors—miscomprehensions, misnamings, and inaccurate repetitions. A similar error pattern would suggest that the child and aphasic follow similar operations when they use and produce language.

Children at each successive developmental stage are basically content with their language output. If the aphasic's language is simply a lower-level but homogeneous system, then, like the child, he should find his utterances acceptable exemplars of his intent. A third implication of the regression hypothesis (mainly in strong form), therefore, is that the aphasic is fundamentally satisfied with his language.

The regression hypothesis makes several suggestions about how and why aphasic dissolution reflects, in reverse, child acquisition. Some traditional lines of evidence are consistent with the hypothesis, but cannot constitute proof of it. Clear evidence would be the demonstrations that children and aphasics:

1. show the same rank order of item difficulty
2. vary their performance with the same stimulus parameters
3. make the same number and type of errors
4. reveal a similar level of satisfaction with their language

Is there such evidence? Does the language dissolution of the aphasic really mirror child acquisition for phonology, speech praxis, the inflectional system, naming, syntactic comprehension and production, and the understanding of complex utterances?

THE PHONOLOGICAL SYSTEM

Jakobson (1968) claimed that aphasic sound disturbances exhibit a strictly regular sequence of stages and are therefore similar to phonological development in the child, a development in which the succession of steps is "universally valid and strictly regulated by structural laws [p. 28]." He (1968, p. 61) adduces several examples of phonemic regression:

　　1. The individual components of the phonemic system are eliminated in
　　　　sound aphasia (although not in dysarthric conditions) in a fixed order
　　　　of precedence, and that order is the mirror image of the one for
　　　　acquisition.
　　　　　a. The distinction between the liquids /r/ and /l/ is a common aphasic
　　　　　　 loss and a late acquisition for children;
　　　　　b. nasal sounds are acquired late in French and disappear earliest in
　　　　　　 French aphasics;
　　　　　c. interdental fricatives are acquired later than corresponding
　　　　　　 s-sounds, and English aphasics lose the first earlier than the sec-
　　　　　　 ond;
　　　　　d. forward articulated consonants are more resistant to lo: , in
　　　　　　 aphasia than palatovelar sounds, with "exact correspondences" in
　　　　　　 child language.
　　2. The order in which speech sounds are restored during recovery from
　　　　aphasia corresponds to their sequence of acquisition.

Jakobson argued, in summary, that the incomplete phonological rosters of
children and aphasics are subject to certain fixed, step-by-step, laws of the
phonemic system and that the dissolution of one language system follows
the course of acquisition of the other. Certain sounds do seem to be
acquired late and lost readily in aphasia, but the issue is whether the
evolution–dissolution concept captures the nature of this parallel.

　　Aphasics and children make errors on **some** of the same sounds (e.g.,
fricatives and affricates), and certain parameters like phoneme frequency of
occurrence influence articulation similarly in both groups (Fry, 1966;
Whetnall & Fry, 1964; Shankweiler & Harris, 1966; Menyuk, 1971; Trost
& Canter, 1974). However, other stimulus parameters affect production
differently in the two groups. Final consonants tend to be easier than initial
consonants in aphasia (Shankweiler & Harris, 1966; Trost & Canter, 1974)
while, for children, the quality of articulation is either independent of the
position of the sound in the word (Snow, 1963) or better on initial consonants (Winitz, 1969). The phones easiest for children are those that are
rapidly articulated (Templin, 1966) but, for aphasics, the most rapid speech
gestures suffer most in phonetic disintegration (Shankweiler & Harris,
1966).

　　Children and aphasics do not always substitute the same sound for the
unavailable target. Although some aphasic simplifications are like those of
children (e.g., the substitution of stop consonants for fricatives), other
errors do not occur in children's speech (e.g., the breaking up of consonant
clusters by inserting a vowel between the normally linked pair)
(Shankweiler & Harris, 1966). Aphasics replace voiced sounds by unvoiced

ones (Shankweiler & Harris, 1966), a substitution which rarely occurs in children (Fry, 1958).

The impairments accompanying disordered phonology are different in children (with either normal or immature speech sound articulation) and aphasics. Word-finding problems may contribute to the aphasic articulation difficulty, since inadequate responses occur more often in naming than in repetition (Trost & Canter, 1974). The presence of a semantic component aids phonological production in aphasia, since subjects make more errors in the repetition of nonsense syllables than in repeating real words (Martin & Rigrodsky, 1974a). The extent to which the child does this is uncertain, but Jakobson noted the parrotlike repetition of sounds by children unable to use those same sounds in conversational speech, suggesting that children's phonological production may be less tied than that of an adult to semantic components of language. Prosodic alterations are a common feature of nonfluent aphasia (e.g., Johns & Darley, 1970; Kerschensteiner, Poeck, & Brunner, 1972). There are no marked prosodic alterations in the speech of children with developmentally immature speech, although older misarticulating children tend to equalize stress (Yoss & Darley, 1974). Trial-and-error movements and audible groping for successful placement of the articulators are prominent in adults with apraxia of speech, but absent in children (Yoss & Darley, 1974). Retrial and self-correction are not normally found in younger children, whereas adults with apraxia of speech typically recognize their errors (Deal & Darley, 1972). Adult apraxics, it appears, are dissatisfied with their utterances when output does not match adult targets. The child with phonological immaturities, by contrast, seems content with his utterances until increased language experience creates an adult sound system to be approximated.

The key question concerns the kind of underlying phonological organization that these error patterns represent. Children in the early stages of phonological development tend to use one sound in place of many. Their early sound roster is impoverished because of an inability to use sounds in all positions in a word, or to use a sound consistently in that word, and there are certain patterns which are simply not produced (Templin, 1957). The later development of the phonological system involves the acquisition of a hierarchy of feature distinctions, beginning with that between consonants and vowels, then that between speech sound sets (nasals, glides, stridents, stops) and finally that between members of the sets. Features with categorical characteristics like nasality or voicing rather than relative characteristics like place (e.g., closure at the lips versus closure near the lips) are produced earliest (Menyuk, 1971; Bricker, 1967). In terms of these distinctive features, the order of loss reverses the acquisition sequence, at least that reported by Jakobson (Blumstein, 1973).

But despite the fact that some features are acquired late and readily lost in aphasia, the errors made by aphasics do not group systematically according to these features. There is no tendency for front consonants like /p/ to be better produced than middle or back consonants such as /t/ or /k/ (Shankweiler & Harris, 1966), yet /p/ differentiates earlier in acquisition than /t/ or /k/ (Menyuk, 1971). The phonemes difficult for aphasics do not share identical manner or place features of production (Trost & Canter, 1974) and no particular distinctive feature opposition is more difficult than another for aphasics (Martin & Rigrodsky, 1974b). Because aphasic errors are close to the target (Trost & Canter, 1974; Martin & Rigrodsky, 1974b), it seems that the aphasic has an adult phonological target, even when he fails to reach it. Aphasic impairment, whether characterized as that of phonological encoding (Shankweiler & Harris, 1966) or that of discriminative selection of encoding elements (Trost & Canter, 1974), seems to concern the accessibility of phonemes rather than the completeness of the phoneme roster (Wepman & Jones, 1964). By contrast, children's errors reflect a lack of differentiation of phonological categories, and they represent the operation of a simpler but lawful system for translating standard adult sounds into the actual speech sounds used. The targets are different.

Thus, although there are phonological regularities in the imperfect articulation of children and aphasics, the parameters modifying articulatory competence are not identical in each. The phonological system of the child reflects a different organization from that of the adult aphasic. The roster of the aphasic, further, reflects two features absent in children: retrial and self-correction, and a readjustment of the residual components of the sound system. Jakobson (1968) himself recognized the latter.

> As long as part of the phonemic system continues to exist, it forms in its turn a system which is still ordered, although impoverished . . . there is in the linguistic systems of an aphasic as well not only a reduction of the former richer system, but sometimes also a remodeling. . . . A constructive readjustment is even manifested, therefore, in the destructions of the aphasic's phonological system [pp. 33–34].

INFLECTIONAL SYSTEMS

Both children and aphasics show incomplete inflectional rosters: they tend to use base lexical forms and often miss the bound inflectional morphemes that indicate person, number, or tense. To consider the aphasic's system as regressed to a developmentally earlier level, we would need to demonstrate similar difficulty orderings on tests of morpheme use, then show that similar parameters modify production in each instance.

Which morphemes do children and aphasics find difficult to produce? De Villiers (1974) scored the spontaneous utterances in a corpus of child and aphasic speech for the presence of 14 different morphemes in obligatory contexts (the use of obligatory contexts being considered a more sensitive measure than the count of the number of times a morpheme occurred in spontaneous speech, which was more likely to be a function of what the subject chose to say). Despite good intra-group consistency, there were many differences between children and aphasics. For example, copula morphemes were usually intact in aphasics but relatively late developing in children; the past irregular was acquired early by children but used poorly by aphasics. In general, phonological complexity proved less important for aphasics than for children in determining the difficulty of the inflection. The aphasics seemed to have difficulty with morphemes whose inclusion was crucial to the grammatical meaning of the sentence. Phenomena like overgeneralization of regular inflections occurred in children but not in aphasics. The rank order correlation between the child and aphasic orderings of difficulty was an insignificant .25.

Berko Gleason (1978) tested knowledge of English morphology by requiring children and aphasics to inflect nonsense or real words. The differences between the two groups were more salient than the similarities. Berko Gleason suggested that the aphasics appeared to be confused by conflicting patterns they had learned, whereas children, who had not been exposed to these patterns, were not confused.

Even more convincing evidence that the dissolution of the inflectional system cannot be adequately described in terms of the sequence of its acquisition comes from studies of the parameters of successful morpheme production. Aphasics are assisted to retrieve an omitted morpheme by the phonological salience of an extra syllable, so that, for example, they find *books* and *played* more difficult than *horses* and *waited* (Goodglass, Gleason, Bernholtz, & Hyde, 1972). Correspondingly, they omit more nonsyllabic than syllabic variations of -s and -d. Children show the opposite result.

The determinants of morpheme difficulty are also different in children and aphasics. De Villiers (1974) ordered her 14 morphemes in terms of the number of transformations involved in their derivation and showed that the rank order between number of transformations and order of acquisition was .85 for children, but only .12 for aphasics. Berko Gleason (1978) noted that the child's difficulties with inflections seemed to reflect their imperfect knowledge of the rarer syllabic forms, whereas aphasics found some rare forms quite easy to produce. It is evident that the transformational complexity and frequency of the morpheme bear more lawful relationships to acquisition than they do to dissolution.

It is not only the morphemes themselves, but also the obligatory contexts in which they occur, that are different in the child and the aphasic. The linguistic situations in which some of the morphemes are needed are not present in the beginning stages of acquisition; they only gradually become identifiable in child speech (de Villiers, 1974). Aphasics, by contrast, possess all the contexts, although they may not use them with the same frequency as the normal subject. Some of the agrammatic quality of child speech reflects not so much the loss of a particular morpheme as the absence of the context in which the morpheme might occur (de Villiers, 1974). This disorder is different in kind from that of the aphasic.

The fact that morpheme is produced by both groups is not of itself evidence that it is used in the same way. The progressive -ing is acquired early and well-retained by aphasics. Berko Gleason (1978) lists some of the reasons for this—the -ing structure occurs frequently, is pervasive, is phonologically salient because it occupies a complete syllable, and comes in one basic shape—and she argues that children and aphasics may rely on different features in producing this ending. In fact, the aphasics' use of -ing in some instances (e.g., *workin'*) appeared to be more a nominalization than a progressive. Thus, even a successfully produced morpheme may represent the operation of different underlying language structures in children and aphasics.

NAMING AND WORD RETRIEVAL

Naming and word retrieval are linguistic skills obviously subject to certain rules in all language users. Objects which are familiar and whose names are frequently employed in the language are more likely to be produced appropriately than those of lesser familiarity and frequency (see, for example, Oldfield, 1966; Rochford & Williams, 1962). Elements that lend themselves to manipulation and a variety of multimodal associations or that are discrete entities are easier to name than elements that blend into their surroundings or are known primarily through the visual modality (see Piaget & Inhelder, 1968; Gardner, 1974). Since naming to visual confrontation and retrieving names to oral information are lawful in the manner indicated, it is important to consider whether the laws dictate behaviour in the same manner for children as for aphasics.

In their study of naming, Rochford and Williams (1962) were specifically interested in parallels between acquisition and dissolution. They compared children and aphasics on confrontation naming tests and found that the names first learned in childhood were least likely to be lost in aphasia. The performance of the children and the aphasics was so close that the authors spoke of a "naming age" in nominal aphasia.

But the fact that the two groups showed similar rank orders of item difficulty neither implies that the determinant of performance was the age of acquisition nor requires that the aphasic misnaming represent regression.

Evidence for the latter would be similar parameters of word retrieval and similar error patterns. Although the children and aphasics did tend to make the same errors, the underlying naming processes could not have been identical, as the authors note, because the cue effective in eliciting an initially inaccessible name was different in each group. Before age 9, sound rather than meaning elicited the target name (i.e., the clue *not a home but a . . .* was more useful than *we do our hair with it* to the young child attempting to name a comb). There was no stage in the aphasics that corresponded to the level of sound responsiveness in the young children. Thus, a name for a young child is not produced by the same processes as those used by the aphasic, even when the actual word generated is the same in the two instances. These data, together with the observation that "sound alike" or "clang" responses dominate childrens' word associations at age 4, but decrease progressively (Entwisle, 1966; Ervin, 1961), suggest that lexical access may be phonological in young children but primarily semantic in older children and adults.

The Rochford–Williams test relies exclusively on one category of names, that of use objects. Naming efficiency has been shown to vary with semantic class, so the question is whether this stimulus parameter operates in the same way in the nominal processes of children and aphasics. Apparently it does not. Colors and animals are easy elements, but letters and numbers are difficult for children to name; colours, animals, and letters are all difficult for aphasics, although they readily retrieve numbers (Gardner, 1974). Denckla and Rudel (1974) in a study of the relationship between rate of acquisition and naming speed found that the ranks of relatively fast and slow naming categories did not parallel—in fact, they nearly reversed—the order in which the names were acquired. Letters and numbers were the last semantic categories to be acquired, but the most rapidly and accurately named by older children; use objects, highly familiar and operative stimuli, were acquired first but named most slowly. In short, age of acquisition did not predict fluency of word retrieval in older children. Nor does it seem to do so in adult aphasics, who make low scores in naming objects and colors and high scores in naming letters and numbers (Goodglass, Klein, Carey, & Jones, 1966). The semantic category of the item to be named modifies performance differently in children and aphasics.

The clearest evidence that the parameters of naming and word retrieval are different in children and aphasics comes from an analysis of the types of errors each group makes in naming. Aphasics are more likely than children to respond with a semantic paraphasia, to produce disordered phonemic approximations to the target word (literal paraphasias), to perseverate on a previous response, or to give a neologistic or totally irrelevant response; they rarely assert that they do not know the name and almost never make visual confusions. Aside from the high percentage of synonyms in each, the ranks of error frequency are different in the two groups. The aphasic's second most common misnamings were semantic paraphasias—the children's *don't know;* literal paraphasias were the third most common error of aphasics, but the least frequent for the children (Gardner, 1974). The aphasic reliably identifies the semantic category; the naming process is defective for intracategory lexical selection or sequencing of the sounds of the target. For the child, misnamings reflect a lack of experience with the name, a tendency to treat the picture as more of a visual than a linguistic stimulus (see also Denckla & Rudel, 1976), or a response to the components of the picture in lieu of the name.

While there are certain common patterns in the naming behavior of children and aphasics, the processes of vocabulary acquisition in childhood are not mirrored in the dissolutions of naming and word retrieval in aphasics. Frequency of occurrence, familiarity, and operativity of the elements to be named modify the performance of both, but the parameters of successful naming are different. The factors that facilitate naming in childhood are not those determining accessibility of names in aphasia. Dissolution of naming cannot be characterized simply as a regression to processes operating early in development.

PRODUCTION AND COMPREHENSION
OF COMPLEX UTTERANCES

Children and aphasics operate with a less than full repertoire of grammatical constructions and each sometimes fails to derive the content and syntax of heard utterances. For agrammatic aphasics, the syntax of language is simplified to a string of grammatically and prosodically disconnected short utterances that contain the content words of the message. Their difficulty in producing certain forms seems to differ along several dimensions from the acquisition of grammar in children.

The child is content with his utterances as instances of his working grammar: he says what he wanted to say and the goal is the actual output even when the utterance is imperfect by standards of an adult grammar. The aphasic will typically produce the correct construction over successive approximations, even if the initial attempt is agrammatic. He will rarely attempt to change an already correct utterance (Berko Gleason, Goodglass, Green, Ackerman, & Hyde, 1975 who also suggest that the correct response is available as a goal for the aphasic). That the aphasic can, over time, produce most of the grammatical constructions of adult language shows that the impairment is not so much in the existence of a particular form as in its relative inaccessibility. As one might expect in such a case, the pattern of grammatical breakdown is not uniform across aphasics and the difficulty or length of the required construction do not predict performance (Berko Gleason *et al.*, 1975). While the ability to self-correct might be argued to be characteristic of both groups, it has been suggested that this skill is prognostic for the aphasic, but is merely indicative of the child's level of syntax development.

The aphasic creates new strategic modes of dealing with his limitations: initiating utterances with stressed vocatives, sequencing content words in a loose pattern, substituting adverbs of degree and time for inflections and functors, and producing predicate adjectives more often than pronominal modifiers (Berko Gleason *et al.*, 1975). The constructive readjustment of language to compensate for missing constructions appears to be a striking feature of aphasic agrammatism. But it is obviously an adult, and not child, grammar that is being reorganized. Goodglass (1968) notes that a clinician reading transcripts of children's utterances would readily identify some as possible, but others as impossible, aphasic productions. A case in point would be the child's selective reductions of adult speech models to chains of contentives, a kind of telegraphic transformation. The child's reductions, unlike those of the adult aphasic, are determined by the reference-making functions of contentives, the fact that they are practiced by the child as single words, and the differential stress these words receive in the adult model. Further, the child's telegraphic utterances may fail to preserve word order (e.g., *Cowboy did fighting me. Where the more grandma*), an error rarely demonstrated by adult aphasics.

This data suggest that aphasic agrammatism cannot be adequately described in terms of a regression to early stages of grammatical acquisition. Sentences generated through transformation rules in the adult grammar may be based on different, and simpler, rules in grammatical acquisition, so that the aphasic and child rule systems are different regardless of the grammatical quality of their output.

Studies of syntactic comprehension reveal a second line of evidence for the claim that the structure of complex utterances is different in the child and the aphasic. The Parisi–Pizzamiglio test measures the ability to discriminate a variety of syntactic contrasts ranging from simple locative prepositions to complex constructions involving passives and direct and indirect objects. Although the rank order of difficulty for children and aphasics is similar (rank order Italian sample .80 [Parisi & Pizzamiglio, 1970], rank order English sample .61 [Lesser, 1974]), such data prove only that some syntactic contrasts are easier or more difficult than others for language users.

Evidence for the notion that the aphasic's grammatical understanding has regressed to that of a child would be a demonstration that children and aphasics have difficulty with the same categories of syntactic contrasts. Lesser (1974) grouped the Parisi–Pizzamiglio contrasts into eight types (word order, verb tense, number, polarity, reflexive–nonreflexive, gender, easy locative prepositions, difficult locative prepositions). Analysis of rank order of difficulty showed no significant correlation between children and aphasics. Different parameters determine difficulty for the two groups. It might be noted that the significant correlation was that between the right hemisphere-lesioned, nonaphasic adults and the children, suggesting that the defects of the children and the aphasics might differ in kind.

Another line of evidence for different comprehension processes in children and aphasics comes from data on the Token Test (De Renzi & Vignolo, 1962), which measures the ability to execute a variety of complex commands varying in information level and syntactic complexity. There is reasonably good correlation between the rank orders of errors in children and aphasics (Whitaker & Selnes, 1978); but little concordance for error distribution. The critical items for children, that is, those that reveal most age variance, account for only one-third of aphasic errors (Poeck, Orgass, Kerschensteiner, & Hartje, 1974). The existing parallels mean only that linguistic complexity is a factor in both acquisition and dissolution of language (Whitaker & Selnes, 1978).

STATUS OF THE REGRESSION HYPOTHESIS

The regression hypothesis makes a proposal about the underlying linearity of language in children and aphasics. The traditional lines of supporting evidence have come from rank order statistics. Such data, logically, cannot constitute proof of an underlying identity of process in the two language systems, but are clear evidence only that certain linguistic functions are rule-governed or lawful for most language users.

Children and aphasics show obviously dissimilar patterns of difficulty for some language functions, indicating that the language of aphasics cannot be described as having regressed to that of children. Even when rank orders of difficulty are the same, the parameters of language performance and the nature of erroneous responses were often different. In the case of naming and word retrieval, it is especially clear that a similar end product has been generated by qualitatively different processing in children and aphasics.

Dissolution of language, then, cannot be described simply in terms of a regression to some earlier level of acquisition. Forced parallels between children and aphasics leave many striking aspects of both language systems unaccounted for. More productive is the study of what the linguistic organization of each can do. For the aphasic, what needs to be more fully studied is the nature of the reorganization within the intact language structures, a process that Jackson (1958c) characterized as "the evolution still going in what is left intact of a nervous system mutilated by disease [p. 411]."

REFERENCES

Berko Gleason, J. 1978. The acquisition and dissolution of the English inflectional system. In A. Caramazza & E. B. Zurif (Eds.), *Language acquisition and language breakdown*. Baltimore: Johns Hopkins University Press. Pp. 109–120.

Berko Gleason, J., Goodglass, H., Green, E., Ackerman, N., & Hyde, M. R. 1975. The retrieval of syntax in Broca's aphasia. *Brain and Language, 2,* 451–471.

Blumstein, S. E. 1973. *A phonological investigation of aphasic speech* (Janua Linguarum Series Minor No. 153). The Hague: Mouton.

Bricker, W. A. 1967. Errors in echoic behavior of pre-school children. *Journal of Speech and Hearing Research, 10,* 67–76.

Deal, J. L., & Darley, F. L. 1972. The influence of linguistic and situational variables on phonemic accuracy in apraxia of speech. *Journal of Speech and Hearing Research, 15,* 639–653.

Denckla, M. B., & Rudel, R. 1974. Rapid "automatized" naming of pictured objects, colors, letters and numbers by normal children. *Cortex, 10,* 186–202.

Denckla, M. B., & Rudel, R. 1976. Naming of object-drawings by dyslexic and other learning disabled children. *Brain and Language, 3,* 1–15.

De Renzi, E., & Vignolo, L. A. 1962. The Token Test: A sensitive test to detect receptive disturbances in aphasics. *Brain, 85,* 665–678.

de Villiers, J. 1974. Quantitative aspects of agrammatism in aphasia. *Cortex, 10,* 36–54.

Entwisle, D. 1966. *Word associations of young children.* Baltimore: Johns Hopkins University Press.

Ervin, S. 1961. Changes with age in the verbal determinants of word associations. *American Journal of Psychology, 74,* 361–372.

Fry, D. B. 1958. Phonemic substitutions in an aphasic patient. *Language and Speech, 1,* 52–61.

Fry, D. B. 1966. The development of the phonological system in the normal and the deaf child. In F. Smith & G. A. Miller (Eds.), *The genesis of language: A psycholinguistic approach.* Cambridge: MIT Press. Pp. 187–206.

Gardner, H. 1974. The naming of objects and symbols by children and aphasic patients. *Journal of Psycholinguistic Research, 3,* 133–149.

Goodglass, H. 1968. Studies on the grammar of aphasics. In S. Rosenberg & J. Koplin (Eds.), *Developments in applied psycholinguistics research.* New York: Macmillin. Pp. 177–208.

Goodglass, H., Berko Gleason, J., Bernholtz, N. A., & Hyde, M. R. 1972. Some linguistic structures in the speech of a Broca's aphasic. *Cortex, 8,* 191–212.

Goodglass, H., Klein, B., Carey, P., & Jones, K. 1966. Specific semantic word categories in aphasia. *Cortex, 2,* 74–89.

Jackson, J. H. 1958a. Evolution and dissolution of the nervous system. In J. Taylor (Ed.) *Selected writings of John Hughlings Jackson.* New York: Basic Books. Pp. 45–75.

Jackson, J. H. 1958b. On some implications of dissolution of the nervous system. In J. Taylor (Ed.) *Selected writings of John Hughlings Jackson.* New York: Basic Books. Pp. 29–44.

Jackson, J. H. 1958c. The factors of insanities. In J. Taylor (Ed.). *Selected writings of John Hughlings Jackson.* New York: Basic Books. Pp. 411–421.

Jakobson, R. 1968. *Child language, aphasia and phonological universals* (Janua Linguarum Series Minor No. 72). The Hague: Mouton.

Johns, D. F., & Darley, F. L. 1970. Phonemic variability in apraxia of speech. *Journal of Speech and Hearing Research, 13,* 556–583.

Kerschensteiner, M., Poeck, K., & Brunner, E. 1972. The fluency–non-fluency dimension in the classification of aphasic speech. *Cortex, 8,* 233–247.

Lesser, R. 1974. Verbal comprehension in aphasia: An English version of three Italian tests. *Cortex, 10,* 247–263.

Martin, A. D., & Rigrodsky, S. 1974b. An investigation of phonological impairment in aphasia. Part I. *Cortex, 10,* 317–328.

Martin, A D., & Rigrodsky, S. 1974b. An investigation of phonological impairment in aphasia. Part 2: Distinctive feature analysis of phonemic commutation errors in aphasia. *Cortex, 10,* 329–346.

Menyuk, P. 1971. *The acquisition and development of language.* Englewood Cliffs, N.J.: Prentice-Hall.

Oldfield, R. C. 1966. Things, words and the brain. *Quarterly Journal of Experimental Psychology, 18,* 340–353.

Parisi, D., & Pizzamiglio, L. 1970. Syntactic comprehension in aphasia. *Cortex, 6,* 204–215.

Piaget, J., & Inhelder, B. 1968. *The psychology of the child.* New York: Basic Books.

Poeck, K., Orgass, B., Kerschensteiner, M., & Hartje, W. 1974. A qualitative study on Token Test performance in aphasic and non-aphasic brain damaged patients. *Neuropsychologia, 12,* 49–54.

Rochford, J., & Williams, M. 1962. Studies in the development and breakdown of the use of names I. The relationship between nominal dysphasia and acquisition of vocabulary in childhood. *Journal of Neurology, Neurosurgery and Psychiatry, 25,* 222–227.

Shankweiler, D., & Harris, K. S. 1966. An experimental approach to the problem of articulation in aphasia. *Cortex, 2,* 277–292.

Snow, K. 1963. A detailed analysis of articulation responses of 'normal' first grade children. *Journal of Speech and Hearing Research, 6,* 277–290.

Templin, M. 1957. *Certain language skills in children.* Minneapolis: University of Minnesota Press.

Templin, M. 1966. The study of articulation and language development during the early school years. In F. Smith & G. A. Miller (Eds.), *The genesis of language: A psycholinguistic approach.* Cambridge: MIT Press. Pp. 173–186.

Trost, J. E., & Canter, G. J. 1974. Apraxia of speech in patients with Broca's aphasia: a study of phoneme production accuracy and error patterns. *Brain and Language, 1,* 63–79.

Wepman, J. M., & Jones, L. V. 1964. Five aphasias: A commentary on aphasia as a regressive linguistic phenomenon. In D.M. Rioch & E. A. Weinstein (Eds.), *Disorders of communication* (Vol. 42, Research Publications of the Association for Nervous and Mental Disease). Baltimore: The Williams & Wilkins Company. Pp. 190–203.

Whetnall, E., & Fry, D. B. 1964. *The deaf child.* London: Heinemann.

Whitaker, H. A., & Selnes, O. A. 1978. Token Test measures of language comprehension in normal children and aphasic patients. In A. Caramazzo & E. B. Zurif (Eds.), *Language acquisition and language breakdown.* Baltimore: Johns Hopkins University Press. Pp. 195–210.

Winitz, H. 1969. *Articulation acquisition and behavior.* New York: Appleton-Century-Crofts.

Yoss, K. A., & Darley, F. L. 1974. Developmental apraxia of speech in children with defective articulation. *Journal of Speech and Hearing Research, 17,* 399–416.

5

VOT Distinctions in Infants: Learned or Innate?

Dennis L. Molfese

Victoria J. Molfese

SOUTHERN ILLINOIS UNIVERSITY

One area of speech perception that has been extensively investigated with adults is voice onset time (VOT). VOT refers to the relation between laryngeal pulsing and the onset of consonant release. Variations in VOT appear to be one of the cues utilized by adults to discriminate between various voiced and voiceless stop consonants. For example, Liberman, Cooper, Shankweiler, and Studdert-Kennedy (1967) noted that adult listeners can discriminate between variations in VOT only to the extent that they can assign unique labels to the sounds. Adults are unable to discriminate between bilabial stop consonant sounds with VOT values of 0 and +20 msec, which they identify as /b/, nor can they discriminate between VOT values of +40 and +60 msec, sounds which are identified as /p/. Discrimination, however, is possible between VOT values of +20 and +40 msec, values which characterized different phoneme categories. Recently, researchers have attempted to study this process in infants in order to determine whether discrimination of the VOT continuum is learned or innate. Such efforts have generally employed one of three different methodologies that have been developed or modified for use with infants: high amplitude sucking (HAS), habituation of heart rate (HR), and auditory evoked responses (AER).

HIGH AMPLITUDE SUCKING

The sucking response has long been known to be reliably under an infant's control from birth. The use of this response as a conditioned

225

operant in discrimination studies gained popularity following the publication of Siqueland and DeLucia's (1969) research on infant visual perception. In that study, presentation of a stimulus was contingent on infants changing their sucking from a baseline level to meet some criterion level established by the experimenter. The infants could view various visual stimuli, which changed every 30 sec, as long as they maintained criterion level sucking. Siqueland and DeLucia found that infants could use the operant to make reliable discriminations.

Eimas, Siqueland, Jusczyk, and Vigorito (1971) utilized a modification of this procedure in their investigations of VOT perception in 1- and 4-month-old infants. Six stimuli with VOT values of -20, 0, $+20$, $+40$, $+60$, and $+80$ were used. Infants in each age group were assigned to one of two experimental conditions or to a control condition. For infants in the experimental conditions an auditory stimulus was presented repeatedly until the sucking rate habituated (decreased to 20% below the criterion sucking level for 2 minutes). Following habituation a new auditory stimulus was presented contingent upon criterion level sucking. Infants in one experimental condition (20D) were presented with VOT stimuli that differed from each other by 20 msec and came from different adult phoneme categories (i.e., $+20$ and $+40$ msec). Infants in the other experimental condition (20S) were presented with VOT stimuli that also differed from each other by 20 msec, but the stimuli were from the same phoneme category (i.e., -20 and 0 or $+60$ and $+80$). Control group infants were presented with one of the six VOT stimuli throughout the testing session with no stimulus change after habituation. Infants in all conditions were found to habituate their sucking rate during repeated presentation of a VOT stimulus. Both the 1- and 4-month-old infants showed dishabituation of the sucking rate when the stimuli belonged to different phoneme categories (20D) and no dishabituation when the stimuli belonged to the same phoneme category (20S). Control group infants showed no dishabituation. Thus, it appears that infants as young as 1 month respond to speech sounds varying in VOT in a manner similar to that shown by adults.

Since the publication of the research by Eimas *et al.* (1971) the HAS procedure has been used by a number of researchers to investigate VOT in infants (Kuhl & Miller, 1975; Moffitt & Pankhurst, 1973; Morse, 1972; Treub & Rabinovitch, 1972). Despite its demonstrated usefulness, however, the HAS procedure has a number of shortcomings. Many studies using HAS have shown a subject attrition rate as high as 40–50% (see, for example, Eimas, 1974). Such high levels may have been due to the demands placed on the subjects' cooperative (or uncooperative) spirits. Because HAS requires the active participation of the subjects, a high attrition rate with young infants is to be expected, due to their highly variable state.

A second difficulty with the HAS procedure concerns its applicability to only a narrow age range of subjects. Although the procedure has been used in VOT studies with infants up to 6 months, it is clearly not appropriate for older children and adults. Furthermore, the HAS procedure has been used with only limited success with newborn infants (Butterfield & Cairns, 1974). Consequently, little data using the HAS procedure are available which might indicate unambiguously that newborns can or cannot discriminate among values along the VOT continuum. Such a step would obviously be important in any attempt to identify VOT discriminations as innate or learned abilities.

HEART RATE HABITUATION

Heart rate habituation, like HAS, is a method that depends on the habituation of a response to a stimulus but, unlike HAS, requires little active participation from subjects. The HR method is based on the role of the orienting reflex in the responsiveness of infants to their environment. Sokolov (1963) describes the orienting reflex as a normal, unconditioned response to a novel stimulus. A cortical model of the stimulus develops progressively with each presentation of the stimulus. When the cortical model is developed, the orienting response habituates. The heart rate response has been used in infant auditory research as an index of the orienting response and was used first by Moffitt (1971). Moffitt presented subjects with a series of trials, each containing 10 presentations of a synthetic speech syllable. The subjects (5–6-months-old) showed heart rate habituation over the first series of trials on which the same syllable was presented, but dishabituated when a new syllable was introduced on later trials.

Like HAS, HR has been used to investigate infant perception of the VOT continuum (Lasky, Syrdal-Lasky, & Klein 1975). The HR method can be used with subjects from infancy to adulthood, although heart rate in very young infants tends to be more unreliable (Gregg, Clifton, & Haith, 1973). Unlike HAS, active subject participation is not required with the HR method. However, state variables are as critical for HR as they are for HAS. One major problem with the HR method is that researchers frequently use a fixed number of trials during the habituation phase, rather than monitoring heart rate on-line to determine when habituation (or return of the response to baseline) occurs. Consequently, in some studies (Miller, Goy, Morse, & Dorman, 1975; Roth & Morse, 1975) habituation had not occurred when stimulus change took place.

AUDITORY EVOKED RESPONSE

Research with auditory evoked responses was conducted as early as 1939 (Davis, Davis, Loomis, Harvey, & Hobart, 1939; Davis, 1939), but it has only been within the last half-decade that systematic attempts have been made to use these measures in the area of speech preception. The AER is an electrocortical response evoked by an external auditory stimulus. Electrodes placed over various areas of the scalp are used to detect the response.

Fewer studies of infant speech perception have employed the AER method than have employed HAS and HR. Nevertheless, there have been investigations of infants' responses to speech parameters such as frequency (Lenard, von Bernuth, & Hutt, 1969), intensity (Barnet & Goodwin, 1965), transition characteristics and format structure (Molfese, 1977; Molfese, Nunez, Seibert, & Ramanaiah, 1976) and to speech syllables and words (Barnet, DeSotills, & Campos, 1974; Molfese, 1972). These studies have found evidence of electrocortical responses that have different characteristics when speech sounds are used as stimuli than when non-speech sounds are used. It has also been found that the two hemispheres of the brain responded differently to speech sounds.

Molfese *et al.* (1976) recorded the AERs from temporal scalp locations of newborn infants during presentation of a series of speech and nonspeech stimuli. Stimulus discrimination was determined by comparing the average AER to each stimulus and noting similarities and differences among the components of the responses. AERs have also been used to investigate VOT perception. Molfese (1978) recorded AERs from scalp locations over the left and right hemispheres of 16 adults in response to four bilabial stop consonants with VOT values of 0, +20, +40, and +60 msec. Two components of the AER that were sensitive to the different VOT stimuli were identified. One component, present only in the AERs recorded from the right hemisphere, differentiated between the VOT stimuli in a categorical-like manner. There was no differentiation between the 0 and +20 msec stimuli or between the +40 and +60 stimuli, but the 0 and +20 stimuli were differentiated from the +40 and +60 stimuli. A second AER component, identified in the right hemisphere, occurred later in time and was also sensitive to differences between phoneme categories. A VOT study conducted with 4-year-old children reported similar findings. Molfese and Hess (1978) identified an early right hemisphere AER component that only distinguished between VOT stimuli from different phoneme categories. However, the later component that was sensitive to within as well as between phoneme differences occurred in both hemispheres. Such consistent findings across different populations suggest that the AER procedures are sensitive to the processing of VOT changes.

Unlike the HAS and HR methods, the AER method does not rely on the habituation paradigm, although such a paradigm can be used (Dorman, 1972; Molfese, 1977). The AER method also differs from HAS and HR in the assumptions made concerning the meaning of the responses. AER is a measure of electrocortical activity in response to auditory stimulation and thus can be used as a direct assessment of cortical processes (Callaway, 1975). HAS and HR rely on the measurement of responses that are hypothesized to reflect cortical processing and consequently represent indirect measures of neural activity. The AER method, like HR, does not require active participation by the subjects and can be used with subjects of any age to facilitate comparisons across different ages.

The HAS, HR, and AER methods have all been shown to be sensitive to variations in VOT. Subjects at all ages tested have shown categorical discrimination of VOT stimuli along phoneme boundaries. However, the issue of whether the discrimination of the VOT continuum is learned or innate remains open, since none of the methods have been used with newborn infants to determine if they respond differentially to VOT stimuli within and across phoneme boundaries. Therefore two studies employing AER procedures were conducted to investigate the responsiveness of infants 2–5 months old and infants within 24 hours of birth to 0, +20, +40, and +60 msec VOT stimuli. Because sex differences in AERs have been found in previous research with infants and children (Molfese *et al.*, 1976; Molfese & Hess, 1978), sex was included as a factor in the present studies.

EXPERIMENT 1

Subjects

Sixteen infants, eight males and eight females, participated in this first study. The male infants ranged in age from 2 months, 19 days to 5 months (mean age was 3 months, 25 days). The age range for the female infants was from 2 months, 3 days to 4 months, 16 days (mean age was 3 months, 4 days).

Stimuli

Four consonant–vowel speech syllables constructed on the parallel resonance speech synthesizer at Haskins Laboratories were used as stimuli. These syllables consisted of an initial bilabial stop consonant (50 msec in duration) with VOT values of 0, +20, +40, and +60 msec and the vowel /a/ (300 msec in duration). Sixteen replications of each stimulus were recorded in a random order on a one-tape channel by a Sony Stereo Tape Recorder (Model TC-560). A 50 Hz square wave ($\frac{1}{4}$ volt in amplitude) was recorded on the second tape channel and time locked to the onset of the speech stimulus. This 50 Hz square pulse served as a stimulus trigger pulse to identify the beginning of each stimulus presentation and the beginning of the auditory evoked potential for a PDP-12 computer. The interstimulus interval varied randomly from 4 to 8 seconds.

Procedure

The infants were tested individually in a sound dampened and electrically shielded room. Each infant was placed in a 40° reclined infant seat. Recording electrodes were then placed on the scalp over the superior temporal regions of the left and right hemispheres at T_3 and T_4 of the 10–20 electrode system of the international federation (Jasper, 1958) and referred to linked ear lobes. Electrode impedances for each side of the head were checked and recorded both before and after each testing session. The mean values of these impedances were 3.81 kOhms before testing (range: 2.0 to 6.8) and 3.82 kOhms (range: 1.7 to 7.5) at the end of the 15-minute testing session. Impedances for the two scalp electrodes were maintained within 1 kOhm of each other throughout the testing session. The recording electrodes were connected to two Analogue Devices Isolation Amplifiers (Model 273J) that protected the infants against possible shock. The output of each amplifier was connected to a modified Tektronix AM502 differential amplifier with the bandpass flat between .1 Hz and 30 Hz and with the gain set to 20 kOhms. The amplified auditory evoked potentials from the two scalp locations and the stimulus trigger pulses were each recorded on separate channels of a four channel Vetter modified Cassette FM tape recorder (Model C-4) for later off-line analyses on a PDP-12 computer and an IBM-370. The stimuli were presented to each infant through a speaker positioned one meter above the infant's head. The stimulus intensity was 80 dB SPL at the infant's ears.

Results

The AERs from each subject were digitized and averaged on a PDP-12 computer using a modified version of "Averager" (Decus 12–84). Averages were obtained at 8 msec intervals over a 1 sec period following stimulus onset (for a total of 125 points) for each AER to the 16 stimulus repetitions for each VOT value (4), each hemisphere (2), and each subject (16). This procedure resulted in 128 averaged evoked potentials. Following the procedures outlined by Molfese *et al.* (1976), a 125 (time point variables) × 128 (averaged evoked response cases) input matrix was obtained. Intercorrelations among the 125 variables were submitted to a principal component factor analysis. Five factors accounting for 96.58% of the total variance were selected on the basis of the Cattell Scree Test (Cattell, 1966) and then rotated using the varimax method (Harman, 1967; Mulaik, 1972) with the

BMDO8M computer program (Dixon, 1972) in order to obtain latent components of evoked potentials that might provide a more parsimonious representation of the complex AER waveform.

The centroid (the average evoked AER of the entire data set) and the five factors obtained by the principal components analysis are plotted in Figure 5.1. The centroid was characterized by a major positive peak 400 msec (P_{400}) after stimulus onset, followed by a negative peak at 768 msec (N_{768}), a positive peak at 848 msec (P_{848}), and a final negative peak 968 msec (N_{968}) after onset. Factor 1 was characterized by a major peak 96 msec after stimulus onset, whereas peaks at 144 and 920 msec distinguished Factor 2. The major peak latencies for Factor 3 were 40 and 528 msec. A major peak at 392 msec characterized Factor 4 and a peak at 696 msec marked Factor 5.

Each of the five factors was submitted to a 2(Sex) × 2 (Hemisphere) × 4 (VOT) analysis of variance. A VOT × Hemisphere interaction was found for Factor 2 ($F = 2.84, df = 3,42, p < .05$). This interaction was due to the ability of only the right hemisphere to differentiate the 0 and +20 msec VOT stimuli from the +40 and +60 VOT stimuli ($p < .05$) as illustrated in Figure 5.2. The group averaged AERs for the right hemisphere that reflect these VOT differences are presented in Figure 5.3. For both the 0 and +20 msec VOT conditions the N_{200} component was more negative than the N_{584} peak. In addition, the amplitudes of the N_{584} and N_{776} components are equal. For the +40 and +60 msec conditions, however, the N_{200} and N_{584} components were equally negative and the N_{584} component was more positive than the N_{776} peak. The last half of the AERs for the +40 and +60 msec conditions are characterized by a general slow negative trend, but

Figure 5.1 The centroid and the five orthogonal factors isolated by the principal components analysis. The centroid is the average evoked potential for all subjects in all conditions and consequently characterized the electrocortical components common to all AERs. The time course for the centroid is 1000 msec, with stimulus onset occurring at the beginning of the waveform. The calibration scale is 5μV with positive up. The five factors each consist of 125 factor loadings that correspond to the 125 time points. The factor loadings reflect the association of the factors to these original time points. The polarity and amplitude of the factors as represented here are arbitrary. They can be calculated for the different conditions by multiplying them by the factor scores (gain factors which served as the dependent variables in the analyses of variance) for the different conditions. All waveforms represented here are based on points at 24 msec intervals.

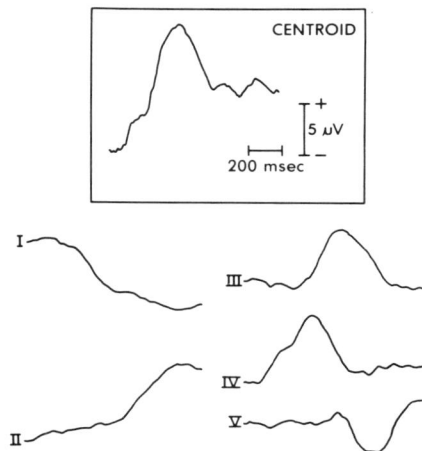

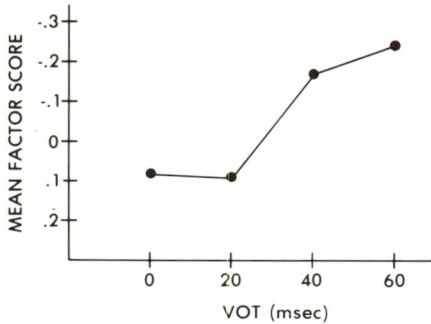

Figure 5.2 The right hemisphere responses as characterized by mean factor scores as a function of different VOT values. The factor scores plotted along the ordinate are the means for the dependent measures in the analysis of variance. These means reflect the weights of the VOT × Hemisphere interaction for Factor 2. The polarity and amplitude of the waveform for a particular condition is determined by multiplying each point of the waveform by the mean factor score for that condition.

those for the 0 and +20 msec stimuli are not. Main effects for VOT ($F = 2.92$, $df = 3,42$ $p < .05$) and Hemispheres ($F = 5.13$, $df = 1,14$, $p < .05$) were found for Factor 3. This Hemisphere effect can be seen in the group average AERs of Figure 5.4. Here the N_{200} component for the left hemisphere response was more negative than the N_{584} peak, but both components were equal in amplitude for the right hemisphere. However, the N_{584} peak reached a more negative point than the N_{776} component. A significant Sex × VOT interaction ($F = 4.59$, $df = 3,42$, $p < .01$) also found for this factor suggests that the VOT main effect was due to the differential ability of female infants relative to males to distinguish the 0 and +20 msec stimuli from the +40 and +60 msec stimuli. This interaction is presented in Figure 5.5. Given the orthogonal nature of the factors, it should be noted that the VOT effect for this last interaction was independent of the VOT × Hemisphere effect of Factor 2. As illustrated in Figure 5.1, the latencies of the major AER components for these two factors were different. No effects were found for Factors 1, 4, or 5.

RIGHT HEMISPHERE

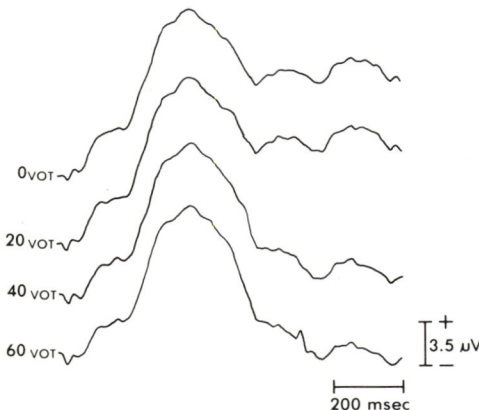

Figure 5.3 Group averaged AERs for the right hemisphere elicited in response to the four VOT stimuli. The calibration marker is 3.5 μV with positive up. Duration is 1 sec. Plots are based on points at 16 msec intervals.

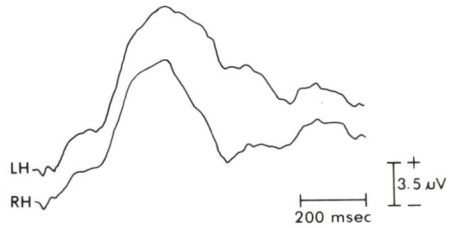

Figure 5.4 Group averaged AERs for the left and right hemispheres. Calibration marker is 3.5 μV. Polarity is positive up. Latency is 1 sec.

The findings of Experiment 1—that certain components of the AERs of infants are sensitive to different VOT characteristics—are remarkably similar to those found in adults (Molfese, 1978) and children (Molfese & Hess, 1978). In all three studies there were two AER components that varied systematically with changes in VOT. Factor 2 characterized a phoneme category discrimination process in the right hemisphere. A second VOT effect indicated by Factor 3 was present in both hemispheres. The latencies of the components of Factor 3, however, were later than those for Factor 2. AERs of the infants, children, and adults consistently differentiate between VOT stimuli along phoneme boundaries and these results are similar to those of studies using HAS and HR procedures.

In Experiment 2 the AER procedure was used with newborn infants to determine if their responses showed the same type of categorical differ-

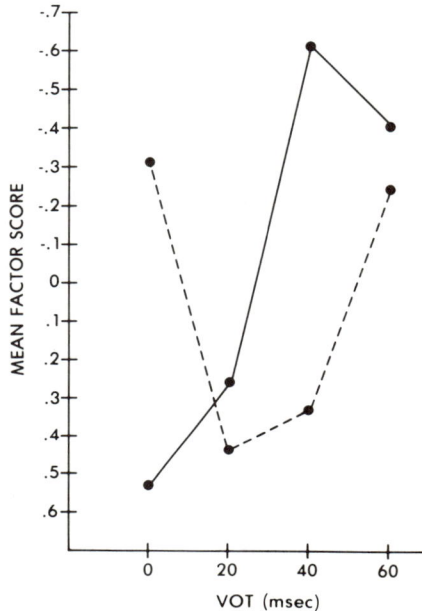

Figure 5.5 Mean factor scores for the male (– – –) and female (——) infants as characterized by Factor 3 in response to the four VOT stimuli.

entiation of the VOT stimuli. The presence of such a differential response would support the notion that VOT perception has an innate basis.

EXPERIMENT 2

Subjects

Eight male and eight female infants were tested within 24 hr of birth. The males had 1 and 5 minute mean Apgars of 8.2 and 8.9, respectively (range = 7–9 and 8–9). The mean 1 and 5 minute Apgar scores for the female newborns were 8.1 and 9.2, respectively (range = 7–9 and 9–10). The mean birth weight for the males was 7 lb., 5 oz. (range = 6 lb., 11 oz. to 8 lb., 12 oz.) and 6 lb., 12 oz. (range = 5 lb., 9 oz. to 7 lb., 13 oz.) for the females. Only local or epidural anesthetics were used during deliveries.

Stimuli

The stimuli employed in Experiment 1 were also used in Experiment 2. Stimulus presentation rate and order were also comparable.

Procedure

The stimuli were presented to each infant individually in a room adjoining the hospital nursery. The stimulus intensity was 80 dB SPL at the infant's ear. The infant was placed in a semireclined infant seat and scalp electrodes were placed over the left and right temporal regions identified as T_3 and T_4, respectively. These were referred to linked ear leads. A fifth electrode, which served as a floating ground, was placed on the forehead. Electrode impedances were measured and recorded before and after the testing session for each infant. Pretest mean impedances were 4.54 kOhms (range = 1.0–8.0). Posttest mean measures were 5.07 kOhms (range = 1.0–8.0). Impedances for the two scalp electrodes were maintained within 1 kOhm of each other throughout the testing session. The amplifying and recording systems were identical to those described in Experiment 1. Infant EEG activity was monitored throughout the recording session. Stimuli were only presented when the infants were in a quiet sleep state.

Results

As in Experiment 1, 128 averaged evoked responses were obtained from 16 repetitions of each stimulus for each VOT value (4), each hemisphere (2), and each subject (16). Each average was based on 125 samples at

8 msec intervals over the 1 sec period following stimulus onset (for a total of 125 points). A 125 (time point variables) × 128 (averaged evoked response cases) input matrix was then constructed. Intercorrelations among the 125 variables were submitted to a principal components factor analysis. Four factors accounting for 52.20% of the total variance were selected on the basis of the Cattell Scree Test (Cattell, 1966) and then rotated using the varimax method with the BMDO8M computer program.

The centroid and the four factors obtained by the principal components analysis are plotted in Figure 5.6. The centroid consisted of an initial negative component 216 msec after onset (N_{216}) that was followed by a positive component (P_{384}), a second negative component (N_{504}), a final positive component (P_{720}), and a late negative component (N_{960}). Factor 1 was characterized by a large late component that peaker 824 msec after stimulus onset. For Factor 2 an early component began 80 msec after stimulus onset, peaked at 224 msec, and was followed by a later peak at 536 msec. A component that peaked at 382 and ended at 585 msec, followed by a small peak at 960 msec, characterized Factor 3. The major component for Factor 4 began 520 msec after onset and peaked 664 msec after onset.

Significant Hemisphere effects were found for Factor 1 ($F = 17.14, df = 1, 14, p < .01$), Factor 2 ($F = 8.56, df = 1, 14, p < .01$) and Factor 4 ($F = 11.33, df = 1, 14, p < .01$). The group average AERs for the two hemispheres are presented in Figure 5.7. The amplitude of the N_{216}–P_{384} left

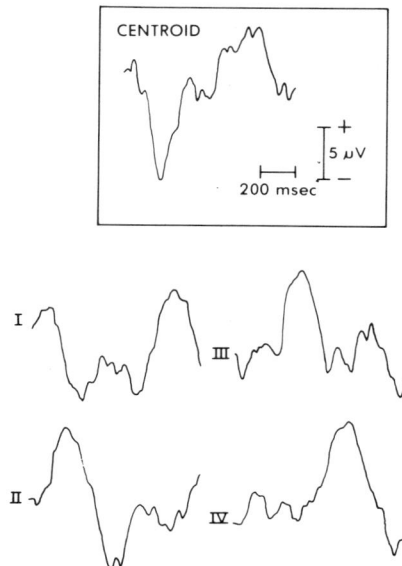

Figure 5.6 The centroid and four factors for Experiment 2. The calibration scale for the centroid is 5 μV. Positive is up. Duration is 1 sec. Plots are based on points at 8 msec intervals.

LEFT
HEMISPHERE

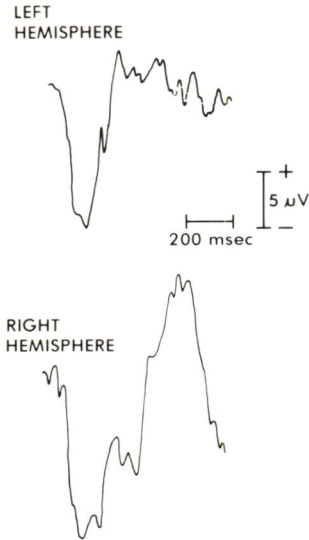

200 msec

5 μV

RIGHT
HEMISPHERE

Figure 5.7 Group average AERs for the left and right hemispheres of the newborns. Calibration is 5 μV with positive up. Latency is 1 sec.

hemisphere response was larger than that for the right hemisphere for all stimuli. This effect was due primarily to the greater development of the late positive component (P_{720}) in the right hemisphere. Such differences reflect the contributions of the three orthogonal factors (1, 2, 4) to the waveforms at different latencies. A sex × hemisphere interaction ($F = 8.14, df = 1, 14$ $p < .01$) was also found for Factor 2. This effect was due to a difference in the hemispheric responses of the female but not the male infants to all stimuli.

DISCUSSION

The purpose of the two experiments described was to determine if the AER procedures could be used with newborn and 2–5-month-old infants to detect differentiation of VOT values. Previous behavioral research using HAS and HR procedures found that infants as young as 1 month differentiate between VOT stimuli along phoneme boundaries. Thus, 0 and +20 VOT stimuli (which adults label as /ba/) got different responses from +40 and +60 VOT stimuli (which adults label as /pa/). No differential response was noted to stimuli within the /ba/ and /pa/ categories. In Experiment 1, the AERs of 2–5-months-old infants showed evidence of electrocortical differentiation of the VOT stimuli along phoneme boundaries. These responses were consistent with the findings of the HAS and HR studies. However, in Experiment 1, two distinct cortical events reflected such VOT effects. One early AER component (144 msec) that differentiated between stimuli from different phoneme categories occurred only in the right hemisphere of all infants. A second cortical component that reflected phoneme boundary effects occurred later in time (264–604 msec) and was present in the AERs of both hemispheres of the female infants but not the males. Such findings suggest that VOT discriminations are based on a number of cortical processes, some which are developed by 2 months of age and others which continue to develop into adulthood.

Because behavioral studies of young infants have found that responses to VOT stimuli are similar to those found with adults, perception of VOT stimuli along phoneme boundaries was thought to be innate (Eimas *et al.*, 1971). The results of Experiment 2, however, provide no evidence of such differences in newborn infants. Nevertheless, components of the newborns' AERs were similar to components of AERs recorded from older infants (Experiment 1), children (Molfese & Hess, 1978), and adults (Molfese, 1978). All four experiments have found evidence that the two hemispheres are actively involved in the processing of auditory stimuli.

However, the hemispheres appear to respond in different ways. This differential hemispheric response shows an interesting developmental change. In newborns the two hemispheres respond differently to the VOT stimuli, but show no evidence of categorical response. Differential VOT responses were found in the infant and child populations, but only occurred in the right hemisphere. In adults, this response was again found only in the right hemisphere, but the left hemisphere differentiated between specific VOT stimuli, that is between end points on the VOT continuum (0 and +60) and between end points and the middle values (+20 and +40). Such changes in AERs may reflect the influence of maturation or experience factors.

The studies also indicate the AER components of newborns, infants, and children reflect sex differences in cortical activity. The presence of sex differences in only the infant and child populations suggests that the sex effect may be due to maturational factors. Such differences have been noted in other areas, as in the case of the anatomical systems of male and female infants and children (Tanner, 1970). The absence of sex differences in adult AERs and the failure to find morphological differences related to sex in the brains of adults (Geschwind & Levitsky, 1968; Wada, Clark, & Hamm, 1975) suggest that maturational differences in brain development may be responsible for the presence of sex differences in AERs.

Overall, the results of the HAS, HR, and AER studies indicate that, although the ability to discriminate VOT stimuli along phoneme boundaries is present by at least the first month of life (Eimas *et al.*, 1971), it is not innate and may require some maturational or experiential influences in order to develop or become functional. It could be argued, however, that the two temporal area scalp locations utilized in Experiment 2 were insufficient in number or did not correspond to cortical areas responsible for categorical responding. Other areas of the cortex in addition to the temporal regions could be involved in the VOT discrimination process and these other areas could be functional at birth. Further research is necessary in order to determine if VOT detectors are located in other cortical areas in newborns. However, it is clear that the VOT effects found at these temporal sites (T_3, T_4) in all older populations were not present in the newborns' responses. Consequently, some development of this perceptual ability occurs only after birth.

The AER procedure has proven to be an effective means of assessing responses to VOT stimuli across subject populations of diverse ages. Furthermore, because of the nature of the AER procedure, the total testing time during which each individual subject is presented with all stimulus values is approximately 10 minutes. Thus, it is possible to analyze within sample designs with infant and child subjects rather than only between sample designs, as is true in typical HAS and HR studies. In addition, since the procedure is the same across all subjects tested, it is possible to examine the results for consistencies and differences in responses across age. In summary, then, such procedures offer not only alternate ways in which to assess neurolinguistic functions, but also quite powerful tools that may provide us with different types of information concerning different levels of cortical and linguistic involvement.

REFERENCES

Barnet, A. B., DeSotills, M. V., & Campos, M. 1974. *EEG sensory evoked potentials in early infancy malnutrition.* Paper presented at the meeting of the Society for Neurosciences, St. Louis.

Barnet, A., & Goodwin, R. S. 1965. Averaged evoked electroencephalographic responses to clicks in the human newborn. *Electroencephalography and Clinical Neurophysiology, 18,* 441–450.

Butterfield, E. C., & Cairns, G. F. 1974. Infant reception research. In R. L. Schiefelbusch & L. L. Lloyd (Eds.), *Language perspectives—acquisition, retardation and intervention.* Baltimore: University Park Press. Pp. 75–102.

Callaway, E. 1975. *Brain electrical potentials and individual psychological differences.* New York: Grune & Stratton.

Cattell, R. B. 1966. The scree test for the number of factors. *Multivariate Behavioral Research, 1,* 245.

Chapman, R. M., McCrary, J. M., Bragdon, H. R., & Chapman, J. A. 1977. Latent components of evoked potentials functionally related to information processing. In J. E. Desmedt (Ed.), *Cerebral evoked potentials in man.* London: Oxford University Press.

Davis, H., Davis, P. A., Loomis, A. L., Harvey, E. N., & Hobart, G. 1939. Electrical reactions of the human brain to auditory stimulation during sleep. *Journal of Neurophysiology, 2,* 500–514.

Davis, P. A. 1939. Effects of acoustic stimuli on the waking human brain. *Journal of Neurophysiology, 2,* 494–499.

Dixon, W. J. 1972. *BMD biomedical computer program: X-series supplement.* Berkeley: University of California Press.

Dorman, M. F. 1972. Auditory evoked potential correlates of speech sound discrimination, *Haskins Laboratories Status Report on Speech Research,* SR – 29/30, 111–120.

Eimas, P. D. 1974. Auditory and linguistic processing of cues for place of articulation by infants. *Perception and Psychophysics, 16,* 513–521.

Eimas, P. D., Siqueland, E. R., Jusczyk, P., & Vigorito, J. 1971. Speech perception in infants. *Science, 171,* 303–306.

Geschwind, N., & Levitsky, W. 1968. Left-right asymmetries in the temporal speech region, *Science, 161,* 166–167.

Gregg, C., Clifton, R., & Haith, M. 1973. *Heart rate change as a function of visual stimulation in the newborn.* Paper presented at the biennial meeting of the Society for Research in Child Development, Philadelphia.

Harman, H. H. 1967. *Modern factor analyses* (2nd ed.). Chicago: University of Chicago Press.

Jasper, H. H. 1958. The ten twenty electrode system of the international federation of societies for electroencephalography: Appendix to report of the committee on methods of clinical examination in electroencephalography. *The Journal of Electroencephalography and Clinical Neurophysiology, 10,* 371.

Kuhl, P. K., & Miller, J. D. 1975. Speech perception in early infancy: Discrimination of speech–sound categories. *Journal of the Acoustical Society of America, 58,* 556 (A).

Lasky, R., Syrdal-Lasky, A., & Klein, E. 1975. VOT discrimination by four-to-six-month-old infants from Spanish environments. *Journal of Experimental Child Psychology, 20,* 215–225.

Lenard, H. C., Von Bernuth, H., & Hutt, S. J. 1969. Acoustic evoked responses in newborn infants: the influence of pitch and complexity of the stimulus. *The Journal of Electroencephalography and Clinical Neurophysiology, 27,* 121–127.

Liberman, A. M., Cooper, F. S., Shankweiler, D. P., & Studdert-Kennedy, M. 1967. Perception of the Speech Code. *Psychological Review, 74,* 431–461.

Miller, C. L., Goy, E. R., Morse, P. A., & Dorman, M. F. 1975. Selected problems in infant burst discrimination. In L. L. Leavitt & P. A. Morse (Eds.), *Infant development laboratory: Research status report* (Vol. 1). Madison, Wisconsin: University of Madison.

Moffitt, A. R. 1971. Consonant cue perception by twenty-to-twenty-four-week-old infants. *Child Development, 42,* 717–731.

Moffitt, A. R., & Pankhurst, D. J. 1973. *Speech perception during infancy.* Unpublished manuscript, Carleton University, Ottawa, Canada.

Mofese, D. L. 1972. *Cerebral asymmetry in infants, children and adults: auditory evoked responses to speech and music stimuli.* Unpublished doctoral dissertation, The Pennsylvania State University.

Molfese, D. L. 1977. Infant cerebral asymmetry. In S. Segalowitz & F. Gruber (Eds.), *Language development and neurological theory.* New York: Academic Press.

Molfese, D. L. 1978. Electrophysiological correlates of categorical speech perception in adults. *Brain and Language, 5,* 25–35.

Molfese, D. L., & Hess, T. M. 1978. Hemispheric specialization for VOT perception in the preschool child. *Journal of Experimental Child Psychology, 26,* 71–84.

Molfese, D. L., Nunez, V., Seibert, S. M., & Ramanaiah, N. V. 1976. Cerebral asymmetry;

changes in factors affecting its development. *Annals of the New York Academy of Sciences, 280,* 821–833.

Morse, P. A. 1972. The discrimination of speech and nonspeech stimuli in early infancy. *Journal of Experimental Child Psychology, 14,* 477–494.

Mulaik, S. A. 1972. *The foundation of factor analysis.* New York: McGraw-Hill.

Roth, P. L., & Morse, P. A. 1975. An investigation of infant VOT discrimination using the cardiac OR. In L. L. Leavitt & P. A. Morse (Eds.), *Infant development laboratory: Research status report* (Vol. 1). Madison, Wisconsin: University of Madison. Pp. 207–218.

Siqueland, E. R., & DeLucia, C. A. 1969. Visual reinforcement of nonnutritive sucking in human infants. *Science, 165,* 1144–1146.

Sokolov, E. N. 1963. *Perception and the conditioned reflex.* New York: MacMillan.

Tanner, J. M. 1970. Physical growth. In P. H. Mussen (Ed.), *Carmichael's manual of child psychology.* New York: Wiley.

Treub, S., & Rabinovitch, S. 1972. Auditory–linguistic sensitivity in early infancy. *Developmental Psychology, 6,* 74–77.

Wada, J. A., Clark, R., & Hamm, A. 1975. Cerebral hemispheric asymmetry in humans. *Archives of Neurology, 32,* 239–246.

6

Disruption of Written Language in Aphasia

Hanna K. Ulatowska

THE UNIVERSITY OF TEXAS AT DALLAS

Temple Baker

THE UNIVERSITY OF TEXAS AT ARLINGTON

Renee Freedman Stern

THE UNIVERSITY OF TEXAS AT DALLAS

The relationship between speech and writing has been a question of interest at least since Aristotle. For many decades, the accepted point of view had been that writing was simply a transcription of spoken language, merely "speech written down." Structural linguistics long considered spoken language to be its primary subject matter, and until recently virtually excluded written language from the proper domain of (synchronic) linguistic science (Bloomfield, 1933). Likewise, the study of pathological language has historically been primarily concerned with disturbances of speech, although dysgraphic phenomena were reported in almost the earliest literature on language disturbances.

In recent years, however, the view that speech and writing are autonomous variants—dialects—of the same language has been gaining acceptance. Proponents of this view do not go so far as to maintain that the two variants are of equal status, but argue that speech has biological and historical precedence over writing and is the unmarked member of the pair (Vachek, 1972). They support their position with examples of differences in the two variants, especially syntactic and lexical ones (Stalker, 1974; Gleason, 1965), and of difficulties in intralingual translation (Vachek, 1972). The proposed basis of these differences varies with the perspective of the investigator. Vachek focuses on the complementary functions of the two forms: spoken utterances serve to give ready, immediate, and emotional response; written utterances allow documentary and easily surveyable reac-

241

tion. Returning to ultimate causes, he suggests that written language emerges only after a society reaches a level of complexity that creates the functional need for it.

Other writers focus on different parts of the communication situation. For instance, Gleason (1965), concentrating on the medium through which the message is transmitted, explains the differences in speech and writing in terms of redundancy. Speech "provides the maximum amount of structure signals to overcome difficulties in transmission and still guarantees an adequate minimum at the hearer's end. The other uses a minimum of signals with much higher precision and efficiency [p. 172]." In a similar vein, but from a perspective slightly shifted toward the receiver of the message, F. Smith (1975) notes that writing permits the reader to determine his own speed and sequence but provides none of the supplementary information that speech makes available. However, the differences should not be over-emphasized. As Smith points out, they are probably not any greater than the differences **within** the spoken form.

Along with the increased status of written language in linguistics, a heightened interest in the analysis of writing has developed in the fields of educational psychology and communication disorders. The present article attempts an integrated survey of normal and pathological written language from all these disciplines.

The first part of this chapter surveys some of the recent literature on the acquisition, structure, and pathology of written language. The second part presents analysis of two types of original data: the writing of a group of subjects responding to a pictorial stimulus and the spontaneous writing of one aphasic patient in the form of letters and diaries.

THE ASSESSMENT AND DEVELOPMENT OF WRITTEN LANGUAGE

Assessments of written language have largely been the work of educational psychologists, whose techniques are essentially methods for measuring complexity or variety in samples of writing from selected populations writing to specific tasks. Using samples written freely to particular stimuli, within certain time limits, investigators describe the writing in terms of a number of conventional grammatical units: the word, the sentence, the phrase, the clause, and the T-unit or "minimal terminable unit" (a structure first defined by Hunt [1965] as one independent clause plus all the modifiers attached to it, the smallest unit that can be punctuated as a sentence). Features of the sample are then stated in such statistics as mean number of words per sentence or T-units per composition. Complexity can be defined by the occurrence of certain syntactic patterns: phrases per clause, clauses per sentence or T-unit, and the internal structure of constituent clauses. Variety can be defined in terms of the number of different syntactic patterns employed. In addition, features of the vocabulary are usually examined. Much of the evaluation that has been undertaken has been directed toward drawing a profile of the normal development of writing abilities and in correlating milestones in this sequence with those in the development of spoken language.

Increase in the length of composition and of its components is one manifestation of increased writing maturity. Sentence length can be increased in three ways: clauses can be joined with coordinating conjunctions; one clause can be subordinated to another with a subordinating conjunction; or a clause can be reduced to a word or phrase and embedded within another. Hunt (1965, 1970) and O'Donnell, Griffin, and Norris (1967), along with many others (Peltz, 1974; Lawton, 1963; Golub, 1964; Evanechko, Ollila, & Armstrong, 1974; Loban, 1963), have examined the development of these techniques with very similar results. First, they have found that the coordination of clauses is developmentally the earliest method of increasing sentence length. It is used often in the early grades, decreasing steadily and reaching adult levels by grade 12. The second method, adding dependent clauses, increases rapidly in grades 4 through 8, when it reaches almost adult level. The final method, embedding clause reductions, increases very slowly with age and is not fully developed until the level of the skilled adult. Sentences in which clauses are both coordinated and subordinated are uncommon at all levels (Bear, 1939; National Assessment of Educational Progress, 1972).

In terms of the internal structure of the sentence, variety and complexity have been measured in several ways. The number of sentence-combining transformations per sentence (excluding coordinating clauses) rises with age (O'Donnell *et al.*, 1967; Hunt, 1970). In addition, older writers use a greater variety of embeddings (Hunt, 1965). In the early stages of writing development, nouns modified by possessives are the most common nominal construction. Nouns modified by prepositional phrases and adjectives are fairly common, while nouns modified by participles or participial phrases are rare; the frequency of these structures increases with age (O'Donnell *et al.*, 1967; Evanechko *et al.*, 1974; Trebuzovskaja, 1974; Nemanich, 1974). Hunt (1970) maintains that all ages use essentially the same phrase structure rules, although older writers elaborate the auxiliary more, using perfectives and a variety of modals. And although most sentence patterns are present in the writing of even the youngest children, SVO and SV account for 85% of sentence types in grades 3 to 7 (O'Donnell *et al.*, 1967).

Vocabulary development is usually measured along three parameters: fluency, diversity, and complexity. The simplest and most common measure of fluency is the number of words written. Without exception, studies of writing development show that older children write more, given the same stimulus and the same time constraints (Hunt, 1970; O'Donnell *et al.*, 1967; National Assessment of Educational Progress, 1975). Vocabulary diversity is usually measured in terms of the type–token ratio, which has been found to increase with age (National Assessment of Educational Progress, 1972). Complexity is measured in terms of the percentage of words that are not in the first thousand or so items on a frequency list or in terms of word length. By any of these measures, vocabulary complexity increases with age (Bushnell, 1930; DeVito, 1965; Choltos, 1944; National Assessment of Educational Progress, 1972). Attempts have also been made to measure development in terms of ratios of the occurrence of various parts of speech (Fairbanks, 1944; Mann, 1944; DeVito, 1967); however, these measures do not seem to yield consistent results.

Comparison of the Development of Written and Spoken Language

Investigations into the development of written language in relation to spoken language indicate that, until about fifth grade, children have weaker control of the written language than of the spoken. At least one study (Golub, 1969) reports a certain time lag between the acquisition of syntactic structures in speech and their occurrence in writing. However, O'Donnell *et al.* (1967) is more typical of studies comparing spoken and written development in finding that "advances in control of syntax in Grades 5 and 7 were accelerated in writing far beyond those reflected in speech [p. 95]." Whether syntactic structures appear first in speech followed shortly thereafter by extended use and elaboration in writing is not clear from these data, although it is likely that those structures that are used almost exclusively in writing do not occur initially in speech.

A number of studies have reported longer samples and longer sentences in speech (Buschnell, 1930; De Vito, 1965). They also report that although sentences containing a single independent clause are more common in written language, compound sentences are more common in spoken language. The use of sentence patterns in speech is similar to that in writing in that SVO and SV are the most common patterns, together accounting for approximately 87% of the sentences used (O'Donnell *et al.*, 1967). In comparison of vocabulary, type–token ratios are always larger in writing (Mann, 1944; Fairbanks, 1944; Gibson, Gruner, Kibler, & Kelly, 1966; DeVito, 1965).

Development of Written Language in the Deaf

Since in normal children writing depends on the acquisition of spoken language, an interesting special case of writing development is provided by deaf children, whose writing cannot be based on speech. Deaf children are from 2 to 4 years behind hearing children in written language development. They write less, have a lower type–token ratio, and their clauses, T-units, and sentences are shorter, with fewer coordinate and subordinate clauses per sentence. However, growth in all of these measures, except coordinate clauses, occurs as age increases at about the same rate in deaf and hearing children. In addition, the relative use of the various types of embedding transformations is very similar in the two groups (Taylor, 1969; Stuckless, 1966).

The writing of the deaf contains many times the number of errors found in the writing of the hearing and this gap increases with age. The largest number of errors involves determiners, articles, and auxiliaries, although use of the latter is rare in the writing of deaf children (Taylor, 1969; Quigley, Mantonelli, & Wilbur, 1976). Morphological errors are the second most common type in the writing of the deaf. Problems include the omission of verb and noun inflections, the overgeneralization of regular verb and noun inflectional patterns, shifts of tense, and occasionally incorrect use of possessive and pronoun inflections (Taylor, 1969; Quigley *et al.*, 1976; Wilbur, Mantonelli, & Quigley, 1976). However, conclusions based on these data should be drawn cautiously: Most of the deaf students in the studies learned American Sign Language, which is substantially different in structure from both written and spoken English, as their first language. Their progress in developing writing might more accurately be compared with mastery of a second language than with writing development in hearing children.

TYPES OF WRITING DISRUPTION

Early Investigations of Agraphia

The first description of central writing disturbances was made by Marcé (1856). Benedikt (1865) used the term agraphia and considered it a complication of aphasia. Trousseau (1864) and Dejerine (1891) also observed writing disturbances in aphasics. Early investigators emphasized the similarity of writing disorders to the accompanying disorders of spoken language. John Hughlings Jackson (1866) considered that impairments of writing, as well as of speech and reading, reflected the same linguistic deficiency in various forms. In his experience, writing was always impaired to some extent in aphasia. Several other investigations have reported that writing disturbances parallel those of spoken language (for example, Weisenberg & McBride, 1935). In addition to the early emphasis on the similarities of written and spoken language abnormalities, attempts to localize a specific writing function in the brain were made (see especially Exner, 1881). Wernicke (1886) also described differential disturbances according to site of lesion.

Classification and Symptomatology of Agraphia

Several classifications of agraphia have been proposed. One method, used for example by Hecaen (1963), describes writing deficiencies under the headings of the major clinical aphasia types (motor, expressive, sensory, parietal syndrome, conduction), with further subclassifications according to level of severity. Another method describes deficiencies in terms of types of writing performance and their components (e.g., copying to dictation or copying written models, spontaneous writing, written spelling, identification of written words). A symtomatology that describes paragraphias of written language as being either different from or identical to those in the spoken language is found in Pick (1973) and in Klein and Mayer-Gross (1957). Further, Leischner (1958), among others, attempted to correlate the similarity or difference in deficits in speech and writing with site of lesion.

Among specific studies of particular syndromes may be mentioned Dejerine (1891), Wernicke (1903), and von Monakow (1914) for motor aphasia; Goldstein (1910) and Klein (1931) for amnesic aphasia; Wernicke (1886), von Monakow (1914), Kleist (1934), and Leischner (1953) for sensory aphasia; and Wernicke (1886), for conduction aphasia.

Written language is the most complicated and fragile of language skills. Lord Brain (1961), discussing the anatomy and physiology of writing, says "clearly, this is a most complex process, considerably more complex than articulate speech [p. 133]." Porch (1967), in testing a large random sample of aphasics, found that written tasks were more difficult than either verbal or gestural. Schuell, Jenkins, and Jimenez-Pablon (1964) found impairments of writing to be characteristic of all five subgroups established in Schuell's Minnesota Test of Differential Diagnosis of Aphasia. In another diagnostic study, Keenan (1971) found writing to be a highly sensitive indicator of aphasic involvement in a group of mildly impaired patients. Smith (1971) noted that in aphasia involving both speech and writing, writing is the last skill to recover, and some aphasics may never fully recover despite improvement of communicative functionality via spoken language.

In view of this, it is not surprising that initial writing performance is a poor predictor of overall language recovery (Keenan & Brassell, 1974). It seems to be the case that any degree of spoken aphasia produces some disruption of writing. Geschwind (1973) argues that all reported cases of spoken aphasia with perfectly preserved writing turn out, on closer inspection, to be examples of insufficient testing. For example, it is common for automatic sequences such as a signature to be preserved in aphasia, but this is not proof of intact written language. Geschwind claims that some aspect of writing will always be disrupted if aphasia is present. The converse situation, "pure" agraphia without accompanying spoken aphasia, is rare.

Luria (1966) views language disruption as functional disorganization and breakdowns in parts of the system as having selective or global effects, depending on the nature of functional relationships or on the ability of the system to compensate for defective components. Weigl applies Luria's model to the experimental manipulation of the spoken and written components of language. The mechanism he proposes in this framework he calls "recoding" and the experimental manipulation of recoding is reflected in his therapeutic technique of "deblocking." Weigl's (1974, 1975) and Weigl and Fradis's (1977) experiments demonstrated that there is a faculty for "transcoding" word structures in the spoken sign system into structures in the written sign system and vice versa.

Isolated and Pure Agraphias

Linguistic errors in writing indicate aphasic involvement even if spoken language is virtually intact. "Pure" agraphia has come to refer to a syndrome of aphasic writing usually associated with well-delimited focal lesions of the dominant hemisphere. According to Hecaen, Angelergues, and Douzens (1963), pure agraphia may be no more than a limited aspect of a more global disorganization, the global aspect preventing compensation.

Hecaen *et al.* (1963) have pointed out that a disproportionate number of left-handers develop pure agraphia as a result of brain lesions. The patients may be left with a residual pure agraphia even after full recovery of other language functions. He suggests that writing in left-handers is more sensitive than other linguistic functions.

Assal, Chapuis, and Zander (1970) describe a case of "almost pure agraphia," resulting from stenosis of the left internal carotid artery. In explaining the independence of their patient's agraphia from disorders of spoken language or praxis, they point to a general intellectual impairment and a selective deficiency corresponding to a more localized disorder.

Lecours (1966) reports the case of Lee Harvey Oswald as an instance of isolated agraphia manifested in written spelling errors only, with preservation of spoken language and bright normal intelligence. The errors involved were sequential in nature and were analyzed as perseverations or anticipations influenced by immediate context. Though the subject is cited as an example of developmental agraphia, the type of error is characteristic of agraphias resulting from focal brain lesions.

The term "isolated" agraphia is less precisely defined, but is usually contrasted with pure agraphia by differences in etiology. The sources of isolated agraphias are varied (but exclude focal lesions) and the symptoms do not necessarily reflect aphasic involvement. Chedru and Geschwind (1972a, 1972b) report cases of "induced" isolated agraphia in subjects suffering acute confusional states. They conclude that an agent with diffuse, global effects (Amytal) produces disruption in writing, including spelling and grammatical errors. They compare the performance of their subjects with cases of "pure agraphia," noting similarities in motor, spatial, and linguistic errors (and some differences of severity) and suggest that isolated agraphia may be the result of diffuse brain dysfunction.

Ferguson and Boller (1977) report three patients who displayed syntactic writing errors in combination with a motor speech disturbance and impaired motor limb function. Two of the patients had amyotrophic lateral sclerosis (ALS). All three had both a motor speech disturbance and motor impairment in the arms and hands. These researchers note that the presence of a nonspecific neural impairment may suggest a situation similar to the confusional states discussed by Chedru and Geschwind. They favor, however, the hypothesis that disturbed feedback from speech and hand movements produced agraphia in these cases. In this connection, they note the experiment of Van Burgeijk and David (1959), who introduced delayed visual feedback into a writing task given to normal subjects and thereby produced an artificial writing impairment.

Aphasic Writing in Conjunction with Aphasia of Spoken Language

Writing disturbances are usually part of a complex aphasic syndrome in which writing is the most disrupted component.

Acquired aphasia in children is an interesting special case. Focal cerebral lesions in childhood can result in language disruptions similar to the aphasic disorders of the adult. The special interest of childhood aphasia is that it involves the nervous system and language function in the process of maturation. In a study of 32 children with aphasia, Alajouanine and Lhermitte (1965) noted that the most striking feature was the reduction of expressive language; spontaneous language was nearly absent. In a majority of cases, spontaneous writing, writing to dictation, and copying were completely suppressed. Where some written language remained, it was in all cases disturbed and this disturbance was more severe than that of oral language. Misspellings noted were often dependent on corresponding phonetic disturbances. The authors suggest that the deficits in writing reflect later acquisition of written language for which, developmentally, new neural circuits have been elaborated to code the phonemic units of language into graphic units. In other words, no automatization of writing has developed.

Disruptions of written language often parallel accompanying disorders of speech, as noted by, among others, Weisenberg and McBride (1935). Goodglass and Hunter (1970) analyzed samples of spontaneous written and spoken responses to picture narratives by a Wernicke's and a Broca's aphasic. The samples showed the same contrasting features in both means of expression. Both subjects produced longer grammatical runs in speech than in writing. The difference between the length of grammatical runs in the writing of the two patients was not statistically significant.

In another study (Hier & Mohr, 1977) comparing the spoken and written performance of a Wernicke's aphasic, written naming was spared although oral naming was not, and there was some superiority of reading comprehension to auditory comprehension. This suggests, contrary to the conventional view, that Wernicke's aphasia may not be an inseparable syndrome of deficiencies in reading, writing, and speech. All the above studies support the view of speech and writing as two different but related modalities of the same linguistic system.

ANALYSIS OF APHASIC WRITING

The present study is influenced by the investigation of functional communication in aphasia conducted by the senior author (Ulatowska *et al.*, 1976, 1977). Functional communication, defined by successful transfer of meaning in verbal and written modalities, was investigated both formally, in a number of simulated real–life situations, and informally, through questionnaires completed by aphasics, their families, and their clinicians. The results of the study revealed that some aphasics, especially those with moderately impaired language, write checks, take phone messages, and occasionally write letters. Aphasics also resort to writing when encountering difficulties in verbal expression.

The primary issue then is how that transfer of meaning is achieved despite the disruption of linguistic structure in aphasia. In order to answer this question, this study describes writing produced under two different conditions: in response to pictures and spontaneously. Whereas the structure of the communicative message is provided by the pictorial stimulus, in spontaneous writing that message must be generated by the writer himself.

Hence, the difference in the eliciting conditions might be reflected in the type of writing produced. However, we have not explored these differences systematically here.

Method

Two samples of writing were collected and analyzed by the authors. The first sample consisted of written descriptions of pictures elicited using two different pictures: the "cookie theft picture" of the Boston Diagnostic Aphasia Examination and a "cat and fishbowl" sequence picture. The "cookie theft picture" was given to 25 aphasics in therapy, 8 employed aphasics, 9 elderly normal subjects, and 9 children (3 of whom had completed the fourth grade, and 6, the fifth grade). All aphasics had suffered one cerebrovascular accident more than 3 months previously and their language impairment ranged from severe to mild. Six of the 8 employed aphasics were within normal range on the Boston Diagnostic Aphasia Examination and all were able to describe the "cookie theft" picture. Of the 25 aphasics in therapy, 20 were able to describe the picture and were included in the study. All 20 of the selected aphasics were able to write words and sentences to dictation. The "cat and fishbowl" sequence picture was given to another group of 25 aphasics in therapy. Data from this group was provided by Josephine Simonson of the Texas Neurological Institute. All except 2, who had had tumors, had suffered a single cerebrovascular accident more than 3 months previously. Their impairment ranged from severe to mild. Twenty of this group were able to describe the picture sequence and were included in the study. Since the data elicited in response to the "cookie theft" are similar to those of the "cat and fishbowl" sequence picture, the studies will be discussed together. The total sample of 58 aphasics provides a range of aphasic impairments that allows at least some generalizations about writing competence in aphasia. The two other samples of elderly normal subjects and young children, though rather small, yield some additional data for comparison.

Set against these data is the material of the second sample of over 10,000 running words of spontaneous writing by one aphasic who sustained a cerebrovascular accident with resulting fluent aphasia 3 months prior to the beginning of the investigation. The writing was produced over a period of 12 months. It includes letters written to the patient's speech therapist, a reconstructed diary covering his entire life, summaries of stories read by him, and anecdotes, all written at home. Over 4000 words, consisting of letters written in the first 5 months of the investigation, were coded for computer manipulation, providing the basis for quantitative description of the writing.

Analysis of the Written Descriptions

Table 6.1 gives the quantitative description of performance in the picture task. Some subjects tested (but not included in the tabulation) were able to produce descriptions in other than narrative form, either by listing nouns representing the participants in the pictured events or by producing the story in a different modality, such as pantomiming or drawing.

The main findings revealed in Table 6.1 can be summarized in the following points:

1. The mean number of sentences produced is similar for all the populations, with the fifth grade children producing the highest number.
2. Mean number of words in the complete description is the highest for employed aphasics and the lowest for the elderly normal subjects.
3. Mean sentence length, T-unit length, and clause per sentence ratio in the adult population are the highest for employed aphasics.

The high productivity of employed aphasics in the length of sentences, clauses, and number of words produced can be accounted for by the combination of two factors: their high educational level (mean 13.5 years) compared to the other groups and the nature of their linguistic impairment (as manifested in the high number of run-on sentences).

Typologically, most of the sentences were simple and affirmative. Only three negative sentences were produced, a fact probably related to the stimuli. It is interesting to note that normal adults produced the lowest number of complex sentences and the employed aphasics the highest. Aphasics in therapy and fifth graders produced a large number of compound sentences (representing a simpler method of conjoining clauses), but normal adults produced none.

In the description of the "cookie theft," concatenation of clauses into larger structures was variously handled. Of all the individuals studied, only one child in the older group produced two paragraphs, while all the other subjects had one paragraph. Four out of six fifth graders and one out of three fourth graders produced the story in a narrative form by introducing topic sentences such as "Once there was a mother and her children in the kitchen. . . ." This tactic provides cohesion by introducing temporal linkage. Another narrative device employed by the children was to name the actors, for example, "Then Jeff was to go to get some cookies and the stool started to fall." Since the attempts at producing "stage setting" sentences were evident even in the very immature writings of the younger group of children, it is likely that their particular style is influenced by the stories read to children at that age.

It is interesting to note that a narrative style was entirely lacking in the

TABLE 6.1 Performance on Writing to Pictorial Stimuli

Populations	N	Sentences			T-units			Clauses		Mean CL/sentence	CL/T-unit	Mean words	Range
		Mean	Range	Mean length	Mean	Range	Mean length	Mean	Range				
Cookie theft													
Aphasics in therapy	20	2.9	1–5	10.7	3.0	1–7	8.9	5.1	1–11	2.1	1.3	28.3	2–80
Employed aphasics	8	3.3	2–6	14.9	3.7	2–9	12.8	8.3	5–14	2.5	1.5	48.1	26–87
Normals (elderly)	9	3.1	2–5	6.6	3.1	2–5	6.6	3.6	2–6	1.1	1.3	20.0	1–29
Children: fourth grade	3	2.6	1–5	7.2	4.2	2–7	6.4	5.0	2–8	1.6	1.1	30.0	14–47
Children: fifth grade	6	4.2	3–5	11.1	6.3	4–8	7.5	8.0	6–10	1.8	1.1	48.0	36–72
Cat Fishbowl													
Aphasics in therapy	20	1.9	1–7	11.0	2.1	1–7	8.6	3.3	1–8	1.9	1.4	16.9	1–46

writing of the normal adults, who produced a list of simple sentences with no overt cohesion apart from that resulting from mere juxtaposition of sentences. This characteristic may be accounted for by the artificiality, for an elderly population, of the task of describing pictures. On the other hand, half of the employed aphasics and six of the aphasics in therapy produced the story in a narrative form, with cohesion achieved by the presence of dependent relative, temporal, or causative (finite and nonfinite) clauses or independent compound clauses with the conjunction "but;" for example, "Little boy was trying to get a cookie for his little sister is falling off the stool," and "The boy is getting into the cookie jar, but he is upsetting the stool and is about to fall."

The "cat and fishbowl" sequence picture given to the other population of 25 aphasics in therapy has a narrative component built in through the sequence of the two connected events depicted in the pictures. However, only seven subjects produced the narrative form. It is interesting to note that two resorted to the devices—employed by some of the children—of involving themselves in the story or imposing evaluative interpretations on the story; for example, "One had a companion of a gold fish and the other was so lonesome and missed a companion that meant the world of happiness that meant so much towards the days passing happy"; "The cat sees the fish and thinks about a good dinner, so he ate the fish."

Analysis of clausal elements disclosed a small number of modifiers, primarily possessive pronouns and the diminutive "little." These were used by all the populations studied. Employed aphasics used the most noun modifiers, normal adults the fewest. Relative clauses were rare. Verb forms consisted primarily of present progressive in the "cookie theft" picture, and simple present and past in the "cat and fishbowl" picture. The restricted use of tenses can be accounted for by the nature of the stimuli: one represents action in progress; the other a sequence of two actions, one in the present, the other in the past. Modals were restricted to markings of future action: *is going to, is about to.*

Error Analysis

At the level of syntax and morphology, three primary areas of errors were isolated: verbs, articles, and prepositions. In the use of verbs, omission of the auxiliary in present progressive was the most frequent error, followed in frequency by tense shift from past to present. In the use of articles, omissions of both definite and indefinite articles were observed, while additions and substitutions were rare. In the use of prepositions, mostly omissions were encountered, with infrequent substitutions and no additions. In all the above cases, omissions acounted for the majority of the errors, a finding consistent with the general reduction of functors in aphasia. There were a few additional sources of difficulty: Agreement errors resulting from the omission of plural markings were noticed in the use of nouns and in pronouns the objective case was replaced by the subjective case.

It should be noted that, on the whole, very few semantic errors were observed. Those present usually involved substitutions within the same semantic category, for example, *consume* instead of *eat* or *overbalanced* instead of *lost balance.*

Spelling errors were relatively infrequent (1%). Most of them were phonetic, for example, "steeling ('stealing') cookies," or involved doubling of consonants, for example, "watter." Punctuation errors consisted of omissions of periods and substitution of hyphens for periods, noticeable especially in the employed aphasics. These errors resulted in the long run-on sentences mentioned before.

Out of the entire number of sentences produced, one-fourth were correct. On the whole, aphasics displayed communicative functionality in their writing, since most of the descriptions were intelligible and coherent. The relevant activities and actors were included even by the subjects who resorted to drawing pictures, using pantomime, or listing words. The primary error types involved the grammatical system to a much greater extent than the semantic system.

SPONTANEOUS WRITING OF A SINGLE APHASIC

The patient studied (MA) is a 60-year-old, right-handed white male, diagnosed as a Wernicke's aphasic. Twelve months prior to this investigation, the man suffered infarction in the posterior branch of the left middle cerebral artery secondary to respiratory failure. EEG and brain scan confirmed left temporal lobe pathology. Residuals of the cerebrovascular accident included fluent aphasia and compensated right homonomous hemianopsia. The patient has a tenth grade education. His overall language performance according to Boston Diagnostic Aphasia Examinations ad-

TABLE 6.2   **Boston Diagnostic Aphasia Examination**

Time	Severity	Auditory comprehension[a]	Naming[a]	Repetition[a]	Writing[a]
3 mpo[b]	1.0	76	35	15	67
6 mpo	1.5	79	59	35	81
12 mpo	2.5	82	71	27	83

[a] In percentages.
[b] mpo = months post onset.

ministered at 3-month intervals following the stroke is presented in Table 6.2.

MA, from the onset of his stroke, had writing as his strongest expressive modality, and used it as the primary vehicle for functional communication and self-expression. He has produced over 10,000 words, which probably constitutes the largest data base ever obtained from any aphasic with such severe involvement in spoken language.

Characterization of MA's Writing

In general, MA's writing can be characterized as fluent and paragrammatic, the first term being a misnomer, since fluency implies facility and it took MA long days of strenuous effort to produce his writing. Paragrammatic language is defined as wrong distribution rather than reduction of grammatical structures. This quality is clearly demonstrated in the sample.

The entire corpus used in the analysis consists of letters written by MA to his therapist (over 4000 words) followed by a reconstructed diary covering his entire life (about 6000 words). That part of MA's writing consisting of 23 letters was coded for computer manipulation. The entire corpus of letters and diaries is described in the qualitative analysis, which is summarized in Tables 6.3, 6.4, 6.5, and 6.6. Table 6.3 gives totals for major syntactic units (paragraphs, sentences, clauses, phrases, and words), and mean number of units in superordinate structures. T-units were not counted because of the infrequency of clause compounding; the number of T-units is approximately the same as the number of sentences. Note a complete inventory of syntactic units and the shortness of T-units and phrases. Most T-units were five or six words long and most phrases were three words long. Table 6.5, which displays the inventory by major grammatical classes, shows that all major classes are represented.

Table 6.6 compares the 50 most frequent words in MA's letters with two standard frequency lists, Jones and Wepman (1966), *A Spoken Word Count*, and *The American Heritage Word Frequency Book* (Carroll, 1975). The

TABLE 6.3 Totals and Means for Units in MA's Writing Sample

Totals	Units	Means	Units
Paragraphs	148	T-units/paragraph	4.34
Sentences	642	Clauses/sentence	1.09
Clauses	700	Phrases/sentence	4.28
Phrases	2749	Words/sentence	6.28
Words	4030	Words/clause	5.76
		Words/phrase	1.47

TABLE 6.4 Frequency Tables for Distribution of Words in
T-Units and Phrases

Number of Words	Number of T-units	Number of phrases
1	17	49
2	41	106
3	63	225
4	75	168
5	85	94
6	92	45
7	60	24
8	47	7
9	41	1
10	28	—
11	17	
12	14	
13	10	
14	4	
15	6	
16	6	
17	1	
18	4	
20	2	
21	3	
23	1	
24	1	
25	1	

Jones and Wepman list was chosen because it represents language produced spontaneously, as opposed to a passive literary vocabulary. The American Heritage list was included for comparison with normal written language. The most frequent words in MA's corpus are quite similar to those in the other lists. The high-frequency items are function words such as pronouns, prepositions, conjunctions, and auxiliary words. The pronoun *I* is the most frequent in MA's letters, which can be explained by the nature of the letter format.

TABLE 6.5 Inventory of Grammatical Classes

Grammatical class	Frequency
Verbs	778
Nouns	717
Pronouns	687
Prepositions	291
Adverbs	178
Adjectives	332
Articles	78
Other determiners	40
Conjunctions	89
Interjections	43

TABLE 6.6 The Fifty Most Frequent Words in MA's Letters Compared with American Heritage and Jones and Wepman

Words	MA (frequency)[b]	American Heritage (U, adjusted)[a]	Jones and Wepman (frequency)[b]	
I	343	18	93	(6)
to	169	95	113	(5)
you	96	39	21	(37)
for	81	31	17	(49)
a	79	98	131	(4)
got	72	2	6	(92)
at	67	19	14	(56)
me	67	4	12	(63)
is	66	47	176	(1)
she	59	9	69	(11)
and	57	105	132	(3)
the	44	292	150	(2)
it	44	37	84	(8)
will	34	8	21	(38)
good	33	4	5	(114)
her	32	6	36	(20)
was	31	30	14	(57)
some	31	9	16	(51)
get	30	4	112	(65)
see	29	7	17	(47)
of	29	114	74	(10)
are	29	27	21	(36)
my	28	5	4	(129)
have	27	17	24	(31)
not	29	15	47	(12)
about	26	10	18	(45)
letter	26	1	—	
don't	25	2	—	
all	24	13	16	(50)
on	24	29	31	(23)
he	24	33	82	(9)
no	23	6	7	(87)
write	23	4	—	
home	20	2	5	(118)
this	20	18	53	(16)
love	19	1	—	
pretty	18	1	—	
today	17	1	—	
we	17	12	6	(101)
one	17	16	17	(48)
just	16	4	22	(32)
be	16	18	59	(13)
Monday	16	1	—	
but	16	14	24	(30)
guess	15	1	3	(152)
like	15	7	40	(18)
am	15	1	6	(95)
much	15	4	8	(82)
hope	15	1	—	
would	14	9	—	

[a] *The American Heritage Word Frequency Book*'s (Carroll, 1975) *U* statistics, adjusted to 4000 words, the size of MA's corpus.

[b] Jones and Wepman's mean frequency, adjusted to frequency per 4000 words. Numbers in parentheses are the rank orders for the words in their sample.

A few further comments on MA's vocabulary can be made. Nouns used were primarily picturable nouns such as *book, candy,* and *chair.* The class of verbs contained such high-frequency items as *get, like, listen,* and *shut.* About one-third of the adjectives used were of the evaluative type, such as *nice, pretty,* and *good.* Pronouns included a complete inventory of personal pronouns and subsets of possessive and reflexive pronouns. Both the definite article *the* and indefinite articles *a* and *an* were used. Determiners used included deictics (*this/these*) and qualifiers (*any, all*); *some* was used as a pronoun but not as a determiner. The class of prepositions contained 23 different items; a high proportion of these expressed location, such as *in,* and *at. To* and *for* also had a high frequency. Conjunctions were represented by the coordinating conjunctions *and, or,* and *but* and some subordinating conjunctions, such as *until, unless, if,* and *since.* Adverbs frequently used included *almost, here, now, too,* and *there.* Auxiliary verbs included *have, be, can, will, would, may,* and *gonna.* The data contained no neologisms and there was a dearth of "empty" words such as *thing* or *something,* which are usually associated with fluent output in Wernicke's aphasia.

The qualitative analysis of the total corpus, displayed in Tables 6.7, 6.8, and 6.9, demonstrates that MA's writing contains an almost complete inventory of grammatical structures. Table 6.7 lists content word classes, illustrating extensive representation of subcategories within each word class. Thus, for example, plural and possessive forms appear within nouns, degree in adjectives and adverbs, and tense, aspect, voice, mood and modality in verbs. Table 6.8 lists function word classes. Pronouns include subcategories of number, gender, person, and case. Determiner subsumes number, definiteness, and quantification. Adverbs are represented by the closed sets of place and time terms. Conjunctions include coordinate and subordinate connectors. Table 6.9 lists major syntactic elements, that is, clauses and sentences. The clause types listed represent those most frequent in MA's writing. Sentences include both compound and complex and, within the latter, finite and nonfinite subordinate predicates.

Error Analysis

Although, as seen from the preceding description, MA has almost a complete inventory of grammatical structures, the paragrammatic nature of his writing is observed in the wrong usage of those structures. The primary areas of errors are in the use of prepositions, verbs, and articles.

PREPOSITIONS

Substitution, deletion, and addition of prepositions occurred. Substitution was by far the most common error, involving, in the majority of cases,

TABLE 6.7 Content Word Classes

Noun	Adjective		Verb					Adverb
	Degree							*Degree*
Number possessive	*Comparative* *Superlative*		*Tense*	*Aspect*	*Voice*	*Mood*	*Modality*	Comparative Superlative
Singular	*Suffixal*		Present	Continuous	Active	Indicative	Intention	
Plural	-er -est		Past	Perfective	Passive	Interrogative	(will)	
	Periphrastic			Habitual	(be +en)	Imperative	Ability	
	more most			(would)	(get +en)	Nonfinite	(can)	
							Inference	
							(must)	
							Condition	
							(would)	
							Obligation	
							(should)	

TABLE 6.8 Function Word Classes

Pronoun	Adverb		Determiner	Conjunction	
Personal possessive reflexive	*Place*	*Time*	*Determiner*	*Coordinating*	*Subordinating*
Person	Here	Now	Number	And	Temporal (when)
Gender	There	Then	ordinal	But	Causal (for)
Number		Today	cardinal	Or	Complement (that)
Case		Tomorrow	Definiteness	Either . . . or . . .	Reason (because)
		Yesterday	Quantification		Relative (who)

TABLE 6.9 Syntactic Elements[a]

Clause	Compound sentence	Complex sentence
NP V NP	S cc S	S sc CL finite
NP V	S, S	S CL nonfinite
NP V NP PP	S; S	(infinitival)
NP V PP (PP)	S S	(gerundial)
NP be COMP		

[a] NP = noun phrase; V = verb; PP = prepositional phrase; COMP = complement; CL = clause; S = sentence; cc = coordinate conjunction; sc = subordinate conjunction.

the preposition *for,* which replaced specific prepositions of place, for example, "He lived his life **for** Clayton, Alabama;" of direction: "They sent him **for** Terrel;" of time: "He was died **for** 1918 or 1919;" of qualification: "He feed a five gallon can **for** sweet milk and cornbread." *For* also substituted for specific verb particles, for example, "I was mad **for** Mansell."

Errors of omission in most cases occurred in adverbs of time, place, and direction when they displayed some redundancy, that is, the nouns that followed indicated either time terms, for example, "They got married 1904," or place terms, for example, "I can get one garage sale," and "I had to go the farm." Similarly, prepositions were deleted after verbs when they functioned as particles and were fully predictable, for example, "He would always to joke her." Errors of addition of prepositions occurred in two situations: when no preposition was required, for example, "½ dozen **of** kids," and when one preposition was already present, for example, "We moved **at from** Ennis," and "I didn't write a lot **for to** you about for a month." A few errors of ordering of prepositions in relation to their objects were observed, for example, "One morning I could see the horizon **on** the raft."

VERBS

The most striking error in verb morphology was the marking of tense by the addition of a past auxiliary before a main verb that was either already in the past or in canonical form, for example, "The people that lived in this little farm **was loved** for basketball;" "I **was dance** and laugh of heaven." Tense shift from past to present was also quite frequent—sometimes as a result of shift into the more immediate present and sometimes as a result of a failure to add the past tense ending—for example, "James **starts** to school in 1930;" "I lived to the neighbor and **work** for him (boss)." Moreover, tense errors in subjunctives and in reported speech were observed. Other tense errors involving morphological forms were deletions and simplifications or over-generalizations of the regular past suffix of the following types: "We **are look** to buy me;" "She **would love** to kill him ('would have loved');" "She was all **bented** over the tub."

Frequent substitutions of **have** for copula **be,** and occasionally of **be** for **have** were present, for example, "We **are** ice on the street;" "I **have** no busy tomorrow." Other substitutions included replacement of specific verbs by the general verbs **do** or **have,** for example, "I **did** to store;" "Me and mother would **have** him some trouble." Deletions included the copula **be,** for example, "I just stubborn" and the omission of main verbs with preservation of only tense marker and object, for example, "made bed, sweep, not dishes yet." "I would TV ('I would watch TV');" "She letters ('she wrote letters')."

ARTICLES

The most common article error was the omission of both definite and indefinite forms. Some substitutions involved replacement of **an** by **a.** However, there were a few instances of incorrect articles, for example, "I had never taste **the** drop of whiskey before." Frequently, the article was omitted between a preposition and its object, "I went Friday to store." A few cases of additions of articles were found, for example, "**The** girls have improved in the years," "I guess I'd better write **a** some of essay." In the whole corpus, 20% of the entire number of articles used showed errors.

OTHER GRAMMATICAL CATEGORIES

In pronouns, errors were mainly substitutions in gender, usually masculine for feminine, and in case, for example, "My mother was too busy for smart. **He** was too busy for getting kids;" "**Me** always forget;" or substitution of personal pronouns, for example, "I got to write **me.**"

In determiners, substitutions of *this/these* for *that/those* were observed with a tendency for the unmarked member to take the place of the marked one, for example, "I walked to Jefferson Street **this** morning." The determiners *this/these* occasionally exhibited violation of number agreement with the following noun.

Omissions of conjunctions were noted, for example, "I ate breakfast was taste good." Sometimes a comma was used in place of the conjunction, for example, "I took 3 shirts, 3 pants from tub." Another substitution of conjunction involved using *wh*-words within the same semantic series as the required conjunction, for example, "The old lady is crying *why* ('because') she doesn't have any money."

WORD ORDER ERRORS

Word order errors in noun compounds were the most consistent and conspicuous, for example, "They would have a crowded for any **match team**;" "Friday had good rain for **game ball**;" "I got a ½ **melon water**;" "I can get one a **sale garage** sometimes." Ocassional errors within noun phrases in the order of modifiers were also found, for example, "The **young tall** man."

Frequent errors of order in clausal elements involved objects or adverbial elements, for example, "One morning I could see **the horizon on a raft**;" "I will **letter mail you** Monday." It is interesting to note that no errors of ordering of subjects relative to their predicates were observed.

AGREEMENT ERRORS

Agreement errors were not very frequent. They involved primarily number agreement between subjects and predicates and determiners and nouns, usually resulting in replacement of plural by singular (another instance of the vulnerability of the marked member, the plural), for example, "The people that live in this little town **was** loved for basketball;" "Our **days was** dry."

SEMANTIC ERRORS

Semantic errors consisted primarily of substitutions involving members of semantically related pairs such as learn–teach, go–come, borrow–lend, for example, "But she **learned** these boys when she word new;" "He would **borrow** me his horse for Tony." Substitutions within time terms were also found, such as, "After about 4 **years** ('hours') he got a hole;" "I wanted to hire him all **next** ('following') year." On the whole, semantic errors were not very frequent, and those occurring followed the principle of in-class semantic substitution of closely related terms. For that reason, the intended meaning was usually recoverable.

SPELLING ERRORS

MA's writing contained relatively few spelling errors (2%). The majority of the errors were phonetic, for example, *Hafta* ('have to'), *brana new* ('brand new'). The above clearly reflect spoken representation. Another type of phonetic error is related to the existence of multiple orthographic representations of the same vocalic elements in English, which produces homophones, for example, *peeches* ('peaches'), *pantrie* ('pantry'), *hirt* ('hurt'). Errors in words with double consonants represent another example of violation of orthographic rules related to particular lexical representations, for example, *carefull*. Visual confusion errors were extremely rare, for example, *teleprap* ('telegraph'), *the* ('he'). It is interesting to note that most of MA's self-corrections were in the area of spelling. These were often successful corrections. In other cases, when he could not correct, he would write "sp?" over the word. This indicates that MA's monitoring was restricted primarily to the orthographic form of his writing, since self-corrections of grammatical forms were extremely rare.

What Is Correct?

In order to complement the preceding section, it will be useful to include some general comments on what is grammatically and semantically correct in MA's writing.

On the average, one out of 25 sentences was completely correct. Most of these were simple affirmative sentences of five or six words, usually in the present or past tense. They represented the "favorite" sentence types with the following syntactic patterns:

NP	V	NP	(*We had a new car.*)
NP	V		(*I washed.*)
NP	be	COMP	(*He was funny.*)
NP	V	ADV	(*I'll finish soon.*)

There were few compound sentences, connected either by a comma or with the conjunctions *but,* or *and,* for example, *Yes, sure I talk to people, but I do not interest them.* Complex sentences were also rare. The subordinate clause could be finite or nonfinite, for example, *I will get shoes if I get money; My papa wanted me to go to school.*

Sentences were combined into paragraphs, which were indicated by indentation. Initiation of a new paragraph corresponded to a change of topic, often marked by a temporal adverbial. Internally, paragraphs were organized by chronological sequence of events and often ended with a summary statement.

In general, the phrase units noun phrase, prepositional phrase, and verb phrase had proper order internally and were about three words long.

All the correct structures at the sentential and phrasal levels were of a restricted length.

CONCLUSIONS

Communicative functionality, even in the face of sometimes severe disruption of language, was generally preserved in the writing of the aphasics. The content of the writing was supplied either by the experimental stimulus (in the case of description of pictures), or by the real world of experiences (in the case of MA's letters). The letterwriting represented a higher level of achievement, but was preceded by extensive rehabilitative effort using pictorial stimuli to facilitate written expression. In all cases, the cognitive ability to recognize the essential components of the message to be communicated was preserved. For example, some patients who could not provide a written description of pictures resorted to an intelligible pantomime or drawing, or to simply listing the participants and actions.

The semantic structure of the message was generally preserved even when the grammar was disrupted. The main feature of language that makes this possible is its redundancy, the multiple overt marking of linguistic features. The use of prepositions referring to time and location is a specific example. Thus, in MA's writing, omission of prepositions can be interpreted as an exploitation of the principle of redundancy, since they are usually only omitted in contexts where they could be supplied (e.g., *They got married 1904.*). Other examples are deletion of copula *be* in present tense (*I just stubborn.*); deletions of verbs when recoverable from their objects (e.g., *I would TV.*); deletion of obligatory particles accompanying verbs (e.g., *I would always to joke her.*); deletion of sentence conjunctions when the relation between clauses is apparent; deletions of definite articles used anaphorically.

The cohesiveness of discourse in MA's writing is another factor that allows the message to be preserved even with deletions and substitutions. Thus the fact that sentences in the same text are topically related makes it possible to understand pronoun reference even if the wrong gender is selected. Tense is usually shifted from past to present when adverbial expressions provide the time reference. Similarly, plural verbs are replaced by singular when noun subjects are marked plural.

The above examples also illustrate the rule-governed nature of many of the disruptions, which results in a certain consistency of the paragrammatisms. The general rule of substitution within the same grammatical class, well-documented in aphasia literature, holds for the data discussed here as well. In addition a number of idiosyncratic rules can be observed to operate with relative consistency throughout the text. For example, MA always reversed the order of components of noun compounds, as in *melon water, sale garage,* and *game ball.* However, correct order was preserved at higher syntactic levels, as in subject–verb–object constructions. Another consistent idiosyncratic rule of MA's writing was the expression of past tense by the past of the auxiliary *be* before the main verb. Further, there was a conspicuous overgeneralization of the preposition *for* to express a variety of relations such as time, place, and direction, and even intersentential relations. *For* was also inserted in prepositional phrases which already contained a preposition (*I didn't write a lot for to you.*).

The claim that MA's writing is rule-governed is strengthened by the results of tests of his judgment of grammaticality. When MA was presented with single sentences from his letters out of context, he accepted the correct ones and rejected the aberrant ones, though he was unable to correct them. Listening to his erroneous sentences, he would say to his clinician, "They do not make sense to you, but they make sense to me." This shows that he was consistent in the use of his own grammar.

MA's diary shows especially clearly that the preservation of cohesion as a result of retained cognitive ability allows for successful transfer of meaning. The events unfold in an orderly chronological sequence, including details such as names of participants and specific locales reaching far back into his childhood. The diary includes interpretative comments of a humorous or introspective nature. Some of these features are shown in the following excerpt from the diary which may serve as a concluding illustration of both the extent of the disruption of his language and the preservation of the cohesive structure.

> I found Butch, I think it was 1968. Bernice and I walk to 7 up for phone. The dog was stood to see me. He was the prettiest for boxer, had three feet white and one black foot. He had a half-dollar for forehead white. The rest was light brown.
>
> We started for home, the dog just walk before me. We walked up the street. The dog stopped to door #3. He looked good for the house. First he found the ice box.

ACKNOWLEDGMENTS

The authors would like to thank Josephine Simonson and Alvin North for their comments on early versions of this paper. Thanks are also due to Anne Weise for analysis of the data and to Josephine Simonson and Emily Anderson for providing us with samples of aphasic writings used in the analysis.

REFERENCES

Alajouanine, T., & Lhermitte, F. 1965. Acquired aphasia in children. *Brain, 88,* 653–662.

Assal, G., Chapuis, G., & Zander, E. 1970. Isolated writing disorders in a patient with stenosis of the left carotid artery. *Cortex, 6,* 241–249.

Bear, M. V.. 1939. Children's growth in the use of written language. *Elementary English Review, 16,* 312–319.

Benedikt, M. 1865. Über aphasie, agraphie and verwandte pathologische Zustände. *Wiener Mediznesche Presse, 6,* 897–1265.

Bloomfield, L. 1933. *Language.* New York: Holt.

Brain, R. 1961. *Speech disorders: Aphasia, apraxia and agnosia.* Washington, D.C.: Butterworth.

Bushnell, P. P. 1930. *An analytical contrast of oral with written English.* New York: Teachers College Press.

Carroll, J. B. (Ed.). 1975. *The American heritage word frequency book*. New York: American Heritage.

Chedru, F., & Geschwind, N. 1972a. Disorders of higher cortical functioning in acute confusional states. *Cortex, 8,* 395–411.

Chedru, F., & Geschwind, N. 1972b. Writing disturbances in acute confusional states. *Neuropsychologia, 10,* 343–353.

Choltos, J. W. 1944. A statistical and comparative analysis of individual written language samples. *Psychological Monographs, 56,* 77–111.

Dejerine, J. 1891. Contribution à l' étude des troubles de l' écriture chez les aphasiques. (A propos d' une observation d' aphasic motrice avec paragraphie pour l' écriture spontanée et sous dictée.) *Comptes Rendus des seances de la Société de Biologie et de ses Filiales, 9,* 97–113.

DeVito, J. A. 1965. Comprehension factors in oral and written discourse of skilled communicators. *Speech Monographs, 32,* 124–128.

DeVito, J. A. 1967. Oral and written style: Directions for research. *Journal of Southern Speech, 33,* 37–43.

Evanechko, P., Ollila, L., & Armstrong, R. 1974. An investigation of the relationships between children's performance in written language and their reading ability. *Research in the Teaching of English, 8,* 315–326.

Exner, E. 1881. *Untersuchungen Uber die localisation der funktion in der grosshirnrinde des menschen.* Vienna: Braumüller.

Fairbanks, Helen. 1944. The quantitative differentiation of samples of spoken and written language. *Psychological Monographs, 56,* 19–38.

Ferguson, J., & Boller, F. 1977. A different form of agraphia: writing errors in patients with motor, speech and movement disorders. *Brain and Language, 4,* 382–389.

Geschwind, N. 1973. *Writing and its disorders.* Paper presented at the Second Pan-American Congress of Audition and Language, Lima, Peru.

Gibson, James W., Gruner, C. R., Kibler, R. J., & Kelly, F. J. 1966. A quantitative examination of differences and similarities in written and spoken languages. *Speech Monographs, 33,* 444–451.

Gleason, H. A. 1965. *Linguistics and English grammar.* New York: Holt.

Goldstein, K. 1910. Amnestische form der apraktischen agraphie. *Neurologisches Zentralblatt, 2,* 635.

Golub, L. S. 1969. Linguistic structures in students' oral and written discourse. *Research in the Teaching of English, 3,* 70–85.

Goodglass, H., & Hunter, M. 1970. A linguistic comparison of speech and writing in two types of aphasia. *Journal of Communication Disorders, 3,* 28–35.

Hecaen, H., Angelergues, R., & Douzens, J. A. 1963. Les agraphies. *Neuropsychologia, 1,* 179–208.

Hier, D. B., & Mohr, J. P. 1977. Incongruous oral and written naming: evidence for a subdivision of the Syndrome of Wernicke's aphasia. *Brain and Language, 4,* 115–126.

Hunt, K. W. 1965. *Grammatical structures written at three grade levels* (Research Report No. 3). Champaign, Illinois: National Council of Teachers of English.

Hunt, K. W. 1970. Syntactic maturity in school children and adults. *Monographs of the Society for Research in Child Development, 35,* 134.

Jackson, John Hughlings. 1866. On a case of loss of power of expression; inability to talk, to write and to read correctly after convulsive attacks. *British Medical Journal, 192,* 326–330.

Jones, L. V., & Wepman, J. M. 1966. *A spoken word count.* Chicago: Language Research Associates.

Keenan, T. 1971. The detection of minimal dysphasia. *Archives of Physical Medicine and Rehabilitation, 52,* 227–232.

Keenan, T., & Brassell, E. 1974. A study of factors related to prognosis for individual aphasic patients. *Journal of Speech and Hearing Disorders, 39,* 257–269.

Klein, R. 1931. Zur Symtomatologie des Parietallappens. *Zeitschrift für die gesamte Neurologie und Psychiatrie, 135,* 589–608.

Klein, R., & Mayer-Gross, W. 1957. *The clinical examination of patients with organic cerebral disease.* London: Cassell.

Kleist, K. 1934. *Gehirnpathologie.* Leipzig: J. Barth.

Lawton, D. 1963. Social class differences in language development: a study of some samples of written work. *Language and Speech, 6,* 120–143.

Lecours, A. 1966. Serial order in writing: a study of misspelled words in "Developmental Dysgraphia." *Neuropsychologia, 4,* 221–241.

Leischner, A. 1953. Analyse einer Alexie mit sensoricher Aphasie. *Archiv für Psychiatrie und Nervenkrankheiten, 190,* 261–296.

Leischner, A. 1958. The agraphias. In I. Wechsler (Ed.), *Textbook of clinical neurology.* Philadelphia: W. B. Saunders.

Loban, W. D. 1963. *The language of elementary school children* (Research Report No. 1.). Champaign, Illinois: National Council of Teachers of English.

Luria, A. 1966. *Human brain and psychological processes.* New York: Harper & Row.

Mann, Mary B. 1944. The quantitative differentiation of samples of written language. *Psychological Monographs, 56,* 41–74.

Marcé, P. 1856. Memoire sur quelques observations de physiologie pathologique tendant à démontrer l'existence dún principe coordinatuer de l'écriture et ses rapports avec le principe coordinateur de la parole. *Comptes Rendus des Seances de la Société de Biologie et de ses Filiales, 3,* 93–115.

National Assessment of Educational Progress. 1972. *Writing mechanics.* Report No. 8. Denver: Education Commission of the States.

National Assessment of Educational Progress. 1975. *Writing mechanics.* 1969–1974: Capsule description of changes in writing mechanics. Denver: Education Commission of the States.

Nemanich, D. 1974. Verbal categories in the writing of children and adults. *Elementary English, 51,* 149–151.

O'Donnell, R. C., Griffin, W. J., & Norris, R. C. 1967. *Syntax of kindergarten and elementary school children: A transformational analysis.* (Research Report No. 8). Champaign, Illinois: National Council of Teachers of English.

Peltz, F. 1974. The effect upon comprehension of repatterning based on students' writing patterns. *Reading Research Quarterly, 9* (4), 603–621.

Pick, A. 1973. *Aphasia.* (Translated and edited by Jason W. Brown.) Springfield, Ill.: Charles C. Thomas.

Porch, B. 1967. *The Porch index of communicative ability.* Palo Alto, Cal.: Consulting Psychologists Press.

Quigley, S. P., Mantonelli, D. A., & Wilbur, R. B. 1976. Some aspects of the verb system in the language of deaf students. *Journal of Speech and Hearing Research, 19,* 536–550.

Schuell, H., Jenkins, J. J., & Jimenez-Pablon, E. 1964. *Aphasia in adults: Diagnosis, prognosis and therapy.* New York: Harper & Row.

Smith, A. 1971. Objective indices of severity of chronic aphasia in stroke patients. *Journal of Speech and Hearing Disorders, 36,* 167–207.

Smith, F. 1975. The relation between spoken and written language. In E. H. Lenneberg & E. Lenneberg (Eds.), *Foundations of Language Development* (Vol. 2) New York: Academic Press.

Stalker, J. C. 1974. Written language as a dialect of English. *College Composition and Communication, 25,* 274–276.

Stuckless, E. R. 1966. Objective evaluation of original written language of deaf students. *Volta Review, 68,* 679–685.

Taylor, L. T. 1969. *A language analysis of the writing of deaf children.* Unpublished doctoral dissertation, Florida State University.

Trebuxovskaja, L. V. 1974. Rabota and sentaksiškim stroem pisḿennoj' reci shkolnikov izucemii pričastija. *Russkii yazyk v Shkole, 4,* 36–39.

Trousseau, M. 1864. De l aphasie, maladie décrite récomment sous le nom impropre d'aphémie. *Gazette des hôpitaux civils et militaires, 1,* 13–14.

Ulatowska, H. K., Haynes, S. M. & Richardson, S. M. 1976. Assessment of communicative competence in aphasia. In R. H. Brookshire (Ed.), *Clinical aphasiology conference proceedings 1976.* Minneapolis: BRK Publishers.

Ulatowska, H. K., Haynes, S. M., Richardson, S. M., & Hildebrand, B. H. 1977. The aphasic: A speaker and a listener, not a patient. In R. H. Brookshire (Ed.), *Clinical aphasiology conference proceedings 1977.* Minneapolis: BRK Publishers.

Vachek, J. 1972. The present state of research in written language. *Folia Linguistica, 6,* 47–61.

Van Burgeijk, W. A., & David, E. E. 1959. Delayed handwriting. *Perceptual and Motor Skills, 9,* 347–357.

Von Monakow, C. 1914. *Die Lakalisation im Grosshirn and der Abbau der Funktion durch Corticale Herde,* Wiesbaden: Bergmann.

Weigl, E. 1974. Neuropsychological experiments on transcoding between spoken and written language structures. *Brain and Language, 1,* 227–240.

Weigl, E. 1975. Neuropsychological approach to the problem of transcoding. *Linguistics, 154/155,* 105–135.

Weigl, E., & Fradis, A. 1977. The transcoding in patients with agraphia to dictation. *Brain and Language, 4,* 11–22.

Weisenberg, T., & McBride, K. E. 1935. *Aphasia.* New York: Commonwealth Fund.

Wernicke, C. 1886. Die neuren arbeiten über aphasie. *Fortschritte der Medizine 4,* 371–377.

Wernicke, C. 1903. Ein Fall von isolierte Agraphie. *Monatsschrift für Psychiatrie und Neurologie, 13,* 241–265.

Wilbur, R. B., Mantonelli, D. S., & Quigley, S. P. 1976. Pronominalization in the language of deaf students. *Journal of Speech and Hearing Research, 19,* 120–140.

7

Linguistic Aspects of Lexical Retrieval Disturbances in the Posterior Fluent Aphasias

Hugh W. Buckingham, Jr.

PURDUE UNIVERSITY

In this chapter I will focus my attention on lexical retrieval disturbances that occur secondary to pathological involvement of the posterior language zones of the dominant hemisphere of the human brain. I will restrict my remarks to posterior fluent aphasics, although I am aware that word-finding difficulties will arise from lesions in the frontal language areas as well. I will argue that there are several linguistic manifestations of blocked access to the phonological shape of lexical items stored in the mental dictionary. Close linguistic analysis reveals that different types of aphasic responses in different types of posterior fluent aphasics—or in the same patient over a period of recovery—all suggest word-finding problems. As the discussion proceeds it will become apparent that semantic issues are inextricably bound to the study of the lexicon in fluent aphasia.

THE MEANING OF "USE"

Before proceeding to the main discussion, a word on the term "use" is called for. By speaking of language "use," I imply that what I say concerns performance, not competence. The immediate task of the linguist who analyzes and describes aphasic behavior is not that of the linguistic theorist who attempts to construct a viable model of competence. The builders of theories of competence do not depend upon performance descriptions, at least for the initial construction. If anything, the case is reversed. It is often

269

said that any description of aphasic speech needs a theory of performance. Nevertheless, it is doubtful that a good theory of performance can be devised without initial speculations formed through competence models. Competence theory building in linguistics has always been far in advance of performance description and modeling. Psycholinguistic experimentation on click location, for example, could only come after theoretical exploration of phrase structure. The derivation theory of lexical and syntactic complexity had to be formulated through theory before psycholinguists could submit it to experimentation.

The linguist describing various aphasic disorders would like to think that his work would have some impact on theories of competence and psychological reality. The problem, however, is deciding which type of evidence is germane to psychological reality in competence modeling. The following quotation from Chomsky (1976) is indicative of the still unresolved question concerning which types of evidence constitute grounds for demonstrating psychological reality for linguistic constructs.

> Let us really let down the bars of imagination and suppose that someone were to discover a certain pattern of electrical activity in the brain that correlated in clear cases with the presence of Wh-clauses. . . . Suppose that this pattern of electrical activity is observed when a person speaks or understands (1) ("Violins are easy to play sonatas on." —HWB). Would we now have evidence for the psychological reality of the postulated mental representations?
>
> We would now have a new kind of evidence, but I see no merit to the contention that this new evidence bears on psychological reality whereas the old evidence (intuitive judgments by informants—HWB) only related to hypothetical constructions [p. 12].

It is clear, then, that for Chomsky **both** types of data bear equally on psychological reality. He goes on to say that, "evidence concerning production, recognition, recall and language use in general can be expected (in principle) to have bearing on . . . what is sometimes called 'linguistic competence' or 'knowledge of language' [p. 12]."

His point is that **no** type of evidence has a "privileged character" that bears on psychological reality in "some unique way." Neurolinguists working on electrophysiological research concerning language may or may not agree with Chomsky on the weight of evidence these different types of findings provide for establishing the reality of mental representations. Perhaps the issue is somewhat obscured because Chomsky speaks of mental "representation," whereas electrophysiological work must of necessity be measuring mental **processes,** which once measured can shed the attribute "mental" for that of "nervous," "brain," "physical" or the like. Here the "mind–brain" distinction becomes quite evident. In any event, as linguists describing aphasic behavior, what we discover may bear on linguistic theories, even though it may not necessarily be of any greater import than the intuitions provided by normal speakers. Let us really let down the bars of imagination and suppose that an aphasia secondary to a lesion in the language zones of the left temporo-parietal region is caused where the only problem the patient has is an inability to produce or comprehend sentences with Wh-clauses. Presumably, at least for Chomsky, our supporting evidence for the reality of this structure would be no more significant than the intuitive judgments or the electrophysiological findings in his hypothetical example. Surely, though, it is the "separate disruption" paradigm which is of primary importance to neurolinguists and to neuropsychologists in general; it is here where our analyses have the most to offer linguistic theory.

CODING LEXICAL ITEMS

In language use words do not occur in isolation, but rather in syntactic matrices, which must themselves be somehow produced by the speaker. John Hughlings Jackson felt that "the mind must be aroused in propositional form and then the words must be fitted to the proposition [cited in Head, 1926, p. 45]." Arnold Pick (1931), influenced by Wilhelm von Humboldt (Spreen, 1973; Buckingham, 1975) postulated a level of "preverbal syntax" for the organization and structuring of ideas for linguistic expression, after which the lexical items are inserted. Syntactic production does not generally represent a problem for the kinds of aphasics that I will be discussing in this chapter, as the data provided will make amply clear. Lexical retrieval blocks most often occur in the declarative sentences, while nonpropositional matrices rarely show retrieval errors.

Lexical items are coded in lexical memory (storage) in various ways. One way is in terms of a semantic feature hierarchy composed of a set of semantic primitives such as *Human, Animate, Abstract,* and the like (H. Clark, 1970). Nouns are usually coded in terms of these types of primitives. Verbs, on the other hand, are often coded with respect to the types of noun phrases with which they can occur (Fillmore, 1968, 1971a, 1971b). Cooccurrence coding is syntagmatic and applies to "frame" coding for verbs as well as linear cooccurrences for nouns such as *peanut butter* and *jelly,* or *needle* and *thread.* All lexical items are bonded together into different similarity matrices (fields) based on shared properties. Nouns can be grouped into fields for cooking (Lehrer, 1969, 1974), kinship and color (Miller & Johnson-Laird, 1976) for example, whereas verbs can be grouped into fields such as motion, possession, vision, and communication (Miller & Johnson-Laird, 1976). Relational lexical fields such as space, time, and causation have also been explored (Miller & Johnson-Laird, 1976). Each of these fields in turn has a set of idiosyncratic primitives, such as the landmark or focal colors *black, white, red, green, yellow,* and *blue.* Key primitives for verbs of motion, for instance, are *travel, arrive, depart, stop, start, to, from,* etc. As we shall see, the notion of semantic field is crucial for understanding lexical use in aphasia (Rinnert & Whitaker, 1973; Luria, 1975; Goodglass & Baker, 1976; Buckingham & Rekart, in press).

Describing the structure of the lexicon has been the task of linguists like Jackendoff (1975) and Katz (1972) or of psycholinguists such as H. Clark (1970), E. Clark (1973, 1974) and Miller and Johnson-Laird (1976). The lexicon has been assumed to exist in the mind of the ideal speaker–hearer. The purpose of this chapter, however, is to focus on the task of the linguist who wants to describe what happens to the lexicon and its use when the brain, which is the organ of the mind, is damaged. Much of what I will say will relate in one form or another to the **retrieval** of stored lexical items from the mental dictionary. I will try to distinguish where possible between retrieval mechanisms and the semantic structure of the lexicon itself. A proper question to ask, of course, is whether the aphasia involves the semantic structure of lexical items, the retrieval of lexical items, or both.

Fedio and Van Buren (1974) have provided strong electrophysiological evidence that the left posterior temporo-parietal cortex plays an important role in the retrieval of stored verbal information. Continued stimulation of this area produced a transient anomic effect. Stimulation of the anterior temporal lobe region and of the homologous posterior temporo-parietal zone in the right hemisphere did **not** produce the retrieval deficiency. The authors concluded that, "If our interpretation is valid, the conjecture follows that Wernicke's expressive aphasia emerges, in part, from a breakdown of the verbal retrieval mechanism which simultaneously creates a retrograde amnesic disorder [p. 40]." This evidence from nonaphasic patients, together with many known cases of anomia and Wernicke's aphasia secondary to lesions in these posterior areas of the dominant temporal lobe, supports the claim that the major disturbance involved for these patients is in the mechanism that allows us to retrieve (or select) words from the lexicon.

An important question to ask at this point is the following: Can we separate words from lexico-semantic structure? This is, can we make a case for considering words as "labels," which when used may draw upon some, all, or none of the actual semantic structure? Many theories of the lexicon hypothesize that words "decompose" into atomic primes. For instance, *pen* might decompose to "instrument for writing and hand-held and fluid-core," (Dillon, 1977). The verb *whiten* might decompose to "cause become white." The question is whether these meaning structures, which are composed of "semantic primes," are inextricably bound to the labels, or whether they exist apart from the labels and **attach** to them differently under different conditions? Or, is decomposition automatically performed as a necessary part of understanding the use or meaning of every lexical item we utter or hear?

I concur with Miller and Johnson-Laird (1976) that proper lexical theory should, as far as possible, consider "definitional" structures composed of various semantic primitives. One immediate concern therefore is to try to constrain, so far as possible, the number and kinds of primes to be incorporated. This is left to lexical theory and will not be discussed further in this chapter. The other issue involved is the complexity metric, which is supposedly predicted by definitional theories. Words with more complex lexical structure should be harder to use (tested by recognition, recall, etc.) than words with simpler structures. Kintsch (1974) showed through experimentation that the complexity predictions do **not** hold. Miller and Johnson-Laird (1976) take the position that the predictions need not hold in every case. The mental computation of lexical decomposition may not be taking place during psycholinguistic experiments of recall, recognition, and so forth with a subject population of non-brain-damaged normal speakers.

TYPES OF RETRIEVAL DISTURBANCES

These issues are obviously involved in word-finding difficulties in aphasia, as will become readily apparent in the following discussion of the various manifestations of blocked access to the lexicon of speakers who have sustained damage to the posterior superior temporal regions of the dominant left hemisphere. The manifestations, to be dealt with in turn, are (1) the definition; (2) the pause; (3) the field error; (4) the unrelated lexical error; (5) indefinite anaphora; and (6) neologisms and confabulations. I will draw upon sources from the literature on anomia, Wernicke's aphasia, conduction aphasia, and from some of my own research. Again, I would like to argue that these six linguistic response types, although each is distinct from the others, all indicate lexical retrieval deficits. Also, I will show that in many instances the underlying lexico-semantic structure is still, at least in part, intact.

The Definition

Most of the studies of anomia have found that, although patients cannot retrieve labels (most often nouns), they can, in many instances, offer definitions such as "for writing" ('pen'), "to tell time with" ('watch'), or "for eating" ('fork'), (Geschwind, 1967; Wepman, Bock, Jones, & Van Pelt, 1973). Furthermore, the patient will often provide a pantomimed action demonstrating the use of some object. For instance, the patient will pretend to write with the hand. Note that the use of the hand (in the case of *pen* or *pencil*), together with the description "for writing," incorporate aspects of the semantic structure postulated by Dillon (1977). Patients not able to retrieve labels such as "eye glasses" or "television" will at times refer to them as "lights." Goodglass and Baker (1976) have pointed out that superordinates were often used in definitions provided instead of retrieved labels. I believe that these facts strongly support definitional theories of the lexicon, and further believe that the definitional structures can be separated from the labels, as evidenced by separate disruptability. Furthermore, and most obvious, the definitional response is indicative of a word-finding block.

The Pause

The pause is another obvious manifestation of a word block and is painfully present in the spontaneous speech of many anomics. Goodglass (1968) provides a good example:

(1)   *Well, I had trouble with . . . oh, almost everything that happened from the . . . eh, eh, ... Golly, the word I can remember, you know, is ah . . . When I had the . . . ah biggest . . . ah . . . that I had the trouble with you know . . . that I had the trouble with, and I still have a . . . the ah . . . different . . . . The things I want to say . . . ah . . . . The way I say things, but I understand mostly things, most of them and what the things are [p. 179].*

If we focus our attention on the pauses (represented by the ellipses, we see immediately that they most often occur directly after noun determiners (most often articles). F. Goldman-Eisler (1964, 1968) has recently corre-lated pausing phenomena to the Jacksonian dichotomy of automatic versus volitional processes in language production. Whereas in most normal unin-terrupted spontaneous speech there is an integrated blend of automatic and volitional processes (where the results of practice and over-learning alter-nate with spontaneous elicitation), in many types of aphasia productivity is dissociated from habitual verbalization (Goldman-Eisler, 1968, p. 10). The pausing is assumed to be an attribute of spontaneity in the creation of new high-information (low-redundancy) verbal forms. Her general thesis is that the pauses are correlated with the more highly volitional or willful aspects of the total linguistic production; few, if any, pauses occur during automatic, non-propositional speech. Buckingham, Whitaker, and Whitaker (1975) suggested that nonpropositional, higher clauses with verbs of propositional attitude such as *I think that S, I know that S,* or with performatives such as *I say that S,* tend to be preserved in severe jargon aphasics, while the lexical selection in the declaratives (the propositional material in the embedded S) is not. In any event, the volitional, spontaneous, and creative nature of lexical retrieval is readily apparent in the spontaneous speech of anomic aphasics. The silent pause itself represents the clearest case of a failure to retrieve.

Field Error

Another manifestation of lexical retrieval difficulties is the semantic field error.[1] Semantic confusion studies have been reviewed and a typology of errors developed in Rinnert and Whitaker (1973). These authors analyzed the relational categories for the confusion pairs and the shared and unshared features of the targets and errors. They maintain that the semantic confusions are often like word association responses of normal subjects.

Before going any further with the Rinnert–Whitaker taxonomy, I would like to draw a basic distinction between "semantic field" and "lexical set." For example, let us take some words and categories: *property, household items, furniture, article for sitting on, chair,* and *sofa.* The "semantic field" may be said to include all terms, and therefore it subsumes hierarchical (superordinate) paradigmatic relations. The "lexical set" (referred to as the "minimal contrastive set" in Miller & Johnson-Laird, 1976) includes only *chair* and *sofa;* the relations within the lexical set are not hierarchical but rather linear.[2] Words in lexical sets may be synonyms or antonyms, as well as "like" objects such as our example of *sofa* and *chair.* It has been pointed out in several places (H. Clark, 1970, p. 275; Fromkin & Rodman, 1974, p. 117) that antonymic forms (polar opposites) usually differ by one feature only.

The confusion pairs within the "same category" (Rinnert & Whitaker, 1973, p. 67) are all from lexical sets, for example, *FRUIT: figs → bananas.*[3] The "category–instance" and "object–description" confusion matrices involve the hierarchy of the semantic field as a whole. An "object–description" pair would be: *oven → hot.* The category "instrument–function" would include confusion pairs such as: *match → to light.* The natural order (or direction) for the errors is usually: **hyponym → superordinate**, although some errors have been reported which go the other direction: *hospital → Montifiore.* The true lexical paraphasia should involve only the members of a lexical set. In fact, the **hyponym → superordinate** switch is not, perhaps, to be considered an error at all but rather a partial description based on the intact hierarchical semantic relations as compensation for a lexical retrieval difficulty. I mentioned previously that Goodglass and Baker

---

[1] Studies of speech errors in nonbrain-damaged normals (Fromkin, 1973) have demonstrated that semantic field "slips" can occur—often under fatigue, emotional unrest, inattention, and the like. The aphasic will, however, produce many more of them. That is, there is a quantitative difference, not a qualitative one.

[2] I refrain from using the term "syntagmatic" for "linear" in this case because it would introduce an ambiguity. Viewed from a slightly different perspective, *chair* and *sofa* are in a paradigmatic class relationship, as opposed to *needle* and *thread.* These latter two words often collocate and therefore share a syntagmatic class relationship (see H. Clark, 1970).

[3] The target stimulus is on the left of the arrow; the response uttered by the patient on the right.

(1976) noted a striking preservation of the ability to recognize superordinates. It would seem, then, that word-finding problems involve lexical sets rather than the whole semantic field. Lexical paraphasia would thus be the production of another member of the lexical set to which the target belongs. The incorrect response that is hierarchically related to the target (i.e., in the semantic field as a whole) is a definitional-type error and as such is significantly different in nature from the lexical set error. Superordinates form the elements of definition of each member of the lexical set; the words in the set itself do not fit into the definitions of each other.

In terms of psycholinguistic operations, attention is first focused on the semantic field and is then shifted to the lexical set, where the selection process retrieves the necessary word. If it cannot do so, there is a pause, or a definitional-type response (*banana* → *fruit*, or *banana* → "It's a type of fruit to eat," etc.) or a lexical set error (*banana* → *apple*).

The distinction between semantic field and lexical set should always be made when analyzing lexical paraphasias. In their study, Goodglass and Baker (1976) used seven sets of lexical relations. One was the identity set; another was a phonic relationship set. The remaining five were semantic relatedness sets. "Superordinate," "attribute," "functional associate," and "functional context" are semantic field relations. Their relational class for lexical set membership is "contrast coordinate." Of these five categories, only errors from "contrast coordinates" would be true lexical field paraphasias. "Clang" (a traditional term in psychological studies of repetitive, rhyming speech) errors are not semantic at all. The Goodglass and Baker (1976) study was therefore not an analysis of verbal paraphasia, but rather a study of associational strengths as a correlate of comprehension and naming, and as such provides a good example of the various types of semantic associations.

Let us now consider A. R. Luria's (1975) theories of anomia and lexical paraphasia.[4] For Luria, the larger the selection possibilities, that is, the larger the number of words semantically related to the target, the more difficult it is to name, because more items must be inhibited from rising to threshold. It would seem logical, then, that if the semantic fields were constricted as a result of brain damage, the patient would have less to inhibit and consequently would be able to name better. However, this is the reverse of what Goodglass and Baker (1976) found. Their study led them to conclude that difficulties with naming (and comprehension) were correlated with a **reduced** semantic field in terms of weaker association strengths. That is, the more complete the convergence of associations the better, the patient could name and comprehend. It would appear that Goodglass and

---

[4] For a discussion and critique of Luria's theories of selection and lexical retrieval, see Buckingham (1977b) and the references cited therein.

Baker's findings are more reasonable and that in order to focus attention on the lexical set of contrast coordinates to select the correct member, the speaker needs full access to the semantic field as a whole through all the association bonds available. By this I do **not** mean to imply that a patient with word-finding problems will be aided by providing him with several words from the same lexical set to solve a "point to" task, for instance. There is some evidence that doing this only further confuses him (Marshall & Halvorson, 1976). Correlating strengths within **semantic field** associative bonds with superior comprehension and naming abilities does not mean that supplying added lexical set cueing will help the patient on confrontation naming and pointing tasks in the clinic. I believe it is preferable, though, to differentiate the lexical set as a subcomponent of the field as a whole and as the specific set out of which lexical items are searched for and selected.

This distinction is not always clearly drawn in the literature. Definitional single lexical item responses should not be considered errors, but rather partial attempts to get at the word through the intact aspects of the field. The lexical set switch, however, is a true selectional error. Nevertheless, both types of response are manifestations of word-finding problems.

Finally, it is possible to isolate the lexical set of color names for separate disruption as part of the syndrome of alexia without agraphia, (Geschwind & Fusillo, 1966; Goodglass, Klein, Carey, & Jones, 1966). The lesions in these cases tend to disconnect the visual cortex of both hemispheres from the language areas. However, primary visual processing is still intact, since the patients can sort colors according to hue. Interestingly enough, they can also match colors and color names with objects having the specific color in question as an intrinsic quality (sky–blue, grass–green). The retrieval difficulties occur when the patients must provide the spoken color labels upon presentation of colored paper, since at best paper is only associated intrinsically with the color white.

Unrelated Lexical Error

The fourth type of manifestation of word retrieval deficit is seen with the so-called unrelated verbal paraphasia. Green (1969) writes that an unrelated verbal paraphasia is "a word (found in the dictionary—HWB) that expresses no phonological or semantic resemblance to any other word suitable to the context [p. 105]." There is not much data on the unrelated lexical error. Some examples are listed in (2).

(2) (a) *I don't know that you can say that you can partly fit what you don't know.* (Buckingham & Kertesz, 1976, p. 59)
   (b) *She had the same mine **arm** I had.* (Green, 1969, p. 107)

(c) *I used to **sit** this, too.* (Buckingham & Kertesz, 1976, p. 59)

(d) *It's kind of **empty** to mark these customers, too.* (Buckingham & Kertesz, 1976, p. 59)

Clearly, the lexical items *fit* (2a), *arm* (2b), *sit* (2c), and *empty* (2d) are in no way relatable—semantically—to the context. Often, however, closer analysis will in some cases reveal that these words are fortuitously recognizable as viable lexical items. When the conversational contexts are further considered, we can often find possible alternative explanations that turn out to be more phonological than lexical. For example, Green (1969) described the patient who uttered (2b) as commenting on his mother's **name**. Although it is possible that the recording Green used makes it clear that *mine* and *arm* are segmentable in the stream of speech, it is possible that the sentence was *She had the same my **narm** I had.* That is, *narm* could have been a phonemic paraphasia on the target word *name.*

A different type of unrelated lexical error stems from the full perseveration of an item (see Buckingham, Whitaker, & Whitaker, chapter 9 of this volume). The sentences (all from Chapter 9 of this volume) in (3) illustrate this phenomenon.

(3) (a) *I got sick and I couldn't **sick** for a couple of weeks.*

(b) *I'm forgetting names that I **forget**, you know.*

(c) *I been sick all the week. But, whatever you're talking about I cannot **week** it.*

The underlined lexical item is perseverated and occupies the slot of the proper targets, *see* (3a), *knew* (3b), and *hear* (3c), all of which can be established easily by the context. It should be mentioned that anticipatory as well as perseverative phenomena can cause this type of lexical switch (see Lecours & Rouillon, 1976). These trans-syntactic errors should be clearly differentiated from the other manifestations of retrieval deficits, since the perseverate may itself be blocking the correct selection process.

Indefinite Anaphora

Still another quite common substitute for unretrievable words is the anaphor. Practically all studies of anomia have indicated that the patient can refer to objects by using *thing, stuff, guy,* or similar words (Wepman *et al.*, 1973; Whitaker, 1969). Unfortunately, few studies make clear distinctions between anaphora involving sense and anaphora involving reference (Caplan & Marshall, 1975). Use of articles is extremely important here, since they control definiteness. *Thing* may refer to a definite object in *I see the **thing** over there,* or to the indefinite sense in *That's a **thing** you tell time with.*

Other indefinite uses involve the forms *anything* and *something*. Relative pronouns often appear in anomic speech, for example, *that* and *which*, which are formed from indefinite head pronouns. The neutral pronoun *it* often replaces the blocked lexical item. In severe jargon aphasia, both subject and object pronouns will often be produced with no clear antecedents whatsoever provided for the hearer. These pronouns have the value of indefinites (see Buckingham & Kertesz, 1976). In addition, *"one* pronominalization" is still intact. Notice that there is a sense–reference distinction with the form *one*. It serves for identity of sense in *I have one at home, She has a blue hat, and I have a red one*. With no article or with the indefinite *a*, *one* pronominalizes under identity of sense. On the other hand, when preceded by the definite article, it serves for identity of reference, as in *That's the* **one** (that) I saw.

Emmon Bach (1968) proposed a structure which he considered to underlie all NP's. That structure is presented in (4).

(4) [ₙₚ *the one* [ₛ *one BE* Pred. Nom.] ₛ]ₙₚ

Since Bach's structure separates the referential index (the highest occurrence of *the one*) from the head noun (the Pred. Nom. in the lower clause), it seems most adequate to explain the anomic's ability to pronominalize with *one* under identity of reference in spite of failure to retrieve the head noun from the lexicon. The structure in (4) is that of a relative clause, and as such must of necessity be restricted to identity of reference, since that is what is needed to derive the relative pronoun *that* for sentences like, *The one* **that** *is a ball*, or *The one that I have at home*. The notion of referential index only deals with identity of reference, not sense. Therefore, the anomic's use of *one* pronominalization of sense has nothing to do with the structure in (4), and that structure is supported only insofar as there is separate disruptability of lexical heads and pronouns of reference. Anomics **can** handle pronouns of sense (indefinite) and pronouns of reference (definite), but Bach's proposal only treats identity of reference. In any event, the striking fact is that, despite failure to retrieve the phonological form for nouns, the patient is still able to produce all these anaphoric structures for both reference and sense and in well-formed syntactic matrices. I would suggest that the anomic's use of anaphoric forms such as *one* supports the concept of pragmatically controlled anaphora introduced by Hankamer and Sag (1976), where the contextual situation determines the antecedent and not some controlling linguistic form in the syntax. For Hankamer and Sag, "nonsyntactic control of indefinite pronouns like *one(s)* seems quite acceptable [p. 407]." Although all speakers can control the pronoun *one* situationally, the evidence from anomics offers even stronger support for Hankamer and Sag's claim since the anomic's difficulty is precisely that he cannot retrieve

from the lexicon the antecedent linguistic form which might have served as
a syntactic controller.

I have provided some examples of this pronominalization ability in (5).

(5) (a) *That's the kahn darn* **thing** *that so many* **things** *have made me
        ladis.* (Spontaneous speech, antecedent unspecified, Bucking-
        ham & Kertesz, 1976, p. 68)

    (b) *It's the same* **thing** . . . *something that you could use to climb* . . .
        I mean to get up on top of **it.** (trying to name "stool", Buckingham,
        in preparation)

    (c) . . . *had* **one** *this morning. The* **one** *that I looked at this morning.*
        (trying to name "calendar", Buckingham, in preparation)

    (d) . . . *the* **thing** *that you view what the time is.* (trying to name
        "clock", Buckingham, in preparation)

    (e) . . . *this* **thing,** *it isn't deg* . . . (Spontaneous speech, antece-
        dent unspecified, Buckingham & Kertesz, 1976, p. 77)

    (f) . . . *get a smalt* **one** *and turn* **it** *to you.* (Spontaneous speech,
        antecedent unspecified, Buckingham & Kertesz, 1976, p. 77)

Similar examples can be multiplied with ease, as anyone who has dealt with
word-finding problems in aphasia can attest to. The point I have tried to
make here is that pronominalization processes are intact despite lexical
retrieval blocks, and that the so-called "indefinites" may serve as anaphors
of sense as well as of reference. Further, the behavior of definite and
indefinite articles is normal in this patient population, and therefore *the
thing* . . . is actually a definite indefinite, while *a thing* . . . is an indefinite
indefinite.

Whitaker (1969) suggests an alternate consideration for analyzing the
indefinites:

> One might consider the indefinites *one, thing,* etc., to be analogous to cover symbols,
> i.e. as general lexical items representing classes of other lexical items. In this view the
> indefinites would be the least specified lexical items of the particular class in question.
> Presumably the aphasic who had lost many of the semantic features differentiating
> items could still make use of the very general features and thus select an indefinite
> from the lexicon [p. 137 n].

Leaving aside the question of whether or not anomic aphasics have "lost
many of the semantic features differentiating items," we might consider a
psycholexical processing model of object labeling such as that proposed by
George Miller and Philip Johnson-Laird (1976). In general, it seems to be
the type of analysis Whitaker had in mind in the above quotation, although
Miller and Johnson-Laird's system comprises computations and procedures.
Their remarks are useful for studying anomic labeling behavior, although

they do not specifically treat aphasic syndromes. The general labeling format in their model would be the following:

(6) Label (x): In order to determine whether some x can be labeled *"W"* at time t, execute the following routine:
(i) test $(t, F(x))$

Accordingly, for the patient to label object x, he must compute $F(x)$. Minimally, then, a routine for labeling some percept as a *thing* would be formulated as follows:

(7)   THING (x): In order to determine whether some x can be labeled "thing" at time t, execute the following routine:
(i) test $(t, \text{OBJ } (x, 3d))$

Obviously, there are objects one perceives as two dimensional, such as streets and windows. Also, the ability to label x as "thing" is often manifested when the object is pictured, that is, in two dimensions. For sake of ease, however, Miller and Johnson-Laird (1976) have used (3d) as an argument of OBJ. Certainly, the patient must be able to associate the item he labels "thing" with some conceptual object which has individuality and permanence, as Miller and Johnson-Laird point out. Also, if OBJ $(x, 3d)$ applies, then $(\exists x)$ is assumed. In addition, objects are imputed to have locations, sizes, and shapes; this is formulated by Miller and Johnson-Laird as follows:

(8) (x) [OBJ $(x, 3d)$ ⊃ $(\exists w)$ PLACE (x, w) & $(\exists y)$ SIZE (x, y) & $(\exists z)$ SHAP (x, z)][5]

Miller and Johnson-Laird allude to some further significant points that apply equally to the anomic use of *thing*. The routine (i) in (7) is found in all other object labeling paradigms but is the **only one** needed for retrieving the label "thing." Because (7) is so short, it will be satisfied by an enormous number of percepts. The authors point out that the routine in (7) might also hold for the labels "object," "article" or "entity." To this list, I would add "stuff," if several objects were the percepts. When a label is sought for some object, a "find" instruction is needed in order to search semantic memory (M(Sem)) for a paradigm that is appropriate. The control instruction is

(9) find $(\text{M(Sem)}, ? \text{ label } ? (x))$

Subsequently, the computation will compare x with all stored paradigms.

---

[5] Miller and Johnson-Laird (1976, p. 224) stipulate that where the ordinary notation for tests and procedures "are frozen into nonoperative assertions," they will be represented within brackets.

THING (x) is more often than not what is satisfied for the anomic; he consequently utters *thing*. But, this is not all. It is rare, indeed, for the anomic to say—in response to *What is this?*—*It is a thing*. Miller and Johnson-Laird write that, "The word 'thing' . . . will not often be used alone to identify an object because it provides no criteria for distinguishing the intended object from all the other objects [p. 221]." This holds equally for the anomic, as seen, for example, in (5b,d).

At this point a very important distinction should be made between labels as labels and labels as words. Miller and Johnson-Laird write "If one thinks of a label as a response to the question 'what's this called?' accompanied by an appropriate pointing gesture, the response is more than a label—it is an answer. To provide answers is to engage in discourse. As an answer, even a one-word response is a word, not merely a label [p. 222]." The anomic's response *The thing that you tell time with* is surely an answer to *What is this?*, although he has supplied a definitional response in a relative clause with an indefinite as the head noun. On the other hand, if the question is *What's this called?*, the response of the anomic could be *clock!* for example, or *thing!* Neither is likely. Rather, *clock* would not be forthcoming—nor the isolated word *thing*—and something more like *I don't*

know . . . it's $\left\{ \begin{array}{l} something \\ a\ thing \end{array} \right\}$ *for telling time* would appear as the response.

Future psycholexical studies similar to those of Miller and Johnson-Laird (1976) will undoubtedly increase our understanding of precisely what is preserved and what is lost with word retrieval difficulties in aphasia.[6]

Neologisms

One of the most important—but least recognized as such—manifestations of word-finding blocks is the neologism. Although the term "neologism" (used to describe some lexical form) has always implied novelty of some sort, difficulties have arisen with its definition, since some writers have chosen to emphasize only the innovative quality of the form, but others have used the term to imply that the word is unintelligible or unidentifiable. "Nonsensical," "gibberish," and "word salad" are other terms which have been used to describe unusual words or groups of words.

There is an important difference between new words introduced into some language (either accidentally or on purpose) and meaningless words. The former are recognizable to the extent that their sources can be uncov-

---

[6] In a review of Miller and Johnson-Laird (1976) I (Buckingham, in press) expressed concern over the fact that such an important procedural psycholexical study did not mention the syndrome of anomia.

ered; the latter cannot be so analyzed. Fromkin (1971, 1975), Lecours and Lhermitte (1972), Chaika (1974), Lecours and Vanier-Clement (1976), Freud (1901), and Laffal (1965) have variously described the neologism as a blend, hybrid, contamination or télescopage form consisting in some way or another of two blended roots or of a lexical root and some incorrectly applied morphological affix, usually a suffix. I have listed some examples in (10).

(10) (a) *groupment* (Fromkin, 1971, pp. 45–46; 1975, p. 499)
　　(b) /finitif/ ("final" + "primitive") (Lecours & Vanier-Clement, 1976, p. 519)
　　(c) *presidium* ("prose" + "idiom") (Laffal, 1965, p. 132)
　　(d) *cuptivate* ("cultivate" + "captivate") (Freud, 1901, p. 41)

These hybrid blends are certainly recognizable in terms of their composition, although the forms do not exist in the dictionary. It should be pointed out that they have been reported in the speech of normal subjects ("slips of the tongue"), jargon aphasics, and in severe schizophrenic language.[7] Blends like (10a) consist of incorrect affixation, not lexical root retrieval; (10b,c,d) are true lexical hybrids and do not imply word-finding problems, but rather two words retrieved and coalesced through anticipation or perseveration.

Many neologisms (quite obviously formed through processes distinct from those above) found in the literature on jargon aphasia do not seem to involve such clear blending as in (10). Consider the sentences in (11).

(11) (a) *I get the funniest forronide*[8] . . . (Kertesz & Benson, 1970, p. 368)
　　(b) *This is a tape of brouse to make buke deproed in the auria.* (Kertesz & Benson, 1970, p. 365)
　　(c) . . . *I buy my* /bIdhag/ in /bIlhId/ /bratals/ (Green, 1969, p. 110)
　　(d) . . . *my* /gupə/ *wasn't too good.* (Green, 1969, p. 113)
　　(e) *I can sit on the* /skampIs/ *and my* /skImp/. . . . (Buckingham & Kertesz, 1976, p. 38)
　　(f) *I had this* /neipʃə/ *on my head.* (Buckingham, 1977a, p. 179)

---

[7] Time and space do not permit a full discussion of the neologism in aphasic versus schizophrenic speech. Recent discussions of the similarities and differences are found in Chaika (1974, 1977), Fromkin (1975), and Lecours and Vanier-Clement (1976).

[8] At times, for the sake of ease, neologisms of this sort will be regularized into English orthography, although the initial transcription should at least be carried out at the phonemic level as far as possible. Obviously, though, any neutralization process will render impossible the uncovering of the proper phoneme. The problem of the phoneme is quite apparent in the transcription of neologisms, since flaps will occur. In those cases, it is purely arbitrary, in English, to assign the flap to /d/ or to /t/.

Since neologisms such as those in (11) have no immediately perceivable underlying form, explanations of their sources have been somewhat speculative. It has often been suggested that they result from severe phonemic distortion of the target word. Clearly, the hybrid type neologism does not stem from phonemic distortion, but those in (11) could. Kertesz and Benson (1970) write that "Linguistically, neologistic jargon appears to consist of phonemic (literal) substitutions which distort the original word to the degree that it becomes a neologism [p. 385]." Benson, Sheremata, Bouchard, Segarra, Price, and Geschwind (1973) state that, "Naming was disturbed, most of the errors being caused by literal paraphasic contamination, often so excessive as to be considered neologistic [p. 343]." Lecours and Lhermitte (1969) have postulated that, ". . . abnormal levels of pre- or post-activation could have something to do with the production of phonemic transformations in jargon aphasia [p. 102]." Notice that Kertesz and Benson's (1970) theory involves substitution, whereas Lecours and Lhermitte's theory considers linear transformations of phonemes, either perseverative or anticipatory. The essential aspect, however, of phonemic distortion theories is that the input to the error mechanism must be retrieved from the lexicon in its underlying phonological shape. It is illogical for these theories to deny that the target word has been initially retrieved, since how can something which is not retrieved at a higher level be distorted? Since it has been found that at later stages of recovery, neologisms reduce significantly and the patient appears more like the anomic (Kertesz & Benson, 1970) with greatly increased numbers of indefinite pronouns (Green, 1969), the following question can be asked: Why, after some recovery, does the patient have **more** retrieval difficulties, as indicated by the plethora of indefinites and pauses? The answer, I believe, is that they do not have any increased retrieval difficulties at later stages, but rather the neologisms **mask** word-finding blocks at the early stages. Consequently, of course, this rules out explaining their genesis by phonemic paraphasia. I will have more to say on the concept of "masking" later on in this chapter.

One other explanation of a neologism is that it derives from a "two-stage" error. That is, first there is a lexical selection error, which is subsequently distorted phonemically. Brown (1972) writes that, "neologistic jargon is a phonemic distortion of severe verbal paraphasia [p. 62]." Lecours and Lhermitte (1972) have stated that

on peut suggérer que ces néologismes sont des paraphasies monémiques[9] dont la composant lexicale est secondairement le siège d'une transformation phonémique

[9] A "moneme" is roughly equivalent to "morpheme;" it is a term borrowed from the French linguist André Martinet (1964) and used by many of the French speaking neurolinguists, such as Lecours and Lhermitte.

[one might suggest that these neologisms stem from morphemic paraphasias where the lexical structure is subsequently the location of a phonemic transformation, pp. 304–305].

Similarly, A. R. Luria (1970) in his description of the sensory aphasic, writes that

If he works with the fragmentary auditory images which he retains, his attempts to find the correct sound patterns result in literal paraphasia. If he abandons this approach and attempts to express the same meanings by other words, he produces verbal paraphasias. . . . Sometimes both strategies occur simultaneously, and the paraphasia which results is quite complex [p. 296].

The first stage (the verbal paraphasia) would represent the word-finding error. Note that the subsequent phonemic paraphasia need not be complex, for in many instances the initial lexical error will yield a form somewhat out of context so that even a simple phonemic switch would render it unrecognizable to the listener. That is, the context will not enable the investigator to "figure out" what the target word (itself a lexical paraphasia) was.

Although the data from the literature indicate that not all neologisms manifest retrieval blocks (i.e., those that stem from hybrids or phonemic paraphasia), many do. The question then arises as to the source of those neologisms. In several studies (Buckingham & Kertesz, 1974, 1976; Buckingham, Whitaker, & Whitaker, Chapter 9 of this volume; Buckingham, 1977a) I have tried to show how neologistic forms may be created by the perseveration of combinations of segments, clusters, and syllables into new forms, which nevertheless abide by the phonotactic constraints of the language in question. Kreindler, Calavuzo, and Milhailescu (1971) described processes of perseveration in the jargon of a Rumanian-speaking aphasic; Green (1969) pointed to the "alliteration" and "assonance" in the speech output of his jargon patient, and "clang" association in jargon aphasia has often been described in the literature (see Brown, 1972, p. 64). Since the publication of Lecours and Lhermitte (1969), much attention has been paid to perseverative **and** anticipatory phenomena in the speech of Wernicke's aphasics (Lecours & Rouillon, 1976).

While developing my analyses of the dynamics of perseveration and the creation of neologisms, I realized that I was dealing with a "masking" phenomenon. That is, it appeared that the neologism could be "covering up" an underlying word-finding block, in other words the neologism was filling a gap (Buckingham & Kertesz, 1974, p. 61). This is clearly supported in a later work (Lecours & Rouillon, 1976) where the authors write, "An important word-finding difficulty is always present but it is somewhat masked by fluency of the speech flow and by paraphasic and neologistic productions [p. 106]." They later describe the speech of Wernicke's aphasics with jargon: "neologisms are (often) so numerous, replacing mainly or nearly exclusively nouns and attributive adjectives thus superficially masking the patient's 'manque du mot' (lack of word), that temporary use of the label *neologistic jargon* is clinically justified [p. 114]." A further search through the literature revealed that the notion of a verbal gap filler was not new.

F. Goldman-Eisler (1968), discussed previously, focuses on pauses in the spontaneous speech of non-brain damaged subjects, but her comments are also applicable to the present discussion of verbal gap fillers, or verbal **pause** fillers. She found that one of the significant uses of pausing was to compute decisions for the selection of words. We may presume that a pause in anomia indicates the mental processing (often totally unsuccessful, however) of lexical selection, that is, an "act of thinking" (Goldman-Eisler, 1968, p. 28). On the other hand, an "act of speaking" (such as the attempts at definition, etc., of the anomic in our case) may stimulate or aid the mental computation during the lexical search process. Conversely, Goldman-Eisler (1968) writes that the act of speaking may serve as, ". . . a substitute for thinking, masking its absence or even inhibiting the thinking process [p. 28]." Therefore, for her non-brain-damaged population, she concludes that ". . . just as speaking may at times mask the absence of thinking, . . . silences (pauses) could mask symbolic processing active within the speaker [p. 30]." Translated into aphasic performance, we would have the glib neologistic jargon speaker in the first case and the hesitating anomic in the second, both having difficulty with access to the lexicon, but manifesting that difficulty quite differently.

Geschwind (1969) develops the notion that the confabulatory response is a ". . . verbal filling in of a gap [p. 119]." Similar arguments are made by Geschwind (1967) in describing different types of naming disturbances. The crucial element is that the material filling these gaps cannot be mapped onto underlying forms. That is, they cannot be related to what would presumably have been the normal underlying content for that specific discourse context. Geschwind (1965) feels that, "it is easy to see that if a particular part of the brain is fully disconnected from the speech area, there is no reason an erroneous name should be related in any way to the correct term. The more complete the disconnection, the more random the errors must be [p. 589]." Confabulation is not necessarily indicative of aphasia—it is often present in severe memory loss (Mercer, Wapner, Gardner, & Benson, 1977)—but it nevertheless masks information voids. Therefore, confabulation may occur secondary to disconnection lesions, as may severe memory loss. Furthermore, "monemic" paraphasias are often not mappable onto underlying forms, as Lecours and Lhermitte (1972) point out:

Les paraphasies phonémiques . . . resultent en effet de la transformation d'un mot précis de la langue, mot en général correctement choisi par l'aphasique bien que transformé sur le plan phonémique, alors que les mots remplacés par les paraphasies monémiques ne sont, selon toute vraisemblance, habituellement pas présents à l'es-pirit du locuteur au moment de la production [Phonemic paraphasias stem from the transformation of a specific word of the language, a word usually chosen correctly by the aphasic but transformed phonemically, while words replaced by monemic paraphasias are not, in all probability, always present in the mind of the speaker at the moment of production, p. 308].

In attempting to show parallels between confabulation and neologistic jargon speech, I would point out that many neologistic jargon patients exhibit the same characteristics shown to correlate with confabulatory be-havior of the population of amnestic patients (see Mercer *et al.*, 1977). Jargon aphasics in general have often been described as logorrhic, with great "pressure" of speech output and an inability to self-monitor (Bucking-ham & Kertesz, 1976). In their study, Mercer *et al.* (1977) state that, ". . . confabulation proved to be strongly related to the inability to withhold answers, to monitor one's own responses, and to provide verbal self-corrections [p. 429]."

In a similar vein, Weinstein and Puig-Antich (1974) discuss the resolu-tion of jargon, which for them masks referential voids, to "analogues" of jargon which **still** mask referential voids at the later stages of recovery. They note that in the early stages of disease the patients produce neologisms and jargon in answers to questions concerning their health. At the later stages of recovery, and in response to the same questions, the patients produce verbal stereotypes, "officialese," cliches, malapropisms, and puns. All of these productions were interpreted by the authors as verbal gap fillers totally lacking referential meaning; they are obviously con-fabulatory responses of circumlocution.

In summary, I have attempted to bring together various studies in the literature, along with some of my own work describing linguistic output abnormalities of posterior fluent aphasics. The patient population included Wernicke's aphasics (with varying degrees of phonemic paraphasia, lexical paraphasias, or neologisms), conduction aphasics, and anomics. I suggested that the different aphasic productions of the distinct groups of aphasics or of one patient throughout stages of recovery may be explained as due to limited access to the phonological shapes of lexical items, most of which were nouns, stored in the mental dictionary. These different aphasic pro-ductions were all shown to be "masking" gaps caused by word-finding problems. A direct correlation was made between the severe word retrieval disturbances and the fact that the aphasia-producing lesions were located in the posterior superior temporo-parietal regions in the dominant hemi-sphere. Electrophysiological evidence was used to support this localization hypothesis, which states that the function of lexical retrieval is vulnerable to disruption secondary to lesions in these cerebral regions.[10] In addition, I outlined those linguistic processes which appear to be intact in these patients, despite their brain damage. I specifically treated the intact syntactic processing with anaphoric elements and distinguished identity of sense versus identity of reference. Having made a basic distinction between lexical sets and the semantic fields as a whole, I then suggested that anomics have better access to hierarchical, superordinate items than to the specific words as they exist with minimal contrast in lexical sets. There was also a brief discussion of a procedural semantics approach to the study of anomic object-labeling behavior. Further linguistic studies of the language of posterior fluent aphasics will no doubt reveal more in terms of dominant temporo-parietal language function.

REFERENCES

Bach, Emmon. 1968. Nouns and noun phrases. In E. Bach & R. T. Harms (Eds.), *Universals in linguistic theory*. New York: Holt.

Benson, D. Frank, Sheremata, W., Bouchard, R., Segarra, J., Price, R., & Geschwind, N. 1973. Conduction aphasia. *Archives of Neurology, 28,* 339–346.

Brown, Jason W. 1972. *Aphasia, apraxia and agnosia: Clinical and theoretical aspects.* Springfield, Ill.: Charles Thomas.

Buckingham, Hugh W. 1975. A review of psycholinguistics and aphasia. *General Linguistics, 15,* 231–257.

Buckingham, Hugh W. 1977a. The conduction theory and neologistic jargon. *Language and Speech, 20,* 174–184.

Buckingham, Hugh W. 1977b. A critique of A. R. Luria's neurodynamic explanation of paraphasia. *Brain and Language, 4,* 580–587.

Buckingham, Hugh W. In press. Metaphorical dictionaries: A review of *Language and Perception* (by George Miller and Philip N. Johnson-Laird). *General Linguistics, 18.*

Buckingham, Hugh W. In preparation. *Studies on anomia.*

Buckingham, Hugh W., & Kertesz, Andrew. 1974. A linguistic analysis of fluent aphasia. *Brain and Language, 1,* 43–61.

Buckingham, Hugh W., & Kertesz, Andrew. 1976. *Neologistic jargon aphasia.* Amsterdam: Swets and Zeitlinger.

Buckingham, Hugh W., & Rekart, Deborah M. In press. Semantic paraphasia. *Journal of Communication Disorders.*

Buckingham, Hugh W., Whitaker, Haiganoosh, & Whitaker, Harry A. 1975. Linguistic structures in stereotyped aphasic speech. *Linguistics, 154/155,* 5–13.

[10] Once again, I do not want to be accused of implying that word-finding problems are restricted to posterior lesioned patients. Even Lichtheim as far back as 1885 claimed that "amnesia" (what he called word-finding problems) was a constant accompaniment of several types of aphasia (motor as well as sensory) and in general was, ". . . not a sign of a focal lesion [p. 474]."

Caplan, David, & Marshall, John C. 1975. Generative grammar and aphasic disorders: A theory of language representation in the human brain. *Foundations of Language, 12,* 583–596.

Chaika, E. 1974. A linguist looks at "schizophrenic" language. *Brain and Language, 1,* 257–276.

Chaika, E. 1977. Schizophrenic speech, slips of the tongue and jargonaphasia: A reply to Fromkin and to Lecours and Vanier-Clément. *Brain and Language, 4,* 464–475.

Chomsky, Noam. 1976. On the biological basis of language capacities. In R. W. Rieber (Ed.), *The neuropsychology of language.* New York: Plenum.

Clark, Eve V. 1973. What's in a word? On the child's acquisition of semantics in his first language. In T. E. Moore (Ed.), *Cognitive development and the acquisition of language.* New York: Academic Press.

Clark, Eve V. 1974. Normal states and evaluative viewpoints. *Language, 50,* 316–332.

Clark, Herbert H. 1970. Word associations and linguistic theory. In John Lyons (Ed.), *New horizons in linguistics.* Harmondsworth, Middlesex, England: Penguin.

Dillon, George L. 1977. *Introduction to contemporary linguistic semantics.* Englewood Cliffs, N.J.: Prentice-Hall.

Fedio, Paul, & Van Buren, John M. 1974. Memory deficits during electrical stimulation of the speech cortex in conscious man. *Brain and Language, 1,* 29–42.

Fillmore, Charles. 1968. Lexical entries for verbs. *Foundations of Language, 4,* 373–393.

Fillmore, Charles. 1971a. Types of lexical information. In D. Steinberg & L. Jakobovits (Eds.), *Semantics: An interdisciplinary reader in philosophy, linguistics and psychology.* Cambridge: Cambridge University Press.

Fillmore, Charles. 1971b. Verbs of judging: An exercise in semantic description. In C. J. Fillmore & D. T. Langendoen (Eds.), *Studies in linguistic semantics.* New York: Holt.

Freud, S. 1901. Slips of the tongue. (Reprinted in R. T. DeGeorge & F. DeGeorge (Eds.) *The structuralists from Marx to Levi-Strauss.* New York: Doubleday, 1972.)

Fromkin, Victoria. 1971. The non-anomalous nature of anomalous utterances. *Language, 47,* 27–52.

Fromkin, Victoria (Ed.). 1973. *Speech errors as linguistic evidence.* The Hague: Mouton.

Fromkin, Victoria. 1975. A linguistic looks at "a linguist looks at 'schizophrenic' language." *Brain and Language, 2,* 498–503.

Fromkin, Victoria, & Rodman, Robert. 1974. *An introduction to language.* New York: Holt.

Geschwind, Norman. 1965. Disconnexion syndromes in animals and man. *Brain, 88,* 237–294; 585–644.

Geschwind, Norman. 1967. The varieties of naming errors. *Cortex, 3,* 97–112.

Geschwind, Norman. 1969. Anatomy and the higher functions of the brain. In R. S. Cohen & M. Wartofsky (Eds.), *Boston studies in the philosophy of science* (Vol. IV). Dordrecht: D. Reidel.

Geschwind, Norman, & Fusillo, M. 1966. Color naming defects in association with alexia. *Archives of Neurology, 15,* 137–146.

Goldman-Eisler, F. 1964. Hesitation, information, and levels of speech production. In A. DeReuck & M. O'Connor (Eds.), *Disorders of language* (The Ciba Foundation Symposium). Boston: Little, Brown.

Goldman-Eisler, F. 1968. *Psycholinguistics: Experiments in spontaneous speech.* New York: Academic Press.

Goodglass, Harold. 1968. Studies on the grammar of aphasics. In S. Rosenberg & J. Koplin (Eds.), *Developments in applied psycholinguistics research.* New York: MacMillan.

Goodglass, Harold, & Baker, Errol. 1976. Semantic field, naming, and auditory comprehension in aphasia. *Brain and Language, 3,* 359–374.

Goodglass, Harold, Klein, B., Carey, P., & Jones, K. J. 1966. Specific semantic word categories in aphasia. *Cortex, 2,* 74–89. (Reprinted in H. Goodglass & S. Blumstein (Eds.), *Psycholinguistics and aphasia.* Baltimore: Johns Hopkins University Press, 1973.)

Green, Eugene. 1969. Phonological and grammatical aspects of jargon in an aphasic patient. *Language and Speech, 12,* 103–118.

Hankamer, Jorge, & Sag, Ivan. 1976. Deep and surface anaphora. *Linguistic Inquiry, 7,* 391–428.

Head, Henry. 1926. *Aphasia and kindred disorders of speech.* London: Cambridge University Press.

Jackendoff, Ray S. 1975. Morphological and semantic regularities in the lexicon. *Language, 51,* 639–671.

Katz, Jerrold J. 1972. *Semantic theory.* New York: Harper & Row.

Kertesz, Andrew, & Benson, D. Frank. 1970. Neologistic jargon: A clinico–pathological study. *Cortex 6,* 362–386.

Kintsch, Walter. 1974. *The representation of meaning in memory.* New York: Wiley.

Kreindler, A., Calavuzo, C., & Mihailescu, L. 1971. Linguistic analysis of one case of jargon aphasia. *Revue Roumaine de Neurologie, 8,* 209–228.

Laffal, J. 1965. *Pathological and normal language.* New York: Atherton.

Lecours, A. R., & Lhermitte, F. 1969. Phonemic paraphasias: Linguistic structures and tentative hypotheses. *Cortex, 5,* 193–228. (Reprinted in H. Goodglass & S. Blumstein (Eds.), *Psycholinguistics and aphasia.* Baltimore: Johns Hopkins University Press.)

Lecours, A., & Lhermitte, F. 1972. Recherches sur le langage des aphasiques: 4. Analyse d'un corpus de neologismes; notion de paraphasie monemique. *L'Encéphale, 61,* 295–315.

Lecours, Andre Roch, & Rouillon, F. 1976. Neurolinguistic analysis of jargonaphasia and jargonagraphia. In H. Whitaker & H. A. Whitaker (Eds.), *Studies in neurolinguistics* (Vol. 2). New York: Academic Press.

Lecours, A., & Vanier-Clement, M. 1976. Schizophasia and jargonaphasia: A comparative description with comments on Chaika's and Fromkin's respective looks at "schizophrenic" language. *Brain and Language, 3,* 516–565.

Lehrer, Adrienne. 1969. Semantic cuisine. *Journal of Linguistics, 5,* 39–55.

Lehrer, Adrienne. 1974. *Semantic fields and lexical structure.* New York: North Holland/American Elsevier.

Lichtheim, L. 1885. On aphasia. *Brain, 7,* 433–484.

Luria, A. R. 1970. *Traumatic aphasia.* The Hague: Mouton.

Luria, A. R. 1975. Basic problems of language in the light of psychology and neurolinguistics. In Eric H. Lenneberg & E. Lenneberg (Eds.), *Foundations of language development: A multidisciplinary approach* (Vol. 2). New York: Academic Press.

Marshall, Robert C., & Halvorson, K. A. 1976. *Influence of semantic relatedness on the auditory comprehension of aphasic adults.* Paper presented at the meeting of The American Speech and Hearing Association, Houston, Texas.

Martinet, André. 1964. *Elements of general linguistics.* Chicago: University of Chicago Press.

Mercer, Brian, Wapner, W., Gardner, H., & Benson, D. F. 1977. A study of confabulation. *Archives of Neurology, 34,* 346–348.

Miller, George A., & Johnson-Laird, Philip N. 1976. *Language and perception.* Cambridge: The Belknap Press of Harvard University.

Pick, Arnold. 1931. *Aphasia.* (Translated by Jason W. Brown. London: Charles Thomas, 1973.)

Rinnert, C., & Whitaker, Harry A. 1973. Semantic confusions by aphasic patients. *Cortex, 9,* 56–81.

Spreen, Otfried. 1973. Psycholinguistics and aphasia: the contribution of Arnold Pick. In H. Goodglass & S. Blumstein (Eds.), *Psycholinguistics and aphasia.* Baltimore: Johns Hopkins University Press.

Weinstein, Edwin A., & Puig-Antich, J. 1974. Jargon and its analogues. *Cortex, 10,* 75–83.

Wepman, Derrel, Bock, R., Jones, L., & Van Pelt, D. 1973. Psycholinguistic study of aphasia: A revision of the concept of anomia. In H. Goodglass & S. Blumstein (Eds.), *Psycholinguistics and aphasia.* Baltimore: Johns Hopkins University Press.

Whitaker, Harry A. 1969. *On the representation of language in the human brain.* University of California, Los Angeles Working Papers in Phonetics, No. 12.

8

Neurologic Correlates of Anomia[1]

D. Frank Benson

BOSTON VETERANS ADMINISTRATION HOSPITAL
and BOSTON UNIVERSITY SCHOOL OF MEDICINE

Almost every individual with aphasia has some reduction in the repertoire of words available for speech and requires more time than normal to produce words in response to either pictures or questions. The problem of producing words appears to be almost universal in aphasia, but word-finding problems also occur in normal individuals and in many types of cerebral dysfunction. In fact, almost all cortical and many subcortical dysfunctions interfere, to some extent, with the process of word-finding. Over the years word-finding difficulty has received many names, one of which is anomia.

Despite the widespread occurrence of word-finding problems in cerebral disorders, there has been little organized research on this topic and only a handful of reports dealing with the neurological aspects of anomia. There is neither an accepted theory or classification of word-finding defect nor an accepted neuroanatomical correlation for anomia. This chapter will discuss anomia by describing a number of variations seen clinically, outline involved neuroanatomical structures and pathways, suggest anatomical–clinical correlations for the varieties of anomia described and, finally, suggest a neurologic framework for the word-finding process.

DEFINITIONS

Before describing the case material, a discussion of terminology is necessary. None of the terms has been used precisely and definitions will, of necessity, be both vague and arbitrary.

[1] Research for this chapter was supported by the Medical Research Service of the Veterans Administration and by Grant NS06209 from the National Institutes of Health to Boston University.

293

Anomia: In general usage anomia is simply the state in which a person has a problem with word-finding. However, there is usually a connotation of loss, that is, the individual at some prior period had the ability to produce the desired word. More elegantly, anomia has been defined as a selective loss of lexical repertoire, primarily nouns and verbs, but adjectives and adverbs as well (Goodglass & Geschwind, 1976). Anomia is often used synonomously with anomic aphasia, but the two conditions can be different. Anomia may be present in individuals who would not be considered aphasic. Failure to differentiate these two terms can lead to confusion.

Word-finding defect: This term is almost self-explanatory and is used to indicate a problem producing a specific word at the time desired. It is similar, if not identical, to anomia and the two terms will be used with little differentiation.

Anomic aphasia: There has been both controversy and confusion in the aphasia literature concerning a specific variety of aphasia in which word-finding defect is the principle or only finding. Some "aphasiologists" totally ignore defective word finding as a distinct aphasic entity, whereas others discuss anomia at length. In particular, Goldstein (1924), Head (1926), and Weisunberg and McBride (1935) emphasized the frequency and discussed the significance of word-finding problems in aphasia. In the classification of the aphasias used at the Boston Veterans Administration Hospital, anomic aphasia is defined merely as that variety in which word-finding problems are the major disturbance (Benson & Geschwind, 1971). Functionally, these patients produce empty, circumlocutory conversational speech, have good or even fully normal comprehension and excellent ability to repeat spoken language. The task of naming, however, is notably abnormal. Many patients with anomic aphasia also have major problems with reading and writing.

Amnesic aphasia: This term was used by Goldstein (1924) and suggests that word-finding difficulty is a memory problem. Theoretically, it is perfectly logical to suggest that the word-finding difficulty reflects an inability to "remember" the words, that is, a memory defect. There is little correlation, however, between amnesic aphasia and amnesia (memory loss). In fact, the presence of any considerable degree of anomia militates against a diagnosis of amnesia. Goldstein's definition of amnesic aphasia (to be given later) is more closely related to anomia (as defined earlier) than to anomic aphasia.

Semantic aphasia: Luria (1966) has described an aphasia characterized by loss of meaning for individual words; that is, the word no longer acts as a symbol for the actual object. The defect is usually described as two-way: Both the meaning of the spoken word and the ability to use the word in speech are disturbed. Semantic aphasia differs from anomic aphasia by the severity of the comprehension problem. "Pure" cases of both semantic aphasia and anomic aphasia occur clinically, although many more aphasics have a mixture, with the word-finding problems outstripping the comprehension defects. Used precisely, anomic aphasia and semantic aphasia describe distinctly different types of aphasia, but some combination is the rule.

Nominal aphasia: Under this term Head introduced a disturbance in which naming and comprehension disabilities were secondary to a disturbance in the use of symbols. This disturbance is quite similar to that outlined by Goldstein and Luria. Brain (1961) used the same term, but carefully noted that word finding for expression was usually much more disturbed than comprehension of the same word. Thus nominal aphasia was originally synonymous with semantic aphasia (as defined earlier), but with time has come to be more closely related to anomic aphasia.

None of the terminology used in discussing word-finding problems is exact, which greatly complicates attempts to outline, classify, and differentiate varieties of word-finding defects. Of greater potential significance, however, are variations within the overall defect of anomia, which appear crucial for the understanding of this aspect of language. Some of these variations will be described, but before this is done, a description of the methods used to evaluate word-finding capability is appropriate.

EXAMINATION FOR ANOMIA

Many tests of word-finding ability can be found in the formal aphasia assessment techniques and many more in research reports. Most such tests are incomplete, usually giving only a plus or a minus (or a numerical grade) to the patient's ability to produce words or comparing a given aspect of word-finding in aphasic and normal control subjects. Most tests offer almost no information that differentiates naming disturbances. Instead of these formal tests, a series of routine bedside tests that emphasize the differences in word finding problems noted in clinical practice will be presented here.

First, but often overlooked, the presence of anomia may be conspicuous in spontaneous or conversational speech. In aphasic output, one of two distinctly different naming problems may be apparent. In one the patient appears to have a problem saying (producing) the word; in the second he appears to have a problem knowing (remembering) the word desired. The first variety is most conspicuously noted in individuals with nonfluent speech (sparse, poorly articulated verbal output, produced with effort and notably dysprosodic). Such patients often appear to be aware of the desired word, but cannot articulate it. This impression is further supported by prompting (offering cues), which frequently help the patient produce the correct word. The cue may be extremely slight. For example, the examiner's lips silently moved into the position of the first syllable of the desired word may be sufficient. The naming defect seems to be based on an inability to initiate pronunciation of the word, not on an inability to remember or "think of" the specific word.

A second, distinctly different, word-finding problem is noted in the conversational speech of fluent aphasia. These patients produce a rambling, noninformative output, containing many words but conveying comparatively little information. Pauses are frequent as the patient attempts to produce a desired word or, failing this, to explain the meaning of a word that cannot be produced. Much of this speech is characterized by generalizations, cliches, prepositional phrases, and indefinite words (*it, things, them,* etc.). Verbal output is accurately described by the term "empty speech." Verbal output is fairly abundant, but the amount of information is small. This type of anomic output is infrequently aided by prompting. In fact, patients with a fluent anomic output often refuse cues and may even refuse the correct word, stating that "some people may call it a _____ but that isn't the word I would use."

Careful monitoring of verbal output not only demonstrates the presence of anomia, but may suggest one of the two types. For further demarcation of word finding difficulties a number of different tests are available. Table 8.1 lists some of the nonstandardized tests used to probe problems of word finding.

Items 2 through 5 in Table 8.1 concern confrontation naming. The patient is asked to name an object or action following visual, tactile, or auditory stimulation. Olfactory and gustatory items can also be tested, although they are not routinely used. Item number 5 specifically tests stress

---

TABLE 8.1 Tests of Word Finding

1. Evaluate conversational speech, noting word-finding problems and dividing them into word production or word gnosis categories.
2. Test ability to name items by visual presentation from the following categories: objects, parts of objects, body parts, colors, geometric shapes, numerals, letters, and actions.
3. Test ability to name items presented to touch.
4. Test ability to name from auditory cues (hand clapping, whistle, etc.).
5. Specifically test items related to illness and hospital (thermometer, nurse, bed pan, etc.).
6. Test ability to name items from a functional description (e.g., What is the machine that a housewife uses to clean carpets?).
7. Test ability to accept and benefit from cues when word finding has failed (i.e., Can the correct name be given if a phonetic cue is offered or if a sentence is given that the desired word would complete?).
8. Test ability to present lists of words by categories (e.g., automobiles, animals, words beginning with a specified letter) in a specific amount of time.

or illness-related items. Test 6 demands that the patient produce the name of an object or action from a description or an outline of function. Item 7 outlines two means of prompting (cuing) to be used when an individual has word finding diffiulty. Phonetic cues involve presentation of the initial sound or syllable only. Contextual cues are most often open ended sentences (e.g., *You pound a nail with a* _____) utilizing the requested word. A number of other means of prompting are recognized (Brown, 1972), but phonetic and semantic cues are most frequently used in clinical testing.

The final test requests production of a list of words in a category suggested by the examiner. Categories such as types of animals, makes of automobiles, names of baseball teams or cities, or articles of clothing may be requested. More difficult categories would be lists of words beginning with a given letter of the alphabet. Word lists are timed, usually for 60 sec, during which the number of words produced by the patient are counted. Word list tests are easily performed at the bedside and allow a degree of standardization. Normal values have been established (Spreen & Benton, 1969), but for general purposes most normal individuals can produce a dozen or more responses in 60 sec. Lists of words beginning with a given letter are more difficult and vary with educational background. Even so, 8 to 10 responses can be considered the lower limits of normal. Sparse word lists suggest word-finding difficulties and often accompany empty or circumlocutory conversational output. Poor word lists are not diagnostic of aphasia, however, since word-finding defects occur in other cerebral dysfunctions and poor word lists reflect this abnormality.

VARIETIES OF ANOMIC APHASIA

Background

Despite more than a century of recognition of word-finding defect as an integral feature of aphasia and the strong inclinations of many investigators to subdivide and classify aphasia, there has been remarkably little interest in variations of word-finding problems. Instead, word finding is usually designated, either overtly or covertly, as a single, unitary process which is either intact or pathological. While no longer universally accepted, this approach to word finding remains prevalent.

The early students of aphasia usually discussed word finding in theories of thinking, imagery, or the neuromechanics of language. Although word-finding defects were emphasized by many early aphasiologists, including Broca, Wernicke, Lichtheim, Isserlin, Pick, Dejerine, Marie, Henschen, Bastian, Jackson, and others, they made little effort to distinguish varieties of anomia. The ability to utilize the proper word in the appropriate context was consistently recognized as a major language function, but variations in this ability received no recognition.

In the early part of this century, two investigators, Kurt Goldstein and Henry Head, produced major studies of word-finding defects. Goldstein (1924) described a specific aphasic condition that he termed amnesic aphasia and characterized as a disturbance in which the patient could not assume an "abstract attitude." The defect in amnesic aphasia was an inability to correlate words, as symbols, with the objects they symbolized. A disturbance of the abstract attitude, thus, would produce devastating effects on both language and thought. Goldstein described a number of patients with amnesic aphasia who had serious problems with comprehension and cognition as well as with word-finding.

Almost simultaneously, Head (1926) published his major work, entitled *Aphasia and Kindred Disorders,* which included description of a disturbance he called nominal aphasia. In this disorder the major disturbance was the aphasic's inability to recognize the word as a symbol for an object, action, or the like. In addition to word-finding problems, Head noted that these patients had related language defects, including alexia, agraphia, autotopagnosia, and others. A double defect, an inability to comprehend a given word plus an inability to utilize the appropriate word in conversation, was also described.

In 1935 Weisunberg and McBride published a study of aphasia based on standardized tests. They demonstrated one language disturbance that could not be placed in their expressive–receptive categorizations. Goldstein's term amnesic aphasia was borrowed, but the authors noted that the disturbance primarily involved word finding without an equal defect in word recognition.

None of these early studies posited variations in word-finding problems. More recently, several investigators have suggested that not all word-finding problems are the same. For instance, Jason Brown (1972) suggested that anomia is a key disturbance in aphasia and that recovery from conduction aphasia, semantic aphasia, and Wernicke's aphasia usually leaves a residual anomic condition. He outlined two distinct varieties, which he designated as anomia and modality-specific anomia. In the latter condition primary sensory areas were separated from the "lexical entry area," producing an anomia only to certain sensory stimuli but normal naming when other sensory systems were utilized. Except for this clear distinction, however, all word-finding problems were called anomia.

Geschwind (1967) outlined four varieties of naming errors. These were

1. aphasic anomia, in which a patient with an aphasic language disturbance had a demonstrable disturbance in confrontation naming

2. word-finding problems caused by disconnection, in which the patient could perceive stimuli but, because of a callosal section or other major pathway separation, could not transmit this information to the language area of the dominant hemisphere to produce the name
3. nonaphasic misnaming, in which a patient without apparent aphasic speech makes gross errors in confrontation naming tests
4. hysterical misnaming, in which the patient mimics aphasia by either failing to name or misnaming in a setting of otherwise normal language output

Geschwind offered clinical examples of each variety and these four syndromes could be considered a classification of word-finding problems. If so, all aphasic naming-disturbances were treated as a single, undifferentiated abnormality.

Without formalizing it as a classification, Luria (1966) described variations of naming disturbance within his subdivision of the aphasias. Table 8.2 presents this information as a classification of the aphasic anomias. By outlining the varieties of aphasia and describing the significant differences in word finding difficulty among them, Luria suggested anatomical

TABLE 8.2 Anatomically Correlated Classification of Anomia[a]

1. Syndromes of sensory (acoustic) aphasia; lesions of the temporal systems
   (a) literal paraphasia
   (b) not aided by prompting
   (c) defect in finding words as noted through imprecision of sound structure
2. Syndromes of acoustic–mnestic aphasia; lesions of the extra-auditory divisions of the left temporal lobe
   (a) an inability to remember names
   (b) associated with other evidences of anmesia
   (c) verbal paraphasia (very little literal paraphasia)
   (d) tendency toward generalizations and/or circumlocution
   (e) not aided by prompting
3. Syndromes of amnestic aphasia; lesions of the inferoparietal (or parieto-occipital) systems
   (a) aided by prompting (especially phonetic)
   (b) otherwise similar to 2
4. Syndromes of orbital aphasia; lesions of the tempero-occipital systems
   (a) naming disturbances on visual confrontation corrected by tactile prompting
   (b) this is considered intermediate between optic agnosia and true aphasia
5. Syndromes of frontal lobe pathologies; lesions of the frontal lobes
   (a) marked decrease in words available for spontaneous conversation
   (b) better at producing name on confrontation testing
   (c) tendency to paraphasia—often producing words of similar sound but different meaning
6. Syndromes of fronto-temporal area; lesions of the left fronto-temporal divisions (also lesions affecting the brain as a whole)
   (a) diminished word traces
   (b) difficulty in word finding

[a] Compiled from data in Luria (1962).

TABLE 8.3   Varieties of Word-Finding Disturbance

1. Word production anomia
   (a) motor
   (b) paraphasic
2. Word selection (word dictionary) anomia
3. Semantic (nominal) anomia
4. Category-specific anomia
5. Modality-specific anomia
6. Anomia of disconnection
7. Word finding disturbance of dementia
8. Nonaphasic misnaming
9. Psychogenic anomia

localizations for varieties of anomia. While there may be disagreement about his correlation of specific word finding symptoms with specific types of aphasia or anatomical localizations, Luria's discussion is certainly the most advanced in the literature to date.

By combining the outlines provided by Geschwind and Luria with additional observations from the Aphasia Research Center, Boston Veterans Administration Hospital, a classification of the anomias can be made (Table 8.3). Although this classification is probably incomplete and some of the suggested varieties may be debatable, it serves as a structure for additional studies of word-finding defects. Each variety of word-finding disturbance mentioned in Table 8.3 has been seen in a pure state clinically; much more often, however, mixtures of several varieties occur in a single patient. Each suggested variety will be described and a short case study will illustrate the specific anomic characteristics.

VARIETIES OF WORD-FINDING DISTURBANCE

The first five varieties of word-finding disturbances in Table 8.3 are associated with aphasia. The final four are not usually considered aphasic, but are frequently mistaken for or misdiagnosed as aphasia. Other varieties of aphasic anomia can be suggested and this list may well be enlarged in the future. It is well to reemphasize that although each type of anomia listed in the classification has been observed independent of any of the other naming problems, it is far more common to have some mixture of types.

Word Production Anomia

Inability to express the desired word constitutes one of the more frequent sources of what appears to be anomia. Whether word production disturbance is a true word finding problem, however, is debatable. When an object is presented, the patient fails to produce the name, but if prompting (cuing) is offered, may utilize the cue and produce the appropriate name. Frequently the amount of prompting needed is so minimal that one must conclude that the word itself is known and the real problem lies in the initiation of articulation. Thus it can be questioned whether this represents a word-finding defect. A stronger cue may be necessary, either pronunciation of one or several of the phonemes or presentation of a contextual cue. Even so, the patient often insists that he "knew" the desired word but could not produce the initial syllable. This type of word production disturbance, along with serious articulatory problems, is most characteristically seen in nonfluent aphasia, secondary to dominant frontal pathology (Benson & Geschwind, 1974; Rubens, 1976).

A somewhat analogous situation, known as the "tip-of-the-tongue phenomenon" (Brown & McNeill, 1966), occurs in normal conversations. The individual "knows" the word he wants to say, but cannot immediately produce it (nor can he "think" of the word). The initial letter—or even the correct number of syllables—may be available and, if given sufficient time, the word may eventually be recalled. The individual with tip-of-the-tongue phenomenon often responds to minimal cues in a manner analogous to the aphasic with word production disturbance. The problem in lexical retrieval underlying the tip-of-the-tongue phenomenon in the normal speaker is unknown and any relationship to aphasic word finding or word production disturbances must remain speculative. Nonetheless, obvious similarities exist.

One type of problem in word-production disturbance appears to be articulatory, but it is difficult to exclude an additional, true, word-finding problem. Considerable cuing may be necessary and at times the patient may fail to produce the correct word on confrontation despite strong cues, suggesting a true disability in thinking of the desired word. On the other hand, the apparent lack of a full repertoire of substantive words in anterior aphasia may be due to a decreased ability to initiate activity, often considered a characteristic of frontal lobe dysfunction (Luria, 1969). That both word production and word-finding problems could occur simultaneously in these patients is quite likely.

One type of word production disturbance, then, can be characterized as a naming disability based on articulatory disturbance, frontal inertia or the tip-of-the-tongue phenomenon. This disturbance is frequently correctable by phonetic or contextual cues. Many patients with word production disturbance, however, fail to produce some names, even after receiving strong cues, suggesting a problem in word finding as well.

Another type of word production anomia that is distinctly different can be described. Some aphasics have fluent verbal output that is seriously contaminated by phonemic paraphasias and neologisms. Paraphasic sub-stitutions may be so prominent during attempts to use names that the responses are restricted to collections of incorrect phonemes. If the patient monitors his output and attempts self-correction, the result may be no response, an apparent inability to produce a name. With less self correction the responses are paraphasic, often to the point of being incomprehensible. Failure to produce the correct word is present in both conditions and may be independent of or added to an inability to "know" the desired word.

In a study of the "tip-of-the-tongue" phenomenon, Goodglass, Kaplan, Weintraub, and Ackerman (1976) demonstrated that aphasic individuals suffering from this paraphasic type of word production anomia frequently recognized the clues. Even though they failed to name the object, they often identified the initial letter and the number of syllables in the target, indicating that the word was at least partially "known" but could not be produced.

The following case reports illustrate the two varieties of word produc-tion defect described. Both individuals had relatively pure problems; many aphasics, however, have word production difficulty combined with other word-finding problems.

CASE 1

At the age of 43 a right-handed construction foreman suddenly suffered right hemiplegia and aphasia. Angiography revealed total occlusion of the left carotid artery. Following transfer to the Aphasia Research Center, examination demonstrated a dense right hemiplegia, almost no verbal out-put, but nearly normal comprehension of spoken language. Focal sharp and slow activity was demonstrated in the left sylvian region of the EEG and an isotope brain scan showed increased uptake in the left frontal-parietal-temporal area. Following four months of rehabilitation, he was ambulatory and self-caring, with considerable improvement in language. Speech re-mained nonfluent with dysarthria, sparse output, considerable effort, and dysprosody. Comprehension was good but both repetition and naming were abnormal. He could name a number of common objects and parts of objects, most colors, and body parts. When he failed to name, he often implied that he knew the name and after a slight cue, either phonetic or contextual, usually produced the correct name. Only rarely was cuing so unsuccessful that even with prompting he could not produce the word wanted. In contrast to the anomia, when names were given by the examiner he could always point to the appropriate object. Ability to produce word lists on request was limited to 2–4 items in 60 sec. Hospital or stress items caused no greater problems in naming than nonstress items. Improvement continued so that within 2 years he named most items, but had word finding pauses in spontaneous speech and remained deficient when asked to produce lists or words.

CASE 2

A 42-year-old male suffered a mild myocardial infarction while on a business trip. After several days in a hospital, he suffered an acute cerebral vascular accident, probably embolic. Initially there was a mild but transient right sided hemiparesis and a severe aphasia. By the time of transfer to the Aphasia Research Center, approximately 4 weeks after onset, there was no discernable neurologic disorder (such as hemiparesis, gait disturbance, or visual-field defect) except for a mild cortical sensory disturbance that involved only the right upper extremity. His major problem was language. Conversational output was jargon: short runs of understandable words, cliches, or prepositional phrases, interspersed with pauses and neologisms. Almost invariably, the neologisms replaced substantive words, so his verbal output conveyed little meaning. In sharp contrast, comprehension of spoken language appeared fully normal. When he attempted to repeat—even to repeat single words—there was total breakdown into neologistic jargon. He was unable to read aloud, but understood the newspaper, business magazines, novels, and the like. Written output was abnormal. The naming disturbance was severe and consistent. When asked to name objects, body parts, colors, and such, there was comparatively little hesitation, but the output was almost entirely paraphasic. Thus, when asked the name of the television set the patient said, *rugabize* for 'a chest of drawers', *rumpfessa* ('dresser'), 'window' *lungfab*, 'nose' *dop*, 'forehead' *clarpil*. In almost every attempt at naming the patient's output was totally wrong, but consisted of real phonemes. Frequently the number of syllables was the same as the target word and often the inflection given to the output closely resembled the expected inflection of the target word. The patient appeared to "know" the requested name, but produced a neologism instead. The aphasia cleared fairly rapidly. Within 6 weeks he communicated relatively well and within 3 months had only minimal paraphasia when repeating and no problem with word finding.

Word Selection (Word Dictionary) Anomia

A pure anomic aphasia, one with no other disturbance of output and no problems in comprehension, repetition, reading, or writing, can be called word selection (or word dictionary) anomia. This patient fails to name objects on confrontation, but readily explains or demonstrates their use, proving that he recognizes the object but cannot produce the verbal symbol (name). In fact, a description of the function of the object is often substituted for the word, producing a circumlocutory response. The circumlocution may even contain the actual target word (e.g., *I don't know what you would call it but it's the thing I would use to comb my hair.*). The patient may realize that he has used the correct word in his description but, not infrequently, even fails to recognize the desired word after he has said it. More often, the functional description is not a sufficient cue to produce retrieval of the desired name. Prompting with either phonetic or contextual cues usually fails and often appears to confuse the patient. Some patients even reject the full cue (the correct name) stating, *You may call it a comb but that's not the word I would use.* In sharp contrast, and a very important feature of word selection anomia, is the rapid and correct response when the name is given and the patient is asked to point to the appropriate object. The response to name recognition testing (comprehension) is immediate and appears to be fully normal. Thus, word selection anomia appears to be a one-way defect, an inability to select the correct word from an internal lexicon but with no problem in recognizing (understanding) the meaning of the word when it is presented by another person.

Most individuals with word selection anomia produce empty speech, often loaded with circumlocution. The use of a functional description as replacement for a word produces long and unwieldy sentences conveying limited information. There has been considerable disagreement concerning the anatomical localization of pathology underlying pure anomia, but most researchers agree on a site posterior to the fissure of Rolando.

CASE 3

A 47-year-old male was admitted with purulent drainage from both ears. The original antibiotic treatment was ineffective and, while under treatment with a more definitive antibiotic, the patient had a major seizure and lapsed into a lethargic state. Full neurologic and neuroradiologic evaluation demonstrated a mass lesion in the left temporal lobe. At craniotomy an abscess involving the midportion of the left second temporal gyrus was drained. Recovery was comparatively uneventful except for residual aphasia. Postoperatively, the patient could not comprehend spoken language and had a jargon output; both conditions cleared rapidly, leaving an almost pure word finding problem as the only residual difficulty. Conversational speech was fluent and effortless until a substantive word, particularly a noun indicative of a specific picturable item, was needed. After a pause he occasionally stated: *I can't think of the word* but more often he would describe the function of the object. Thus, to speak about a pencil he would say: *I pick up that thing I use to write with.* He had no problem with comprehension or repetition of spoken language and read adquately. Specific word finding tests demonstrated considerable problems. He rarely gave a correct name but, almost invariably, described the item or its function adequately. The description might include the name of the desired word. Thus, when a comb was held up the patient said, *That's the thing I use to comb my hair. Hey, that's the word I want, that's a comb.* At other times, he would use the correct word and not realize it. Thus, shown a hammer, he said, *That's the thing I use to hammer in a nail. I can't remember what it's called.* The word finding difficulty slowly improved but never returned to normal. His verbal output became increasingly sparse, as he no longer attempted to produce specific words. He has been followed for many years and, while able to function adequately, continued to have a problem with word finding.

CASE 4

A 52-year-old salesman was admitted for evaluation of aphasia. Three months previously he noted onset of a left-side headache following exertion. Carotid angiography demonstrated a small arteriovenous malformation in the left parietal-occipital region, surrounded by hematoma. Surgical removal of the clots was followed by an excellent recovery except for a residual language problem.

Physical and neurologic examinations showed only minimal defects, the most prominent a right visual field defect that varied in scope but was most often described as a right inferior quadrantopsia. His greatest difficulty was in language production. Conversational speech was distinctly aphasic, with excessive wordiness but relatively little content. While comprehension and repetition were both normal, there were difficulties in naming tasks. He could name most common objects, but failed to name less common objects and most parts of objects (such as the stem of watch, the barrel of a gun). He could name colors and body parts and most geometrical figures. When asked to produce word lists, he gave 10 animals in 60 sec, a borderline response, and only 8 words beginning with the letter *r*. He complained of a mild disturbance in reading, but if given sufficient time could understand paragraph-length material. Within 3 months speech and reading ability had improved considerably and his ability to produce word lists was within normal levels.

Semantic (Nominal) Anomia

The word finding defect in this category resembles the one just discussed, an apparent inability to retrieve the appropriate word from the lexicon. Patients with semantic disturbance, however, also have difficulty understanding the name when spoken or written, that is, a defective appreciation of the symbolic value of the word (as suggested by Goldstein, Head, and Luria). In the most florid clinical examples, the patient will show a fluent, empty output with a tendency to echo, poor comprehension, excellent repetition, and severe defects in naming, reading, and writing. While semantic anomia is usually accompanied by some neurologic deficiency, this may be minimal, with the most significant defects limited to language. Various names for syndromes featuring this word-finding problem include transcortical sensory aphasia, nominal aphasia, and semantic aphasia.

Superficially the anomias of semantic disturbance and word selection disturbance appear closely related. Momentary reflection, however, demonstrates significant differences. The anomia of semantic disturbance apparently represents an inability to use the name as a symbol. While the patient can indicate the use of an object in both conditions, in semantic anomia the "name" of the object fails to convey meaning, whereas in word selection anomia the name offered by the examiner is immediately linked with the object for which it is a symbol. It may be that the anomia of the two conditions is identical and that the additional symptoms of semantic anomia are secondary to a more extensive lesion. In truth, many patients with word selection anomia do have comprehension problems in the early stages and only with recovery attain the state of "pure" anomia, which supports a thesis that the two anomias are similar, differing only in degree. On the other hand, it is just as possible that the two disturbances represent breakdown of separate mechanisms in the activity of word finding. The latter postulate is consistent with existing pathological studies (see later) and is of importance for the theory of word finding to be developed in this chapter.

CASE 5

A 47-year-old professional piano player was admitted for evaluation of aphasia and weakness of the right hand of unknown duration. Although he could give no history, an acute onset was suspected. Routine neurologic examination showed only mild hyperreflexia, clumsiness, posturing, astereognosis, defective two-point discrimination, and defective position sense, all limited to the right upper extremity. Response to pin prick was intact and no field defect could be demonstrated.

His verbal output was fluent, circumlocutory and loaded with interjections such as *you know, oh boy,* and paraphasic substitutions including neologisms. Conversational speech was truly jargon and conveyed almost no information. Comprehension was successful only for general meaning; he could not understand most conversational speech. He consistently failed to understand sentences that described objects, sentences whose meaning was dependent upon the relationships of several words, and sentences dependent upon a specific word for meaning, but did recognize a few common object names. Repetition of spoken language, on the other hand, was intact; he could repeat long and complex sentences and nonsense material without error. Naming was limited to a few common objects, even fewer parts of objects, and very few body parts or colors; he consistently failed when lower frequency items were presented. His ability to name appeared equivalent to his ability to recognize object names; with less frequently used items he failed in both ways. He comprehended some short written phrases, but failed if there was even slight complexity and was totally unable to write. He was unable to present lists of words, usually offering no more than one or two items in 60 sec.

Carotid arteriography demonstrated total occlusion of the left carotid artery at the bifurcation. Both EEG and brain scan demonstrated left frontal-parietal abnormality that was thought to be located in the cortical "border zone," above and posterior to the immediate perisylvian region.

Category-Specific Anomia

There are a number of case reports of patients who cannot name items in certain categories but perform well in other categories. The most commonly reported category-specific disturbance concerns color and has been called color anomia, color agnosia, and color naming disturbance (Geschwind & Fusillo, 1966; Oxbury, Oxbury, & Humphrey, 1969). Isolated body part naming, particularly finger naming, disturbance is reported (Gerstmann, 1924) and many other varieties of category-specific anomia have been suggested. For instance, some authors (Hecaen & Ajuriaguerra, 1956) reported a difference in the ability to name animate and inanimate objects, based on superior or inferior location of pathology in the dominant parietal lobe. Category-specific anomias, however, are distinctly uncommon and rarely pure. The two examples quoted here can be considered typical. The first case had a fairly distinct problem in color naming, but the defect was incomplete; the second case was far from pure, but had some problems in using names in a specific category.

CASE 6

At age 45 a truckdriver with a sixth-grade education noted the acute onset of a right-side visual field defect. Angiography demonstrated occlusion of the left posterior cerebral artery. Among many complaints offered by the patient was an inability to read and he was eventually seen in neurologic consultation.

The patient was obese, poorly motivated, and a chronic complainer, but examination revealed clearcut abnormalities. The right homonymous hemianopsia, originally quite dense, resolved to an upper quadrantopsia with partial defect in the lower quadrant. There was no paresis or sensory loss; ambulation and coordination were intact. There were no noteworthy language problems and spontaneous speech was fluent with an adequate vocabulary. Comprehension and repetition were excellent. He had some difficulty naming uncommon objects, but many of his naming problems might have been based on low educational level. Originally he could not read at all, but over several years he began to recognize letters of the alphabet, say them out loud, and recognize a word he had spelled. From the onset he could recognize words spelled out loud by an examiner and could write meaningful sentences and paragraphs (alexia without agraphia). Both grammar and spelling were poor, but consistent with premorbid capabilities. In contrast to the intact ability to name almost all objects and body parts, he showed profound difficulty in naming colors. He either refused to name the color demonstrated or gave a noncommittal response like grey or greenish-brown. Similarly, he was unable to point to colored chips when the color name was given by the examiner. He could, however, match similarly colored objects and could use color names in conversation without difficulty. There was a mild general naming deficiency that contrasted with the severe difficulty in naming colors and in pointing to colors named by the examiner (so-called "color agnosia").

CASE 7

A 38-year-old housewife suffered intractable psychomotor seizures following injury to the left temporal lobe. Inability to control seizures with medications prompted neurosurgical removal of the left temporal lobe. The operation was limited to the anterior 5 cm of the temporal lobe. Prior to surgery the patient had no demonstrable language disturbance, but postoperatively a language problem was noted. Her speech was fluent but with obvious uncertainty in the use of some words. Similarly, comprehension of spoken language was adequate except for certain words. When asked to point to objects about the room she often failed, even though she could repeat the word correctly and even spell the word out loud. She would state that she could not understand what was meant. Thus, when asked to point to the wall the patient said, *Wall, wall, I don't know what that is. It is spelled W-A-L-L. I just don't know what it is.* While she failed to point to many room objects, she could point to most body parts, colors, articles of clothing, geometrical shapes, coins, and the like. Repetition was fully normal, she could read adequately, both aloud and for comprehension, but had a problem in confrontation naming similar to the problem in comprehension. If unable to understand the name of an object she could not name the same object when it was demonstrated. The anomia, however, was not limited to room objects. She had difficulty in naming some body parts, some colors, some denominations of coins, and other categories. Attempts to produce word lists of almost any category were limited to 8 to 12 words in 60 sec. Unfortunately, the patient was discharged home immediately after the initial examination and no follow-up information is available.

Modality-Specific Anomia

A related but separable specific anomia has been called modality- or stimulus-specific anomia. In this condition the patient has difficulty naming objects presented by one sensory modality (e.g., vision) but not others. The most characteristic cases have been called "visual agnosia" or "visual aphasia" (Rubens & Benson, 1971; Lhermitte & Beauvois, 1973). The patient does not name (or recognize) an object presented visually but immediately names it when allowed to feel or hear it make a characteristic noise. Similar modality-specific naming disturbances have been recorded in tactile and auditory spheres. Most often the patient has a full speaking vocabulary and experiences difficulty in producing names only in response to the specific stimulus system. Whether disturbances of this type should be considered anomia is a debatable point; there can be no question, however, that appropriate testing demonstrates a word finding defect that is limited to a specific sensory modality.

CASE 8

A 42-year-old physician suffered a severe anoxic episode as a result of excessive use of alcohol and drugs. Upon recovery from the acute phase the only notable neurologic defect was a dense right hemianopsia. The patient's behavior, however, was considered abnormal and, because of suspected suicidal tendency, he was referred for psychiatric care. A severe alexia was noted and neurobehavioral evaluation requested. Examination, about three weeks after onset, revealed alexia without agraphia (he was unable to read but could write flawlessly) and a severe disturbance in naming objects on visual presentation. When items such as a pencil, spoon, or comb were shown he could neither tell what the item was nor what it was used for. If the item was then placed in his hand, he immediately named it correctly. The naming problem could not be blamed on primary visual–sensory disturbance, since he made accurate and recognizable drawings of the objects he could not name. Though unable to name visualized items, he had no problems naming the same item when presented in a tactile or auditory manner. With time, this striking modality-specific naming disturbance resolved but, even years later, when asked to recognize simple line drawings of common objects in a tachistoscopic presentation, he either failed or demanded much longer presentations than control subjects.

Anomia of Disconnection

A distinctly different naming disorder was described by Geschwind in his publications on disconnexion syndromes (1965) and naming problems (1967). The characteristic example was the patient with division of the corpus callosum by surgery or natural lesion. When, without using vision, such a patient was asked to name an object placed in the left hand, he either produced nothing or an incorrect name (confabulation). However, if the patient was then allowed to use the left hand to palpate an array of objects the correct object would be retrieved. The latter phenomenon has been called after-selection and demonstrates both sufficient sensory input for recognition of the object and sufficient memory to retain the impression; the failure is in the ability to give the object a name. The explanation offered is that separation of the nondominant somato–sensory area from the dominant language area by section of the corpus callosum precludes naming a correctly perceived sensation. That similar disconnections may exist within a single hemisphere (separation of a sensory area from the language area), and thereby produce a word finding disturbance, is certainly plausible. In fact, this would appear to be an acceptable explanation for the stimulus-specific naming disturbances described above.

CASE 9

Over a period of several years, a 37-year-old man suffered a number of acute central nervous system insults variously diagnosed as cerebral vascular accidents, multiple sclerosis, vasculitis, and the like. At one time there was a transient right-side paresis with language problems, later there was a distinct left-side paresis. Interspersed were grand mal seizures, including one episode of status epilepticus. In general, recovery from each episode was good, but the patient was left in a state of decreased intellectual competency. No specific etiologic diagnosis was ever made. Following one series of seizures an unusual dissociation of right- and left-side activities was noted. Careful evaluation demonstrated callosal apraxia, identical to that described in patients following callosal section (Geschwind & Kaplan, 1962; Gazzaniga, Bogen, & Sperry, 1962). To verbal command he could carry out any type of activity with his right hand (e.g., make a fist, wave goodbye, demonstrate the use of a hammer, pen, teaspoon). None of these commands could be performed with the left hand, which always responded by making the same stereotyped movement, somewhat between saluting and making a fist. The patient himself noted the discrepancy and would attempt to cue himself by surreptitiously performing the appropriate movement with the right hand and quickly imitating it with his left hand. He could write fluently with his right hand, whereas his left hand made only a stereotyped writing movement. No matter what he was asked to write with the left hand, he always produced the first few letters of his name and would then stop; attempts to start over produced exactly the same output. He could not even copy well with the left hand. Dichotic listening tests demonstrated total extinction of left ear stimuli under bilateral stimulation. Disorders of naming were very specific. He had no difficulty with visual confrontation naming and used a fairly adequate vocabulary in spontaneous conversation. He easily named objects placed in the right hand. In contrast, he rarely named correctly an object placed in his left hand. He often confabulated (e.g., *pencil* when a safety pin had been placed in the left hand). When not allowed to confabulate and urged to after-select, his choice was usually accurate. The naming problem was limited to tactile naming with the left hand and astereognosis or other sensory disturbance as a cause was ruled out by the successful after-selection. An isotope brain scan revealed a fairly sizable area of uptake deep in the right frontal lobe just lateral to the genu of the corpus callosum. This abnormality disappeared in several months. The patient has been followed for almost 10 years and maintains the callosal section symptomatology, including the tactile naming disturbance with the left hand.

Word Finding Defect of Dementia

A decrease in available vocabulary is a widely recognized finding of degenerative dementias such as Alzheimer's Disease. The word finding defect of dementia has distinct characteristics, most clearly seen during the early stages of the process. The patient performs well on tests of confrontation naming, giving the appropriate name for most objects, parts of objects, body parts, colors, actions, and so forth. When asked to present a list of words in a given category, however, the number produced is well below normal levels. The discrepancy between near normal confrontation naming and seriously deficient word lists is striking. With progression of the disease the verbal output becomes empty, consisting of many cliches, incomplete phrases, prepositional phrases, and an excessive use of indefinite words. Even at this stage the patient may show few problems with confrontation naming. Only late in the course of dementia does confrontation naming also falter. A similar pattern of word finding problems can be seen in the dementias caused by obstructive hydrocephalus and metabolic, toxic, posttraumatic, and postencephalitic encephalopathies.

CASE 10

A 53-year-old police officer failed to remember orders and was placed on temporary leave approximately nine months before entering the hospital. His family had noted a change in behavior, particularly forgetfulness, for at least two years prior to hospitalization. Physically, he was healthy, robust, alert, and cooperative. A full neurological examination was entirely normal, except for the mental status evaluation. There was a distinct memory problem, he was poorly oriented for time and place, had great difficulty in remembering the names of his ward physicians, unrelated names that were taught to him, and the like. There was a disturbance of constructional skills, with oversimplification and omission and almost no ability to draw or copy three-dimensional figures. The ability to manipulate old knowledge—such as calculating, proverb interpretation, or pointing out differences and similarities—was almost totally lost. Only the most elementary rote calculations could be performed and attempts at proverb interpretation were concrete. Conversational speech was fluent but empty with a rambling, disjointed quality and some tendency for circumlocution. Repetition, comprehension, reading, and writing were all adequate, but there were distinct problems in naming. The emptiness of conversational speech clearly resulted from a lack of specific words, often replaced by an indefinite word. With tests of visual, tactile, or auditory confrontation naming, however, he performed almost flawlessly. In sharp contrast, there was a marked failure to present word lists. He produced the names of only three animals, two makes of automobiles, two articles of clothing, and only one or two words beginning with specific letters of the alphabet. Air encephalography demonstrated a mild increase in ventricular size and considerable cortical atrophy. A presumptive diagnosis of Alzheimer's degeneration was made. Follow-up evaluation revealed increasing dementia.

Nonaphasic Misnaming

This entity has been described in many articles by Weinstein and colleagues (Weinstein & Kahn, 1952; Weinstein & Keller, 1964), who considered nonaphasic misnaming a major variety of word-finding defect. Most of the patients they described were acutely ill, usually in a state of reduced consciousness resulting from widespread cerebral dysfunction (such as increased intracranial pressure, metabolic encephalopathy, or intoxication). Nonaphasic misnaming in the obtunded is usually easy to differentiate from aphasic anomia in a clear mental state. The two conditions can overlap, however, and an individual patient may have aphasic and nonaphasic naming problems simultaneously. Weinstein emphasized that the misnamed words are often stress or illness oriented. In some instances, the misnaming appears confabulatory and additional confabulations may be produced based on the original misnaming. Thus, if the patient calls the individual in the white coat who examines him a repairman, then various pieces of nearby hospital equipment, such as wheelchairs, stretchers, and hospital beds, might be called work bench, tool box, and the like. Nonaphasic misnaming usually occurs in patients whose decreased level of consciousness or attention interferes with memory, but the amount of misnaming greatly exceeds that noted in amnesia such as Korsakoff's psychosis. Nonaphasic misnaming is most often a symptom of an acute confusional syndrome and is usually transient.

CASE 11

A 53-year-old male was evaluated 4 days after surgical removal of a subdural hematoma lying over the left temporal parietal area. There was no residual paralysis or sensory loss and the visual fields were full. The patient remained lethargic, was easily distracted and tended to drift away from any topic of conversation. Aphasia evaluation was normal except for naming. He correctly named many common objects, but misnamed objects related to the hospital. Thus, when a urinal was shown he said that it was a *paint pot*. When asked what a paint pot was doing in his bed, he replied that this was part of his job, that he painted automobiles and always worked with a paint pot. He was disoriented in place and time and denied any recent surgery. The only naming difficulty concerned items that were hospital oriented. Within 2 days the confusional state cleared: There was no longer a denial of surgery and no evidence of a naming disturbance.

Psychogenic Anomia

Of recognized causes of anomia, the psychogenic variety is probably the least common. Psychogenic anomia should not be a cause of diagnostic difficulty; not only is the disorder rare, but aphasia is extremely difficult to mimic and attempts to stimulate anomia are usually obvious to the examiner.

CASE 12

A 35-year-old female was seen in consultation because of suspected temporal lobe epilepsy. Along with her history she gave an intelligent and fairly learned discussion of temporal lobe epilepsy and expressed a desire to have a temporal lobectomy performed in Montreal. She also discussed, at length, her husband's activities as an engineer working in computer sciences and doing advanced work in his field. Her discussion of his activities contained an excellent technical vocabulary and was presented with considerable feeling and interest. Among her complaints, however, was a problem in speaking. No such problem was observed during spontaneous conversation, but on confrontation testing she demonstrated considerable difficulty naming common objects. Thus, when shown objects such as a pencil, comb, and wristwatch, she failed to produce the name and stated: *See, I just can't remember the names of simple things like that.* It was felt that her anomia was unreal, a hysterical symptom related to some underlying disease process. Psychiatric evaluation demonstrated considerable depression, based on marital discord. With appropriate recognition and therapy for this problem, the patient's word-finding difficulty totally disappeared.

CASE 13

A 25-year-old male was admitted to the psychiatry service for evaluation of abnormal behavior and right-side weakness. Examination revealed a "paralyzed" right side without objective evidence of weakness, hyper-reflexia, pathological reflex, or sensory change. There was a notable tendency to give approximate answers. Thus, when asked to add 5 and 2, the patient said 6, when asked how many days in a week, he replied 8, when asked how many legs a cat had, he responded 3. A diagnosis of the Ganser syndrome with hysterical paresis was made and the patient was transferred to the Neurobehavioral Center for additional study. Here he came in contact with individuals with aphasia and within a few days his speech became markedly reduced and grossly abnormal. When asked about his speaking difficulty, he replied slowly and with effort: *Me no can talk so good. Me no know what to say.* Similar grossly abnormal speech was noted throughout the aphasia evaluation. He usually claimed inability to name an object on confrontation, was unable to give word lists, could not name objects from description, and so forth. When he did name objects, the responses were incorrect names of real objects (e.g., shown a pencil he called it a comb). Questioning of family members revealed that his wife was about to deliver a second child, a situation with which he was apparently unable to cope. In addition, a history of significant congenital brain damage was obtained. Air studies showed an asymmetrical ventricular system with the left ventricle considerably enlarged, suggesting injury to his left cerebrum, probably at birth or in early childhood. Objective neurologic evidence of left brain abnormality was masked, however, by the profound hysterical overlay. Neither psychotherapy nor organic therapy was fully effective, although by the time of discharge the patient could converse in a more normal manner and walked freely.

DISCUSSION OF CLINICAL CASES

As already noted, the case reports just given were specifically selected from several thousand aphasia cases evaluated by personnel at the Aphasia Research Center. Obviously, the cases were selected because they most clearly demonstrated the type of naming disturbance being described, but for most of the types of anomia outlined there were many other cases in the files with similar findings. While the majority of aphasic patients have some mixture of word-finding problems, it is usually possible to demonstrate the presence of one or several of the types of word-finding problem described. On the basis of this clinical material, it is obvious that word-finding difficulty, so-called anomia, cannot be considered a single, specific aphasic disturbance. Distinctly different word-finding problems have specific clinical parameters of their own. The cases described can be correlated, at least in many respects, with the varieties of naming disturbance described by Geschwind and Luria. It also appears, on the basis of the above material, that an anatomical–clinical correlation can be posited. This deserves further discussion at this point.

As an initial example of an anatomical–clinical correlation, word production anomia appears to occur primarily, in fact almost exclusively, in individuals whose pathology is located anterior to the parietal-temporal language area. Case 1 of this study had clinical findings of Broca's aphasia plus right hemiplegia and an anterior sylvian focus on the EEG and brain scan, all suggestive of pathological involvement of the posterior inferior aspect of the left frontal lobe, often called Broca's area. Almost invariably this patient knew the word he wanted to say, but could not initiate word production without help from the examiner. A somewhat similar situation was present in Case 2. This individual had conduction aphasia with clear-cut clinical and anatomical findings. The pathology underlying conduction aphasia has been studied (Benson, Sheremata, Burchard, Segarra, Price, & Geschwind, 1973; Green & Howes, 1977) and in the present case, as in many others in the literature, the pathology was located in the anterior inferior parietal area. This patient also appeared to know the word that he desired to say, but his output was so contaminated by paraphasic substitution that the names produced were often completely incorrect. These two varieties are similar, if not identical, to Luria's efferent motor and afferent motor aphasias. The location of pathology in both cases can be considered anterior and the difference in neuroanatomical location of pathology may well account for the variation in the word output difficulty. While the disturbance in naming is dissimilar, in both it is the abnormality of word production that causes the anomia. Word production anomia, then, appears to indicate an anterior lesion.

Case 3 had an almost pure anomia following structural damage to the middle gyrus of the left temporal lobe. Case 4 also had an almost pure anomia, except for minimal reading and writing disturbances, but in this case the pathology was located in the parietal-occipital junction below the angular gyrus, area 37 in the Brodmann terminology. In both cases the primary problem was in word selection. It can be postulated that the problem centered on entry into or use of the hypothetical word dictionary (to be discussed later). Certainly, the word-finding problems in Cases 3 and 4 were distinctly different from that in Cases 1 and 2 and, correspondingly, the locations of pathology were also different. From our own clinical evidence and from review of the literature, it appears that "pure" cases of word selection anomia usually follow pathology involving the posterior part of the second temporal gyrus or the inferior portion of the parietal lobe, the lower angular gyrus or area 37.

Case 5 can be considered an example of semantic aphasia in the terminology of Luria. The striking finding in Case 5 was that the patient's inability to understand the words said to him roughly equalled his inability to produce appropriate names on confrontation. That the comprehension defect was not based on disturbed reception of the auditory language signal is indicated by the intact ability to repeat what was said. He was unable to understand words that he easily pronounced. The pathology appeared to center on the angular gyrus, just superior to the temporal-occipital junction area (area 37). Only occasionally are pathological lesions limited to one or the other of these areas, and it can be anticipated that mixtures of the word selection and semantic varieties of anomia would be the rule rather than the exception. Nonetheless, the occasional demonstration of a relatively pure case of one or the other type of word-finding problem supports the hypothesis that the specific clinical findings stem from involvement of closely adjacent but separate areas in the cerebral cortex.

Color naming disturbance (color agnosia) demonstrated by Case 6 (in which the only significant naming problem involved colors), is most frequently associated with disconnection of an intact right hemisphere visual area from an equally intact left hemisphere language area. The inability to name colors or choose them by name when they can be correctly sorted and used correctly in purely verbal context is a prime example of category-specific anomia. Color naming is defective only in the visual–verbal or verbal–visual association tasks. Similar category-specific naming problems can occur with tactile or auditory stimuli, but the findings are usually clouded by involvement of contiguous areas, producing a much more complex clinical picture.

Case 7 is less clear from an anatomical point of view, but deserves consideration. The location of the pathology that produced the category-specific word-finding problems in this case remains uncertain. The left temporal lobe had been removed, but similar temporal lobectomies have been performed on many patients without residual word-finding difficulties. Additional pathology, in some area presently unrecognized, must be conjectured for the category specific anomia of Case 7. From a review of the literature it would appear that other cases of so-called category-specific anomia are similarly uncertain in lesion localization (Yamadori & Albert, 1973; Dennis, 1976). Quite possibly a combination of lesions involving several specific areas may be involved. Appropriately, category-specific anomia is rarely reported.

In Case 8 a series of separate but related infarcts involved the occipital lobes bilaterally, producing a dramatic symptom picture. This patient had adequate vision but could not name on visual presentation items which he readily named after palpation. This condition has been called visual agnosia. Again, it has been conjectured that selected bilateral lesions are necessary to produce this rare syndrome and post-mortem examination in Case 8 demonstrated damage to the inferior longitudinal fasciculus bilaterally (Benson, Segarra, & Albert, 1974). However, more clinical correlations are necessary before making any definitive statement about the minimal lesions underlying visual agnosia.

Case 9 suffered a number of insults to both hemispheres, particularly involving white matter. One lesion involved the anterior portion of the corpus callosum and appeared to produce a unique word-finding problem. The patient could not name following tactile stimulation to the left hand, despite good ability to name when offered similar stimulation to the right hand. Case 8 can be considered modality-specific anomia and Case 9 callosal section anomia, both apparently dependent on the specific locations of one or more lesions separating the language area from the relevant sensory cortex.

Category-specific anomia, modality-specific anomia, and callosal section anomia are all comparatively uncommon, but each type exists and is clearly different from the other varieties of anomia outlined. Specifically, in each of these varieties the pathology interferes with the stimulus before it reaches an intact language area. In addition, the structural pathology underlying these disorders is located in areas different from the areas involved in the other types of anomia described. It is obvious that combinations of one or more of these anomias with the other varieties must exist to account for some of the many variations of anomia seen clinically.

The other varieties of anomia mentioned have less clear-cut anatomical–clinical correlations. Case 10 is a good example of one common variety. Almost without question this patient had the degenerative disease of brain called Alzheimer's disease. When seen in the early stages, the word-finding problem of Alzheimer's disease can be differentiated from other types of anomia by the comparative retention of confrontation naming in the face of a sharp drop in the ability to present names in category lists. The symptoms in Alzheimer's disease follow marked degeneration of cortical cells, primarily in the association cortex. It is tempting to state that the anomia results from biparietal pathology. This must remain a conjecture, however, as similar pathology is present in the temporal and frontal association areas. With pathology involving so many different association areas, it could be expected that a word-finding problem would appear.

The nonaphasic word-finding abnormality described in Case 11 is also fairly common. Whether this truly represents an anomia is a matter of controversy, but that this disturbance can be mistaken for an anomic aphasia is certainly true. In our experience, nonaphasic misnaming occurs almost exclusively in acute confusional states, a characteristic which helps separate nonaphasic misnaming from the other anomias. No specific structural lesion can be said to underlie this word-finding abnormality, but both subcortical and cortical malfunction can be assumed.

Finally, Cases 12 and 13 are self-explanatory. As noted, word-finding difficulty is not a common hysterical sign and should not be difficult to differentiate from the other varieties mentioned. Obviously, no specific anatomical locus is postulated for the spurious word-finding problem.

To summarize, it appears that the process of producing names can be affected by abnormality involving a number of widely separated neuro-anatomical areas. Pathology in some areas apparently affects only one type of sensory input whereas pathology in other locations may produce problems in intermodal associations, in entering or using the lexical repository, or in the mechanics of producing the word. In clinical practice a mixture of several varieties of anomia is frequent, but differentiation can often be made, particularly when related clinical signs are taken into account.

THEORETICAL CONSIDERATIONS

Clearly, anomia cannot be considered a single, unitary defect. The examples of anomia defined and illustrated above demonstrate unequivocally that the word-finding problem noted in one patient with a neurobehavioral problem may be distinctly different from the anomia in another patient. The evidence that this difference is related to, if not fully dependent upon, the neuroanatomical site of cerebral malfunction is strong. Based on this demonstration a hypothetical explanation of the process of word-finding will be presented.

Actually, a number of fundamentally different hypotheses have been offered to explain variations in anomia through the years. Such obvious and proven factors as word frequency (Rochford & Williams, 1965), picturability (Goodglass, Barton, & Kaplan, 1968), operativity (Gardner, 1973), semantic field (Goodglass & Baker, 1976), and developmental acquisition of target words (Rochford & Williams, 1962) have been discussed. These hypotheses will not be considered here. Instead, a mechanical explanation will be presented, focusing on the neuroanatomical substratum by correlating the variations of anomia with the known locus of pathology. While the proposed theory incorporates some recent clinical and anatomical data concerning cortical–cortical connections, it omits most psychological and physiological theories of mental function. In this respect this hypothetical explanation of word-finding is admittedly limited and incomplete. Rather than representing a complete and inclusive theory, the explanation postulated here should be considered a tentative step, a model for subsequent theories to utilize.

The cornerstone of the proposed theory of word finding is the simultaneous synthesis of both simple and complex percepts from multiple sensory modalities, a process called inter-modal association. A number of contemporary investigators (Geschwind, 1964, 1965; Ettlinger, 1967; Butters & Brody, 1969) note the importance of inter-sensory synthesis for human language function and both clinical and laboratory studies demonstrate that the major cross-modal link takes place in the parietal lobe (Hecaen, Penfield, & Malmo, 1956; Butters & Brody, 1968). A phylogenetically recent portion of the parietal lobe, the angular gyrus, appears to be unique in its ability to act as an area for association of sensory modalities. Clinical evidence indicates that the dominant hemisphere angular gyrus is essential for language and a strong case can be made for the nondominant hemisphere parietal lobe (again, probably centering in the angular gyrus) having a similar key function in complex visual–spatial associations. In particular, the theory of apractagnosia proposed by Hecaen *et al.* (1956) emphasizes the importance of the parietal lobe in visual–spatial activities. Without additional review, the importance of cross-modal associations for language and visual–spatial discrimination and the importance of the angular gyri of the two hemispheres for this activity will be accepted in the following theoretical considerations.

Before attempting to outline other anatomical areas which appear essential for the process of word-finding, it would be good to review, in theory at least, what occurs when a human produces a name. A sequence of activities that **may** occur can be postulated. For instance, what occurs when a person looks at a picture such as Figure 8.1? What mental activities must occur so that a name or description can be offered for this picture? It would appear that many quite different associations are almost instantaneously available. While not all lead directly to production of the name, most reflect upon the name actually selected and the many additional names that are available. Thus, almost immediately upon looking at Figure 8.1 a word becomes available. Often the word selected is the most common name that can identify the figure, but this simple, almost reflex, response fails to indicate

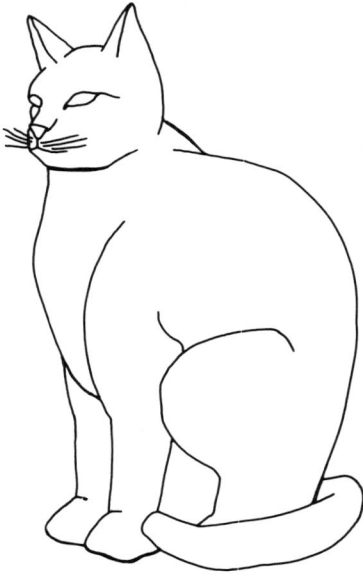

Figure 8.1   Stimulus (see text for explanation).

the complex activities occurring. Some observers will simultaneously vis-
ualize the spelling of the word, either in capital, lower case, or script letters.
Some, familiar with the subject of the picture, will subclassify and produce
the name of a given breed or specific variety. Many observers, based on
personal experience, will produce a given name for an animal of this type,
the name of an old or present pet. Thus, the name first suggested may not
be the most common name at all.

Simultaneous with the production of one of the names many observers
will recollect a specific incident with a specific animal, possibly an incident
with considerable emotional impact that is strongly remembered. Thus,
with selection of a name an affective response may develop; this may be a
feeling of love, of tenderness, of sympathy, of fear, or of sharp distaste
based on a previous experience or on training. Other sensory modalities
(memories) would also be stimulated by visualization of the picture, producing additional associations. The observer may recollect the noises or sounds
made by the animal such as purring, meowing, scratching, or some sound
associated with a specific animal. Somesthetic memories such as the sensation when the animal purrs under the hand, the softness of the fur to
stroking, or the sharpness of the claws may be aroused. The latter associations and many others would be accompanied by altered feeling tone.
Kinesthetic senses such as the movements necessary to pick up or caress the
animal may be stimulated. Visual memories may be alerted. For instance,

after seeing Figure 8.1, animals of this type may be visualized eating, sleeping, playing with a ball, climbing furniture, and so forth. With so many associations almost immediately available after visualization of a simple line drawing, the process can properly be described as a complex, simultaneous synthesis. Naming (word finding) is only one aspect of this complex activity and the actual name chosen will, to some extent, depend upon the strength of the individual associations.

If the stimulus had been received through some other sensory channel, such as auditory (the characteristic noise made by the animal), somesthetic (the feel of the animal's fur) or others, a similar group of almost instantaneous associations would occur. The same name would probably be produced and many of the same associations would be made even though a totally different sensory stimulus initiated the activity. Thus, production of a name appears to be only one of many activities in a complex function (often called concept formation) that is fairly independent of the stimulating sensory modality. For clarity, the following attempt to correlate naming with neuroanatomical sites will focus on naming to visual stimulation; the same basic principles apply to stimuli from the other sensory channels.

Almost no one will be consciously aware of the many associations that occur after visualizing Figure 8.1. Apparently many associations are filtered out below the level of conscious realization. It appears probable that a great many associations do occur, however, and that some or all may enter into production of a name for the subject. The actual act of naming an object thus represents only a minimal portion of this highly complex mental activity. Activities of such complexity should be subject to breakdown or alteration under many different conditions and the variations in word finding reported clinically do reflect this multitude of variables. In this presentation only one variable, the location of the pathology underlying a particular variety of anomia, will be discussed.

If the multiple associations suggested above do occur, can the anatomical structures necessary for such complicated neural circuitry be outlines? The following paragraphs, along with Figures 8.2, 8.3, and 8.4 will illustrate, in a crude manner, some of the interlocking neural associations that can be envisioned in a purely mechanical–anatomical model of word finding.

Upon visualizing an illustration such as Figure 8.1, the initial cortical stimulation occurs in the visual cortex, area 17 (see Figure 8.2). While some crude visual associations may be initiated at a subcortical level, the complex mental functions necessary for word finding demand cortical activation. From area 17 the impulse is directed to the surrounding visual association cortex (areas 18 and 19). This is a mandatory step, as these cortical areas receive virtually all stimuli emanating from the primary visual cortex. The

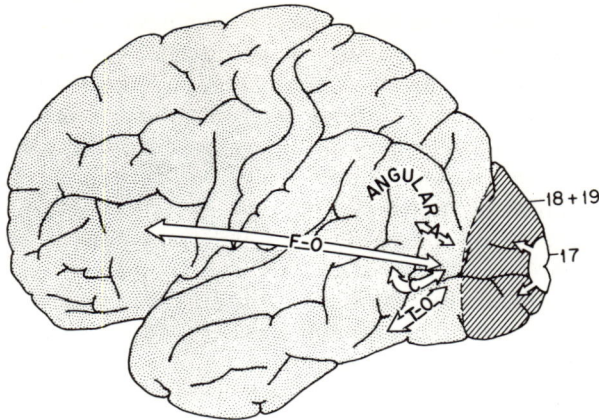

Figure 8.2 Schematic representation of major cortical-cortical connections of visual cortex. The number **17** refers to primary visual cortex, **18** and **19** to visual association cortices and **angular** to the angular gyrus. **A** represents visual angular gyrus connections, **C** the callosal interconnection, **F** the fronto-occipital pathways and **T** the connection with the inferior temporal cortex. Only the left hemisphere is illustrated, but identical connections occur in the right hemisphere.

secondary visual association cortices, on the other hand, have many connections, including a number of major pathways connecting directly to distant cortical areas. These long cortical–cortical connections are of major importance in highest level mental activities.

Each of the major primary sensory areas (visual, somesthetic, auditory) has a similar set of long cortical pathways but only the connections of the visual system have been illustrated in Figure 8.2. One major pathway traverses the corpus callosum to the analogous association cortex in the opposite hemisphere. This sizeable connection is of importance in integrating stimuli activating the two hemispheres. In the visual system this allows a single image to be formed from stimuli activating the visual areas of the two hemispheres. In addition, the callosal pathway allows interchange of stimuli between visual association cortices, producing activation of the cortical areas of both hemispheres from stimuli received at area 17 of only one hemisphere.

A second major pathway connects the visual association cortex and the motor association cortex of the frontal lobe and similar pathways link the other secondary sensory association areas to the frontal motor association area. This connection apparently acts as a sensory–motor reflex pathway and would appear to have little direct effect on naming. The sensory–motor connection, however, rapidly spreads a visual stimulus to the frontal association cortex and through additional frontal interconnections, may effect additional complex associations.

A third major pathway links the sensory association cortex and the inferior part of the temporal lobe, connecting the sensory processing area and the limbic system. It has long been conjectured that this pathway is essential for formation of new memories based on specific sensory information (Scoville, 1954). This link may also be necessary for retrieval of previously learned material. Animal experiments (and a small number of human case studies) implicate the infero-temporal region in visual recognition tasks, a finding of significance in one type of word finding defect (Keating & Horel, 1972; Gross, 1973).

In the human being there is one more major connection from the sensory association cortices: a direct link to the angular gyrus. Anatomically, the angular gyrus is located between (and actually abuts) the sensory association cortex of each of the primary sensory modalities (Figure 8.3). It is probable that association between the different sensory stimuli, the function called cross-modal association, occurs in the angular gyrus. The angular gyrus communicates with most association areas of the ipsilateral hemisphere, including the major somesthetic, auditory, visual, and kinesthetic association cortices (Figure 8.3). Disseminating sensory stimuli from one modality to the association cortices of other modalities (cross-modal association) is a function for which the angular gyrus is ideally situated. Even the most superficial personal introspection shows that stimulation via one sensory modality immediately promotes ideation in other modalities, a linkage of sensory modalities (as illustrated by the response to Figure 8.1). Such associative activities would appear essential for production of a name from a visual (or any other modality) stimulation.

While it is probable that cross-modal associations are necessary for production of a name following external stimulation, it is unlikely that

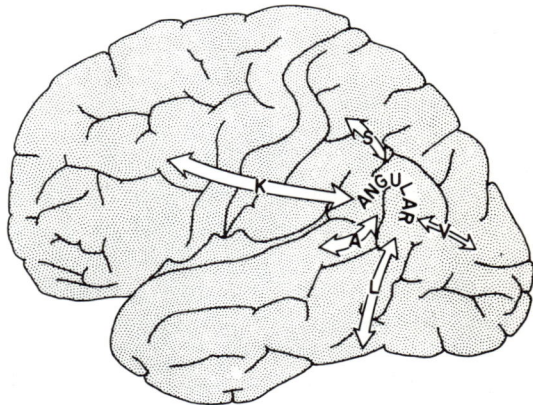

Figure 8.3 Schematic representation of cortical connections of the angular gyrus. **A** represents the pathway to the auditory association cortex, **V** to visual cortex, **L** to limbic area, **S** to somesthetic cortex, and **K** to kinesthetic (motor) region.

naming is a passive product of this process. To select a word or words that identify the picture in Figure 8.1, several additional activities are necessary.

Among the many associations found through stimulation of the angular gyrus, word-finding is unique, demanding selection of an appropriate word (name, symbol) from a lexical repository (word dictionary). Whether entrance into the hypothesized lexical repository occurs through the dominant hemisphere angular gyrus only or is also possible directly from one or more of the sensory or motor association cortices of either hemisphere remains unknown. In fact, whether a lexical repository in the brain, separate from the angular gyrus, actually exists is controversial and unanswered. The conjecture that there are two separate functions, cross-modal association and word selection, can be supported by both theory and clinical evidence. If so, it can be further conjectured that the two acts are the product of two separate anatomical areas.

What proof is there that a specific neuroanatomical location exists for the hypothetical word dictionary? Several of our own cases (specifically Cases 3 and 4) and others in the literature suggest that an isolated and specific naming disturbance, a "pure" anomia, not only occurs, but almost exclusively follows lesions that affect the basal-temporal region of the dominant hemisphere. In Case 3 the anomia appeared to result from a focal lesion of the second temporal gyrus. An almost identical word finding problem was observed following focal pathology in area 37, the temporal-occipital junction area of the dominant hemisphere (Case 4). Whether the postulated word dictionary actually exists in either of these areas or whether pathology involving some combination of these areas and their connections is necessary for full word finding capability is not clear from present information. Clinical data suggests, however, that entry into and use of a functionally discrete lexical repository is a significant portion of the task of word finding and that the temporal–occipital junction area of the dominant hemisphere appears essential for that task.

One striking clinical feature indicates that the "pure" anomia following basal-temporal pathology is not an abnormality of cross-modal associations. Patients such as Case 3 not only demonstrate use of an object they cannot name, they will describe its function, imitate sounds made by the object and, if the name is given by the examiner, will easily point to the correct item. Their problem appears to be only in extracting a word from the lexical repository to identify the object. Confident recognition of the object and its function suggests that cross-modal associations are being performed readily and recognition (understanding) of the specific name distinguishes the "pure" anomia from semantic aphasia.

Following activation of the lexical repository, the next step—forwarding the selection for the process of producing the name—commences. If the name of Figure 8.1 is to be said aloud, the selection from the lexical repository must reach the motor speech area of the frontal cortex, the correct motor speech areas be activated and in turn activate the brain stem nuclear centers for articulation (Figure 8.4 figuratively diagrams these acts). Prior to activation of the final pathway, an internal monitoring system apparently allows the individual to "hear" the name before it is actually articulated. At least, statements (particularly names) are often corrected or altered before or during articulation, an act which demands some type of feedback system (cortical–cortical reverberating circuit). And if, instead of simply identifying Figure 8.1 with a single word, a descriptive sentence is produced, additional language and speech areas must be activated to provide correct relational and syntactical structure to the output. If more complex ideation, such as a functional descriptive definition, a pun, or a metaphor, is presented, additional cognitive and language areas must be involved, again demanding additional interconnections.

Many problems can occur in the final steps of word production and each may interfere with naming. In such instances, however, the resultant anomia is recognizably different from naming problems due to defects in earlier steps. While different problems are grouped under the heading of word production anomia in this chapter, they share one common and significant feature: The desired word is "known," but cannot be produced correctly.

In summary, the process through which one identifies and produces a name following a sensory stimulus involves multiple, widespread neuroanatomical areas. Pathology in some areas would affect only one type of sensory input (visual, auditory, etc.) or a specific pathway causing a modality-specific, category-specific, or callosal section anomia. Interference with cross-modal associations by damage to the angular gyrus appears to reduce both the ability to produce a name and to understand the meaning of the name and can be termed semantic anomia. Isolated word finding problems ("pure anomia") suggest disturbance of a lexical repository or its

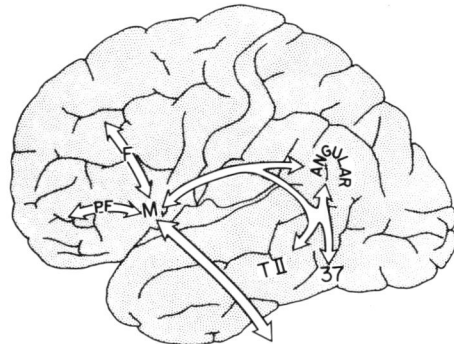

Figure 8.4 Schematic representation of hypothetical word dictionary (lexical repository) and motor speech areas and their connections. **Angular** represents the angular gyrus, **II** the second temporal gyrus, **37** indicates Brodmann area 37, and **M** the motor speech area. **F** and **PF** represent frontal and prefrontal influences on the motor speech area and **A** the final pathway to the articulators.

immediate connections and can be called word selection anomia. Finally, abnormality in the mechanics of forming or articulating the word may cause yet another type of naming defect (word production anomia). Nonfocal cerebral dysfunction such as the acute confusional states or dementias, which affect multiple areas, can also cause anomia. Selected case material from the files of the Boston Veterans Administration Hospital Aphasia Research Center illustrates each of these variations of word finding abnormality.

A theoretical outline of the neuroanatomical structures needed for word finding has been offered, a postulate which correlates various word finding problems with pathology in specific anatomical locations. A number of totally different but fully valid approaches to variations in word finding defect have not been treated in this presentation. Without question there is much to be gained by additional research on word finding utilizing many other parameters. The explanation offered here cannot fully explain a task as complex as word finding, but it is hoped that the suggested model can act as a structure for study and experimentation in future attempts to understand the process of word finding.

REFERENCES

Benson, D. F., & Geschwind, N. 1971. Aphasia and related cortical disturbances. In A. B. Baker & L. H. Baker (Eds.), *Clinical neurology.* New York: Harper & Row.
Benson, D. F., Segarra, J. M., & Albert, M. L. 1974. Visual-agnosia—prospagnosia. *Archives of Neurology, 30,* 307–310.
Benson, D. F., Sheremata, W. A., Buchard, R., Segarra, J., Price, D., & Geschwind, N. 1973. *Archives of Nuerology, 28,* 339–346.
Brain, R. 1961. *Speech disorders–aphasia, apraxia and agnosia.* London: Butterworth.
Brown, J. 1972. *Aphasia, apraxia and agnosia.* Springfield, Illinois: Charles C. Thomas.
Brown, R., & McNeill, D. 1966. The tip-of-the-tongue phenomenon. *Journal of Verbal Learning and Verbal Behavior, 5,* 325–337.
Butters, N., & Brody, B. 1968. The role of the left parietal lobe in the mediation of intra- and cross-modal associations. *Cortex, 4,* 328–343.
Butters, N., & Brody, B. 1969. Familiarity as a factor in the cross-modal associations of brain-damaged patients. *Perceptual and Motor Skills, 28,* 68.
Dennis, M. 1976. Dissociated naming and locating of body parts after left anterior temporal lobe resection. *Brain & Language, 3,* 147–163.
Ettlinger, G. 1967. Analysis of cross-modal effects and their relationship to language. In C. Millikan & F. Darley (Eds.), *Brain mechanisms underlying speech and language.* New York: Grune & Stratton.
Gardner, H. 1973. The contribution of operativity to naming capacity in aphasic patients. *Neuropsychologia, II,* 213–220.
Gazzaniga, N. S., Bogen, J. E., & Sperry, R. W. 1962. Some functional effects of sectioning the cerebral commisures in man. *Proceedings National Academy of Science, USA, 48,* 1765–1769.

Gerstmann, J. 1972. Fingeragnosia: Eine um schniebene störung der Orienterung am eigenen Korper. *Wiener Klinische Wochenschrift, 31,* 1010.

Geschwind, N. 1964. The development of the brain and the evolution of language. In C. I. J. M. Stuart (Ed.), *Report of the 15th annual R.T.M. on linguistic and language studies* (Monograph series on languages and linguistics, no. 17). Duquense, Iowa: Duquense University Press.

Geschwind, N. 1965. Disconnexion syndromes in animals and man. *Brain, 88,* (II), 237–294; (III) 585–644.

Geschwind, N. 1967. The varieties of naming errors. *Cortex, 3,* 97–112.

Geschwind, N., & Fusillo, M. 1966. Color naming defects in association with alexia. *Archives of Neurology, 15,* 137–146.

Geschwind, N., & Kaplan, E. 1962. A human cerebral disconnection syndrome. *Neurology, 12,* 675–685.

Goldstein, K. 1924. Das Wesen der Amnestischen Aphasie. *Schweizer Archiv Fur Neurologie und Psychiatrie, 15,* 163–175.

Goodglass, H., & Baker, E. 1976. Semantic field naming and auditory comprehension in aphasia. *Brain & Language, 3,* 359–374.

Goodglass, H., Barton, M., & Kaplan, E. 1968. Sensory modality and object naming in aphasia. *Journal of Speech and Hearing Research, 11,* 488–496.

Goodglass, H., & Geschwind, N. 1976. Language disturbance (aphasia). In E. C. Carterette & M. P. Friedman (Eds.), *Handbook of perception,* (Vol. 7). New York: Academic Press.

Goodglass, H., Kaplan, E., Weintraub, S., & Ackerman, N. 1976. The "tip-of-the-tongue" phenomenon in aphasia. *Cortex, 12,* 145–153.

Green, E., & Howes, D. 1977. Conduction aphasia. In H. Whitaker & H. A. Whitaker (Eds.), *Studies in neurolinguistics* (Vol. 3). New York: Academic Press.

Gross, C. R. 1973. Visual functions of infero-temporal cortex. In R. Jung (Ed.), *Handbook of sensory psychology,* (Vol. VII 3b). New York: Springer-Verlag.

Head, Henry. 1926. *Aphasia and kindred disorders* (Vols 1 and 2). London: Cambridge University Press.

Hecaen, H., & Ajuriaguerra, J. de 1956. Visual agnosia for inanimate object due to left occipital disease. *Revue Neurologique, 94,* 222–233.

Hecaen, H., Penfield, W., & Malmo, R. 1956. The syndrome of apractagnosia due to lesions of the minor cerebral hemisphere. *Archives of Neurology and Psychiatry, 75,* 400–434.

Keating, E. G., & Horel, J. A. 1972. Effects of prestriate and striate lesions on performance of simple visual tasks. *Experimental Neurology, 35,* 322–336.

Lhermitte, F., & Beauvois, M. F. 1973. A visual–speech disconnexion syndrome. *Brain, 96,* 695–714.

Luria, A. R. 1966. *Higher cortical functions in man.* New York: Basic Books.

Luria, A. R. 1969. Frontal lobe syndromes. In P. J. Vinken & G. W. Bruun (Eds.), *Handbook of clinical neurology* (Vol. 2). Amsterdam: North-Holland.

Oxbury, J. M., Oxbury, S. M., & Humphrey, N. K. 1969. Varieties of color anomia. *Brain, 92,* 847–860.

Rochford, G., & Williams, M. 1962. Studies in the development and breakdown of the use of names. I. The relationship between nominal dysphasia and the acquisition of vocabulary in childhood. *Journal of Neurology, Neurosurgery and Psychiatry, 25,* 222–227.

Rochford, G., & Williams, M. 1965. Studies in the development and breakdown of the use of names. IV: the effects of word frequency. *Journal of Neurology, Neurosurgery, and Psychiatry, 28,* 407–413.

Rubens, A. B., 1976. Transcortical motor aphasia. In H. Whitaker & H. A. Whitaker (Eds.), *Studies in neurolinguistics* (Vol. 1). New York: Academic Press.

Rubens, A. B., & Benson, D. F. 1971. Associative visual agnosia. *Archives of Neurology, 24,* 305–315.

Scoville, W. B. 1954. The limbic lobe in man. *Journal of Neurosurgery, 11,* 64–66.

Spreen, O., & Benton, A. 1969. *Neurosensory center comprehensive examination for aphasia.* Victoria, B.C.: Neuropsychology Laboratory, University of Victoria.

Weinstein, E. A., & Kahn, R. L. 1952. Non-aphasic misnaming (paraphasia) in organic brain disease. *Archives of Neurology and Psychiatry, 67,* 72–79.

Weinstein, E. A., & Keller, N. J. S. 1964. Linguistic patterns of misnaming in brain injury. *Neuropsychologia, 1,* 79–90.

Weisenburg, T. S., & McBride, K. L. 1964. *Aphasia.* New York: Hafner.

Yamadori, A., & Albert, M. L. 1973. Word category aphasia. *Cortex, 9,* 112–125.

9 On Linguistic Perseveration[1]

Hugh W. Buckingham, Jr.
Purdue University

Haiganoosh Whitaker
The University of Rochester

Harry A. Whitaker
The University of Rochester

INTRODUCTION

According to Allison and Hurwitz (1967), Neisser, in 1894, first formulated the term "perseveration" to indicate the persistent repetition or continuation of an activity once started. Since then, there have been many personality and psychological studies concerning this behavioral phenomenon, as reported in Yates (1961). Clinically, perseveration involves the recurrence, out of context and in the absence of the original stimulus, of some behavioral act. A number of investigators have worked with brain damaged patients who perseverate. These subjects seem to perseverate involuntarily, often under conditions of weakness, inattention, or out of frustration due to an inability to perform a specific task. Goldstein (1948) writes that,

> fatigue is more likely to occur the more the task is suited to bring the patient into a castrophic condition. . . . Fatigue is related to distress; it is behavior in distress. It is evident that tasks produce fatigue because the difficulty or impossibility to fulfill a task produces distress. . . . In a condition of fatigue, perseveration occurs [pp. 17–18].

[1] Research for this chapter was supported in part by Grant N00014–68–A–0091 Task 001 from the Office of Naval Research to Haiganoosh Whitaker.

329

Eisenson (1971, 1973) discusses perseveration in aphasics and warns the therapist to be aware of its occurrence, since it signals a behavioral breakdown. He states (1971) that, "Perseveration, in general, may be the human mechanism's way of reacting to situations which demand adaptations and call for responses which the individual is not capable, momentarily or chronically, of making [p. 1258]." Moreover, he points out that non-brain-damaged persons also perseverate when fatigued or when required to perform some behavior more rapidly or with more frequent changes than can be achieved. He further mentions that epileptics increase perseverative acts post-ictally.

Pick (1973) discusses perseveration in terms of "a functional form which is ordinarily supplanted by the next in succession (but which) persists unaltered and leads repeatedly to the same product, or perseverate [p. 63]." Pick considers that fatigue and reduced capacity foster the tendency to perseverate. Allison and Hurwitz (1967) describe perseveration as "the continuation or recurrence of an experience or activity without the appropriate exciting stimulus [p. 429]."

Halpern (1965) studied the effects of stimulus variables or verbal perseveration. He did not analyze the perseverate itself, its composition and relation to other perseverates, but rather the stimulus items that elicited perseveration. Nor did he look at the stimulus–response parameters for the initial occurrence of the item later perseverated. All of his responses were printed words; they varied in abstractness, number of letters, frequency, and grammatical category (noun, verb, adjective). Stimulus items were presented visually for reading aloud, auditorily for repeating, and simultaneously auditorily and visually for both reading and repeating. Perseveration due to the abstractness of the lexical item was only significant in the visual modality; length of word was significant in all modalities; grammatical category and word frequency were not significant for any modality of presentation.

Helmick and Berg (1976) studied perseveration in brain-injured adults and provided a rank-order of tasks according to percentage of perseverative responses. They found that naming items in a series (e.g., days of the week) and reversing that series brought about the highest percentage of perseverative responses (29.26%). In descending order there were writing sentences and a letter (22.80%); drawing designs from memory (17.44%); drawing designs from verbal commands (16.03%); constructing designs (5.66%); naming and describing the function of sighted objects (5.37%); describing a picture (5.11%); defining words (3.40%); and answering questions (1.10%). In this article, the authors did not control for type of aphasia, nor was any attempt made to correlate the perseveration with the site of the lesion.

Underlying Mechanisms

Several factors account for the vague and often contradictory statements concerning the anatomical and physiological mechanisms which are presumed to underlie perseveration. Jasper, as reported by Yates (1961), states that perseveration is "the tendency of a set of neurons once excited, to persist in the state of excitation autonomously, showing resistance to any change in this state [p. 44]."

Depending upon the type of perseverated behavior and the set of muscles involved, it would therefore follow that the anatomical location of the neuronal firing could be almost anywhere in the motor system. On the other hand, many researchers feel that the organization of motor "plans" is mediated in certain frontal structures rostral to the motor strip, and thus damage here would likely lead to disorganized motor behavior, without paralysis.

Luria (1965) analyzes two types of motor perseveration secondary to involvement of the frontal lobes. The first kind of perseveration is caused by damage to prefrontal zones that extends to the subcortical motor ganglia. According to Luria, this gives rise to an "efferent" perseveration in which there is a pathological inertia of prior initiated motor movements, but total "programs of action" are well preserved. These patients have no serious difficulties in switching from one program of action (or task) to another. The second type of perseveration is due to extensive injury to the convexity of the superior posterior midline region of the frontal lobes, not extending subcortically. In this case, the performance of somewhat complex motor programs is severely disturbed and is usually replaced by some perseverating response that the patient does not correct. However, the pathological inertia does not involve any specific link in the chain of motor action, but rather substitutes the repetition of an "inert stereotyped action" (the perseverate) for the correct response.

Brickner (1940) elicited perseverative behavior in a patient (a 32 year-old, right-handed woman) when he stimulated a cortical zone a little less than 1 cm. in diameter. This zone was on the mesial surface of the left hemisphere, low down in area 6, near its juncture with the posterior tip of area 32. In the experiment, the patient was asked to recite the alphabet. When the area in question was stimulated, the letter being uttered at the moment of application was repeated over and over again until the stimulation was withdrawn, at which point the patient would continue reciting normally. The patient reported that she was aware she was perseverating, but that she could do nothing about it.

Brickner was puzzled, since this region was so far from Broca's area. It would appear, however, that the area in question was in the supplementary motor cortex. Penfield and Roberts (1959) showed that transient aphasia will result from the extirpation of supplementary motor regions. The supplementary motor region may also be anatomically connected with parts of the pre-Rolandic motor cortex. Geschwind (1969b) points out that Deepak Pandya demonstrated in his anatomical studies of the monkey that the face portion of the supplemental motor area is clearly connected with the face portion of the classical motor cortex.

Discussing motor apraxia,[2] Keiller (1927) wrote,

> Through deficit in the left pre-frontal area or interruption in association fibers therefrom, the patient may have difficulty in voluntarily starting an action, which, once begun, is fairly well carried out, or he may have trouble in giving up one form of activity for another when told to do so [p. 284].

It is in this way that an apraxic patient will perseverate as part of his abnormal behavior.

Parietal lobe injuries have also been correlated with perseveration. Hécaen (1967) notes the work of Schiller (1947), who emphasized the importance of perseveration phenomena in World War II patients with lesions in parietal and parietal-rolandic regions.

To further complicate matters, Pick (1973) states that perseveration "appears mainly with disorders resulting from lesions of the temporal lobe (usually on the left side) [p. 63]."

It would therefore seem that the phenomenon of perseveration is varied and not necessarily caused by lesions in a certain structure. There appears to be at least two generalized types (iterative and discontinuous) and different regions of the brain have been implicated. Furthermore, if we are to believe Goldstein, it would seem reasonable that if perseveration is conditioned by a "catastrophic" situation, then there need be no certain cerebral location at all. Patients with lesions in distinct regions may be unable to perform correctly; this may induce fatigue, which may then lead to perseveration. Even Penfield and Roberts (1959) have stated that "Difficulty in naming, also perseveration, are recorded in practically all cases of aphasia [p. 73]." The localization issue is further complicated by the fact that even normals perseverate under certain circumstances. Some researchers have deemphasized the role of abnormal physiological function as a cause for perseveration. Leichester, Sidman, Stoddart, and Mohr (1971) write that

---

[2] Apraxia is defined as the loss of the ability to perform voluntary, purposive skilled acts in the absence of any primary sensory or motor loss. One of the characteristics of apraxic behavior is perseveration. Apraxic patients do not necessarily perseverate, but many do. Pick (1973) writes that perseveration is, " . . . not totally absent in other functional forms (even in the field of apraxia) . . . [p. 63]."

Previous workers have believed that perseveration was caused by abnormal physiology—abnormally facilitated and persistent after-effects of ideation, memory, or motor performance. We have described perseveration due to repeating previously correct and reinforced responses and perseveration controlled by irrelevant stimulus patterns. Both these types are consistent with established principles of behavior, and neither requires any abnormal physiology. There are probably a number of different processes by which perseveration is produced [p. 154].

Finally, Hudson (1968) analyzes "intentional" perseveration. This term, he notes, comes from Liepmann who regarded it as "an ideational disorder in which there is an impasse in the area of sensory preparation of movement with the result that new stimuli excite a previous idea and the movement caused thereby [p. 572]." Hudson concludes that "Intentional perseveration may be due to impairment of an inhibitory system which causes an increase in facilitatory activity and involuntary recall of recently established memory [p. 582]."

Intentional perseveration, according to Hudson, is observed when some new performance is **intended** but is not realized; the term should not be taken to mean that the patient intentionally, that is, voluntarily, perseverates. Hudson's findings are based on data collected from experimental testing where there was a constant changing of stimulus items presented to the subject. The subject was consequently required to switch from one response to another when **intending** to produce the proper answer to the stimuli. A large part of our data also derives from confrontation testing; throughout, we have paid special attention to this "intentional" aspect of perseveration and will discuss it further.

THE CASES STUDIED

Since perseveration is a characteristic of a breakdown in skilled, purposive behavioral acts, we would expect to see it in certain language disorders. The present study describes linguistic perseveration in two patients with aphasia secondary to left posterior cerebral lesions.

Patient JT, a 74-year-old right-handed woman, sustained a posterior middle cerebral artery thrombosis with infarction in the left posterior parietal region. A brain scan revealed increased uptake in the distribution of the parietal branch of the left middle cerebral artery, easily seen in both frontal and lateral views. The patient was left with a right homonomous hemianopia, fluent jargon aphasia with neologisms, and many semantic verbal paraphasias. There was no paralysis. Verbal comprehension was difficult to assess with any precision, since before her stroke she wore a hearing aid in the right ear. When speaking, JT did not appear to be self-monitoring; the paraphasic speech was never observed to be self-corrected.

Patient DL, a 61-year-old right-handed woman, suffered a middle cerebral artery thrombosis of the posterior branches. A brain scan revealed increased uptake in the left temporo-parietal region. The patient was left with a severe anomia, a marked repetition difficulty, and no paralysis. Her comprehension appeared to be much better than JT's. She had acute difficulty retrieving nouns, both on naming tasks and during spontaneous speech and frequently produced indefinites in place of nouns. She produced no neologisms. DL's speech was relatively fluent; she demonstrated no clear field cut. We administered apraxia tests to this patient. She perseverated at least once on the motor acts, including the commands: (1) wave goodby; (2) put out your tongue; (3) use a spoon to eat with; and (4) walk forward.

UNITS SUBJECT TO PERSEVERATION

It is important to isolate the type of linguistic structure which can be perseverated. Words are the linguistic units most often perseverated and the perseveration frequency occurs on specific task oriented situations—confrontation naming, repetition, reading aloud, and the like. For instance, JT, when asked to repeat 'window', said *red window.* Next, when asked to repeat 'banana", she said, *a back window . . . a window.* The perseverate, in its first occurrence, was produced as the correct response to the stimulus item, except for the extraneous adjective. The perseverate has usually been observed to occur **correctly** initially by Penfield and Roberts (1959, p. 198) and several others. We decided, therefore, to look carefully at the context of the first occurrence of an item that is later perseverated to see if there were any common characteristics. We found that the perseverate does not have to have occurred correctly in its initial appearance. Helmick and Berg (1976) also noted that the perseverate in its initial occurrence is not necessarily some correct response.

DL, on 3-25-74, was asked to name a picture of a hand. She responded with *more drink . . . drink. Drink* was perseverated throughout the rest of the interview. Asked to name the days of the week on an interview 3 days later, DL said, *six, seven, eight.* Afterwards, on ensuing tasks, she recited numbers. On 5-17-74, DL was asked to repeat *sing;* she responded, *dri . . . drink . . . drink.* The partial phonetic similarity will be discussed below. She perseverated on *drink* again throughout the interview.

JT, on 11-13-73, was asked to name a picture of cherries, in color, to which she said *this is apples.* The word *apple* was later perseverated on other naming tasks. On 10-5-73, JT was asked to identify various body parts. The examiner pointed to the patient's ankle and asked her what it was. She responded, *feet . . . teeth.* Later, for other body parts, she perseverated on both *feet* and *teeth.* From these examples it should be clear that the perseverate is not necessarily produced correctly on its first occurrence, although several of the initial responses appear to be semantically or phonologically related to the stimulus. Note that the perseverate *drink* first appeared when DL was shown a *hand,* which may or may not be a semantic error. On the other interview, *drink* is produced in response to *sing;* they share a common vocalic and nasal sequence. A clearer case in which the perseverate initially occurred as a semantic paraphasia comes from patient JT on 8-30-73. The following was a repetition task; the stimulus item is on the left of the arrow, the subject's response to the right.

(1) STIMULUS   RESPONSE

snowball $\longrightarrow$ /sædnɔ̌l/ *white . . . white, white . . .*
                                          some with them was white.

two $\longrightarrow$ *white*

95% $\longrightarrow$ /ǽksnɪ̆/ *white*

Furthermore, a form which is later perseverated may never be produced as a proper response to the initial stimulus, even in the form of a semantic or phonological switch. The following example is illustrative. This is a picture naming task administered to DL on 5-17-74.

(2) STIMULUS   RESPONSE

hand $\longrightarrow$ ∅ (patient could not name it at all)

car $\longrightarrow$ /hæʔ/ /hæʔ/, *uh . . .*

girl $\longrightarrow$ *that's a* /hæʔ/, *uh . . .*

cup of coffee $\longrightarrow$ . . . /kæn/ . . . /hæn/

In (2), a picture of a hand was presented. 20 sec elapsed, but the patient could not name it. After 20 sec, the printed word "Hand" was placed beside the picture as an additional cue. Another 20 sec passed, but the patient still could not give the proper response. After an interval of 5 sec, a picture of a car was presented. After 4 sec, the first /hæʔ/ appeared. This is a phonetic variant of the ensuing perseverate. It is an incorrect response in its first occurrence, and seems to be the result of delaying processing of the prior input stimulus for hand. Forty-nine seconds had elapsed between the initial presentation of the picture of a hand and the first utterance of /hæʔ/.

The hypothesis that perseveration is involuntary receives some support from patient DL's tendency to catch herself perseverating and stop after producing the first few segments. The glottal quality of the final vowel often indicates this. While DL was perseverating on *drink,* she would often produce /drɪʔ/ as she did /hæʔ/ in (2). When asked on 5-17-74 if she used to work in the convent where she was convalescing, subject DL answered,

(3) *uh, I can't even say it. . . . Isn't that funny . . .* /drɪʔ/, *uh . . . used to . . . Isn't that funny, I can't . . . I* /drɪʔ/ *I used to . . .*

This demonstrates that in spontaneous speech when she could not find certain words, DL would, after moments of silence, attempting to retrieve the word (indicated by . . .), begin to produce the perseverate *drink,* which had carried over from an earlier task. It appeared, however, that the patient would catch herself in the act of perseverating and cut it off abruptly, producing the glottal quality. These findings lend credence to the hypothesis that perseveration is involuntary. Moreover, to the extent that the patient's comprehension and self-monitoring abilities are intact, we would expect instances of self-correction such as seen here. DL's comprehension was much better than JT's; JT rarely, if ever, corrected herself in this fashion.

On occasion the patients produce phonetically similar lexical items apparently derived from the sound structure of the perseverate. DL, having perseverated on *drink* for a while, was asked to repeat the sentence *I am going home.* She responded with, *blank . . . drank* (3-25-74). Again, on 5-27-74, she perseverated on *drink,* and when asked to repeat the word *crack,* she uttered, *drank . . . drack* /dræ:/. Subject JT, on 11-29-73, began to perseverate on the item *bread.* Later on when asked to read aloud the sentence *The yellow pencil writes,* JT said, *bread . . . head.* Two test items later, the sentence to be read was *I saw the big house,* which JT rendered as *red . . . head.* The word *red,* thereafter, became the perseverate. There is a high degree of "clang association" scattered throughout the process of lexical perseveration.

At times a part of some lexical item or of some phonemic paraphasia becomes the perseverate. When attempting to name the object *horseshoe,* patient JT said,

(4) *This is a* /bréi hɔ́ks/ . . . /pléi hɔ́z/ . . . /réi hɔ́ks/.

[hɔks/ conceivably is a phonemic paraphasia for *horse.* She then perseverated on this form with further paraphasias on an isolated-word reading task, saying /hɔk/, /kɔ:/, /ɔk/, and /hɔ́kɪ̆/. The subject read nothing correctly until she was given the word *coffee,* which she read immediately and correctly as /kɔ́fɪ̆/. Forms such as /ɔ́fɪ̆/, /ɔf/ and /ɔ́ksɪ̆/ were later perseverated throughout this task. A formula expresses the phonemic structure of this perseverate:

$$/\binom{h}{k} ɔ \begin{Bmatrix} f \\ k \\ z \end{Bmatrix} (s) \ (ɪ̆)/.^3$$ An additional note of interest is that the preservation of

---

[3] We note that the majority of the segments appearing in the second consonant (inter-

these forms occurred during the reading task on 11-29-73, when the patient, as mentioned earlier, was perseverating on the phonologically similar items *bread, red,* and *head.* Therefore, sets of perseverate forms appear interspersed with one another. When asked to read the sentence *The city is near here,* JT read aloud,

(5) /ɔ́fĭ/ *bread* /kéipə̌/ . . . /ɔ́f ká: kéip/ /ɔ́fĭ/ *red,* /kɔ́i/ *red* . . . /ɔ́fĭ/. (Forms related to *cape* and *kay* had begun to be perseverated four items earlier.)

Similar interaction among sets of perseverates was not uncommon in JT's speech.

When we observe segments being perseverated, such as /ɔ́fĭ/, we may relate their structure to an earlier form, for example, /hɔks/. Initial consonant clusters may also be perseverated. In still other cases the full lexical perseveration will interfere with production of the correct item and the result will be a blend of the initial part of the perseverate and the terminal parts of the correct response item. In this regard, Hudson (1968) writes that,

> In more complex activity complete repetition of performance is less apt to occur. Instead, the perseverational response suggests a partial recall of ideas related to the proceeding performance and a combination of these with the idea related to the current performance [p. 579].

The example that Hudson provides involves the initial drawing of a chair, followed by the drawing of a cat, which consisted of certain features of both the cat and the chair.

Allison and Hurwitz (1967) noted that, "in naming sighted objects . . . curious blending in responses of information relating both to the foregoing and current stimuli (occurs) [p. 437]." The example which they provide is the following.

(6) | STIMULUS | | RESPONSE |
|---|---|---|
| fountain pen | ⟶ | *a kind of pen.* |
| watch | ⟶ | *a pen . . . no . . . your pen for telling the time.* |

As the authors mention, this "information blending" is phrasal. On the lexical-phonological level, Eisenson (1973) has the following remarks.

> Sometimes perseveration produces a partial interference which carries over from one response to another, as when a patient identifies a series of objects such as *key, button, spoon, fork* by calling them *key, cutty, skoon, sfork* [p. 74].

---

vocalic) position share the feature [cont]. This suggests that the phonetic aspect of the perseveration involves more than the obvious vocalic identities.

Similarly, Hudson (1968) writes that, ". . . the patient may perseverate on some part of a word that he appends to other words [p. 579]." Analogous blending is observed in the perseverations of both our patients. DL had been perseverating on *drink* /drɪŋk/; the following were some of her blended responses on a repetition task.

(7)   STIMULUS   RESPONSE
      cross   ⟶   /drɔʔ/ /drɔ:/
      please   ⟶   /dəlɪʔ/ /də/ /li/ /drɪʔ/ /drɪʔ/
      crack   ⟶   /dræk/

It is interesting to observe that the perseverative blend of /d-/ from *drink* and the second element of the initial consonant cluster of *please, /-l-/,* results in the unpermitted initial sequence */dl-/. Note that the subject produced the epenthetic vowel /ə/, which provides proof that, despite the severe aphasia, English morpheme structure constraints are operating normally. English permits word-initial /pl-/, /bl-/, /kl-/, and /gl-/, but does not permit */tl-/ or */dl-/. That is, English has /plei/ and /klei/, but not */tlei/ or */dlei/. One can then write a sequential "if-then" morpheme structure condition for English in the following manner (Hyman, 1975):

$$
(8) \ \text{If:} \quad \#\# \begin{bmatrix} -\text{cont} \\ +\text{cons} \end{bmatrix} \begin{bmatrix} +\text{cons} \\ +\text{voc} \\ +\text{ant} \end{bmatrix}
$$

$$\downarrow$$

Then: $[-\text{cor}]$

This constraint means that if a word-initial noncontinuant is followed by /l/, then it must be either labial or velar; it can not be alveolar. The feature [+ant] distinguishes /l/ from /r/ among the liquids, at least according to the feature specifications of Chomsky and Halle (1968), since both liquids /l, r/ are marked [+cor]. Therefore, to prevent this unpermitted initial consonant cluster from occurring, DL inserted the epenthetic vowel—a perfectly normal process. The forms in (7) are actually lexical hybrids. An interesting perseverate phrasal blend like (6) above was produced by DL on a picture naming task administered on 3-25-74. She was perseverating on *drink,* but for the picture of a cup of coffee, the patient responded, *that drink,* good *drink.* Nine items later, when presented with a picture of an umbrella, DL said *drink of water.* Phrasal blends of this type are intriguing for two reasons. First, they represent the linking of semantic information pertaining to the new stimulus with the perseverate in a grammatically acceptable phrase. Second, they are analogous to the segmental blends of partial perseverates and new stimuli into phonotactically acceptable strings.

Full lexical combinations will also occur. JT named pictures of objects as follows:

(9) STIMULUS   RESPONSE
     knife   ⟶   knife
     hammer   ⟶   hammer knife

Perseveration of this sort may be cross-modal; JT's verbal response *hammer knife* in (9) parallels the written response of a patient reported in Hudson (1968). Hudson's patient, shown a drawing done by the examiner, was asked to copy it and identify it in writing. For *house,* the patient copied it correctly and wrote *an ice house.* For the drawing of a *car,* he copied it correctly and then wrote *an ice house.* For the drawing of an *elephant,* the patient once again reproduced it correctly, but he caught himself perseverating on the written word *house,* and wrote nothing. For the next item, which was a drawing of a flower in a pot, the subject correctly copied it, but then wrote *flower house.* It would be difficult to argue that either of these examples is primarily phonetic or graphic in character. This suggests, of course, that higher level units may be a structured basis for perseveration.

There is some evidence for the perseveration of initial consonant clusters. JT produced the segments /fr-/ and /kr-/ during an interview on 11-13-73. This task was confrontation naming; (10) shows the first occurrence of the forms later perseverated.

(10) STIMULUS   RESPONSE
     limes   ⟶   either a /frə́béi/ or /krémə̃n/

This was early in the interview; no neologisms or any forms had been uttered previously with initial /fr-/ or /kr-/ clusters. The item /frə́béi/ appears to be neologistic; /krémə̃n/ may be a paraphasia for *lemon.*[4] These perseverates are interesting because their first occurrences are in highly deviant forms. Listed in (11) are some of the utterances with perseverated initial /kr-/. The stimuli shown were not presented contiguously on the actual task. For some intervening stimulus items the subject either performed correctly or gave a paraphasic response which did not involve the material under discussion here. Furthermore, we have only included a sample of responses with these initial clusters.

---

[4] This phonemic paraphasia /l/ → /kr/ is complex and involves considerably more than substitution of a few features; however, sensory aphasics often produce paraphasias substantially far from the target.

(11) STIMULUS   RESPONSE[5]

apple	⟶	/krêibjə́sĭ
grapes	⟶	/króuz bèik/
lemons	⟶	/kréibə̌s/ . . . *it's not* /kǽmə̌/
milk shake	⟶	/krǽb dʒù:/
corn	⟶	/kríz/
pancakes	⟶	/kréi pə̌r krèg/
toast	⟶	/fréiz krɔ̀pĭ/
péanŭt bùttĕr	⟶	/krǽk ə̌ krèbĭg/ (note stress similarity)
white shirt	⟶	*a man's* /krú:ks/ . . . *a white* /krú:s/

Tendency to perseverate on /kr-/ was so strong that it even imposed upon an otherwise correct response. When shown a banana, JT said /krə̀bə̌nǽnə̌/. This is similar to the blends in (7), except that /kr-/ is a paraphasia which later becomes the perseverate, unlike the /dr-/ of patient DL from the normal English word *drink*. Interspersed with /kr-/ perseverates are /fr-/ perseverates on this naming task.

(12) STIMULUS   RESPONSE

oranges	⟶	/fróuzĭz/
bottle of soda pop	⟶	/fréi fæ̀t/
cheese		/frú:z/
spinach	⟶	/fréikə̌bĭ/
crackers	⟶	/fréikə̌r/
jello	⟶	*hot* /fréikĭ/
fish	⟶	/fréks/ /frǽksə̌/ . . . *is that a* /frǽkĭs/?
refrigerator	⟶	/fréidə̌m/ /freidə/
stove	⟶	/fréit/
gun	⟶	/fróubə̌r/

Since the stimuli in (11) and (12) are interspersed, one again sees existence of simultaneous perseverate sets.

In an interview on 10-16-73, JT was asked to read isolated words aloud. Her perseverated sequence of segments are consistant with Green's (1969) stereotypic sequence for neologisms. This sequence can be generalized as in (13).

---

[5] Most often there was more material in the response than we have indicated; we simply highlight those forms with initial /kr-/. Note that the diphthong /ei/, which appeared first in /frə̀béi/, is often present.

$\left\{ \begin{smallmatrix} \cdot \\ \cdot \end{smallmatrix} \right\}$

(13) /a + r + C/, where C is some consonant

In this task the stimulus words were clearly printed on 3 × 5 cards, and the patient was asked to read them aloud. These stimuli are shown in (14). Note that, beginning with the stimulus *overlook,* JT introduced a second perseverate set related to /ǽkwìt/, and from then on alternated between it and those forms related to the stereotypic pattern in (13).

(14) STIMULUS   RESPONSE

mine	⟶	/ârf báinz/ . . . /árb/ /árbaín/
against	⟶	/árbɚwáiz/
undershirt	⟶	/árbĭɛ́k/
for	⟶	/ártʃ/
overlook	⟶	/ârtʃ mífìt/ . . . /ǽkwìt/ /ǽkwìt/ /ǽkwít/
somehow	⟶	/árbɚwàiz/
here	⟶	/ǽkwì/
postpone	⟶	/árbɚwàiz/ . . . /árp/ /ârpíwɚz/ /ârpíwìz/
tomorrow	⟶	ártʃũəl/
disorder	⟶	/ǽkwìɛ́rɚbɚ/ /ǽkwĭèibɚ/ /ǽkwĭeibĭ/
there	⟶	/ártʃĭəl/
inhuman	⟶	/ǽkwĭìb/ /ǽkwĭèb/
recall	⟶	/ârzìɚl/ /ârsìɚl/
.		(11 items were presented between *recall* and *most*. The patient responded in a similar fashion.)
.		
.		
most	⟶	/ártʃfild/ /ârtʃfild/
less	⟶	/ǽkwìb/ /ǽkwíb/
worse	⟶	/ártʃfild/
it	⟶	/ǽkwìb/

Once again, all stimulus items except *recall* and *most* were presented consecutively. Special note should be taken of the responses to: (1) *there* and *inhuman* and to (2) *most* and *less*. In the first pair, the responses show a shift in the perseverate set, but *not* in the stress pattern. In both, the stress pattern is primary-weak-secondary (as in the normal pronunciation of the word *suffering* /ˊ ˘ ˋ/. Other utterances having the pattern /ˊ ˘ ˋ/ appeared in this interview, as noted in (14). Similarly, there is a change in perseverate set for the second pair but no change in stress; for both perseverates JT produced stress sequences of / ´ `/ / ^ ´/ (as in the normal contɪ ıst in pronunciation between the compound noun versus the adjective plus noun as in the *Whítehòuse* and *whîte hòuse*).

The combinatory dynamics of perseverates is also a very important aspect of the various responses under analysis here. The data in (15) come from the same interview as in (14).

(15) STIMULUS   RESPONSE
     which   ⟶   /ártʃì:/ /ártʃ-/
     forward   ⟶   /ártʃə́fild/
     .
     .
     .
     everywhere   ⟶   /éifild/ /ǽfíld/
     .
     .
     .
     worse   ⟶   /ártʃfild/

The syllable /-fild/ combined with either /artʃ-/ or /ei-/, which happen to be members of different perseverate sets; it always appeared in the second syllabic slot. These processes are creative in nature and are apparently involved in the genesis of many neologisms, as discussed in Buckingham *et al.* (1978). Perseverative combinations should be distinguished from perseverate interferences in several important ways. A full production of the perseverate, as in (9), would be a combination; partial occurrences of the perseverate, such as (7), are considered interferences. Another difference is that in combinations the perseverate might occur after the correct item, as it does in (9). It may also be produced initially as in (16), where JT was doing a naming task on 11-13-73.

(16) STIMULUS   RESPONSE
     hot dog   ⟶   *hót dòg*
     ice cream   ⟶   *íce crèam*
     jello   ⟶   *hôt* /fréikī/

Interferences are hybrids whose initial segments are the initial segments of the perseverate. For example, if the patient is perseverating on /drɪŋk/ and is asked to repeat /pliz/, it is more likely that, if a perseverative interference takes place, the result will be /dəliz/, not /plɪŋk/.

In this section we have found that many units which turn up as perseverates are not even correct responses on their first occurrence. Some support was offered for the claim that perseveration is involuntary. Throughout the perseverative behavior we witnessed the constant blending of various perseverated elements into new forms as well as the production of alternating perseverate sets.

PERSEVERATION IN SPONTANEOUS SPEECH

Linguistic perseveration is not only seen during specific psychometric testing, but it can also be observed during stretches of spontaneous speech. The perseveration may be either segmental or lexical. When it involves segments, the result is an output which has a "poetic" quality to it. We have already seen the tendency toward "clang" associations throughout task responses.[6] Perseveration among consonants and vowels has been often referred to as alliteration and assonance (Green, 1969; Buckingham *et al.*, 1978). Since this phenomenon has been dealt with in depth in the latter article, we will treat it only briefly here to complete our picture of perseveration. The examples in (17) of alliteration and assonance are from subject JT.

(17) a) *about the* /pǽmə̃nì/ *of my* /fǽmlǐ/
  b) *I did have this* /sáid/ *of* /áid/

---

[6] Describing writing abilities of his patients, Pick (1973) states that, "In writing, there is also **perseveration derived from speech** (after 'spiel' appears 'sbischbeil'). One patient writes 'getorito potogeto geriti' [p. 64, emphasis added]." Apparently, Leichester *et al.* (1971) would not call this perseveration. In their article they present data from writing. The patient was presented visually with a digit numeral and told to write the digit name:

STIMULUS		RESPONSE
5	$\longrightarrow$	5, E
		EAT, EATT
8	$\longrightarrow$	8, GAT
6	$\longrightarrow$	6, FAT
3	$\longrightarrow$	3, CAT
4	$\longrightarrow$	4, DAT
7	$\longrightarrow$	7, GAT
2	$\longrightarrow$	2, BAT
1	$\longrightarrow$	I, 1.00, 1, ACT
9	$\longrightarrow$	9, IAT

The authors were struck by the fact that most of the words that the patient wrote began with alphabet letter which corresponds with the stimulus number; that is "C" is the third letter of the alphabet; "D" is the fourth, and so on. They felt that the ". . . responses related to irrelevant parameters (and) not perseveration." They did not mention the perseveration of the "-AT" for almost all of the written items. Interestingly enough, the initial occurrence of "-AT" is in the word *eat* /it/; the subsequent perseverates with "-AT" involve the phoneme /æ/. It would therefore appear that the initial perseverate, "GAT" was based on orthographic similarity rather than sound. Hudson (1968) also noted perseveration in writing. He stated that the patient showed, ". . . perseveration consisting of a repetition of words with some modification and tendency to alliteration [p. 577]."

    c) *in the Rochester* /mítər/ *there . . . for the* /wârʃə́ fítər/
    d) /fú: fǽn fǽnət̆ĭ/ *at the* /fút/
    e) *there's a lot of* /rúwm/, *a lot of* /rúwm/ *in the* /grúwm/

As the examples show, much of the perseveration involves syllables, such as /ǽm/, /áid/, /rúwm/, and the bisyllabic /ítər/ as well as initial consonants such as /f-/. Our studies have revealed that the perseverated items are quite often in syllables which carry primary sentence stress.

    Full lexical items may be perseverated in grammatically intriguing ways either within a sentence or across contiguous sentences. We have provided some examples in (18).

(18) a) *I got **sick** and I couldn't **sick** for a couple of weeks.* (DL)
      b) *I said bring me some **apples**, and nobody comes **apples**.* (JT)
      c) *I wish that girl would come back and see how my lights are **reading** . . . the girl that was **reading** this. I wonder if the thing is **reading?*** (JT)
      d) *I can't hear a word you're **saying**. I can't **say** a word of it.* (JT)
      e) *but I can't **rain** any **rain** around here.* (JT)
      f) *I did have a cold, and I been sick all the **week**. But that, whatever you're talking about, I cannot **week** it.* (JT)
      g) *I don't hear you **talking**. I know you're **talking**, but I not **talking** you like I can **talk** you 'bout. I can see you **talking** that way. That's if I'm **talking** when I'm . . . I see you **talking** that way then if I'm **talking** my head.* (JT)
      h) *and that's the trouble I'm **forgetting** names that I **forget**, you know.* (JT)
      i) *It's down near the **water** where they live the north **water**.* (JT)

In examples (18a, b, d, f, g, h, i) the first occurrence of the perseverate is grammatically correct; in (18c, e) the initial occurrences of the item to be perseverated are anomalous, since *light* and *I* are selectionally restricted from coocurring with the verbs *to read* and *to rain*, respectively. In order to fully understand (18c), the discourse context must be considered. JT had just finished a reading task. Due to semantic confusions between *eye* and *ear*, *see* and *hear*, and the like, she often referred to her hearing aid as her *ear hides* or her *lights*. She also referred to her glasses at times as her *lights*, an obvious semantic connection. However, when she called her hearing aid her *lights*, she was confusing the perceptual modalities seeing–hearing and eye–ear. In addition, that morning a nurse had been in to adjust her hearing aid. Immediately preceding (18c) was the following exchange.

(19) Interviewer: I want you to just . . .
      JT: I can't hear what you're saying. . . . I wonder if this thing

> (indicating her hearing aid) is working? (I wish that girl would come back and see how my lights are reading . . . the girl that was reading this. I wonder if the thing is reading?)

In its first occurrence in (18c), *reading* appears to replace *working*. Notice that in the preceding sentence this is exactly what she said: *I wonder if this thing is working?* The second occurrence of the perseverate *reading* seems to have replaced a verb like *fix* or *repair*. The third production of *reading* once again seems to replace *working*. By stripping away these intrusive perseverates and by considering the discourse context, one can often arrive at a much better understanding of what the patient is trying to say.

For a clearer understanding of (18e), it must be pointed out that the subject had been trying to name a picture of an umbrella. The following dialogue took place.

(20) Interviewer: (providing cue) . . . for the rain.
      JT: for raining.
      Interviewer: umbrella.
      JT: But I can't rain any rain around here.

The anticipated occurrence of *rain* in (18e) could have replaced some verb *see*, although it is difficult to be completely certain. Here the second appearance of *rain* is contextually correct. Consequently, we have anticipation intersententially but perseveration extrasententially.

In (18a) it is almost certain that the second occurrence of *sick* has replaced *see*, since immediately afterwards the subject said, *I couldn't see or anything*. Incidently, note that the target word and the perseverate have identical initial segments. Regarding (18b), her brother had just brought her a basket full of apples; it is reasonable to assume she was thinking about them. Immediately prior to the utterance (18b), she had been shown a picture of cherries and asked to name them. She responded, *This is apples. Is that an apple?* Example (18b) was produced shortly thereafter. It is also conceivable that (18b) does not involve perseveration of *apple,* but rather a verbal switch of the verb *bring* to the verb *come* in the second conjunct. There is certainly a semantic connection in the deixis of *bring* and *come* (as opposed to *take* and *go*). If this is the case, then the error would be a verbal semantic paraphrasia and not the perseveration of *apple.*

To properly understand the last sentence in (18g), we must not only unravel the perseverations, we must also uncover the target words behind the semantic paraphasias. The first *talking* is correct if we analyze *see* as a semantic confusion of *hear,* which is highly likely in this case since the topic of discussion was the patient's malfunctioning hearing aid. The perseverated item *talking,* with its high probability of recurrence, most likely replaced the verb *turning*. The patient that at time was deliberately turning the side of her good ear towards the interviewer, all of which supports the present analysis of the meaning of this sentence. We also note that again we have an example where the probable target word and the perseverate have identical initial segments.

What makes the sentences in (18) seem strange is the semantic anomaly which arises when the selection restrictions are disobeyed by the perseverate. Consider just the semantically anomalous phrases in (18), listed in (21).

(21) a) *I couldn't sick.*
  b) *Nobody comes apples.*
  c) *I wonder if the thing is reading.*
  d) (no anomaly because in this matrix both *say* and *hear* may occur)
  e) *I can't rain.*
  f) *I cannot week it.*
  g) *I'm talking my head.*
  h) (no anomaly but a contradiction)
  i) *They live the north water.*

The utterances in (18) are clearly not examples of repetitive stereotypic words and phrases. In other words, they are different from the examples in (22), where DL was trying to describe her anomia. (Also, see (3) given earlier.)

(22) DL: *I can see it and everything, but it's **funny**. I can't—uh—I can't say it. It's sort of **funny**. . . . but I can't say it. It's hard to . . . you know . . . but I don't know, it's **funny**. It's a **funny**,—uh—. . . I can't—uh—know why it makes you feel . . . **funny**.*
  Interviewer: *Do they have television here?*
  DL: *Yeah, but it's **funny**—uh—**funny**—uh—**funny** way. You can't . . . uh . . . it's a **funny**—uh—such a—uh—so **funny**.*
  Interviewer: *But you see things all right.*
  DL: *Yeah, I understand. Yeah, but it's **funny**. I just can't tell you, it's sort of **funny**.*

DL's substantives are severely limited; she tends to use certain words from her impoverished lexicon over and over again, especially indefinites. Interestingly enough, DL's spontaneous speech is virtually devoid of nouns. The adjective *funny* occurs all through DL's speech; words perseverated in the manner of (18) do not continue to reoccur for very long stretches. Furthermore, her tendency to use *funny* never results in anomaly or contradiction; it is a general descriptive adjective used, on various occasions during each interview, to give account of her "strange" feelings probably caused by her agnosia.[7]

In addition, "stereotypic" lexical items are not like the forms in (18), nor are they like *funny* in (22). Stereotypes are in some manner contributed de novo by the patient, or, one might say, as part of his pathological competence. For example, another of our patients, not reported here, was observed to produce two stereotypic lexical items: *brave* and *body*. She did so throughout several interviews, although no specific eliciting stimulus could be identified. The overuse of verbal stereotypes may, like the items in (18), lead to semantic anomalies. Note further that in (3) the form *funny* is clearly separable from the true perseverate /drɪʔ/.

Spontaneous speech samples demonstrate perseveration through alliteration and assonance at the segmental or syllabic level and through full lexical postactivation at the word level. Stereotypic lexical items will occur as well as idiosyncratic overused words; we have chosen not to label these perseverative.

THEORIES EXPLAINING PERSEVERATION

The general paradigm for perseveration is represented in (23).

(23) STIMULUS   RESPONSE

$$
\begin{array}{ccc}
A & \longrightarrow & X_1 \\
B & \longrightarrow & Y \\
C & \longrightarrow & X_2
\end{array}
$$

This phenomenon has been most frequently treated as a task oriented behavior where stimuli and responses are very easily specified. In this paper we have concentrated our analysis exclusively on verbal responses; we pointed out, however, that perseveration can occur with equal frequency in many kinds of motor responses. We paid especially close attention to the first occurrence X_1 of items which were later perseverated. The first finding was that X_1 need **not** necessarily be a correct response to A, although in many cases it is. X_1 may be a neologism, a phonemic paraphasia, or a phonic or semantic verbal paraphasia. Sometimes X_1 may not be overtly produced. X_1 is usually lexical, but it may at times be segmental. X_2 may be a slightly altered form of X_1 or it may form a phonological, lexical, or semantic blend with some Y. X_2 may be abruptly cut off during production, often imparting a glottal quality to the last vocalic segment produced.

---

[7] Geschwind (1969a) discusses the strange feelings reported by patients with different types of agnosias, who perceive the stimuli but not the meaning.

Perseveration in spontaneous speech should be treated somewhat differently, because the response mechanisms are not the same. However, there are some common aspects. Considering the example (18a), using the schematic in (23), $X_1 = sick$; $Y = and\ I\ couldn't$; C should have elicited the verb *see*,[8] but instead $X_2 = sick$. X_1 in spontaneous speech can be prompted by either the current or a prior topic. In utterances such as those in (18) X_2 frequently resulted in semantic anomaly. Furthermore, X_2 may carry over from some X_1 produced during a specific task and occur during spontaneous speech at points where the patient becomes frustrated on not being able to retrieve some lexical item.

Alliterative and assonantal sequences do not easily fit the paradigm in (22). We have stated elsewhere, in Buckingham *et al.* (1978), that heavy stress may increase the likelihood of X_1 being perseverated (where X_1 is now some syllabic unit). For the full lexical items which are perseverated, both on specific tasks and spontaneous speech like those in (18), there may very well be an element of stress involved; many of the X_1's in (18) received primary sentence stress.

One might propose that the inappropriate production of perseverate X_2 is an unconscious and involuntary act performed in response to an inability to produce some required response. "Catastrophic response" theory was developed from the study of perseveration on experimental tasks involving presented stimuli. We say that DL produced her perseverate /drɪʔ/ during spontaneous speech when apparently attempting to retrieve certain nouns. She abruptly cut off the perseverate, imparting to the /ɪ/ a glottal quality, thus supporting the theory that perseverates arise involuntarily and unconsciously, but nevertheless may be monitored. The perseverates in (18) were not uttered during periods when the patient was effortfully searching for words. Also note that when DL produced the perseverated and inappropriate *sick* in its second occurrence, she did not cut it short as she did *drink*.

Often, there is a long pause when the patient tries to produce the appropriate behavior. Perseverates frequently occur after these long pauses; this might be the "catastrophic response." On the other hand, in the utterances shown in (18) there was never any pause before the production of the perseverate; all these sentences had normal intonation and stress patterns.

An abnormality in the nervous system may lead to post-activation of behavior; that behavior may be some simple motor or speech unit. The difficulty in interpreting perseveration is in deciding whether it is purely

---

[8] We do not, however, want to imply that we hold to an association chain model for sentence production. In fact, there are discontinuous relational properties between perseverate lexical items in (18).

motor, primarily sensory and *secondarily* motor, or purely sensory. Observationally, perseveration is an output disorder—but is it? For example, as opposed to (23), let us look at another response paradigm, (24).

(24) STIMULUS   RESPONSE

A $\longrightarrow$ $X_1X_2X_3 \ldots \ldots X_n$

Here, only **one** X is required as a correct response. Clearly, this is perseveration, but the response mechanisms appear to be quite different from those in (23). The perseveration of (24) is comparable to Liepmann's second type of perseveration, which he terms "clonic." As discussed in Hudson (1968), clonic perseveration involves a behavior which, once initiated, is repeated indefinitely without interruption. The patient, Hudson writes, will, "continue to draw circles when asked to draw only one [p. 571]." As Hudson mentions, this is parallel to Luria's (1965) first type of perseveration which we discussed earlier and is not ideational or intentional, but rather a form of motor perseveration caused by a defect in an efferent system and nòt in some more abstract "plan." Clonic perseveration, as defined here, is quite like what others have called "palilalia," except that palilalia is confined to the lingual musculature and refers to the repeated iteration of some small unit of speech (often one or two syllables, a word, or a short phrase) without pause. It will be recalled that Brickner (1940) used the term perseveration in describing his patient's iterative behavior secondary to electrical stimulation of the supplemental motor region; the actual behavior exhibited by the patient might be better defined as palilalia. Alajouanine Castaigne, Sabouraud, and Contamin (1959) demonstrated palilalia during a patient's seizures brought on by a lesion in the supplementary motor area. In any event, palilalic perseveration would best conform to the response paradigm in (24), not (23).

It is rather difficult to compare Luria's second type of perseveration with the ideational type of Hudson and Liepmann. As Hudson (1968) reports, Liepmann wrote,

> Intentional perseveration (is) an ideational disorder in which there is an impasse in the area of sensory preparation of movement with the result that new stimuli excite a previous idea and the movement caused thereby [p. 572].[9]

Similarly, Hudson (1968) concludes his study by saying, "Intentional perseveration may be due to impairment of an inhibitory system which causes an increase in facilitatory activity and involuntary recall of recently established memory [p. 582]."

---

[9] These quotations have been repeated here for clarity of discussion.

Luria, on the other hand, states that his type-II[10] perseveration, "is a disorder of the motor function with impairment of a 'program of action' [p. 572]." Of course, Hudson has, perhaps prematurely, interpreted Luria's second type of "motor" perseveration as comparable to "intentional" perseveration, which is the term used by Liepmann. Hudson does not feel that Luria's second type of perseveration should be referred to as a motor disorder. He argues that "highest centers" are not so well differentiated into motor and sensory components. He believes that higher cerebral structures are quite complex sensory-motor phenomenon. It would at least appear that this is the case for intentional perseveration, especially if one adheres to the Liepmann–Hudson hypothesis that new stimuli somehow excite old traces, which then lead to the repeated behavior. Both Hudson (1968:578) and Allison and Hurwitz (1967:434) noted that the requirement to switch linguistic modes from reception to production was highly correlated with the appearance of perseveration. It should also be noted that Hudson's patient was not aphasic and had no speech problems except for perseverations.

From the linguistic data discussed in this chapter, it would appear that, given the stimulus–response parameters used, intentional perseveration results from a sensory–motor ideation disorder in which new stimuli do not necessarily evoke repeated responses, but rather induce recall processing, the result of which is the perseverated behavior. Clonic or efferent perseveration seems less abstract and more peripheral and does not appear to appropriately describe our patients' linguistic perseveration. As Luria (1966) notes, it takes the form of the "liberation of primary automatisms [p. 198]."

Our data are best characterized as representing difficulties in going from one program of action (some task or response requiring a set of movements) to another. We may still ask, however, whether or not the nature of the stimulus in any way affects intentional perseveration. The degree of difficulty of various tasks has been shown to be related to its appearance in some cases; this of course is related to Goldstein's "catastrophic response." There is a problem, however, with theories relating stimulus complexity to perseverating behavior. It is often the case that when a patient "locks in" on a perseverate, it will be produced for difficult as well as for simple stimulus items.

We have focused attention on the phenomena involved in verbal intentional perseveration and have shown where it has analogues in other forms

---

[10] We should point out that Luria (1965) did not use the terms "clonic" or "intentional" in describing his types of "motor" perseveration. Liepmann (1905) is not even listed among the references at the end of Luria's article.

of perseverative behavior. According to Luria, both forms of "motor" perseveration arise from frontal lobe involvement. The first type is caused by lesions in prefrontal areas, and regions deep to those areas, thus cutting off sub-cortical motor regions from the frontal lobes. The second type of perseveration arises from mesial frontal lesions near the Rolandic fissure. Luria (1965) implies that his type-II perseveration does not involve lesions in or disconnections of the basal ganglia. Hudson (1968) feels that perseveration is intimately tied up with lesions that disconnect the limbic system from the frontal lobes. It should be noted that Hudson's patient (who manifested intentional perseveration) had suffered from a grade III glioma that had extended into the left frontal and anterior temporal lobes and the deep structures within the left hemisphere, including the entire thalamus and hypothalamus. Thus, Hudson's intensional and Luria's type-II perseveration seems to have come about secondary to a different array of lesions. For this reason, Hudson may have overstated the case in comparing his patient's perseveration to that of Luria's second type. If this is true, then we may perhaps have three types of perseveration. Moreover, Allison and Hurwitz (1967) have stated that, "It is conceivable that disruption of connections of limbic system with regions of the cerebrum other than the frontal lobes produces perseveration in specific functions [p. 582]."

The frontal lobes did not appear to be involved in our two aphasic patients (based on EEG's, angiograms, and brain scan data); the temporal and parietal lobes did. Furthermore, the lesions could very well have extended deeper into these lobes, possibly cutting some of the thalamic projection fibers.

In summary, there appear to be different types of perseveration secondary to damage in distinct regions of the central nervous system. We have found that posterior lesions in the dominant hemisphere can give rise to linguistic perseveration; the language units involved tend to be segments, syllables, and full words. We do not, however, claim that fluent posterior aphasics are the only ones who perseverate. Needless to say, further analysis of linguistic perseveration in other aphasic populations is required.

REFERENCES

Alajouanine, T., Castaigne, P., Sabouraud, O., & Contamin, F. 1959. Palilalie paroxystique et vocalisations itératives au cours de crises épileptiques par lésion intéressant l'aire motrice supplémentaire. *Revue Neurologique, 101,* 685–697.

Allison, R. S., & Hurwitz, L. J. 1967. On perseveration in aphasics. *Brain, 90,* 429–448.

Brickner, Richard M. 1940. A human cortical area producing repetitive phenomena when stimulated. *Journal of Neurophysiology, 3,* 128–130.

Buckingham, H. W., Avakian-Whitaker, Haiganoosh, & Whitaker, Harry A. 1978. Alliteration and assonance in neologistic jargon aphasia. *Cortex, 14,* 365–380.

Chomsky, Noam, & Halle, M. 1968. *The sound pattern of English*. New York: Harper & Row.

Eisenson, Jon. 1971. Therapeutic problems and approaches with aphasic adults. In L. E. Travis (Ed.), *Handbook of speech pathology and audiology*. New York: Appleton-Century-Crofts.

Eisenson, Jon. 1973. *Adult aphasia: Assessment and treatment*. New York: Appleton-Century-Crofts.

Geschwind, Norman. 1969a. Anatomy and the higher functions of the brain. In R. S. Cohen & M. W. Wartofsky (Eds.), *Boston studies in the philosophy of science* (Vol. IV). Dordrecht: D. Reidel.

Geschwind, Norman. 1969b. Problems in the anatomical understanding of the aphasias. In A. L. Benton (Ed.), *Contributions to clinical neuropsychology*. Chicago: Aldine.

Goldstein, Kurt. 1948. *Language and language disturbances*. New York: Grune & Stratton.

Green, Eugene. 1969. Phonological and grammatical aspects of jargon in an aphasic patient. *Language and Speech, 12*, 103–118.

Halpern, Harvey. 1965. Effect of stimulus variables on verbal perseveration of dysphasic subjects. *Perceptual and Motor Skills, 20*, 421–429.

Hécaen, Henry. 1967. Brain mechanisms suggested by studies of parietal lobes. In C. H. Millikan & F. L. Darley (Eds.), *Brain mechanisms underlying speech and language*. New York: Grune & Stratton.

Helmick, Joseph W., & Berg, Carolyn B. 1976. Perseveration in brain-injured adults. *Journal of Communication Disorders, 9*, 143–156.

Hudson, Arthur. 1968. Perseveration. *Brain, 91*, 571–582.

Hyman, Larry M. 1975. *Phonology: Theory and analysis*. New York: Holt.

Keiller, William. 1927. *Nerve tracts of the brain and cord*. New York: Macmillan.

Leichester, J., Sidman, M., Stoddart, L. T., & Mohr, J. P. 1971. The nature of aphasic responses. *Neuropsychologia, 9*, 141–155.

Liepmann, H. 1905. *Ueber störungen des handelns bei gehirnkranken*. Berlin: Karger.

Luria, A. R. 1965. Two kinds of motor perseveration in massive injury of the frontal lobes. *Brain, 88*, 1–10.

Luria, A. R. 1966. *Higher cortical functions in man*. New York: Basic Books.

Penfield, Wilder, & Roberts, Lamar. 1959. *Speech and brain-mechanisms*. Princeton, N. J.: Princeton University Press.

Pick, Arnold. 1973. *Aphasia*. (Translated by Jason W. Brown.) Springfield, Ill.: C. C. Thomas.

Schiller, F. 1947. Aphasia studied in patients with missile wounds. *Journal of Neurology, Neurosurgery and Psychiatry, 10*, 183–197.

Yates, A. J. 1961. Abnormalities of psychomotor functions. In H. J. Eysenck (Ed.), *Handbook of abnormal psychology*. New York: Basic Books.

Subject Index

.